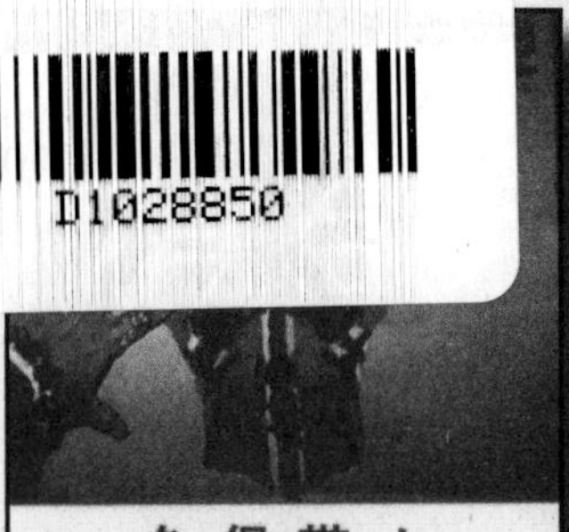

久保帯人

Hello, Kubo here. This is my first graphic novel. Mainly, it's all battles. It's completely OK to just read through it without thinking about anything. But if you feel like it, go ahead and recall some of these details as you read. Like for example, in here, the one thing that brings the dead back to life is not God, or an angel, or a Phoenix, but Zombie Powder. A powder that has a really annoying name.

-Tite Kubo, 2000

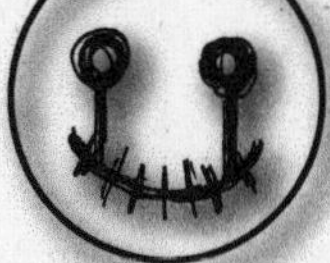

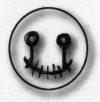

Tite Kubo is best known as the creator of the smash hit *SHONEN JUMP* manga series *Bleach*, which began serialization in *Weekly Shonen Jump* in 2001. *Zombie Powder*, his debut series, began serialization in 1999.

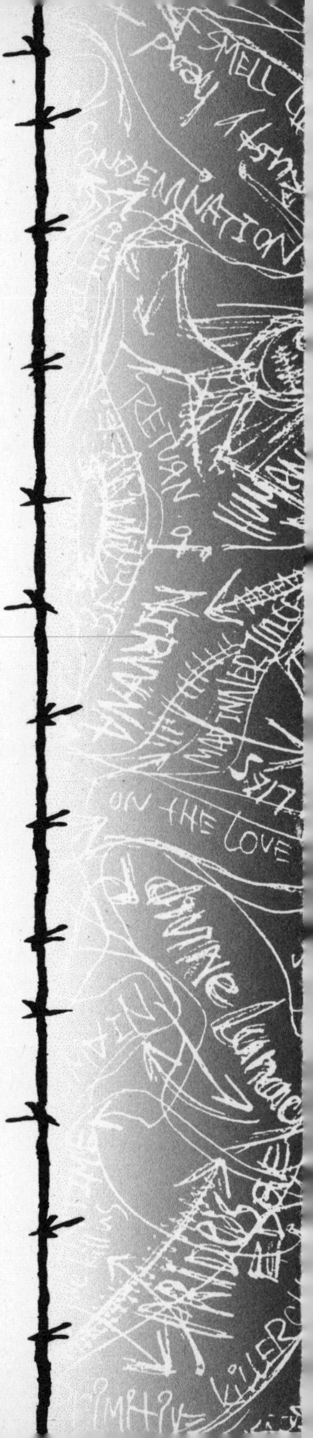
CONDEMNATION
ON THE LOVE

ZOMBIEPOWDER. VOL. 1
The SHONEN JUMP Manga Edition

STORY AND ART BY
TITE KUBO

Translation/Akira Watanabe
Touch-up Art & Lettering/Stephen Dutro
Design/Sean Lee
Editor/Jason Thompson

VP, Production/Alvin Lu
VP, Publishing Licensing/Rika Inouye
VP, Sales & Product Marketing/Gonzalo Ferreyra
VP, Creative/Linda Espinosa
Publisher/Hyoe Narita

ZOMBIEPOWDER. © 1999 by Tite Kubo. All rights reserved. First published in Japan in 1999 by SHUEISHA Inc., Tokyo. English translation rights arranged by SHUEISHA Inc. Some artwork has been modified from the original Japanese edition. The stories, characters and incidents mentioned in this publication are entirely fictional.

No portion of this book may be reproduced or transmitted in any form or by any means without written permission from the copyright holders.

The rights of the author(s) of the work(s) in this publication to be so identified have been asserted in accordance with the Copyright, Designs and Patents Act 1988. A CIP catalogue record for this book is available from the British Library.

Printed in the U.S.A.

Published by VIZ Media, LLC
P.O. Box 77010
San Francisco, CA 94107

SHONEN JUMP Manga Edition
10 9 8 7 6 5
First printing, September 2006
Fifth printing, May 2009

www.viz.com

THE WORLD'S MOST POPULAR MANGA

www.shonenjump.com

PARENTAL ADVISORY
ZOMBIEPOWDER. is rated T+ for Older Teen and is recommended for ages 16 and up. This volume contains graphic violence.

ratings.viz.com

ZOMBIEPOWDER.

Vol. 1
THE MAN WITH THE BLACK HAND

Story & Art by
Tite Kubo

*They all look like the merciless ring that was modeled after
a shining love.*

*I have been captured like a young child who fearfully clings
to my right hand in the darkness.*

ZOMBIEPOWDER.
Vol. 1
THE MAN WITH THE BLACK HAND

CONTENTS

Track 1: The Young Boy and the Black Right Arm

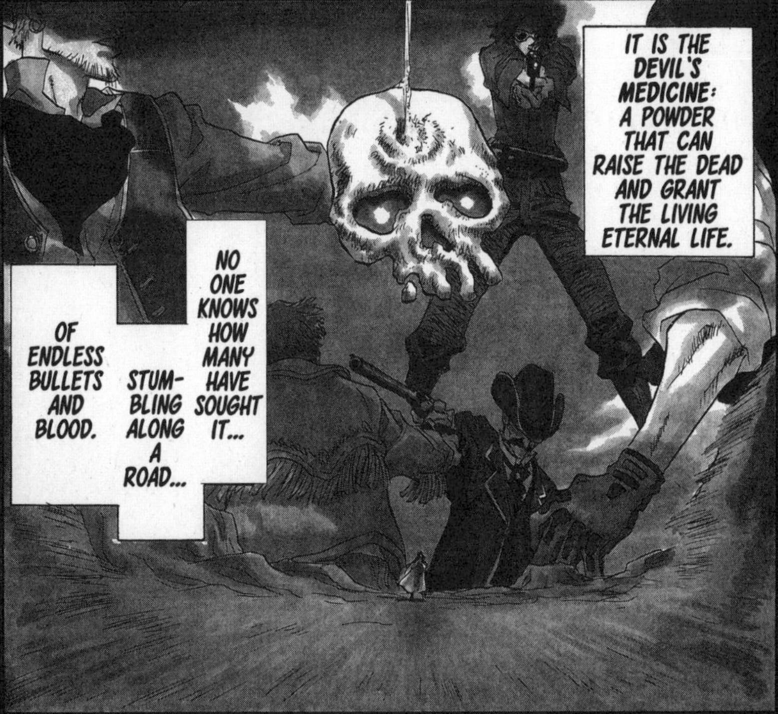
IT IS THE DEVIL'S MEDICINE: A POWDER THAT CAN RAISE THE DEAD AND GRANT THE LIVING ETERNAL LIFE.
NO ONE KNOWS HOW MANY HAVE SOUGHT IT...
STUMBLING ALONG A ROAD...
OF ENDLESS BULLETS AND BLOOD.

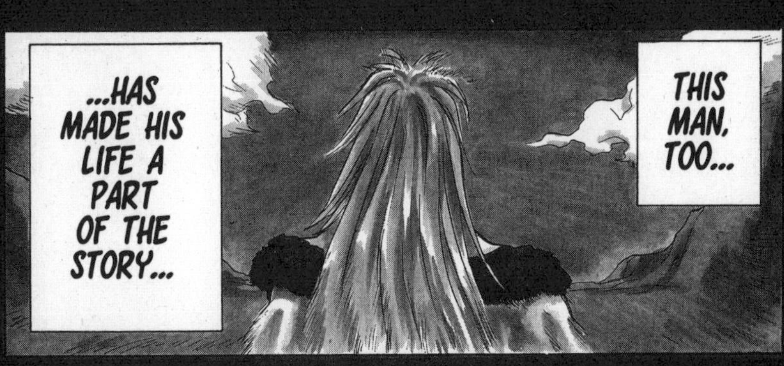
THIS MAN, TOO...
...HAS MADE HIS LIFE A PART OF THE STORY...

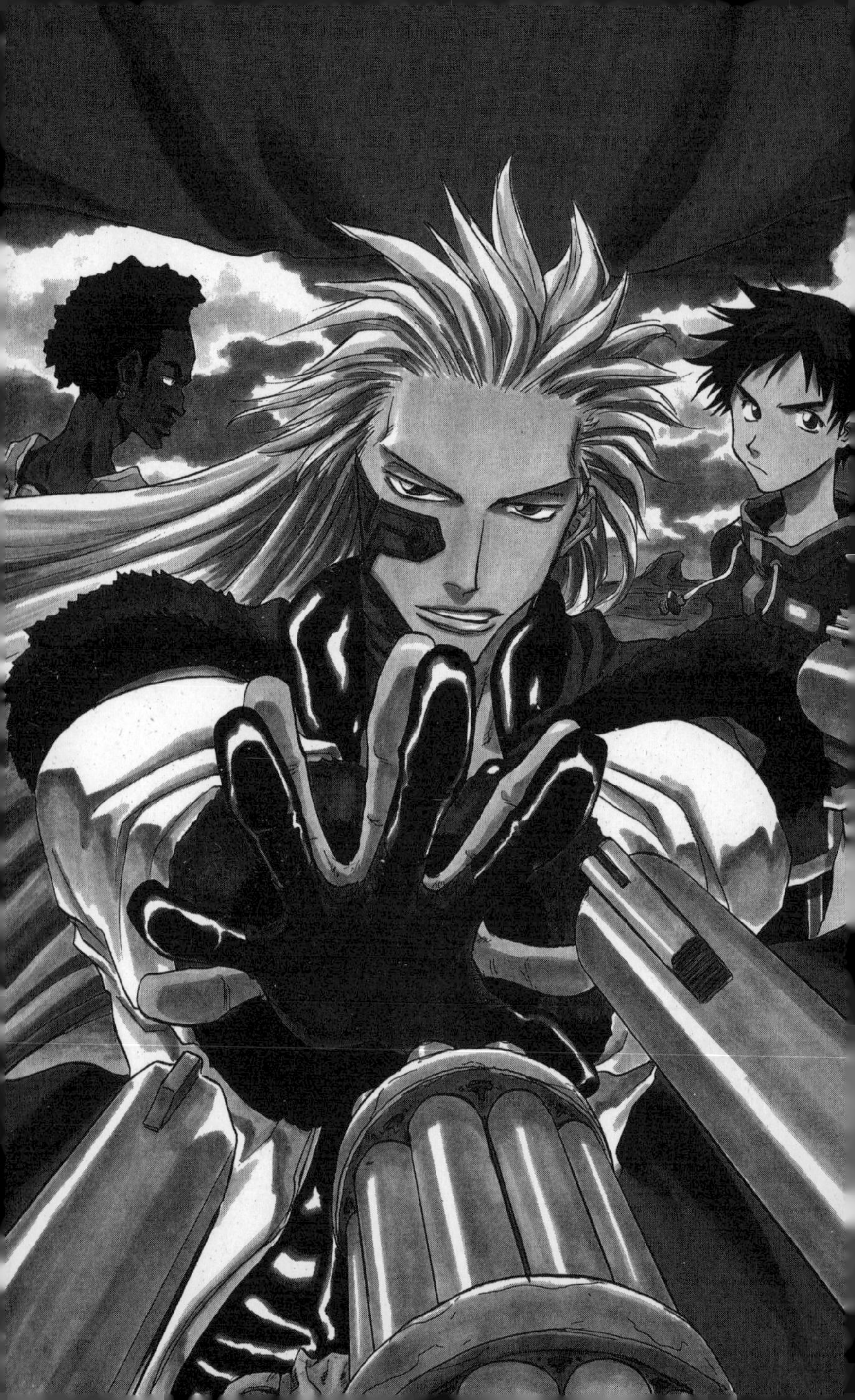

Track 1: The Young Boy and the Black Right Arm

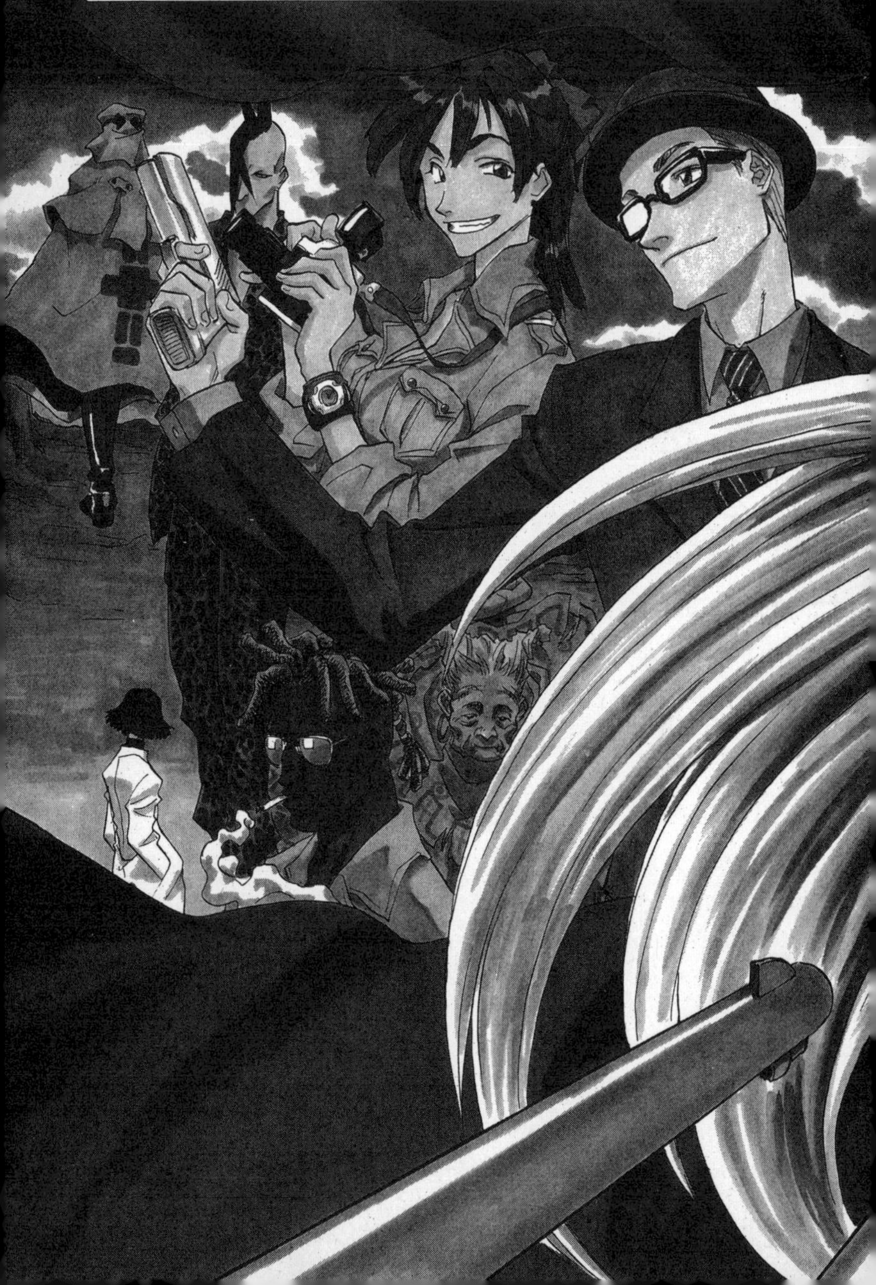

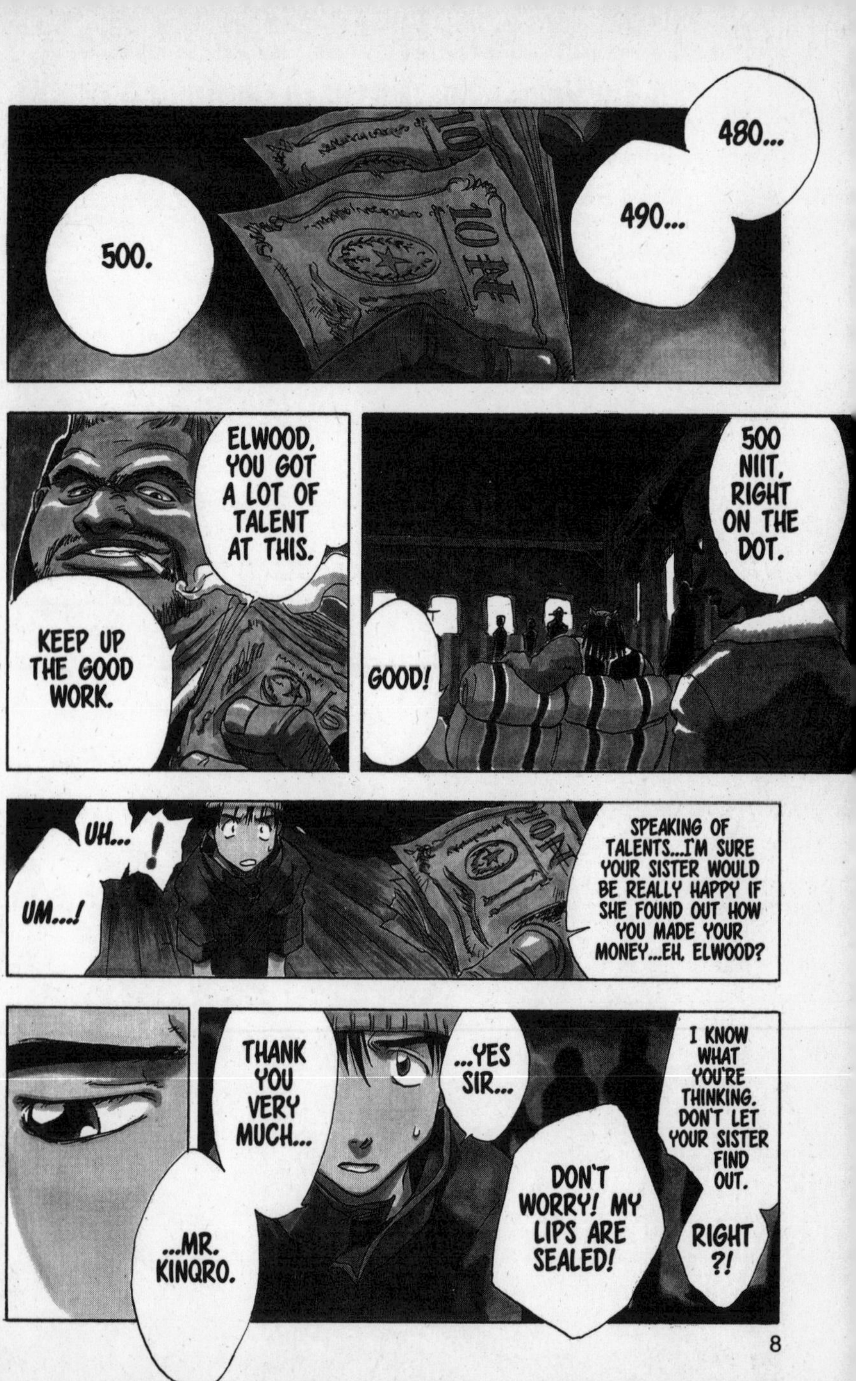
480...
490...
500.
500 NIIT, RIGHT ON THE DOT.
GOOD!
ELWOOD, YOU GOT A LOT OF TALENT AT THIS.
KEEP UP THE GOOD WORK.
SPEAKING OF TALENTS...I'M SURE YOUR SISTER WOULD BE REALLY HAPPY IF SHE FOUND OUT HOW YOU MADE YOUR MONEY...EH, ELWOOD?
UH...
!
UM...!
I KNOW WHAT YOU'RE THINKING. DON'T LET YOUR SISTER FIND OUT.
RIGHT ?!
...YES SIR...
DON'T WORRY! MY LIPS ARE SEALED!
THANK YOU VERY MUCH...
...MR. KINQRO.

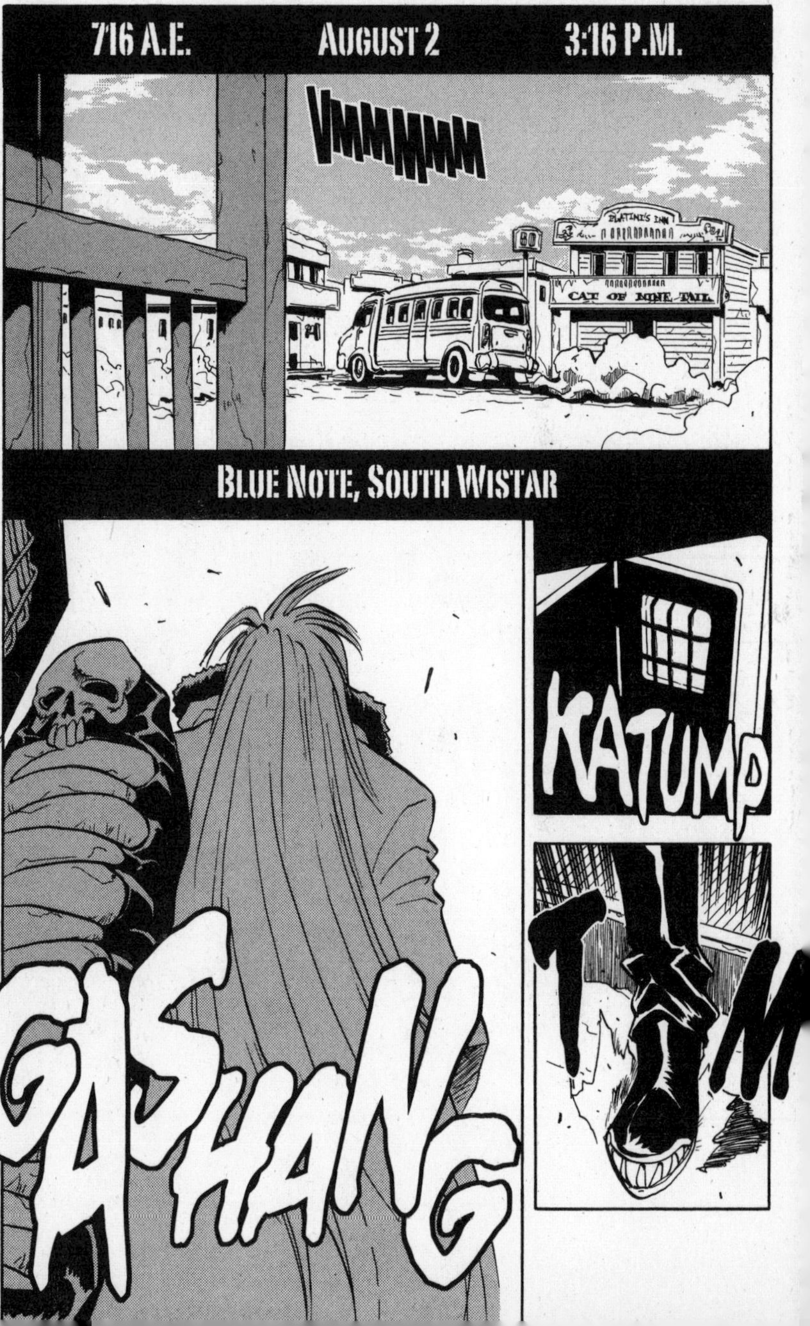
716 A.E.
AUGUST 2
3:16 P.M.
VMMMMM
CAT OF NINE TAIL
BLUE NOTE, SOUTH WISTAR
KATUMP
GASHANG

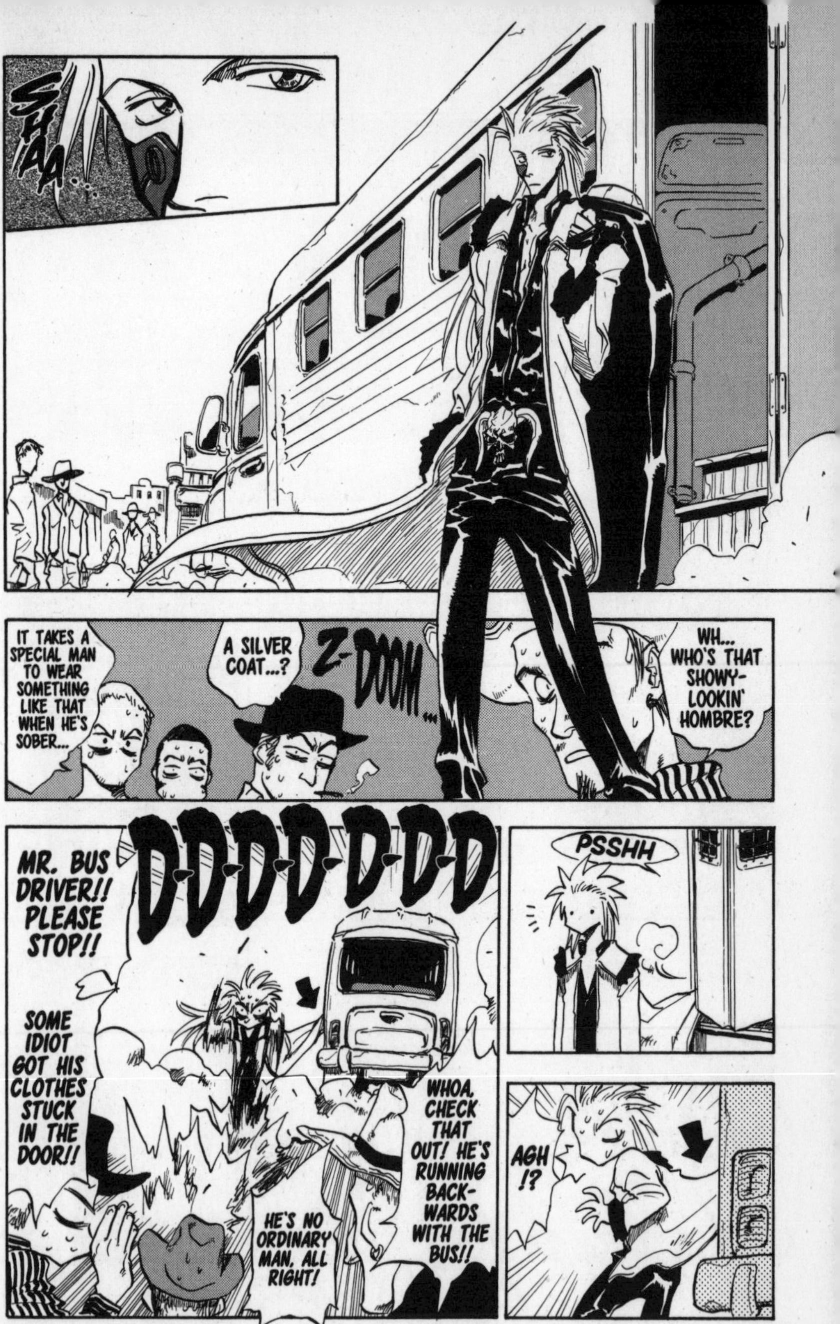
SHAA...
WH... WHO'S THAT SHOWY-LOOKIN' HOMBRE?
Z-DOOM...
A SILVER COAT...?
IT TAKES A SPECIAL MAN TO WEAR SOMETHING LIKE THAT WHEN HE'S SOBER...
PSSHH
AGH!?
D-D-D-D-D-D-D
MR. BUS DRIVER!! PLEASE STOP!!
WHOA, CHECK THAT OUT! HE'S RUNNING BACKWARDS WITH THE BUS!!
SOME IDIOT GOT HIS CLOTHES STUCK IN THE DOOR!!
HE'S NO ORDINARY MAN, ALL RIGHT!

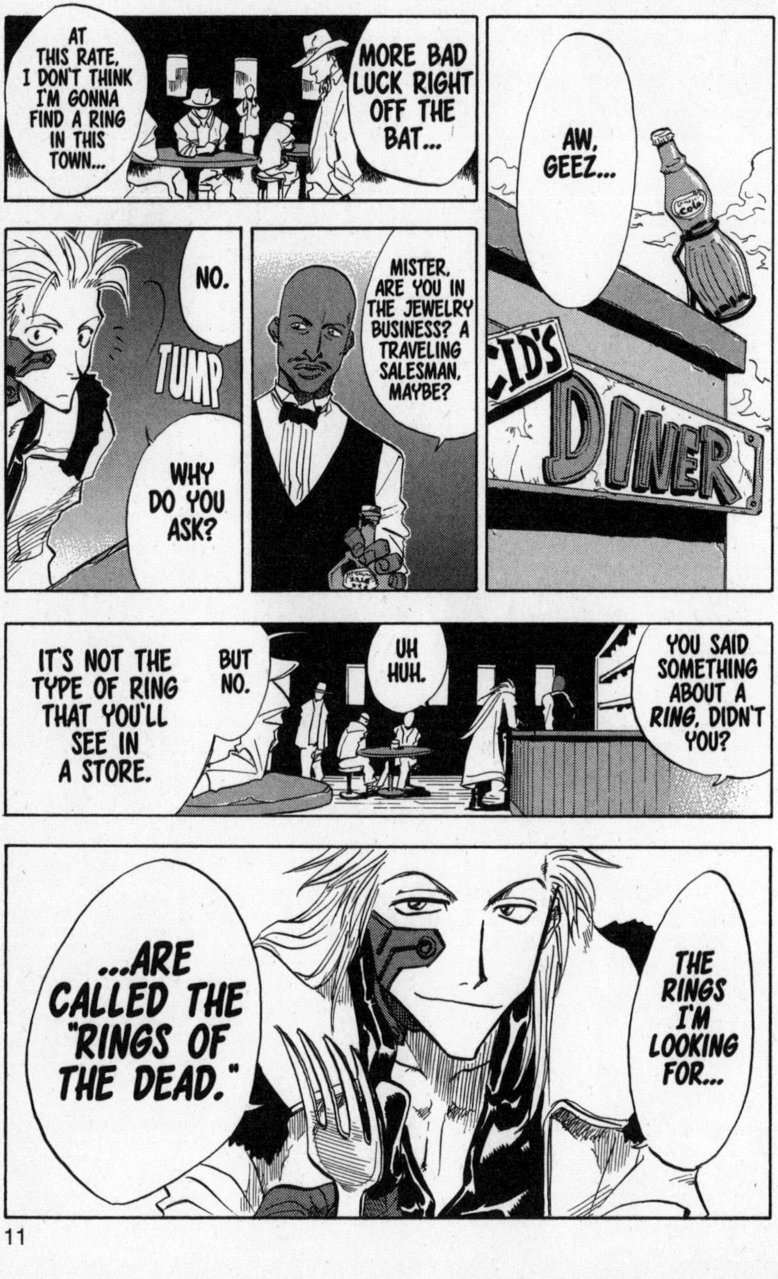
AW, GEEZ...
Cola
CID'S
DINER
MORE BAD LUCK RIGHT OFF THE BAT...
AT THIS RATE, I DON'T THINK I'M GONNA FIND A RING IN THIS TOWN...
MISTER, ARE YOU IN THE JEWELRY BUSINESS? A TRAVELING SALESMAN, MAYBE?
NO.
TUMP
WHY DO YOU ASK?
YOU SAID SOMETHING ABOUT A RING, DIDN'T YOU?
UH HUH.
BUT NO.
IT'S NOT THE TYPE OF RING THAT YOU'LL SEE IN A STORE.
THE RINGS I'M LOOKING FOR...
...ARE CALLED THE "RINGS OF THE DEAD."

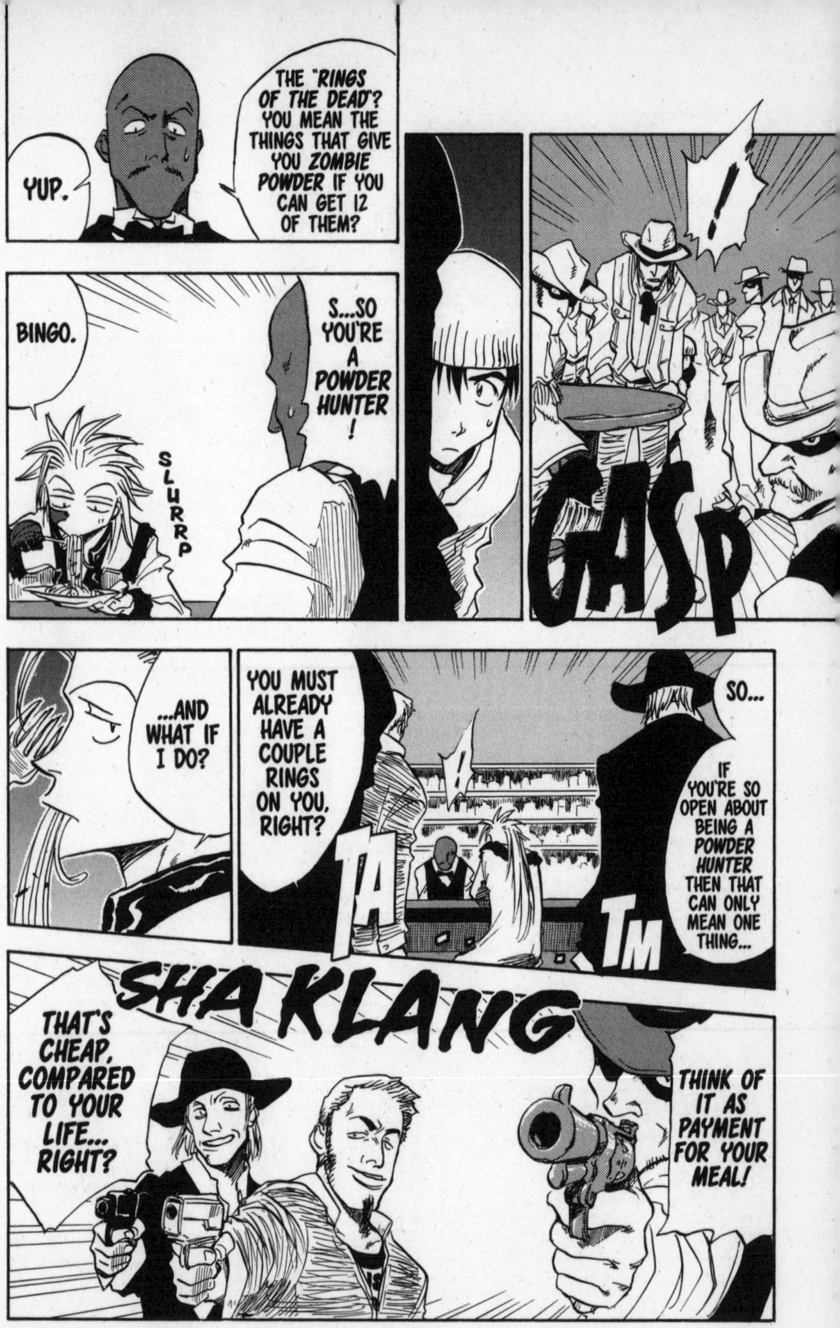
!
GASP
THE "RINGS OF THE DEAD"? YOU MEAN THE THINGS THAT GIVE YOU ZOMBIE POWDER IF YOU CAN GET 12 OF THEM?
YUP.
S...SO YOU'RE A POWDER HUNTER!
BINGO.
SLURRP
SO...
IF YOU'RE SO OPEN ABOUT BEING A POWDER HUNTER THEN THAT CAN ONLY MEAN ONE THING...
YOU MUST ALREADY HAVE A COUPLE RINGS ON YOU, RIGHT?
!
TM
TA
...AND WHAT IF I DO?
SHA KLANG
THINK OF IT AS PAYMENT FOR YOUR MEAL!
THAT'S CHEAP, COMPARED TO YOUR LIFE... RIGHT?

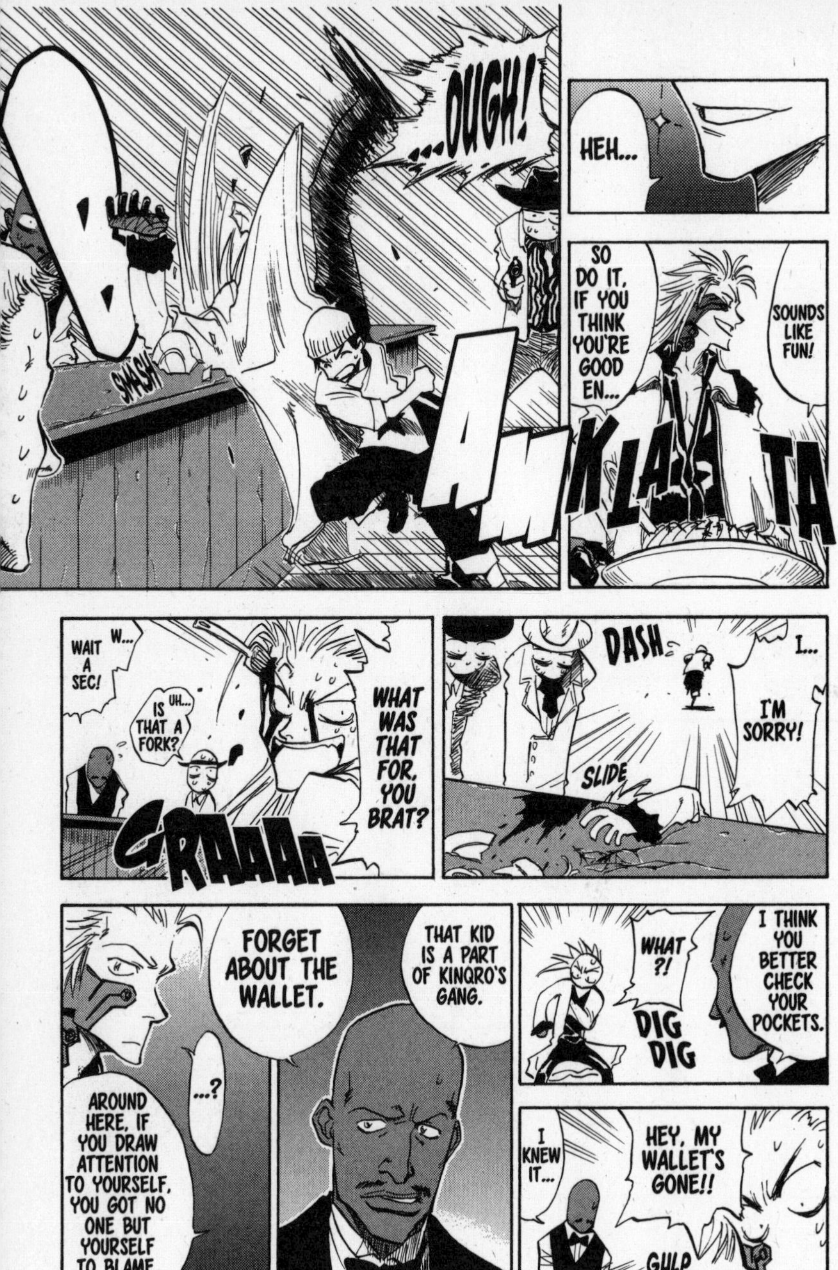
HEH...
SO DO IT, IF YOU THINK YOU'RE GOOD EN...
SOUNDS LIKE FUN!
AMKLA TA
...OUGH!
SMASH
I... I'M SORRY!
DASH
SLIDE
WHAT WAS THAT FOR, YOU BRAT?
W... WAIT A SEC!
UH... IS THAT A FORK?
GRAAAAA
I THINK YOU BETTER CHECK YOUR POCKETS.
WHAT?!
DIG DIG
HEY, MY WALLET'S GONE!!
I KNEW IT...
GULP
THAT KID IS A PART OF KINQRO'S GANG.
FORGET ABOUT THE WALLET.
...?
AROUND HERE, IF YOU DRAW ATTENTION TO YOURSELF, YOU GOT NO ONE BUT YOURSELF TO BLAME.

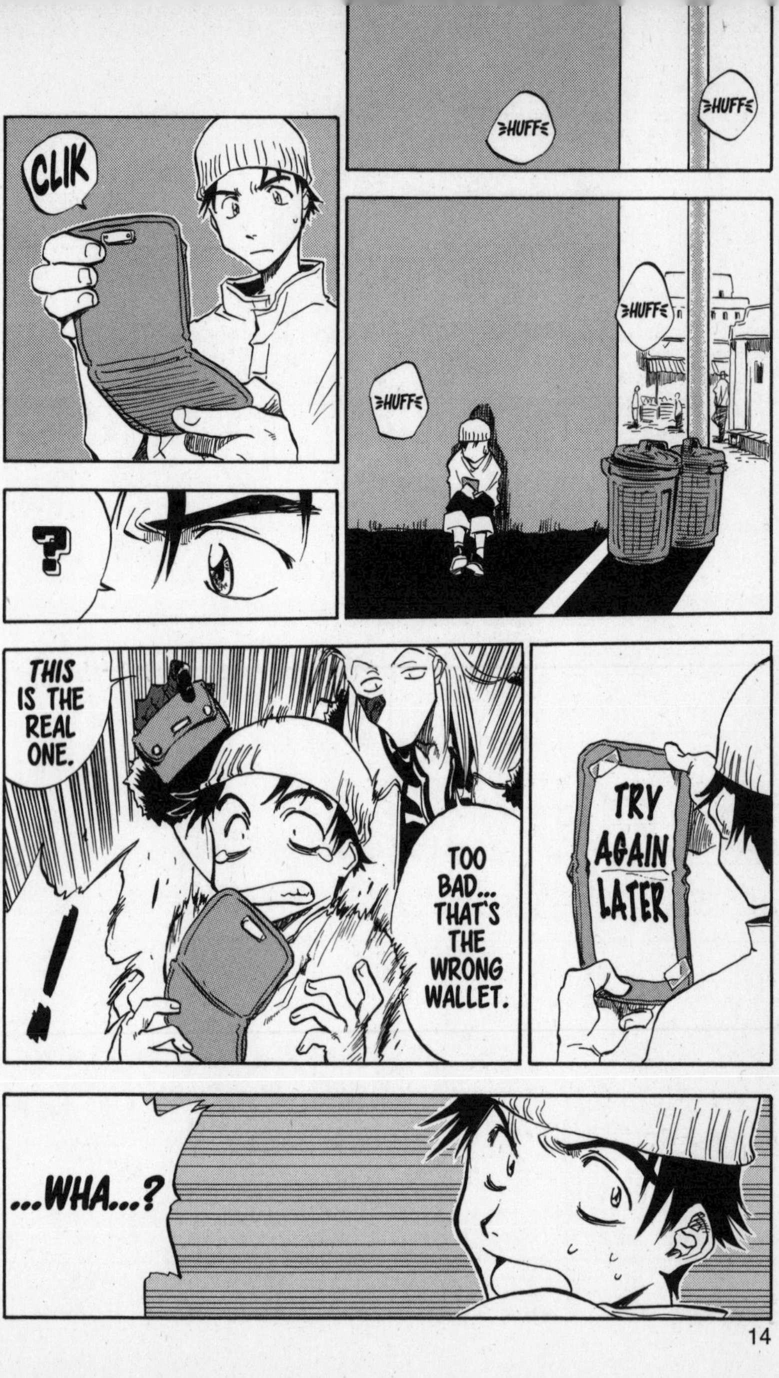

HUFF
HUFF
HUFF
HUFF
CLIK
?
TRY AGAIN LATER
THIS IS THE REAL ONE.
TOO BAD... THAT'S THE WRONG WALLET.
!
...WHA...?

READ THIS WAY

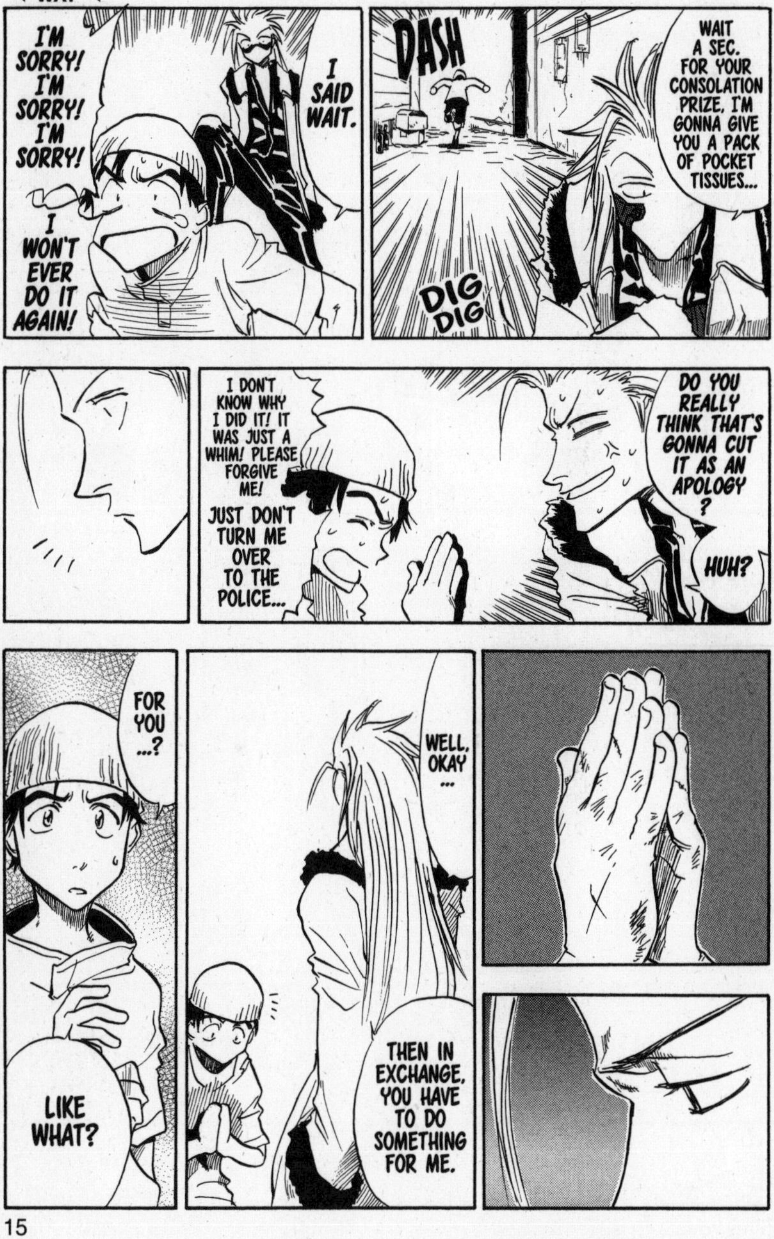
WAIT A SEC. FOR YOUR CONSOLATION PRIZE, I'M GONNA GIVE YOU A PACK OF POCKET TISSUES...
DASH
DIG DIG
I SAID WAIT.
I'M SORRY! I'M SORRY! I'M SORRY!
I WON'T EVER DO IT AGAIN!
DO YOU REALLY THINK THAT'S GONNA CUT IT AS AN APOLOGY?
HUH?
I DON'T KNOW WHY I DID IT! IT WAS JUST A WHIM! PLEASE FORGIVE ME!
JUST DON'T TURN ME OVER TO THE POLICE...
WELL, OKAY...
THEN IN EXCHANGE, YOU HAVE TO DO SOMETHING FOR ME.
FOR YOU ...?
LIKE WHAT?

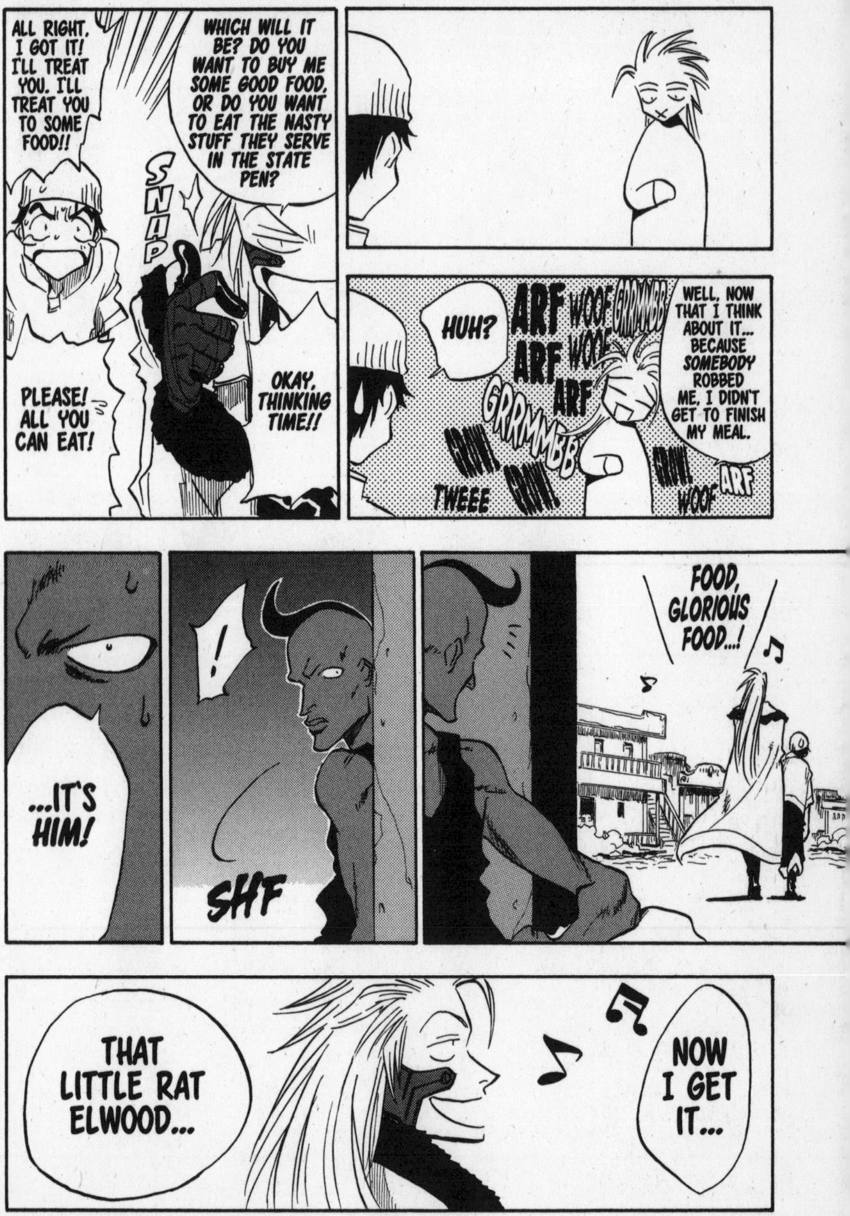
WELL, NOW THAT I THINK ABOUT IT... BECAUSE SOMEBODY ROBBED ME, I DIDN'T GET TO FINISH MY MEAL.
GRRMMBB
WOOF
WOOF
ARF
ARF
ARF
HUH?
GRRMMBB
ARF
WOOF
TWEEE
WHICH WILL IT BE? DO YOU WANT TO BUY ME SOME GOOD FOOD, OR DO YOU WANT TO EAT THE NASTY STUFF THEY SERVE IN THE STATE PEN?
ALL RIGHT, I GOT IT! I'LL TREAT YOU. I'LL TREAT YOU TO SOME FOOD!!
SNAP
OKAY, THINKING TIME!!
PLEASE! ALL YOU CAN EAT!
FOOD, GLORIOUS FOOD...!
!
SHF
...IT'S HIM!
NOW I GET IT...
THAT LITTLE RAT ELWOOD...

READ THIS WAY

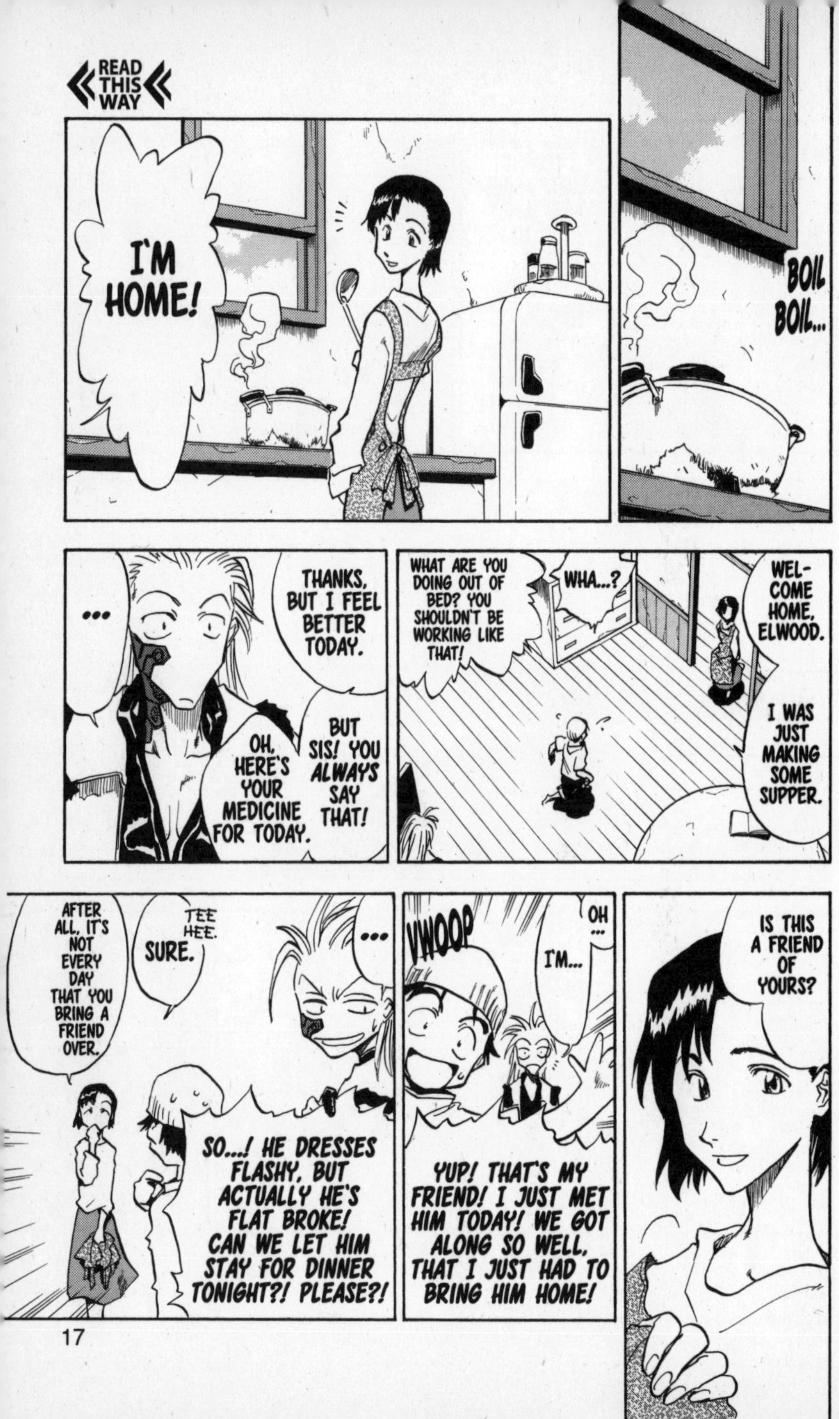

BOIL BOIL...
I'M HOME!
WEL-COME HOME, ELWOOD.
I WAS JUST MAKING SOME SUPPER.
WHA...?
WHAT ARE YOU DOING OUT OF BED? YOU SHOULDN'T BE WORKING LIKE THAT!
THANKS, BUT I FEEL BETTER TODAY.
...
BUT SIS! YOU ALWAYS SAY THAT!
OH, HERE'S YOUR MEDICINE FOR TODAY.
IS THIS A FRIEND OF YOURS?
OH...
I'M...
VWOOP
YUP! THAT'S MY FRIEND! I JUST MET HIM TODAY! WE GOT ALONG SO WELL, THAT I JUST HAD TO BRING HIM HOME!
...
TEE HEE.
SURE.
AFTER ALL, IT'S NOT EVERY DAY THAT YOU BRING A FRIEND OVER.
SO...! HE DRESSES FLASHY, BUT ACTUALLY HE'S FLAT BROKE! CAN WE LET HIM STAY FOR DINNER TONIGHT?! PLEASE?!

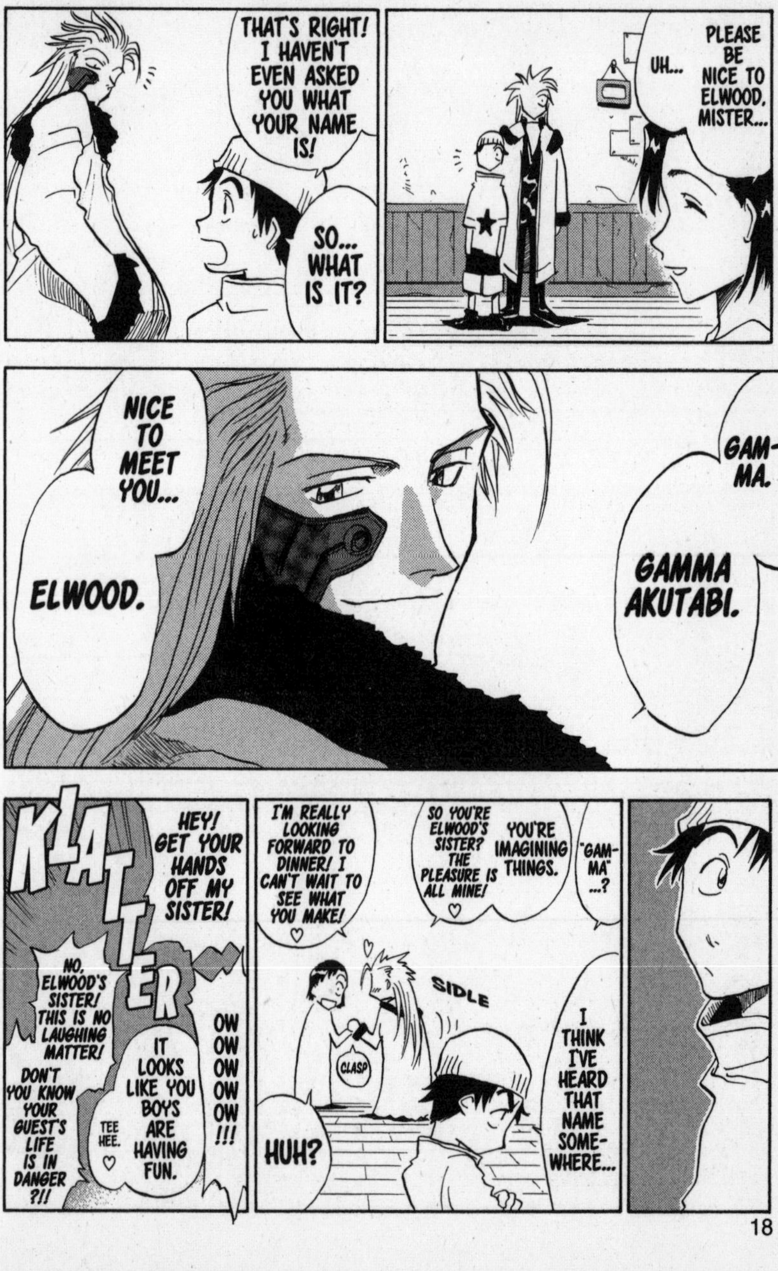
UH...
PLEASE BE NICE TO ELWOOD, MISTER...
THAT'S RIGHT! I HAVEN'T EVEN ASKED YOU WHAT YOUR NAME IS!
SO... WHAT IS IT?
GAM-MA.
GAMMA AKUTABI.
NICE TO MEET YOU...
ELWOOD.
"GAM-MA" ...?
I THINK I'VE HEARD THAT NAME SOME-WHERE...
YOU'RE IMAGINING THINGS.
SO YOU'RE ELWOOD'S SISTER? THE PLEASURE IS ALL MINE! ♡
I'M REALLY LOOKING FORWARD TO DINNER! I CAN'T WAIT TO SEE WHAT YOU MAKE! ♡
SIDLE
CLASP
HUH?
KLATTER
HEY! GET YOUR HANDS OFF MY SISTER!
OW OW OW OW OW!!!
NO, ELWOOD'S SISTER! THIS IS NO LAUGHING MATTER!
DON'T YOU KNOW YOUR GUEST'S LIFE IS IN DANGER?!!
IT LOOKS LIKE YOU BOYS ARE HAVING FUN.
TEE HEE. ♡

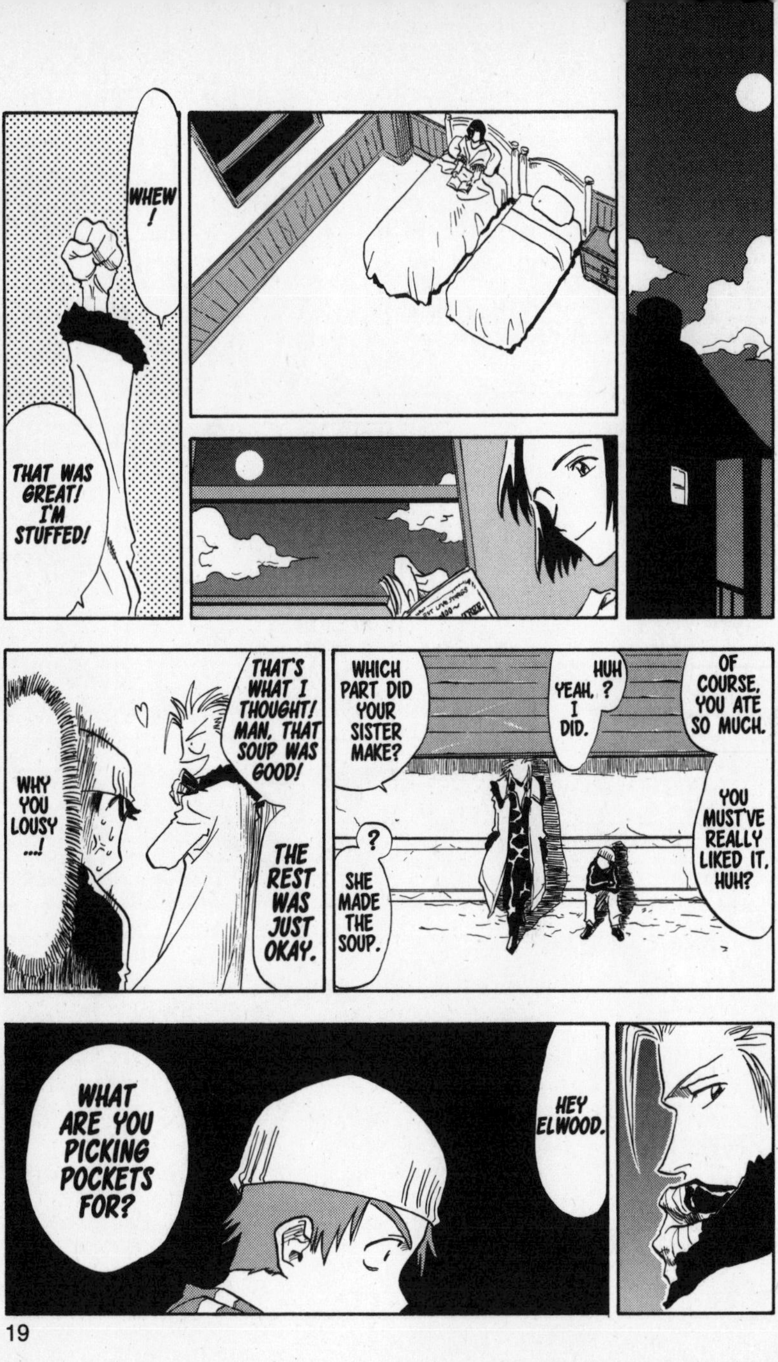
WHEW!
THAT WAS GREAT! I'M STUFFED!
OF COURSE. YOU ATE SO MUCH.
YOU MUST'VE REALLY LIKED IT, HUH?
HUH?
YEAH, I DID.
WHICH PART DID YOUR SISTER MAKE?
?
SHE MADE THE SOUP.
THAT'S WHAT I THOUGHT! MAN, THAT SOUP WAS GOOD!
THE REST WAS JUST OKAY.
WHY YOU LOUSY ...!
HEY ELWOOD.
WHAT ARE YOU PICKING POCKETS FOR?

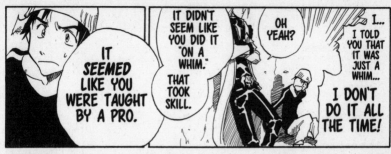

I... I TOLD YOU THAT IT WAS JUST A WHIM...
I DON'T DO IT ALL THE TIME!
OH YEAH?
IT DIDN'T SEEM LIKE YOU DID IT "ON A WHIM."
THAT TOOK SKILL.
IT SEEMED LIKE YOU WERE TAUGHT BY A PRO.
...I WAS.
A PRO TAUGHT ME...
...HOW TO PICK POCKETS AND THROW KNIVES!
...WHO?
A GROUP OF ARMED BANDITS HAVE A HIDEOUT AROUND HERE...
GRIP
THEY'RE CALLED THE "GREY ANTS." AND THEIR BOSS'S NAME...
...IS KINQRO!!
...I GET IT.
SO THAT'S ELWOOD'S PLAN...

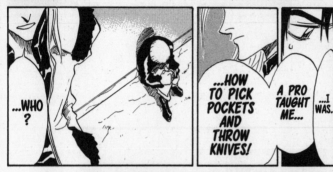

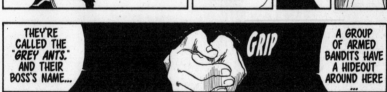

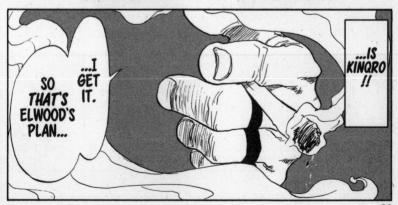

READ THIS WAY

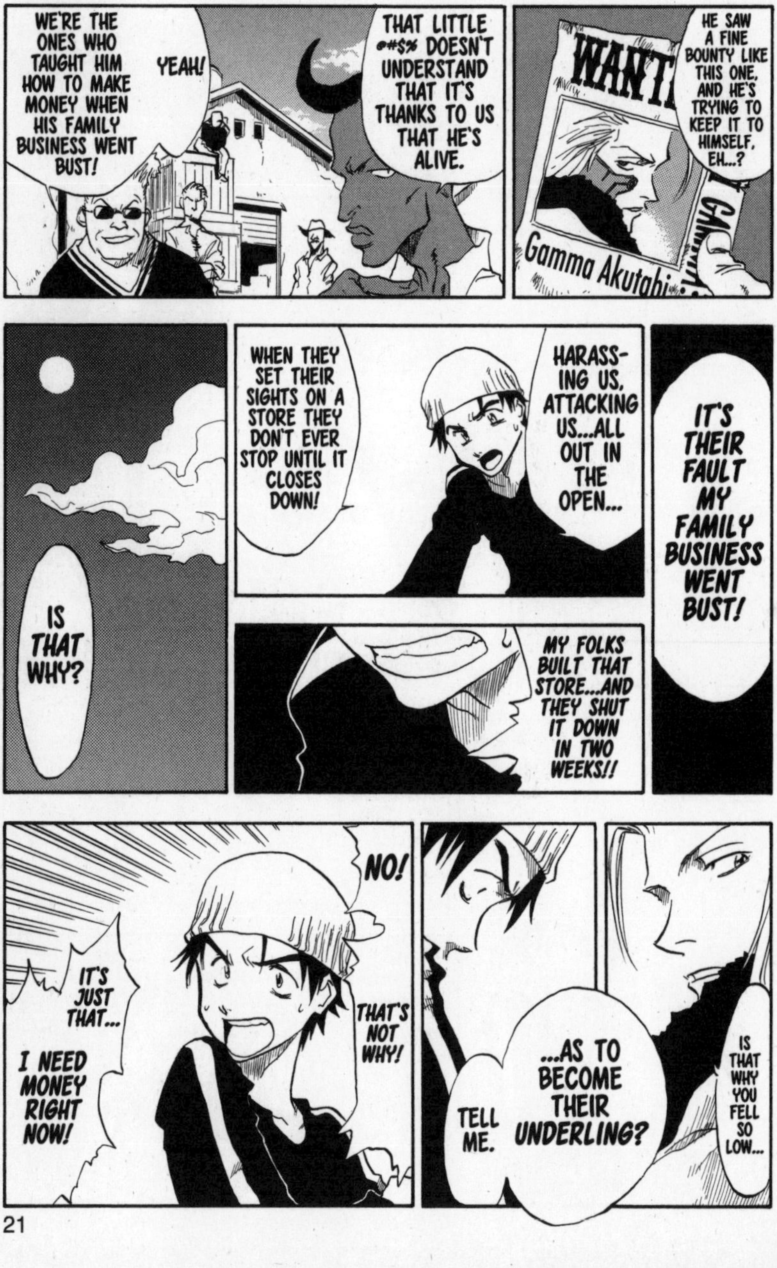

HE SAW A FINE BOUNTY LIKE THIS ONE, AND HE'S TRYING TO KEEP IT TO HIMSELF, EH...?
WANT
Gamma Akutabi
THAT LITTLE @#$% DOESN'T UNDERSTAND THAT IT'S THANKS TO US THAT HE'S ALIVE.
YEAH!
WE'RE THE ONES WHO TAUGHT HIM HOW TO MAKE MONEY WHEN HIS FAMILY BUSINESS WENT BUST!
IT'S THEIR FAULT MY FAMILY BUSINESS WENT BUST!
HARASSING US, ATTACKING US...ALL OUT IN THE OPEN...
WHEN THEY SET THEIR SIGHTS ON A STORE THEY DON'T EVER STOP UNTIL IT CLOSES DOWN!
MY FOLKS BUILT THAT STORE...AND THEY SHUT IT DOWN IN TWO WEEKS!!
IS THAT WHY?
IS THAT WHY YOU FELL SO LOW...
...AS TO BECOME THEIR UNDERLING?
TELL ME.
NO!
THAT'S NOT WHY!
IT'S JUST THAT...
I NEED MONEY RIGHT NOW!

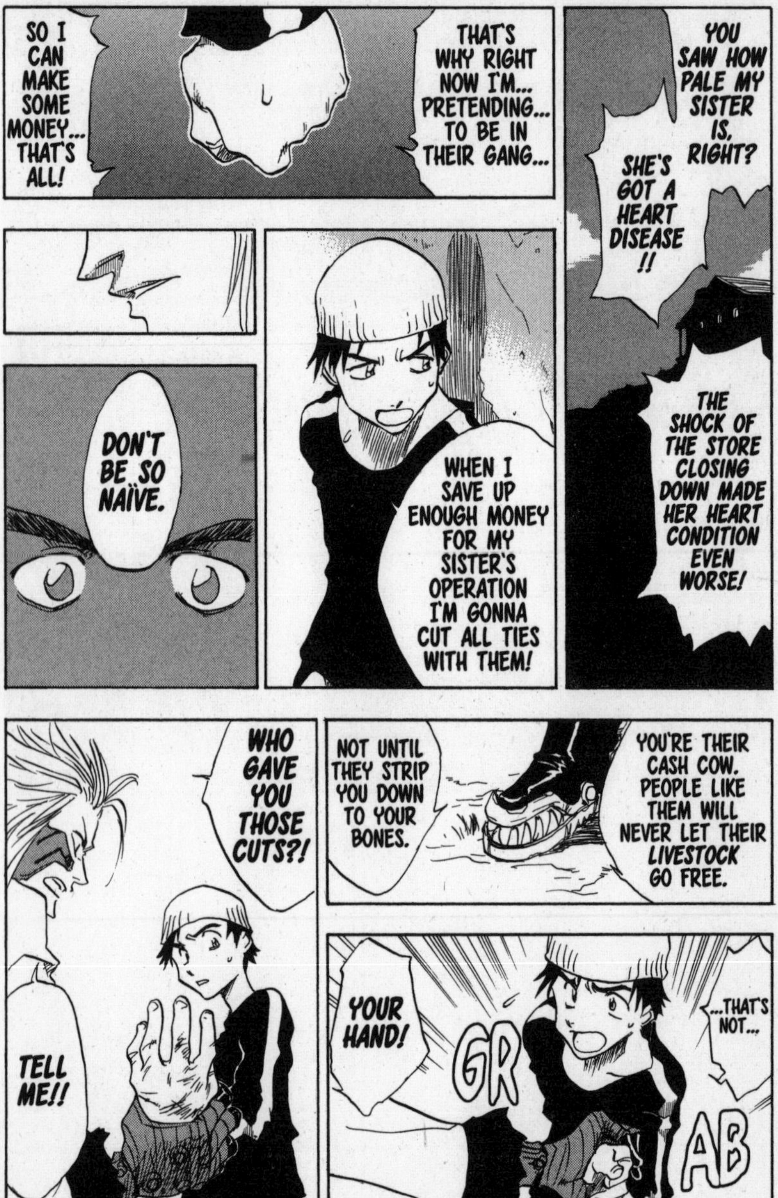
YOU SAW HOW PALE MY SISTER IS, RIGHT?
SHE'S GOT A HEART DISEASE !!
THE SHOCK OF THE STORE CLOSING DOWN MADE HER HEART CONDITION EVEN WORSE!
THAT'S WHY RIGHT NOW I'M... PRETENDING... TO BE IN THEIR GANG...
SO I CAN MAKE SOME MONEY... THAT'S ALL!
WHEN I SAVE UP ENOUGH MONEY FOR MY SISTER'S OPERATION I'M GONNA CUT ALL TIES WITH THEM!
DON'T BE SO NAÏVE.
YOU'RE THEIR CASH COW. PEOPLE LIKE THEM WILL NEVER LET THEIR LIVESTOCK GO FREE.
NOT UNTIL THEY STRIP YOU DOWN TO YOUR BONES.
...THAT'S NOT...
YOUR HAND!
GR
AB
WHO GAVE YOU THOSE CUTS?!
TELL ME!!

READ THIS WAY

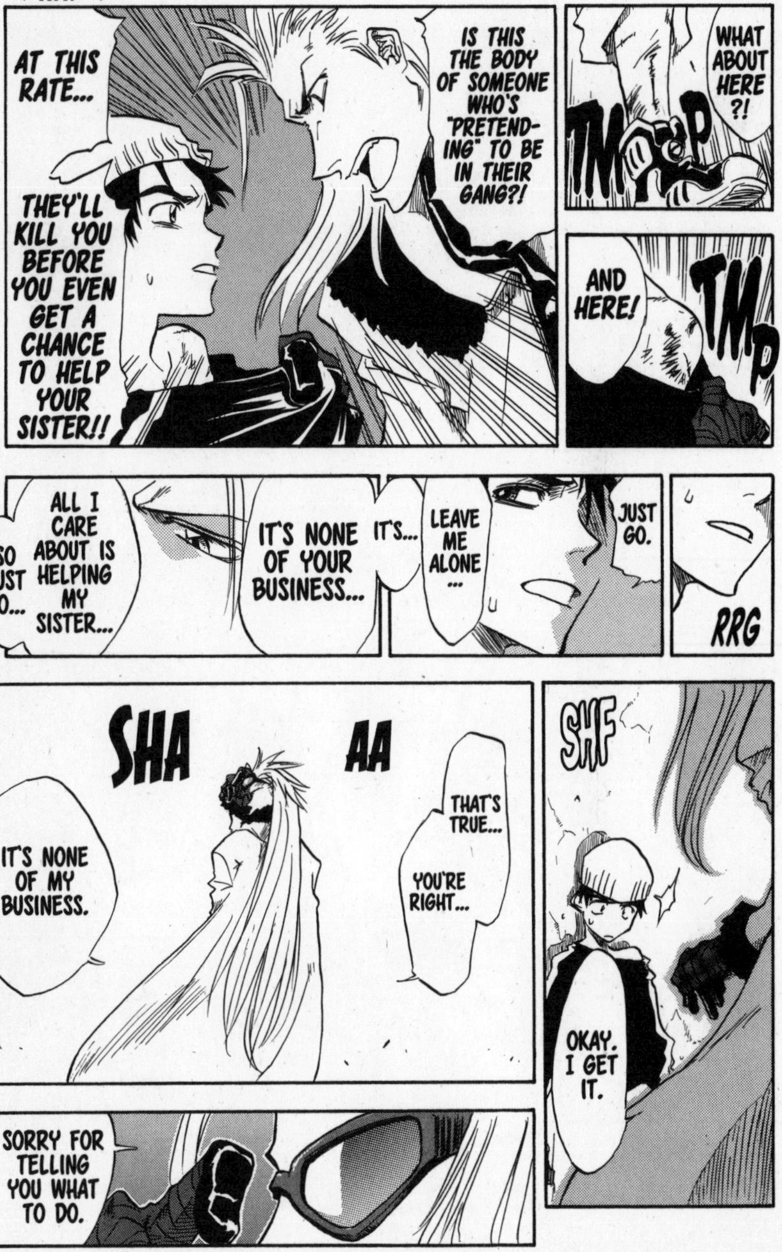
WHAT ABOUT HERE?!
TMP
AND HERE!
TMP
IS THIS THE BODY OF SOMEONE WHO'S "PRETENDING" TO BE IN THEIR GANG?!
AT THIS RATE...
THEY'LL KILL YOU BEFORE YOU EVEN GET A CHANCE TO HELP YOUR SISTER!!
RRG
JUST GO.
LEAVE ME ALONE...
IT'S...
IT'S NONE OF YOUR BUSINESS...
ALL I CARE ABOUT IS HELPING MY SISTER...
SO JUST GO...
SHF
OKAY. I GET IT.
SHAA
AA
THAT'S TRUE...
YOU'RE RIGHT...
IT'S NONE OF MY BUSINESS.
SORRY FOR TELLING YOU WHAT TO DO.

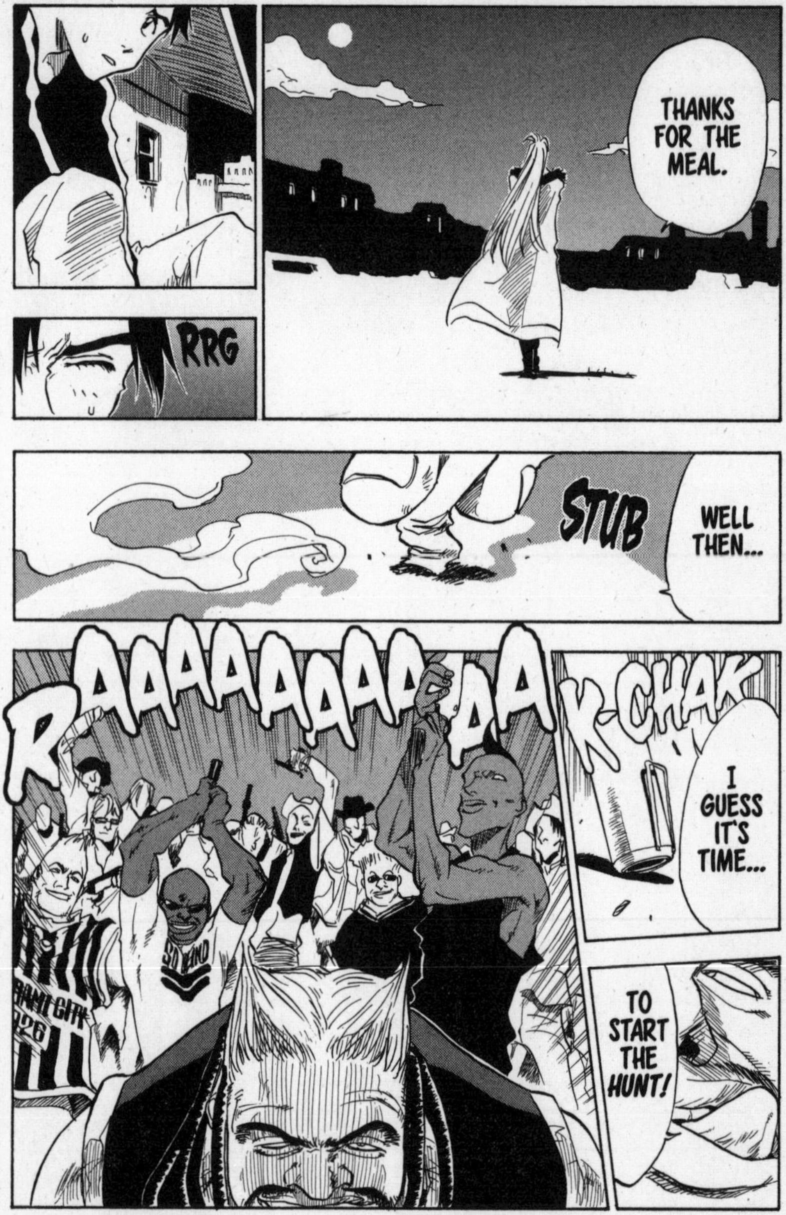
THANKS FOR THE MEAL.
RRG
STUB
WELL THEN...
K-CHAK
I GUESS IT'S TIME...
TO START THE HUNT!
RAAAAAAAAAA

READ THIS WAY

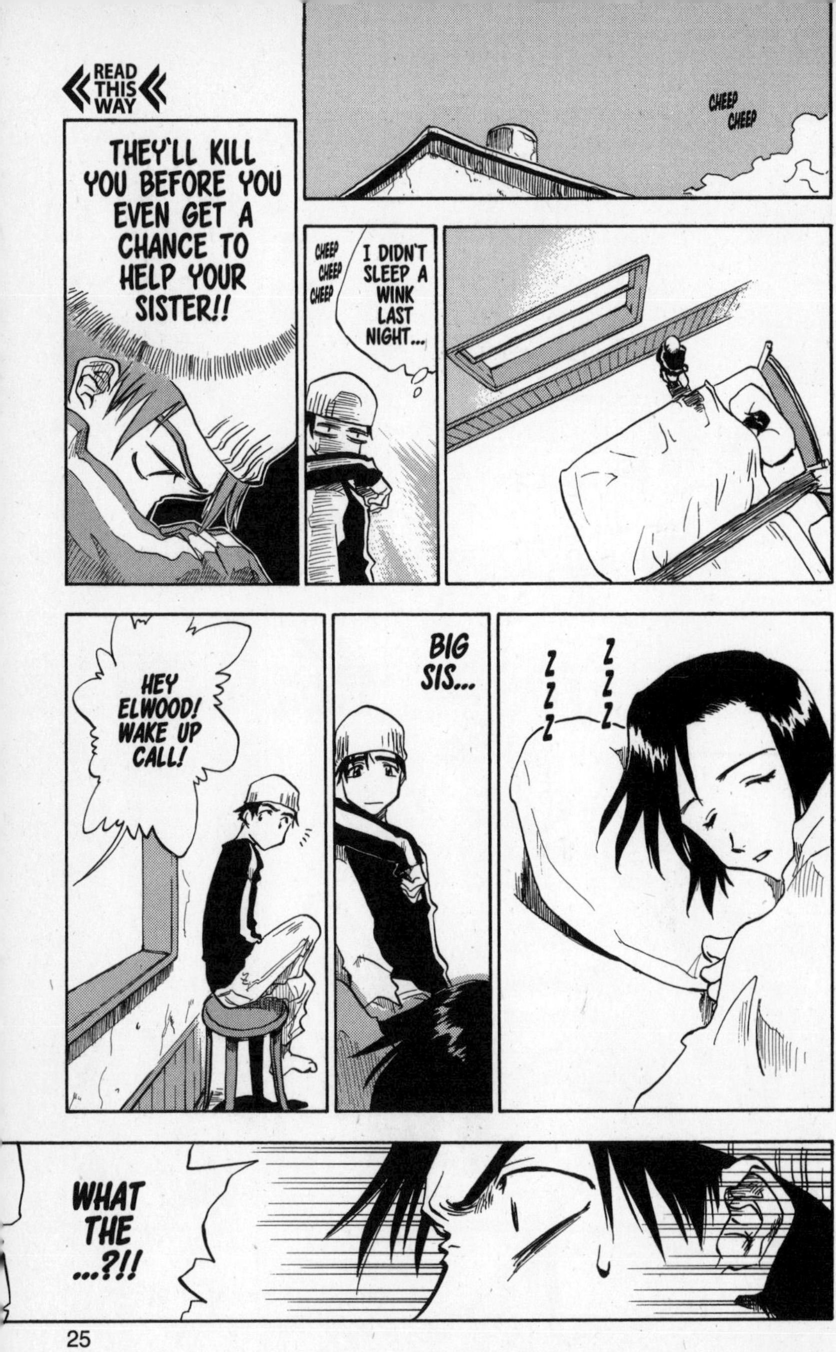
CHEEP CHEEP
CHEEP CHEEP CHEEP
I DIDN'T SLEEP A WINK LAST NIGHT...
THEY'LL KILL YOU BEFORE YOU EVEN GET A CHANCE TO HELP YOUR SISTER!!
Z Z Z Z
Z Z Z
BIG SIS...
HEY ELWOOD! WAKE UP CALL!
WHAT THE ...?!!

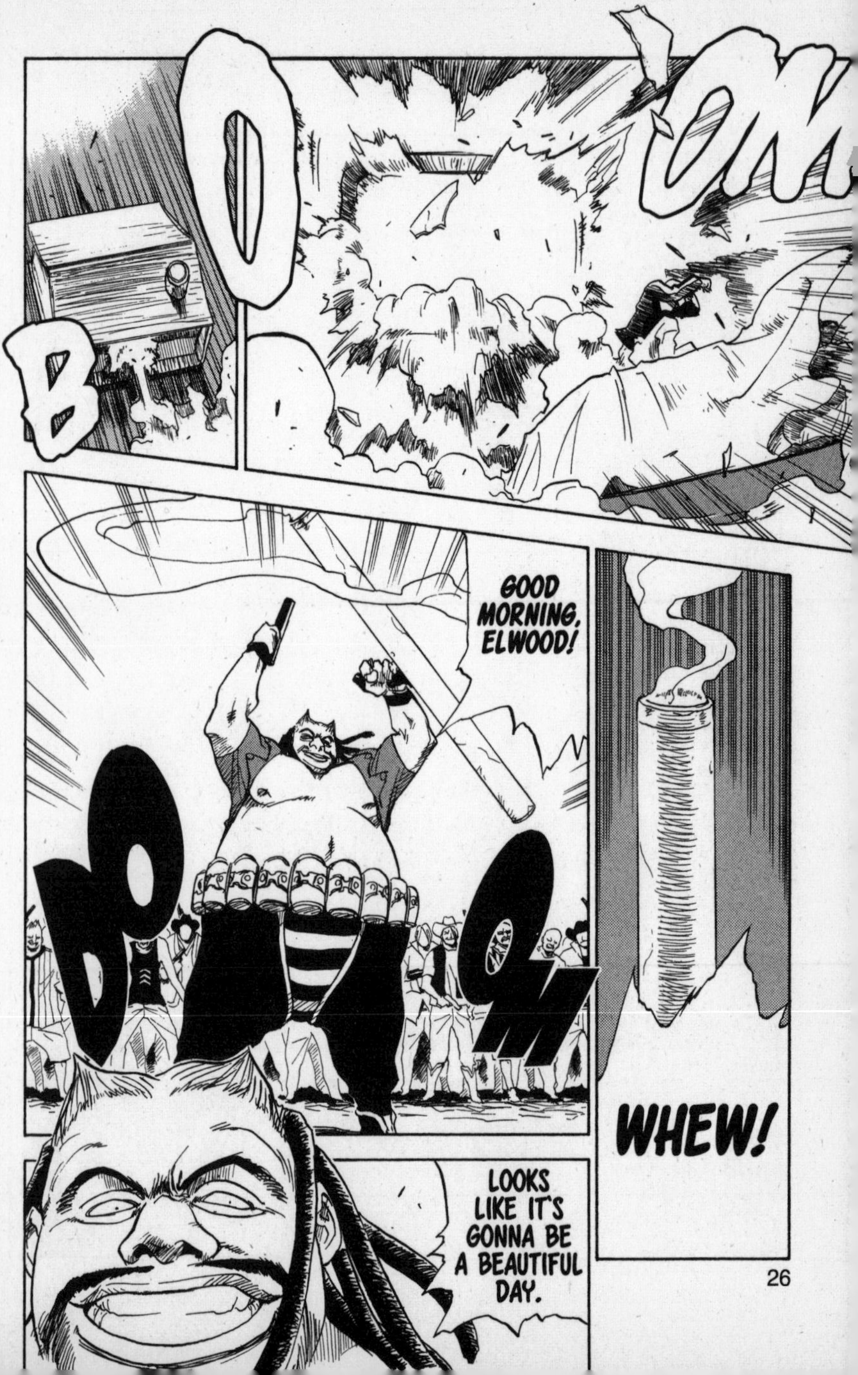
BOOM
WHEW!
GOOD MORNING, ELWOOD!
BOOM
LOOKS LIKE IT'S GONNA BE A BEAUTIFUL DAY.

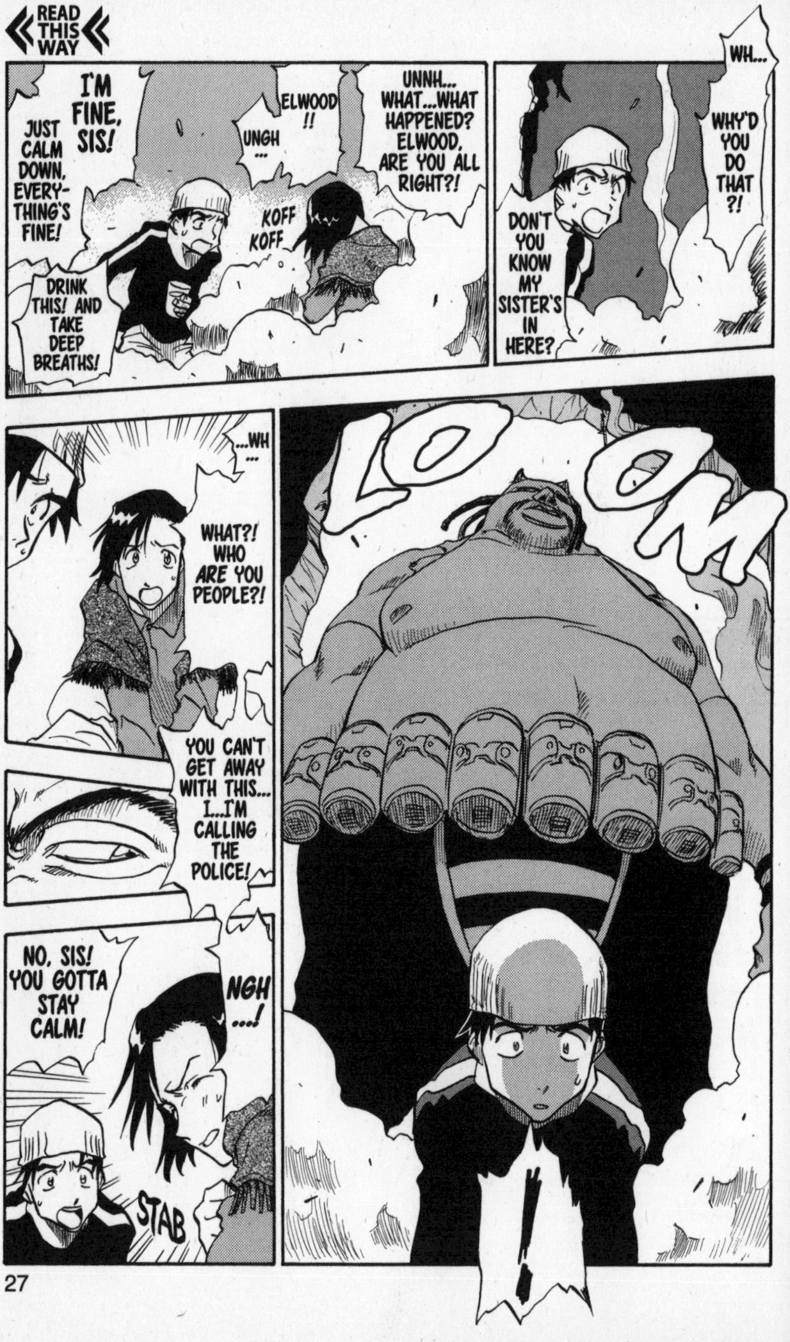
READ THIS WAY
WH...
WHY'D YOU DO THAT?!
DON'T YOU KNOW MY SISTER'S IN HERE?
UNNH... WHAT...WHAT HAPPENED? ELWOOD, ARE YOU ALL RIGHT?!
ELWOOD!!
UNGH...
KOFF KOFF
I'M FINE, SIS!
JUST CALM DOWN, EVERYTHING'S FINE!
DRINK THIS! AND TAKE DEEP BREATHS!
LOOM
...WH...
WHAT?! WHO ARE YOU PEOPLE?!
YOU CAN'T GET AWAY WITH THIS... I...I'M CALLING THE POLICE!
NGH...!
NO, SIS! YOU GOTTA STAY CALM!
STAB

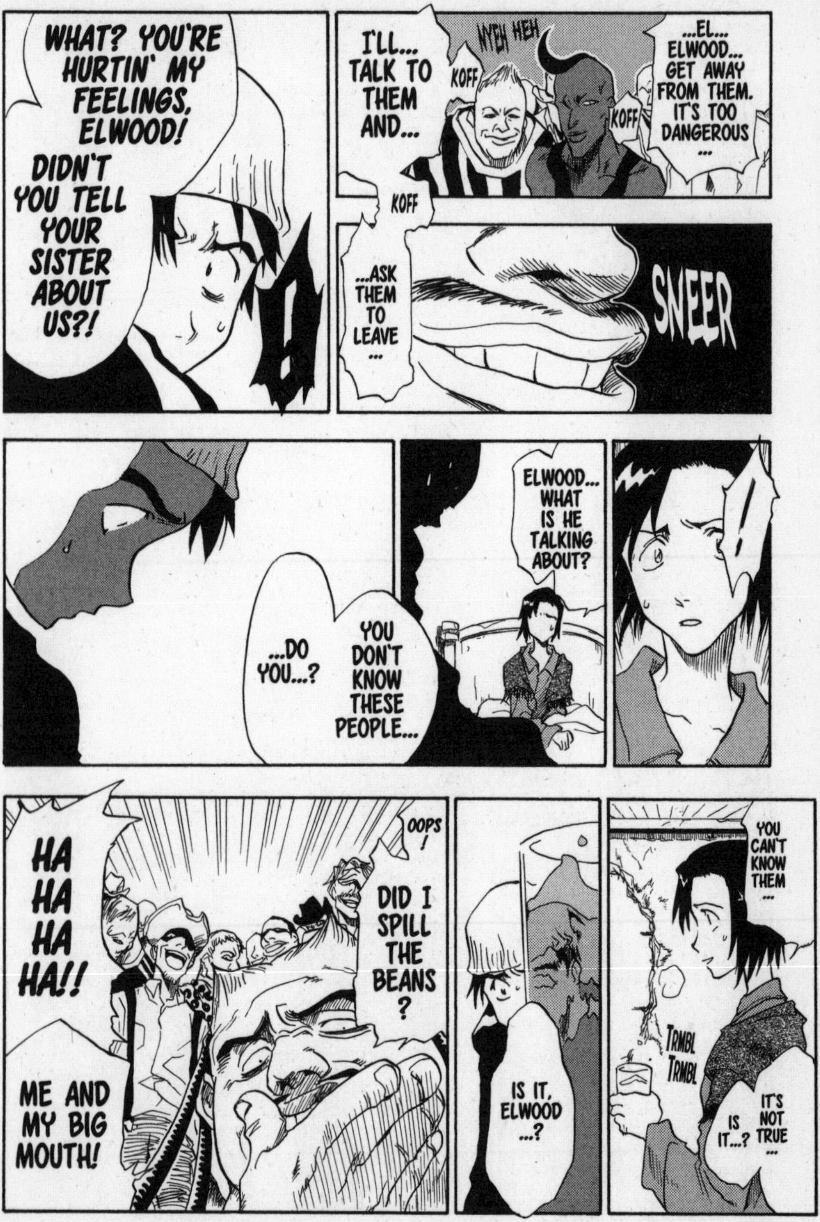
...EL... ELWOOD... GET AWAY FROM THEM. IT'S TOO DANGEROUS...
NYEH HEH
KOFF
KOFF
I'LL... TALK TO THEM AND...
KOFF
...ASK THEM TO LEAVE...
SNEER
WHAT? YOU'RE HURTIN' MY FEELINGS, ELWOOD!
DIDN'T YOU TELL YOUR SISTER ABOUT US?!
!
ELWOOD... WHAT IS HE TALKING ABOUT?
YOU DON'T KNOW THESE PEOPLE...
...DO YOU...?
YOU CAN'T KNOW THEM...
TRMBL TRMBL
IT'S NOT TRUE...
IS IT...?
IS IT, ELWOOD...?
OOPS!
DID I SPILL THE BEANS?
HA HA HA HA HA!!
ME AND MY BIG MOUTH!

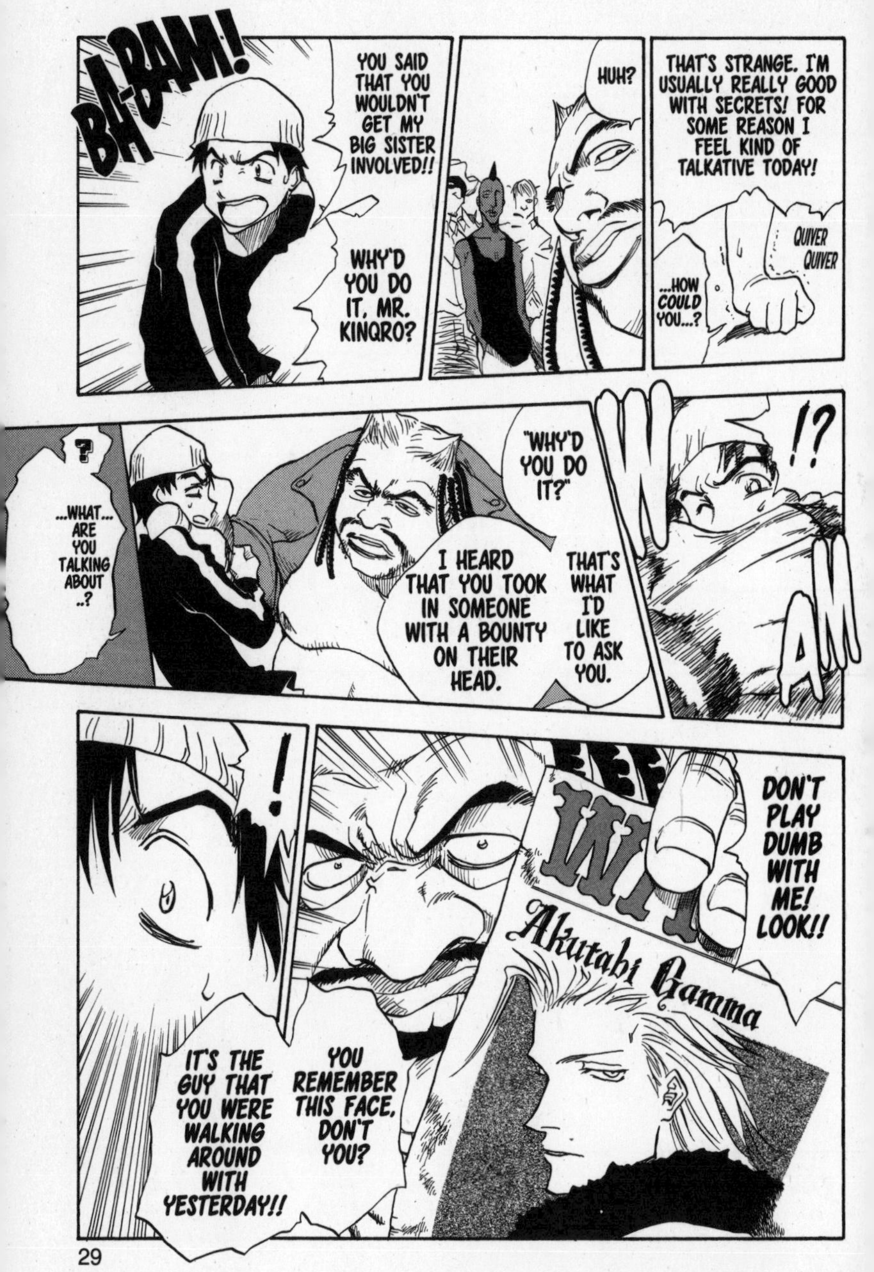
THAT'S STRANGE. I'M USUALLY REALLY GOOD WITH SECRETS! FOR SOME REASON I FEEL KIND OF TALKATIVE TODAY!
QUIVER QUIVER
...HOW COULD YOU...?
HUH?
BA-BAM!
YOU SAID THAT YOU WOULDN'T GET MY BIG SISTER INVOLVED!!
WHY'D YOU DO IT, MR. KINQRO?
!?
WAM
"WHY'D YOU DO IT?"
THAT'S WHAT I'D LIKE TO ASK YOU.
I HEARD THAT YOU TOOK IN SOMEONE WITH A BOUNTY ON THEIR HEAD.
?
...WHAT... ARE YOU TALKING ABOUT ..?
DON'T PLAY DUMB WITH ME! LOOK!!
Akutabi Gamma
YOU REMEMBER THIS FACE, DON'T YOU?
IT'S THE GUY THAT YOU WERE WALKING AROUND WITH YESTERDAY!!
!

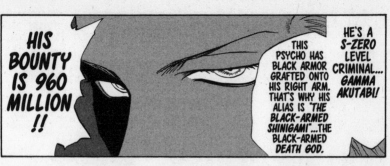

HE'S A S-ZERO LEVEL CRIMINAL... GAMMA AKUTABI!
THIS PSYCHO HAS BLACK ARMOR GRAFTED ONTO HIS RIGHT ARM. THAT'S WHY HIS ALIAS IS "THE BLACK-ARMED SHINIGAMI"...THE BLACK-ARMED DEATH GOD.
HIS BOUNTY IS 960 MILLION!!
WHERE IS HE NOW?!
I... I DON'T KNOW!
HE CAME TO THE HOUSE ONCE YESTERDAY... BUT HE LEFT RIGHT AWAY!!
I DON'T KNOW WHERE HE WENT AFTER THAT!
...
...IS THAT RIGHT?!
SZZZ
AGGH!
HOW'S YOUR MEMORY NOW?
WHERE IS HE?
P...PLEASE BELIEVE ME! I'M TELLING THE TRUTH!!
HON-EST...!
I DIDN'T KNOW THAT THIS GUY HAD A BOUNTY ON HIS HEAD EITHER!!

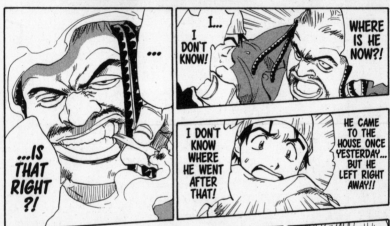

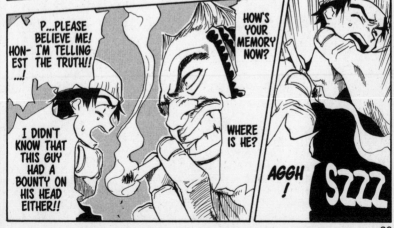

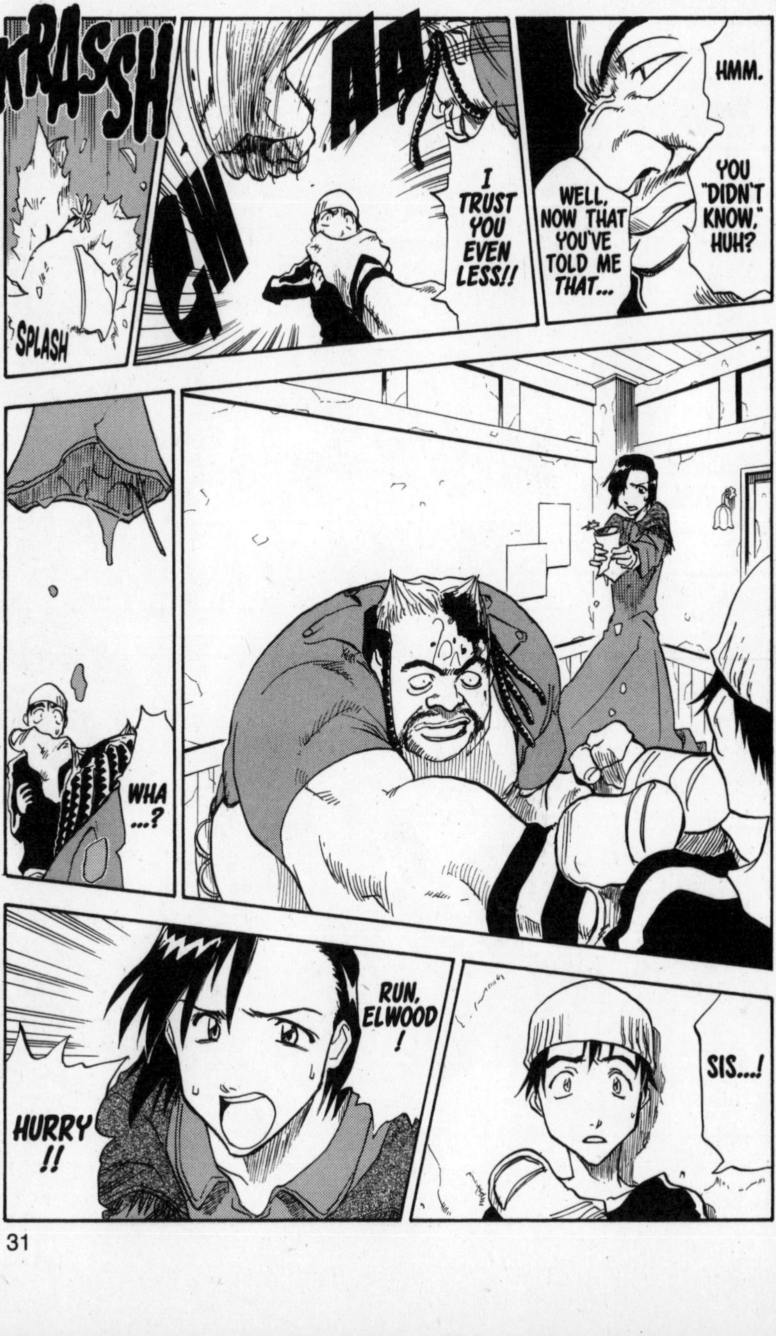
HMM.
YOU "DIDN'T KNOW," HUH?
WELL, NOW THAT YOU'VE TOLD ME THAT...
I TRUST YOU EVEN LESS!!
KRASSH
SPLASH
WHA ...?
SIS...!
RUN, ELWOOD!
HURRY!!

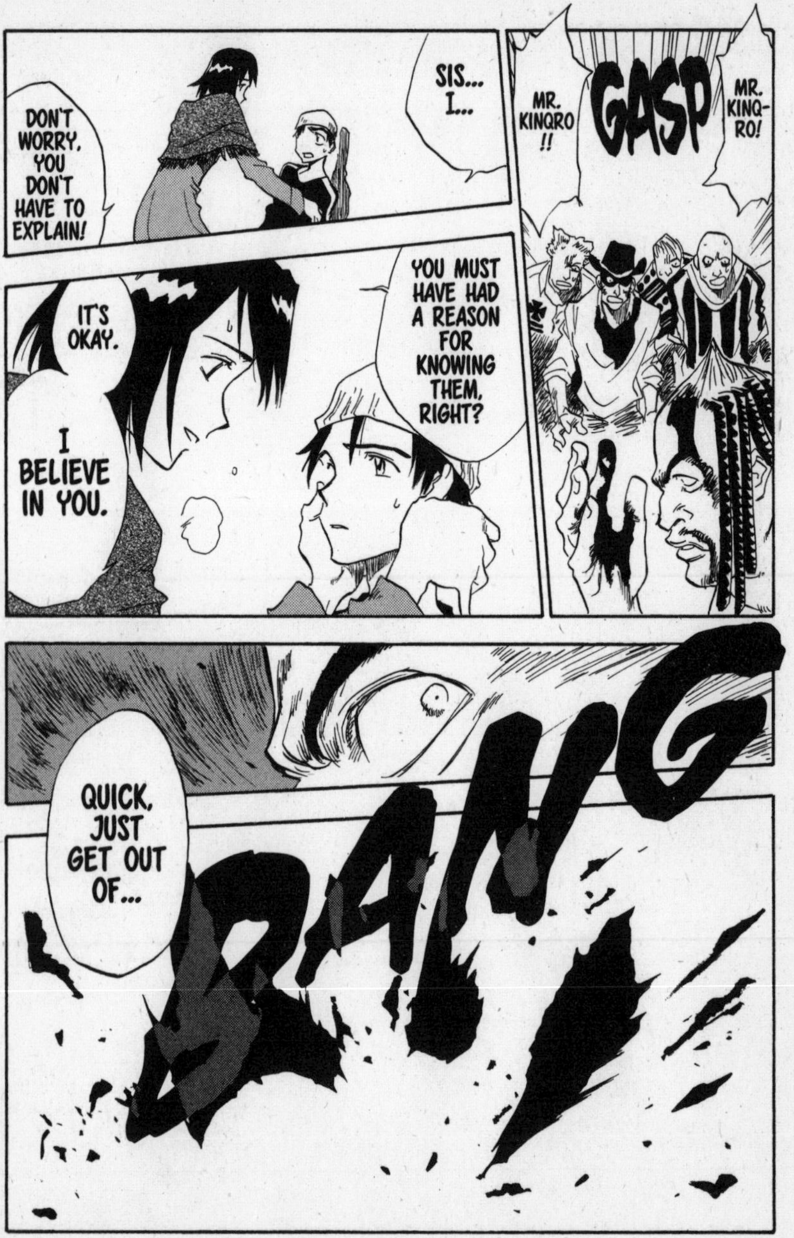
MR. KINQRO!
GASP
MR. KINQRO !!
SIS... I...
DON'T WORRY. YOU DON'T HAVE TO EXPLAIN!
YOU MUST HAVE HAD A REASON FOR KNOWING THEM, RIGHT?
IT'S OKAY.
I BELIEVE IN YOU.
QUICK, JUST GET OUT OF...
BANG

READ THIS WAY

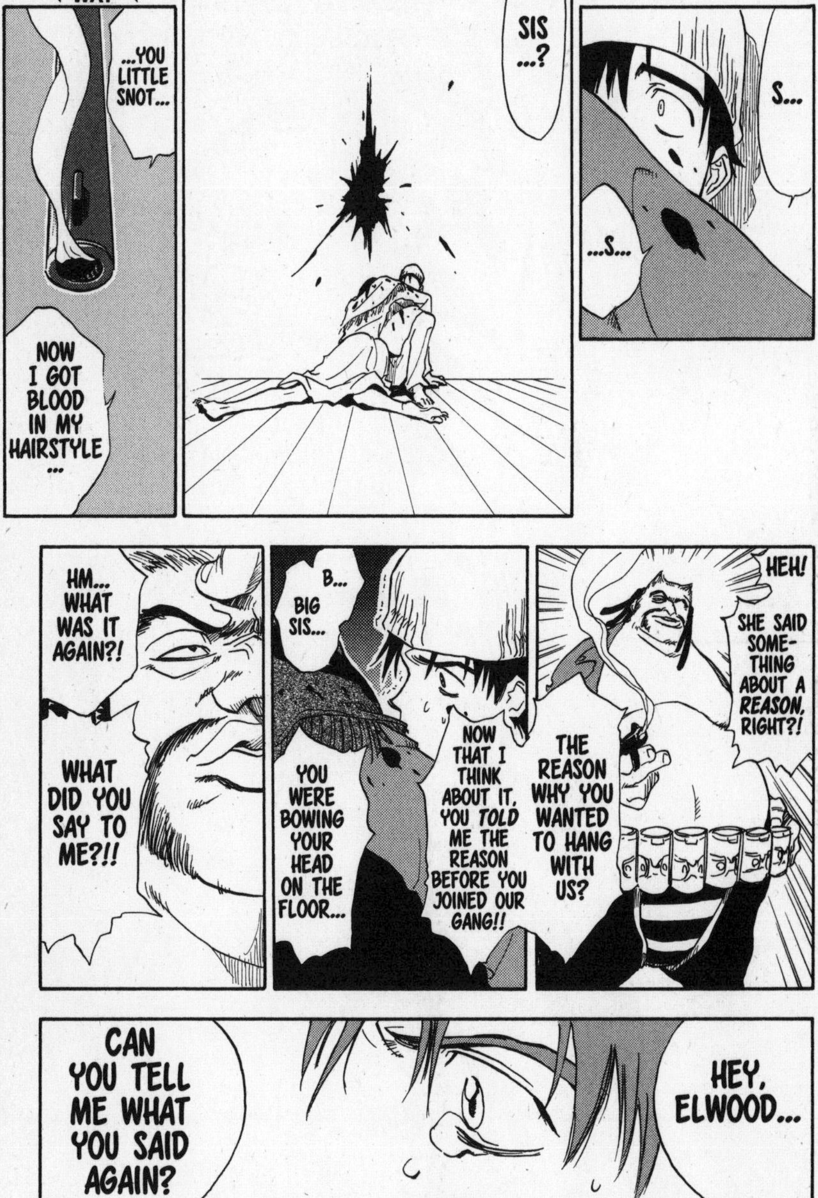
S...
...S...
SIS ...?
...YOU LITTLE SNOT...
NOW I GOT BLOOD IN MY HAIRSTYLE ...
HEH!
SHE SAID SOME-THING ABOUT A *REASON*, RIGHT?!
THE REASON WHY YOU WANTED TO HANG WITH US?
B...
BIG SIS...
NOW THAT I THINK ABOUT IT, YOU *TOLD* ME THE REASON BEFORE YOU JOINED OUR GANG!!
YOU WERE BOWING YOUR HEAD ON THE FLOOR...
HM... WHAT WAS IT AGAIN?!
WHAT DID YOU SAY TO ME?!!
HEY, ELWOOD...
CAN YOU TELL ME WHAT YOU SAID AGAIN?

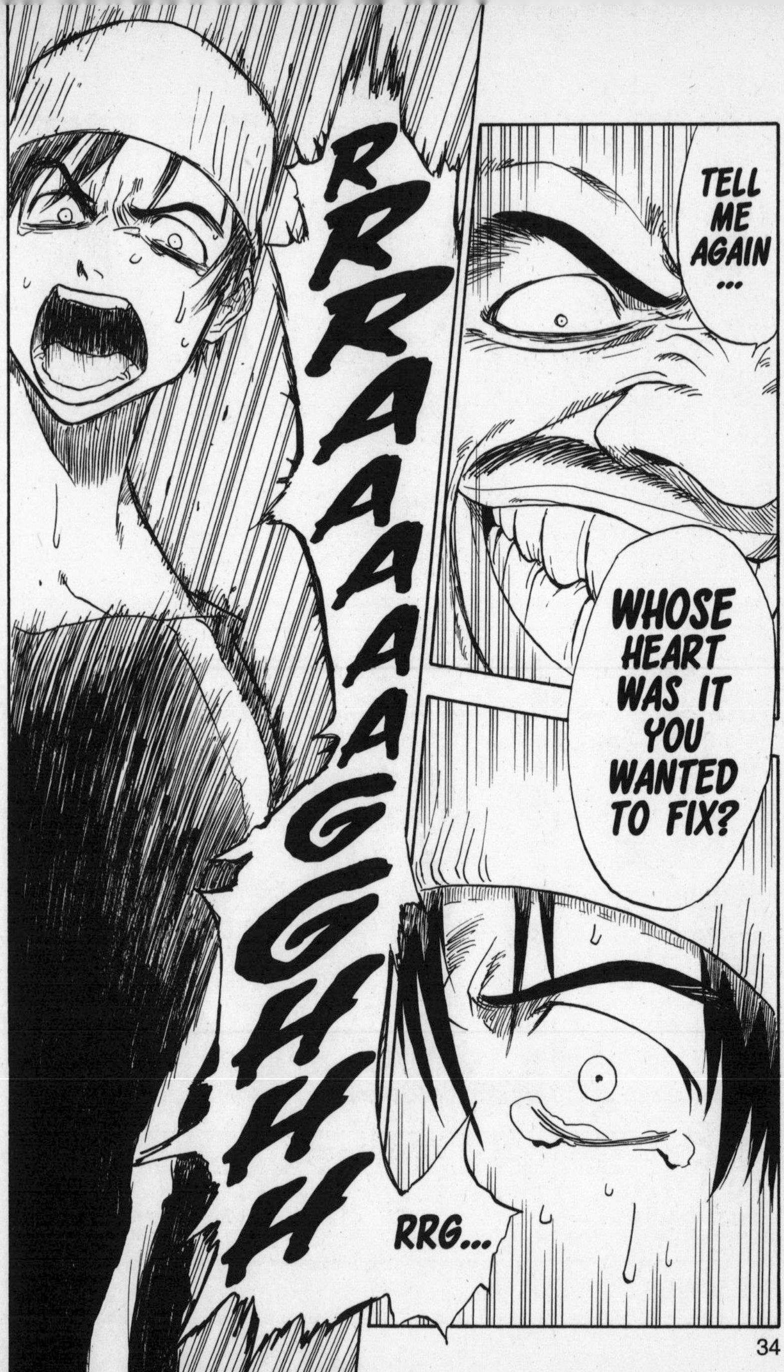
TELL ME AGAIN ...
WHOSE HEART WAS IT YOU WANTED TO FIX?
RRG...
RRRAAAAAGGHHHH

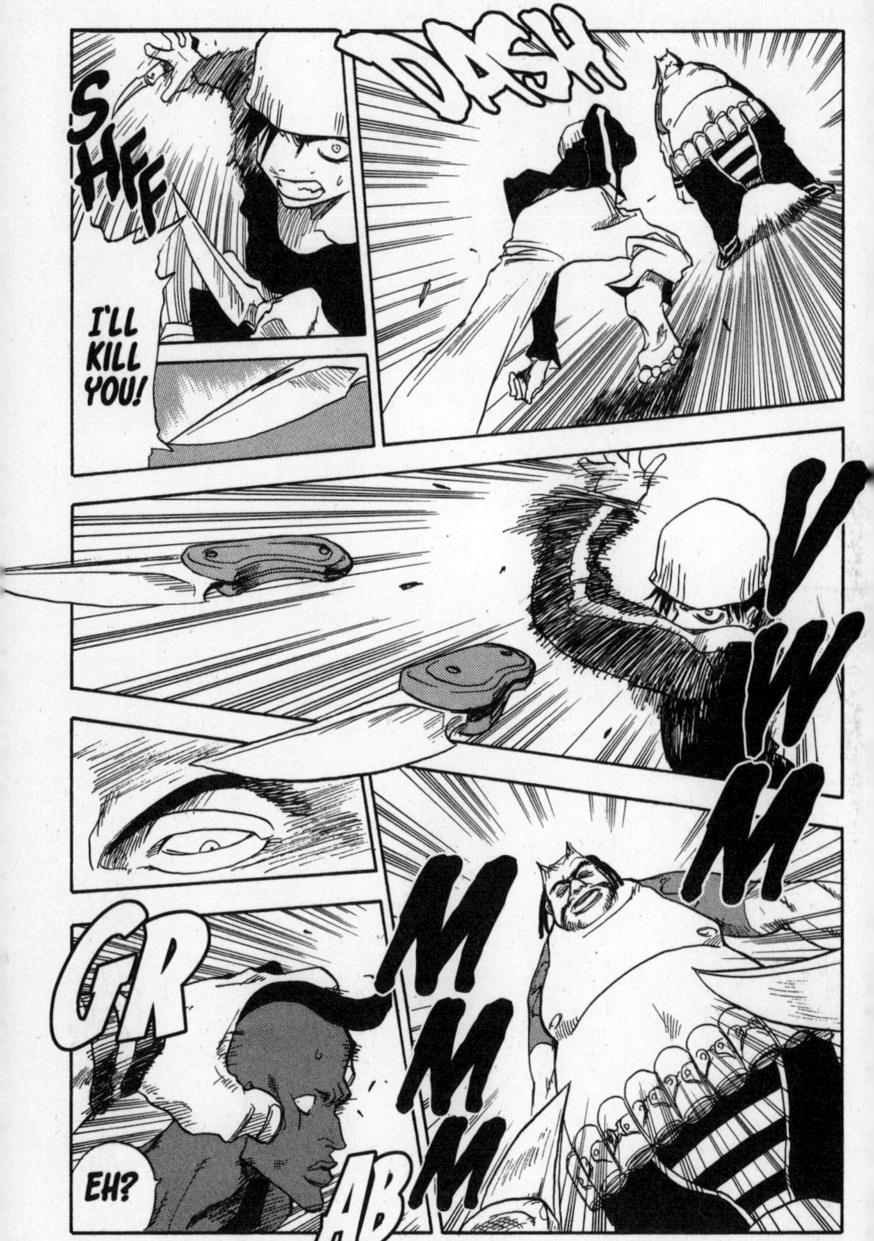
DASH
SHFF
I'LL KILL YOU!
VWM
MMMM
GR
AB
EH?

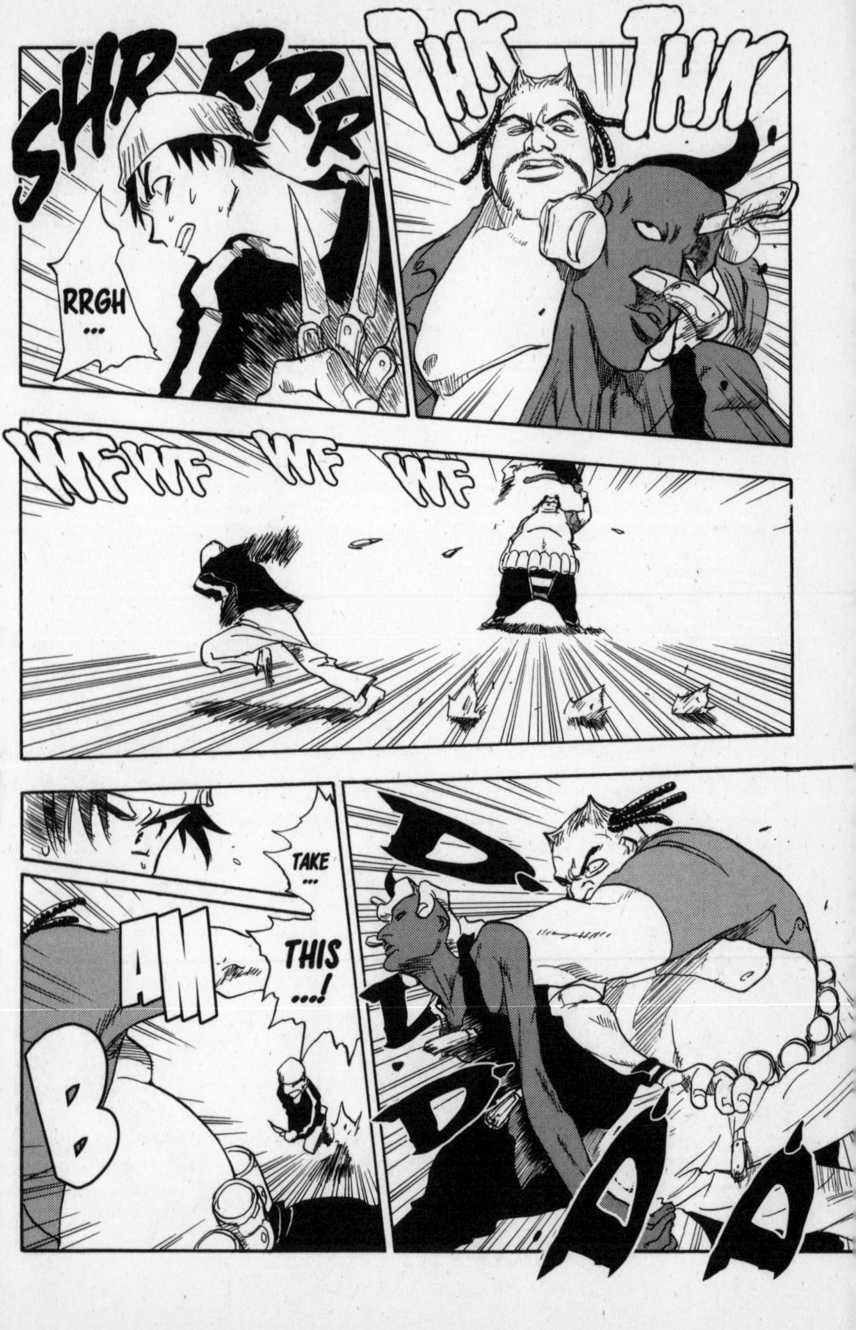

THN THN.
SHRRRR
RRGH ...
WFWF WF WF
DDAA
TAKE ... THIS ...!
BAM

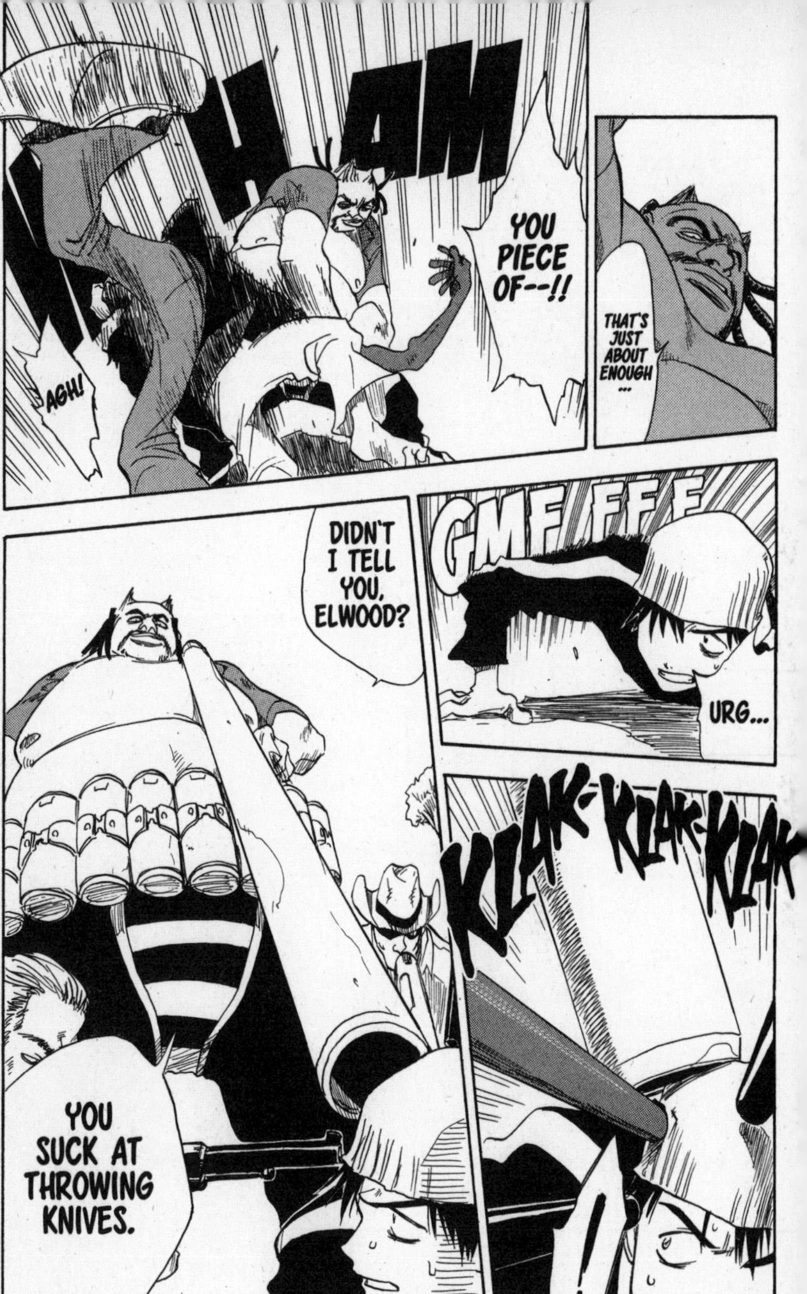
THAT'S JUST ABOUT ENOUGH...
YOU PIECE OF--!!
AGH!
GMFFFF
URG...
KLAK-KLAK-KLAK-KLAK
DIDN'T I TELL YOU, ELWOOD?
YOU SUCK AT THROWING KNIVES.
!

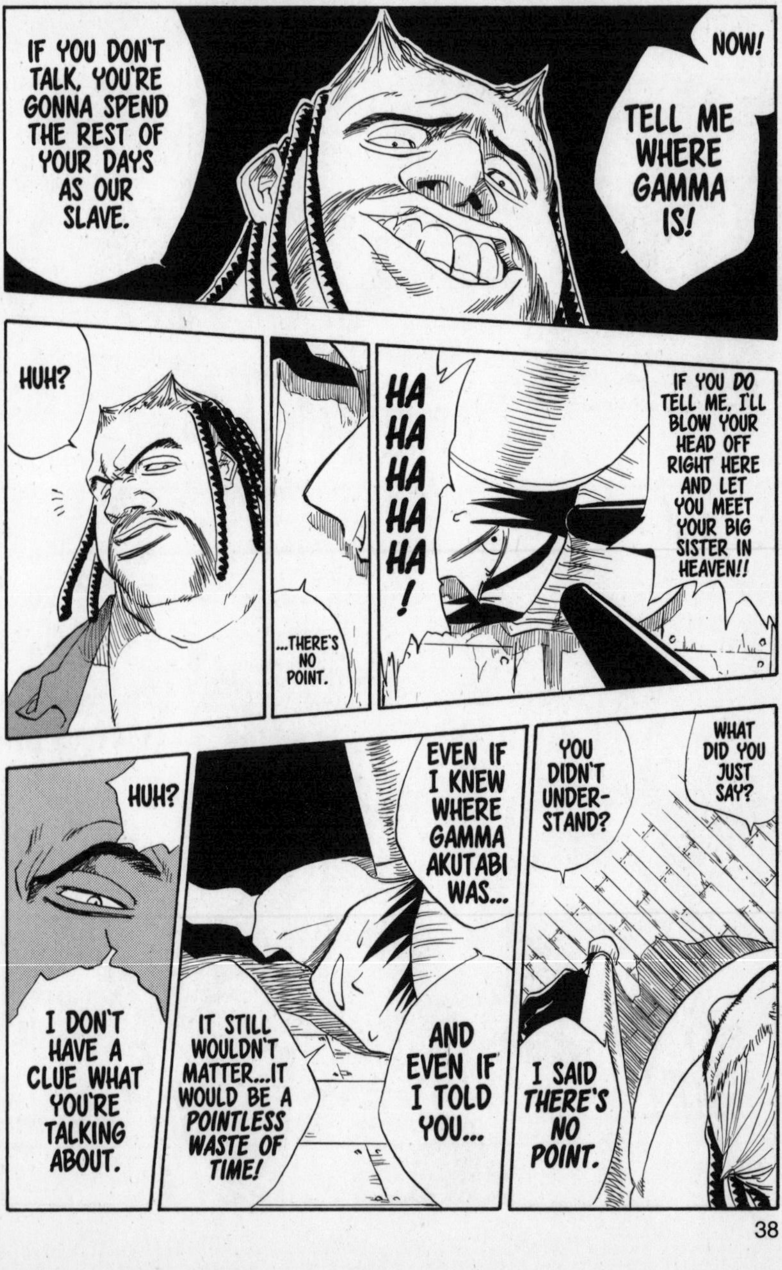
NOW!
TELL ME WHERE GAMMA IS!
IF YOU DON'T TALK, YOU'RE GONNA SPEND THE REST OF YOUR DAYS AS OUR SLAVE.
IF YOU DO TELL ME, I'LL BLOW YOUR HEAD OFF RIGHT HERE AND LET YOU MEET YOUR BIG SISTER IN HEAVEN!!
HA HA HA HA HA HA!
...THERE'S NO POINT.
HUH?
WHAT DID YOU JUST SAY?
YOU DIDN'T UNDER-STAND?
I SAID THERE'S NO POINT.
EVEN IF I KNEW WHERE GAMMA AKUTABI WAS...
AND EVEN IF I TOLD YOU...
IT STILL WOULDN'T MATTER...IT WOULD BE A POINTLESS WASTE OF TIME!
HUH?
I DON'T HAVE A CLUE WHAT YOU'RE TALKING ABOUT.

OF COURSE YOU DON'T!!

HOW COULD A PIG LIKE YOU UNDERSTAND HUMAN SPEECH?!!

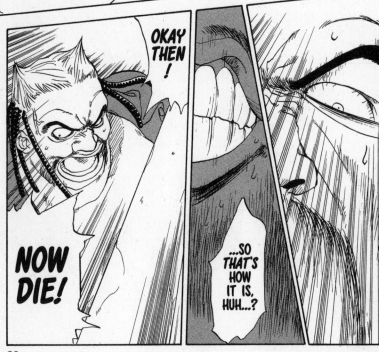

OKAY THEN!

NOW DIE!

...SO THAT'S HOW IT IS, HUH...?

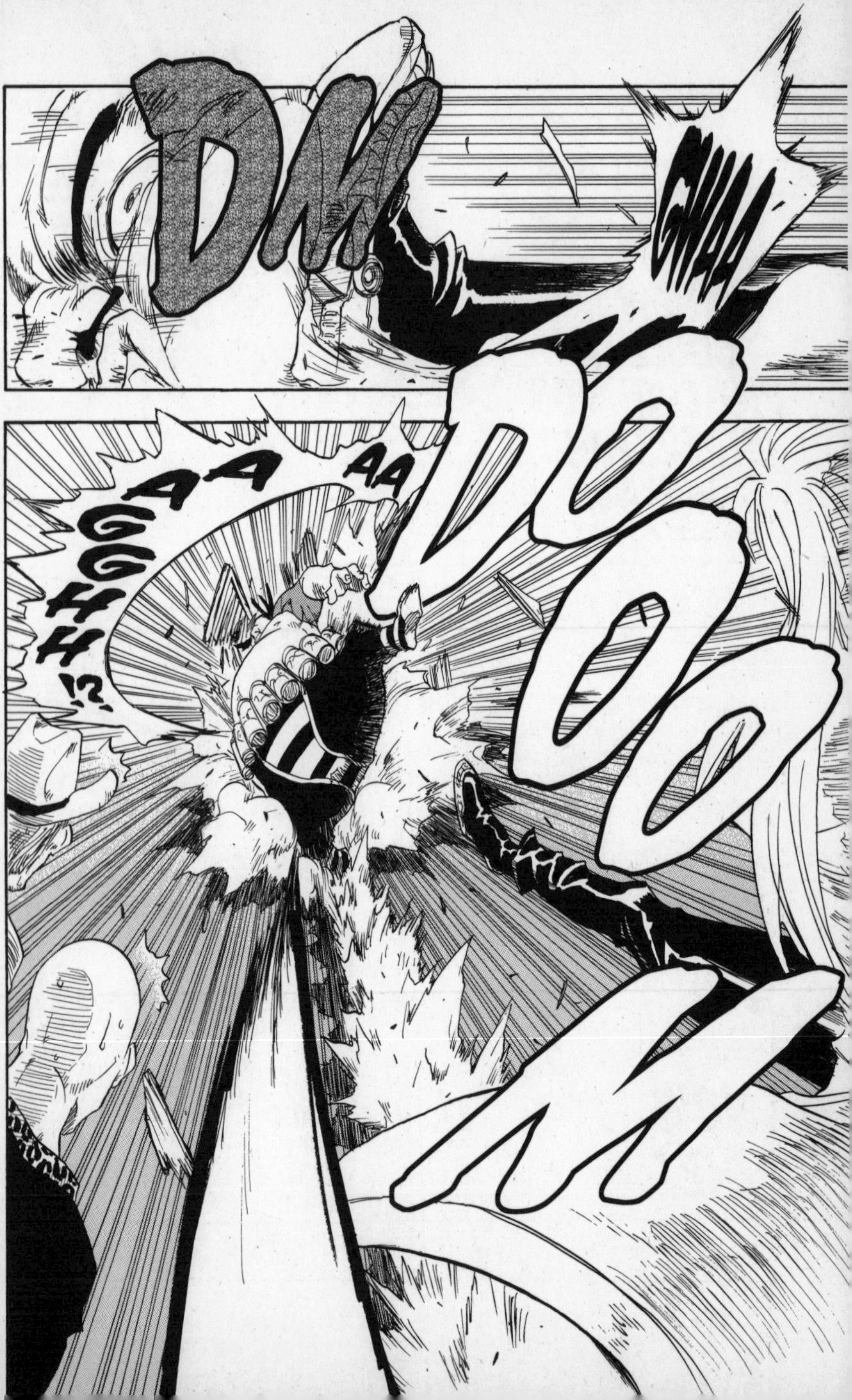
GWAA
DM
DOOOOM
AA
AAGGHH!?

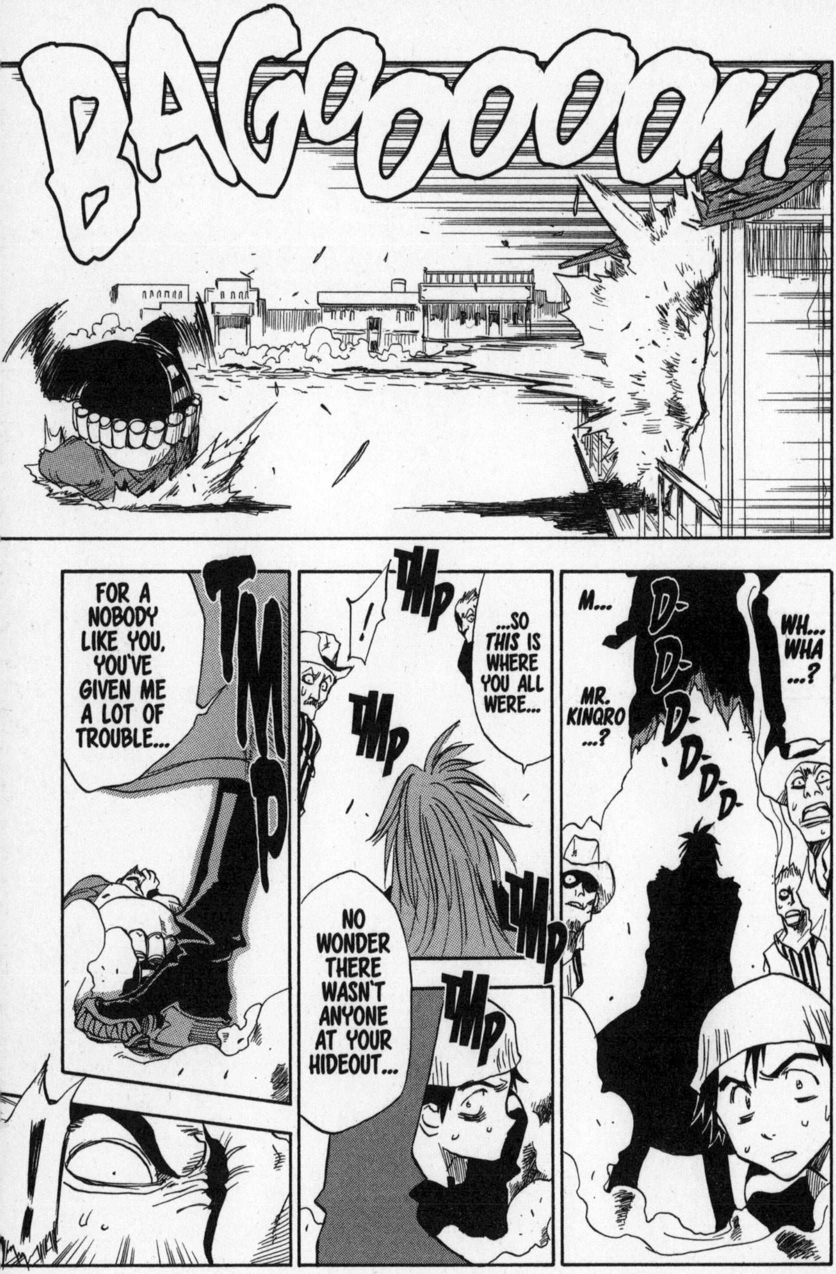
BAGOOOOOM
WH... WHA ...?
M...
MR. KINQRO ...?
D-D-D-D-D-D-D-D
...SO THIS IS WHERE YOU ALL WERE...
TMP
!
TMP
TMP
NO WONDER THERE WASN'T ANYONE AT YOUR HIDEOUT...
TMP
FOR A NOBODY LIKE YOU, YOU'VE GIVEN ME A LOT OF TROUBLE...
TMP
!

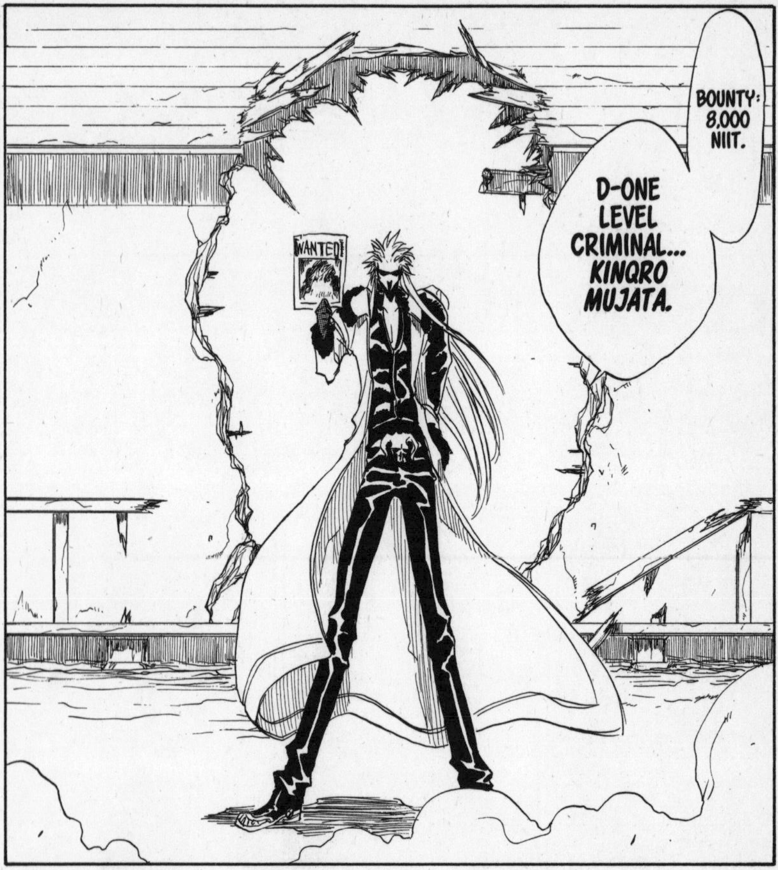
BOUNTY: 8,000 NIIT.
D-ONE LEVEL CRIMINAL... KINQRO MUJATA.

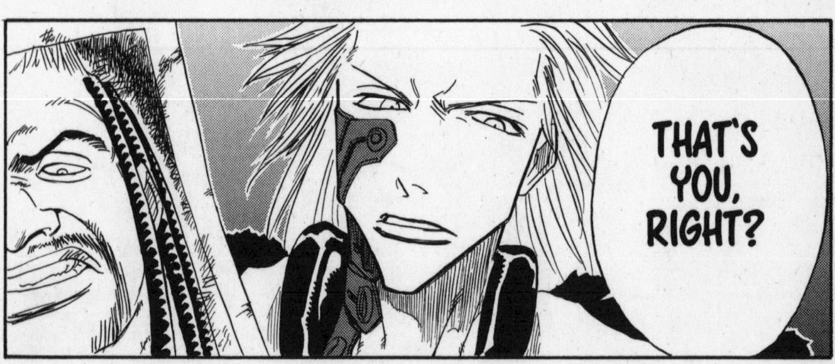
THAT'S YOU, RIGHT?

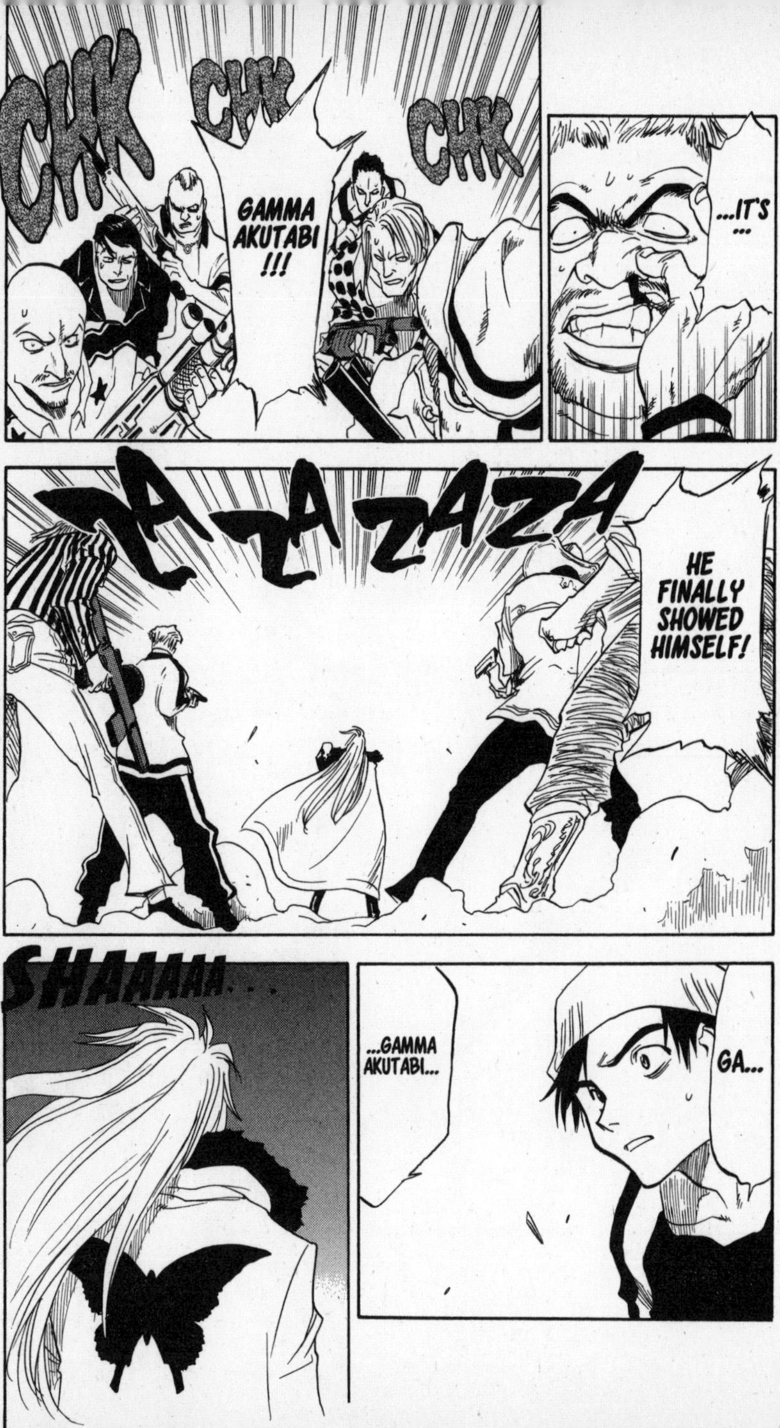
...IT'S ...
CHK
GAMMA AKUTABI !!!
CHK
CHK
HE FINALLY SHOWED HIMSELF!
ZAZAZAZA
GA...
...GAMMA AKUTABI...
SHAAAAA...

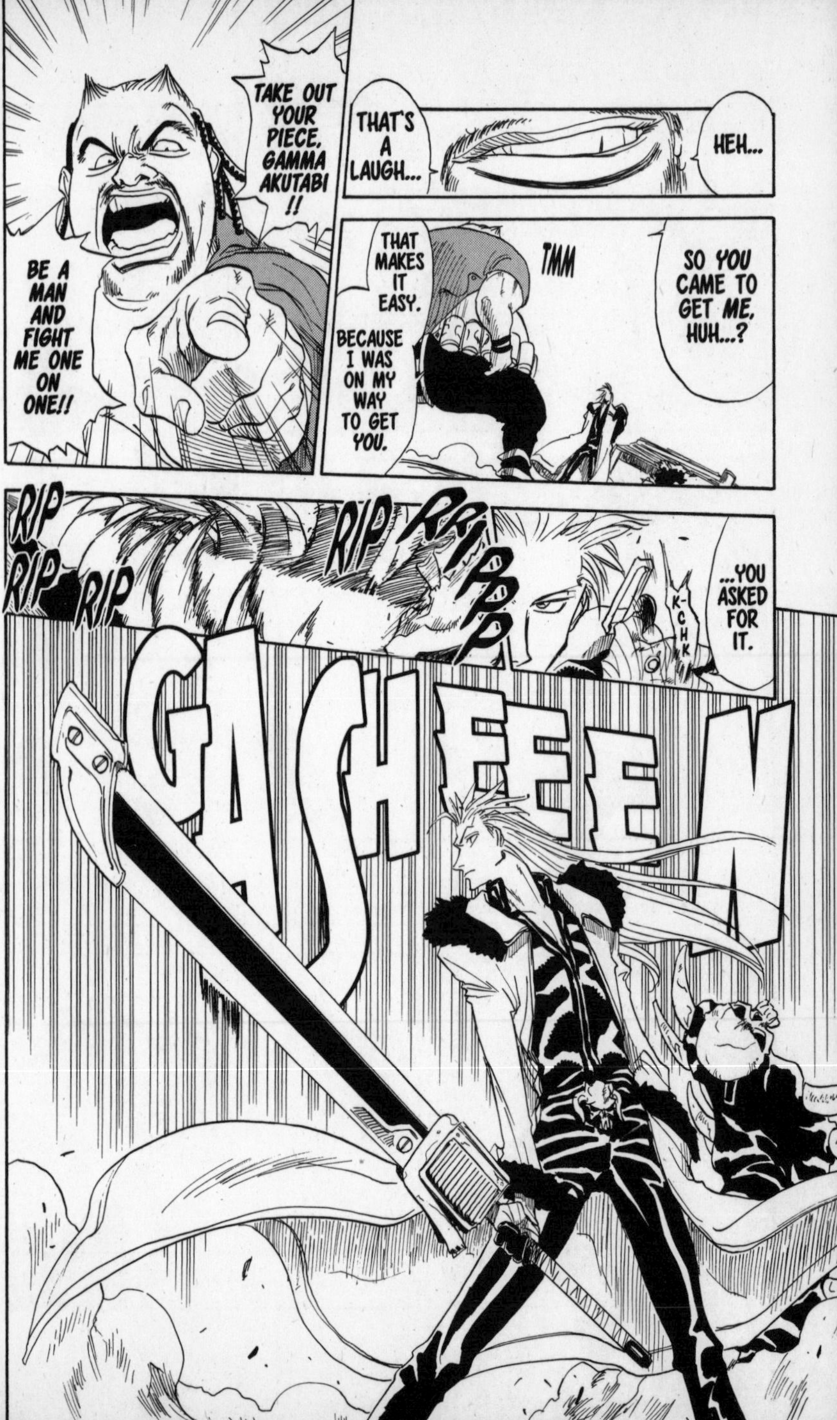
HEH...
THAT'S A LAUGH...
SO YOU CAME TO GET ME, HUH...?
TMM
THAT MAKES IT EASY.
BECAUSE I WAS ON MY WAY TO GET YOU.
TAKE OUT YOUR PIECE, GAMMA AKUTABI !!
BE A MAN AND FIGHT ME ONE ON ONE!!
...YOU ASKED FOR IT.
K-CHK
RRIPPP
RIP
RIP
RIP
RIP
RIP
GASHEEEN

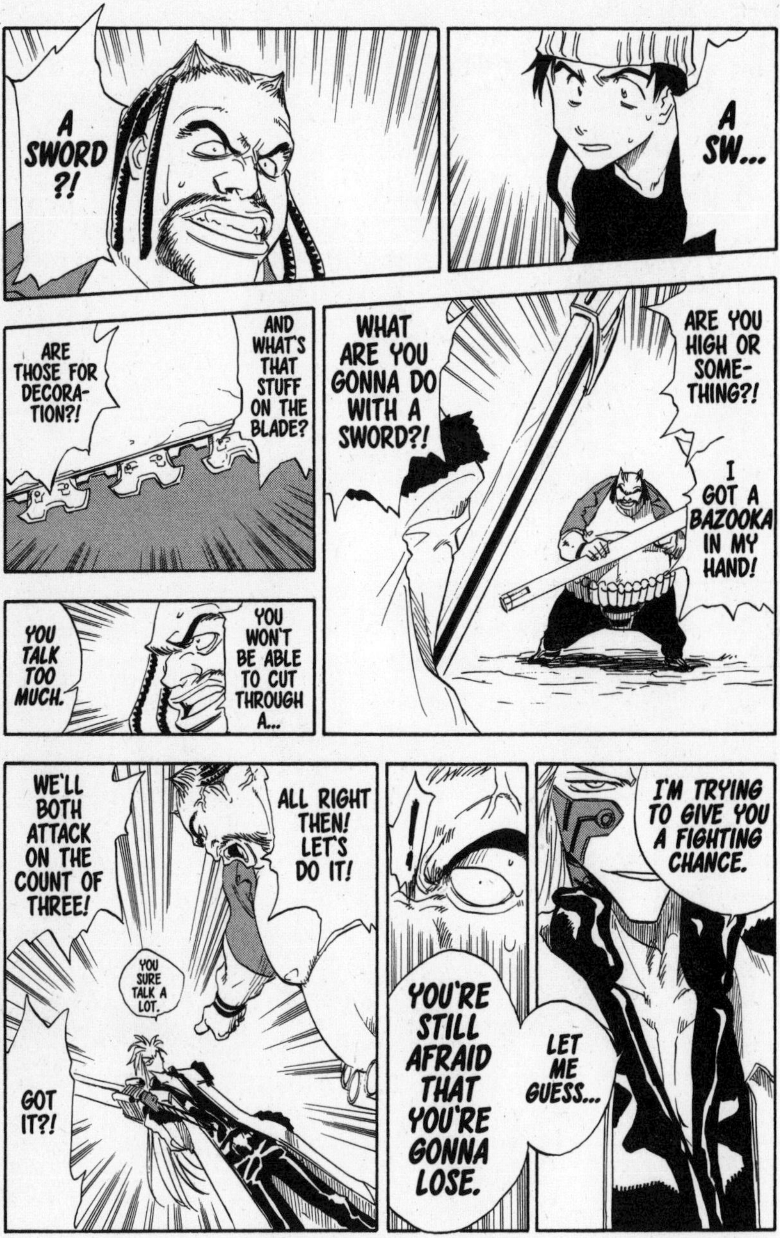
A SW...
A SWORD ?!
ARE YOU HIGH OR SOME-THING?!
I GOT A BAZOOKA IN MY HAND!
WHAT ARE YOU GONNA DO WITH A SWORD?!
AND WHAT'S THAT STUFF ON THE BLADE?
ARE THOSE FOR DECORA-TION?!
YOU WON'T BE ABLE TO CUT THROUGH A...
YOU TALK TOO MUCH.
I'M TRYING TO GIVE YOU A FIGHTING CHANCE.
LET ME GUESS...
YOU'RE STILL AFRAID THAT YOU'RE GONNA LOSE.
!
ALL RIGHT THEN! LET'S DO IT!
WE'LL BOTH ATTACK ON THE COUNT OF THREE!
YOU SURE TALK A LOT.
GOT IT?!

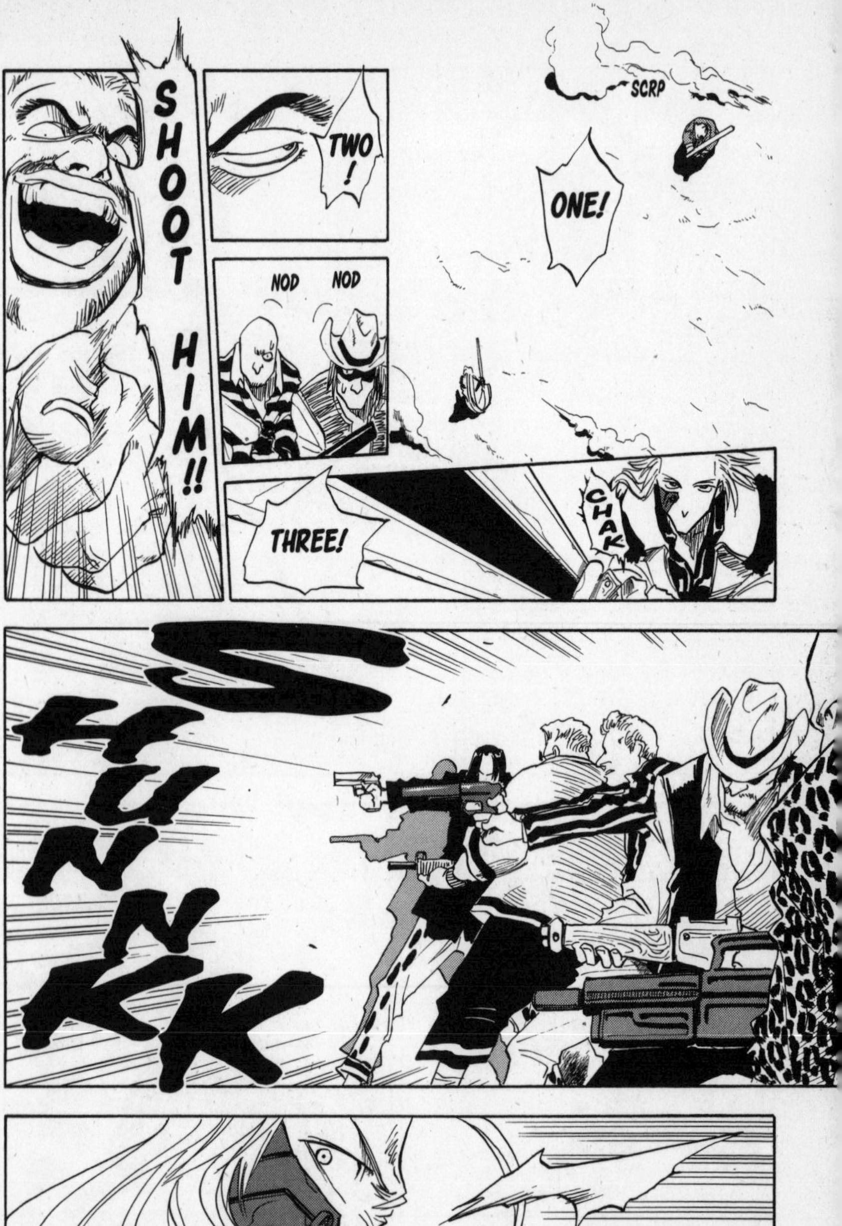
SCRP
ONE!
TWO!
NOD
NOD
THREE!
CHAK
SHOOT HIM!!
SHUNNKK

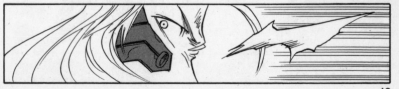

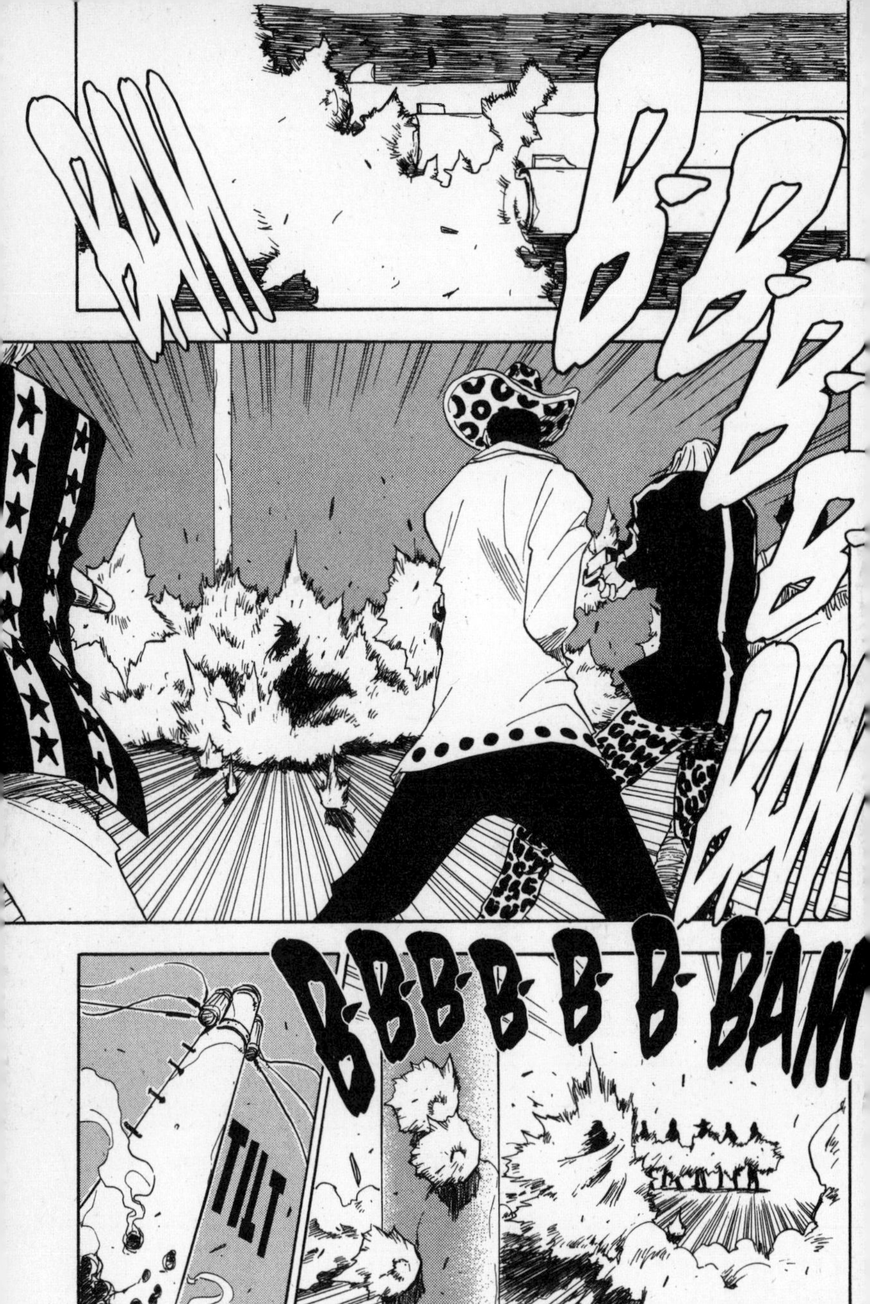
B-B-B-B-BAM
BAM
BBBB B B BAM
TILT

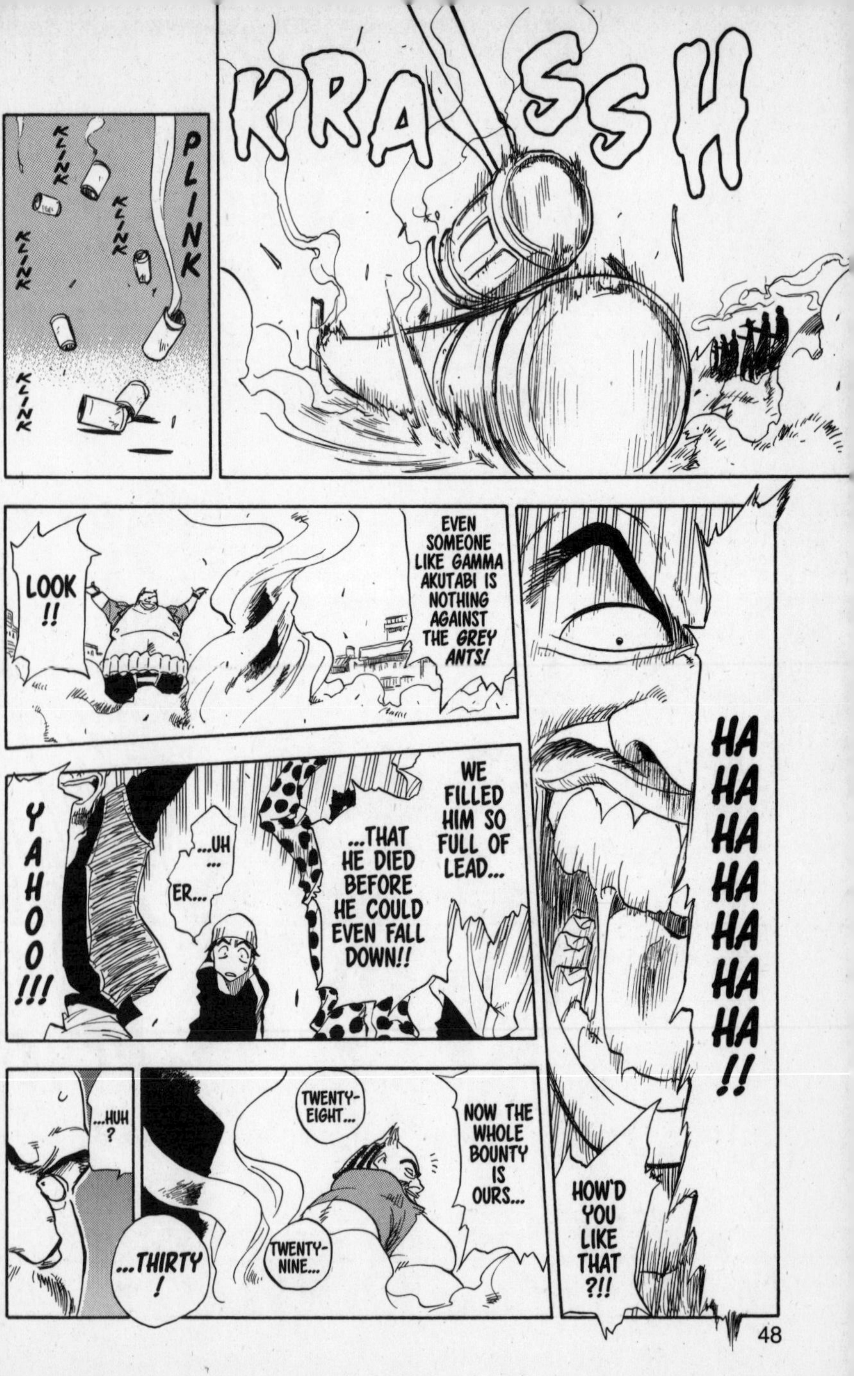
KRASSH
PLINK
KLINK
KLINK
KLINK
KLINK
HAHAHAHAHAHAHAHAHA!!
HOW'D YOU LIKE THAT?!!
EVEN SOMEONE LIKE GAMMA AKUTABI IS NOTHING AGAINST THE GREY ANTS!
LOOK!!
WE FILLED HIM SO FULL OF LEAD...
...THAT HE DIED BEFORE HE COULD EVEN FALL DOWN!!
...UH ... ER...
YAHOOO!!!
NOW THE WHOLE BOUNTY IS OURS...
TWENTY-EIGHT...
TWENTY-NINE...
...HUH?
...THIRTY!

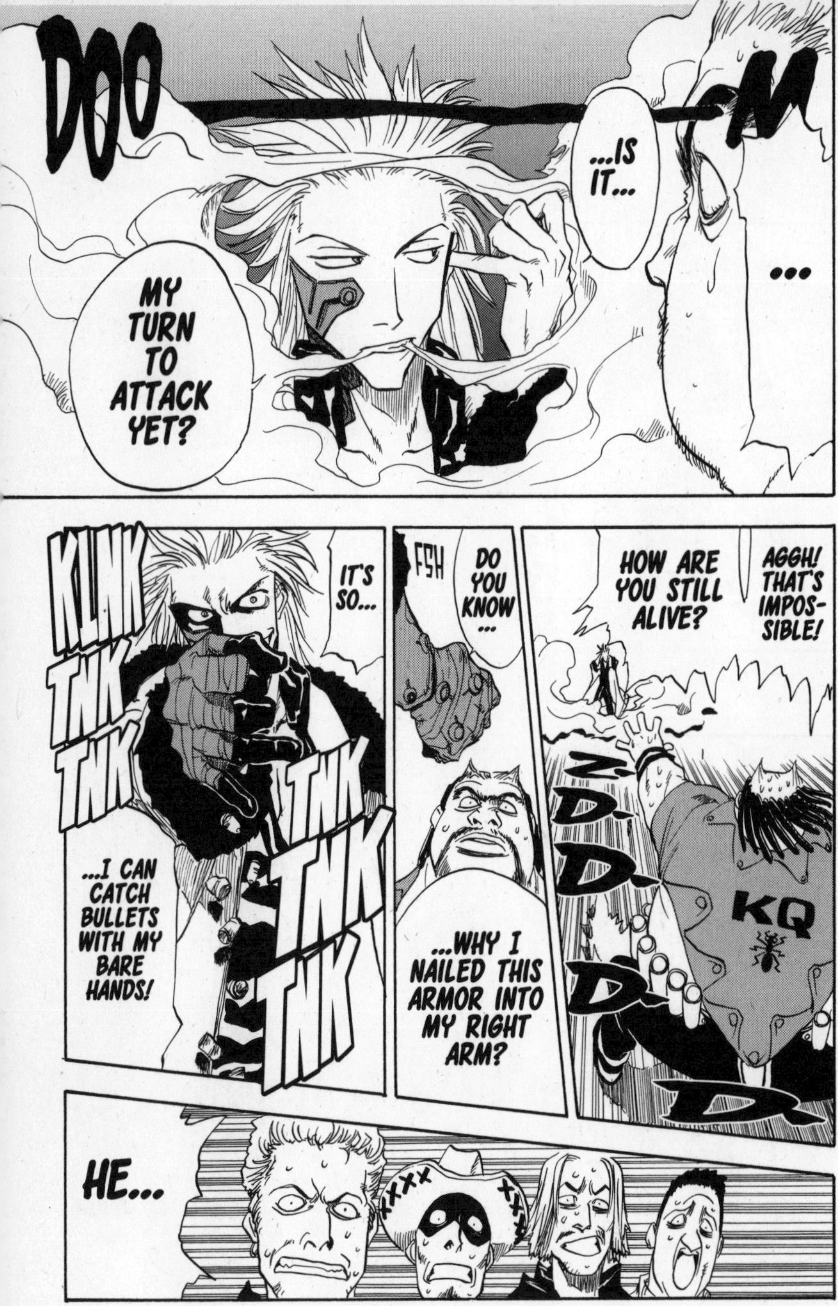
DOOM
...IS IT...
...
MY TURN TO ATTACK YET?
AGGH! THAT'S IMPOSSIBLE!
HOW ARE YOU STILL ALIVE?
ZDDDD
KQ
DO YOU KNOW...
FSH
...WHY I NAILED THIS ARMOR INTO MY RIGHT ARM?
IT'S SO...
KLINK TNK TNK
TNK TNK TNK
...I CAN CATCH BULLETS WITH MY BARE HANDS!
HE...

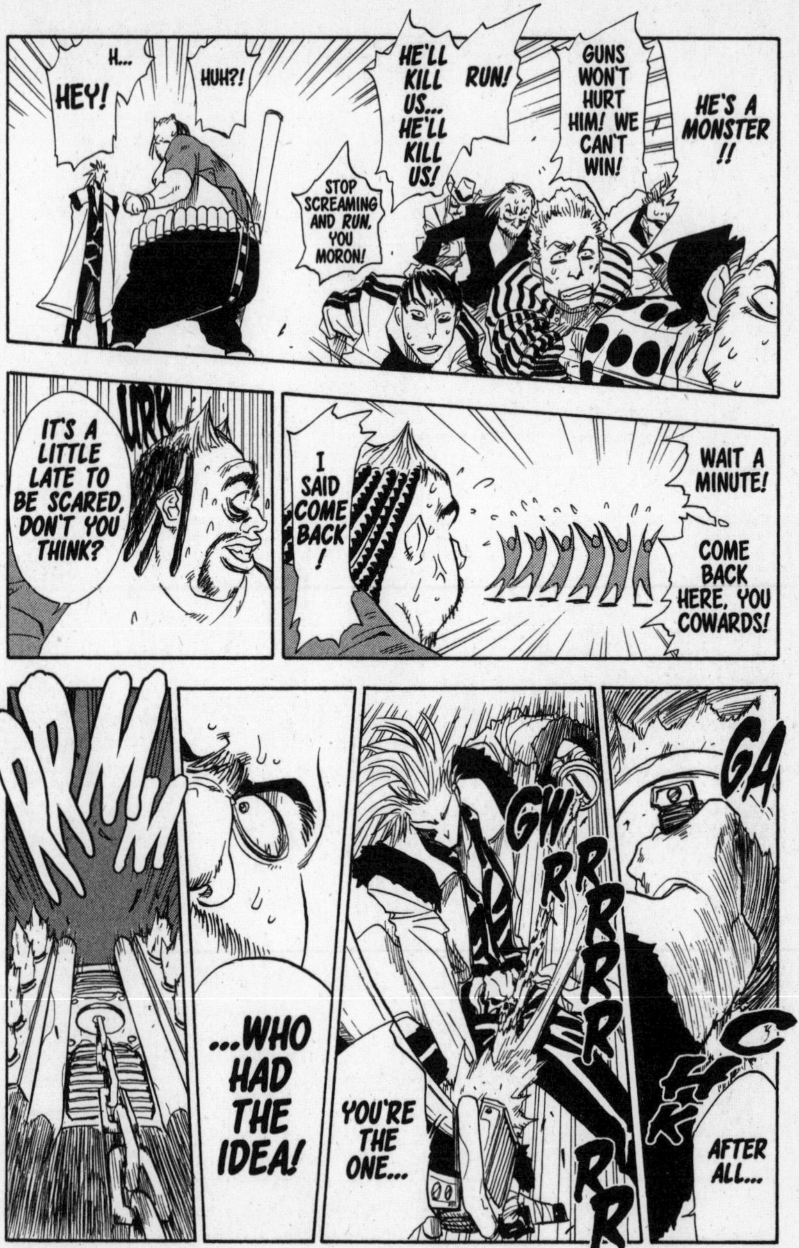

HE'S A MONSTER!!
GUNS WON'T HURT HIM! WE CAN'T WIN!
RUN!
HE'LL KILL US... HE'LL KILL US!
STOP SCREAMING AND RUN, YOU MORON!
HUH?!
H... HEY!
WAIT A MINUTE!
COME BACK HERE, YOU COWARDS!
I SAID COME BACK!
URK
IT'S A LITTLE LATE TO BE SCARED, DON'T YOU THINK?
GA
AFTER ALL...
YOU'RE THE ONE...
...WHO HAD THE IDEA!

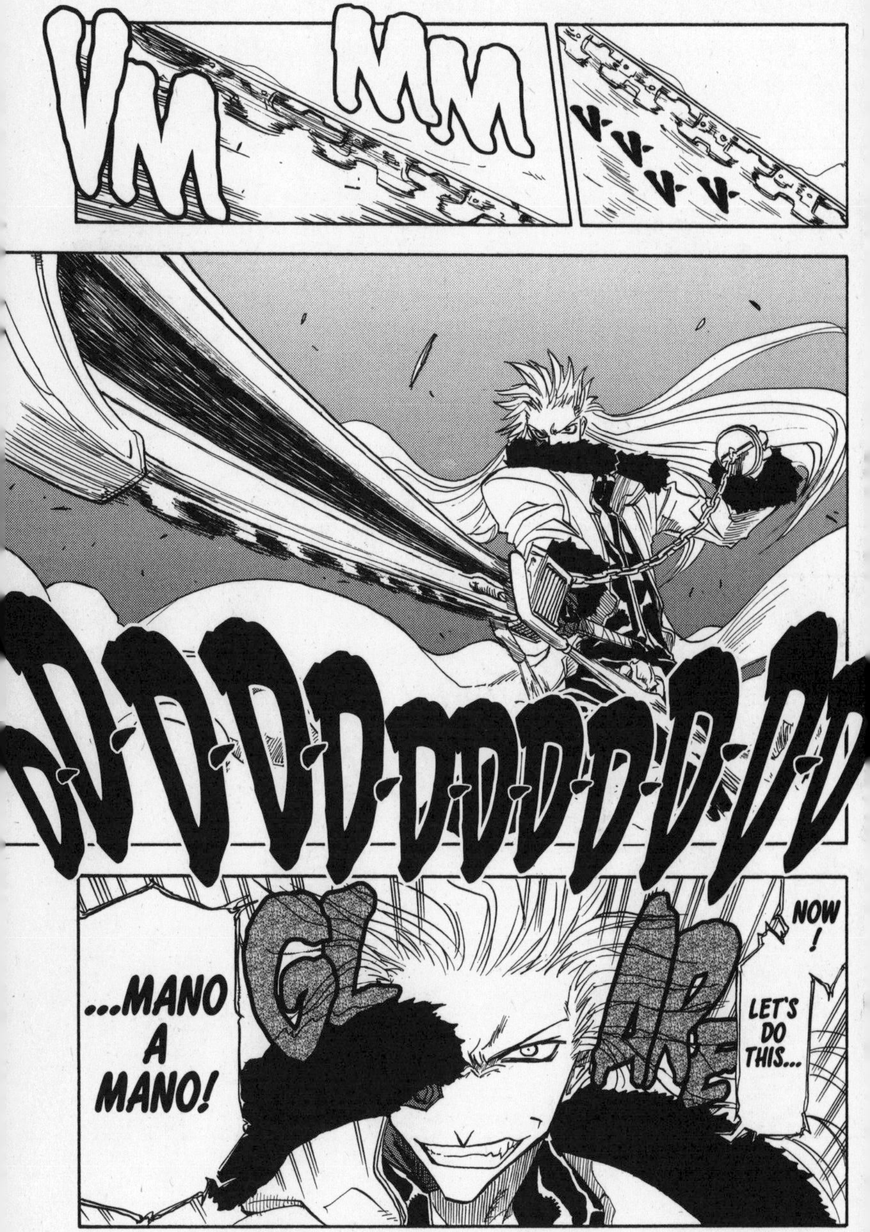
VVVVV
VM MM
DDDDDDDDDDDDD
NOW!
LET'S DO THIS...
GLARE
...MANO A MANO!

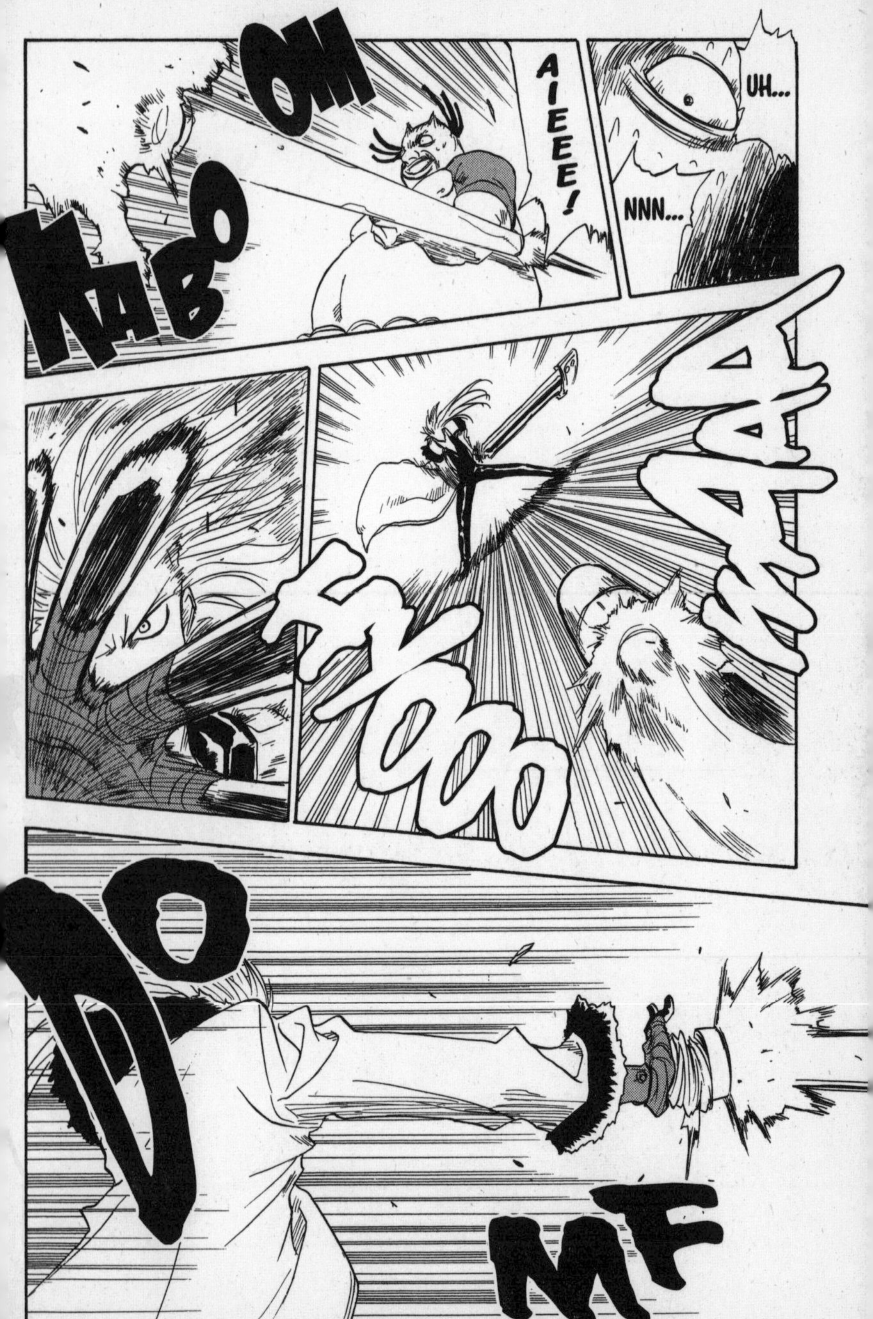
UH...
NNN...
AIEEEE!
KABOOM
WAAA
FYOOO
DO
MF

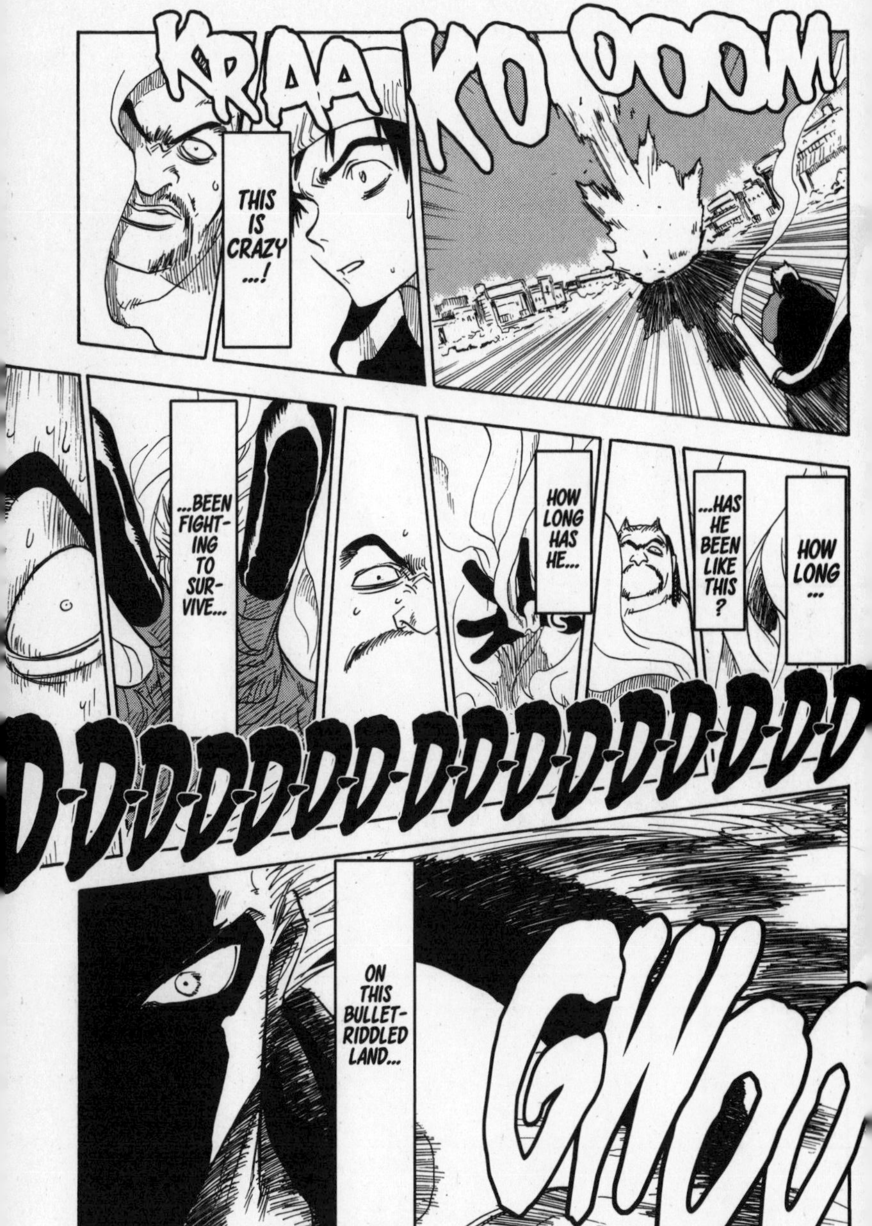
KRAAKOOOOM
THIS IS CRAZY...!
HOW LONG...
...HAS HE BEEN LIKE THIS?
HOW LONG HAS HE...
...BEEN FIGHTING TO SURVIVE...
D-D-D-D-D-D-D-D-D-D-D-D-D-D-D
GWOO
ON THIS BULLET-RIDDLED LAND...

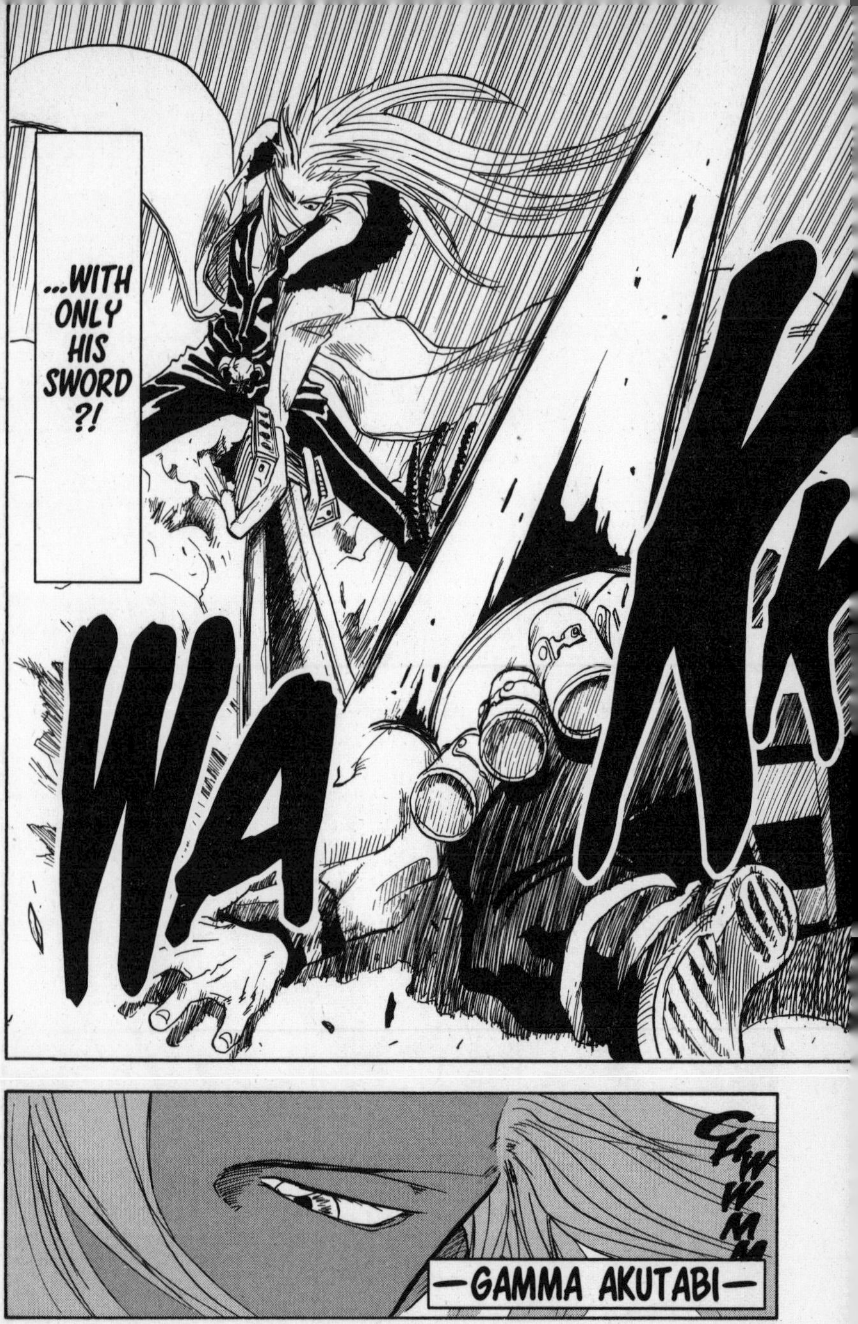
...WITH ONLY HIS SWORD ?!
WAKK
GHWWMM
—GAMMA AKUTABI—

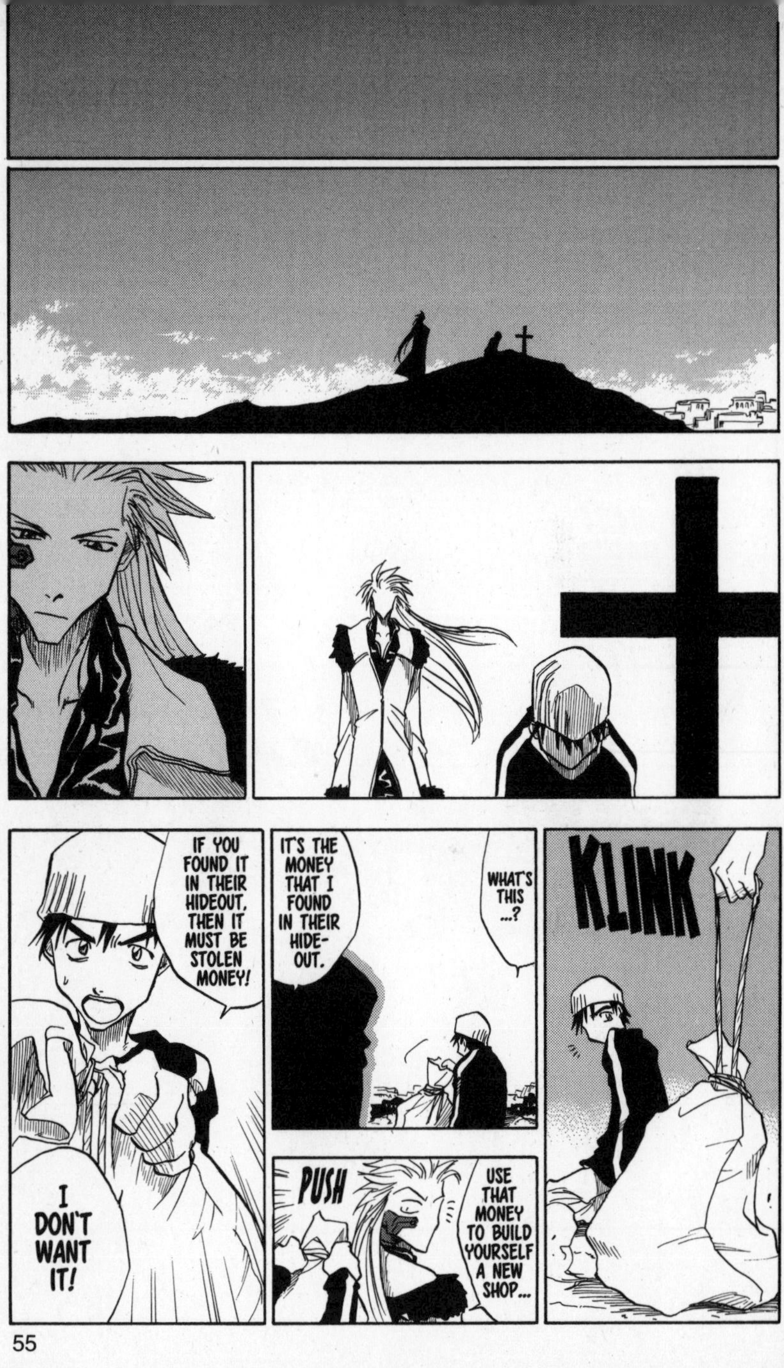
KLINK
WHAT'S THIS ...?
IT'S THE MONEY THAT I FOUND IN THEIR HIDE-OUT.
USE THAT MONEY TO BUILD YOURSELF A NEW SHOP...
PUSH
IF YOU FOUND IT IN THEIR HIDEOUT, THEN IT MUST BE STOLEN MONEY!
I DON'T WANT IT!

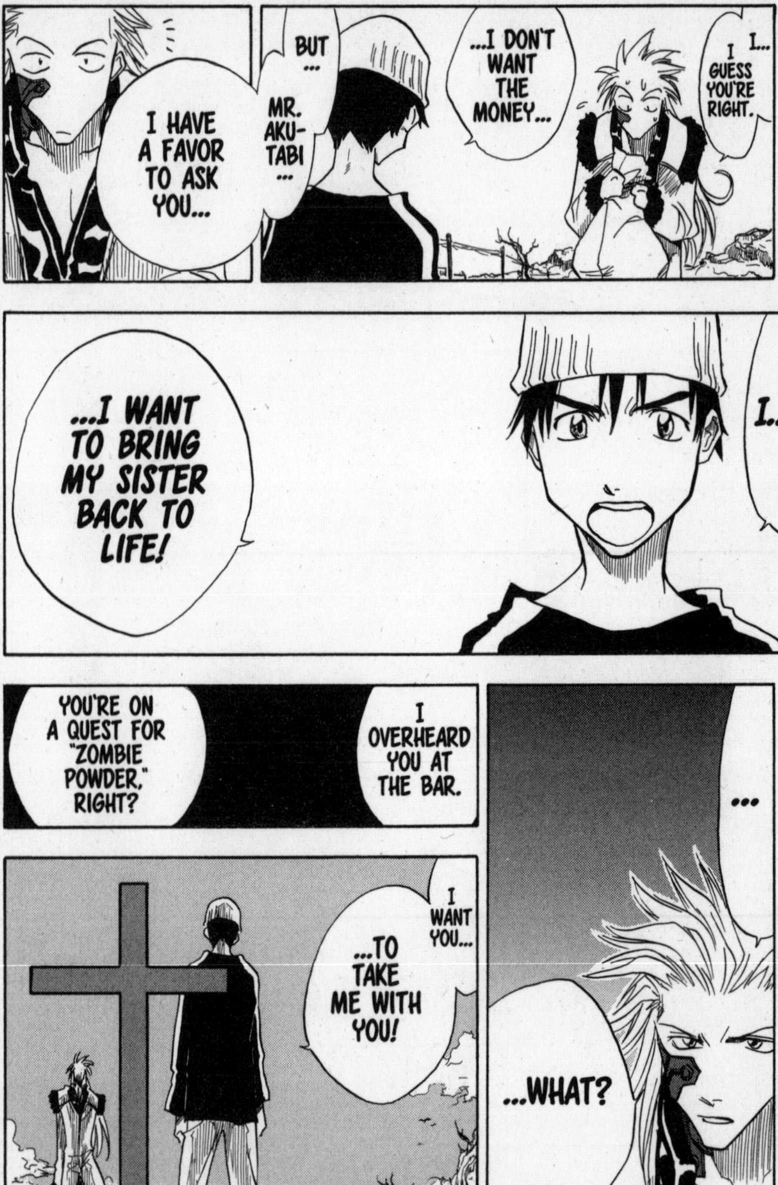
I... I GUESS YOU'RE RIGHT.
...I DON'T WANT THE MONEY...
BUT...
MR. AKU-TABI...
I HAVE A FAVOR TO ASK YOU...
I...
...I WANT TO BRING MY SISTER BACK TO LIFE!
...
...WHAT?
I OVERHEARD YOU AT THE BAR.
YOU'RE ON A QUEST FOR "ZOMBIE POWDER," RIGHT?
I WANT YOU...
...TO TAKE ME WITH YOU!

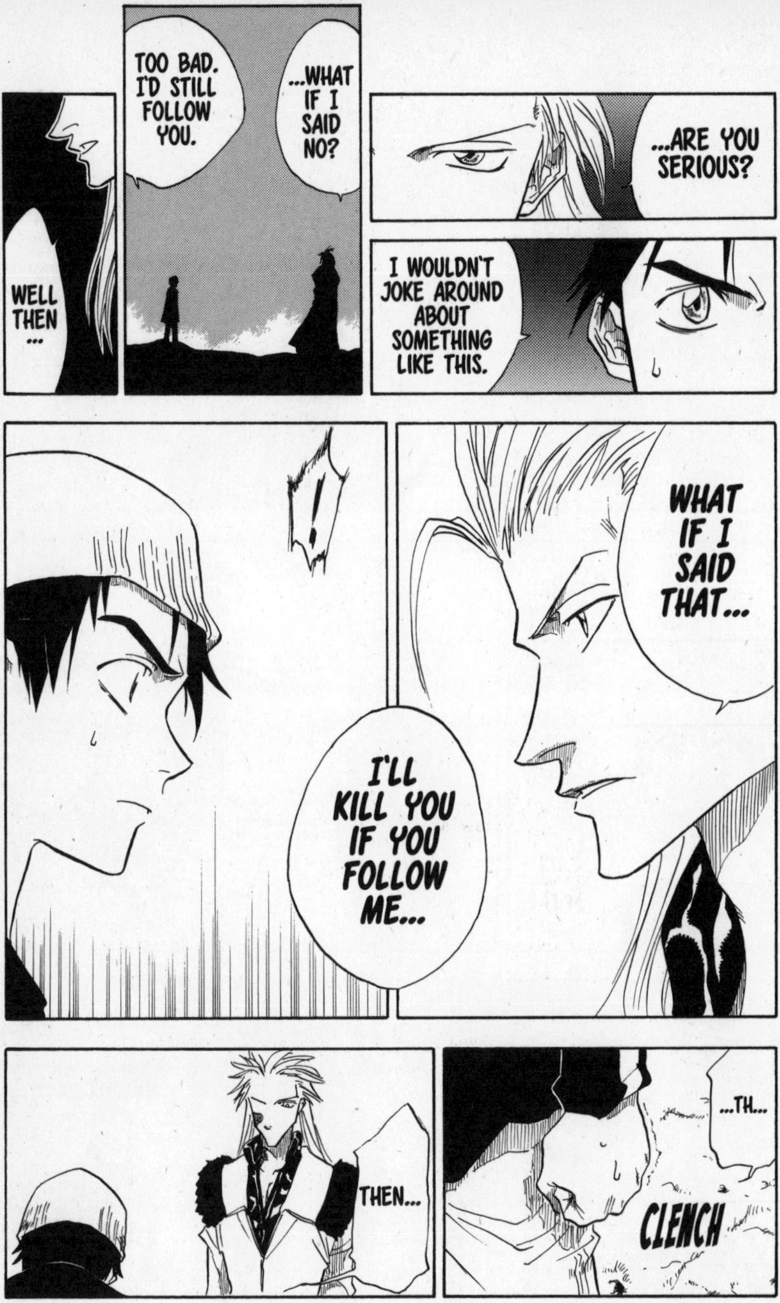
...ARE YOU SERIOUS?
I WOULDN'T JOKE AROUND ABOUT SOMETHING LIKE THIS.
...WHAT IF I SAID NO?
TOO BAD. I'D STILL FOLLOW YOU.
WELL THEN ...
WHAT IF I SAID THAT...
I'LL KILL YOU IF YOU FOLLOW ME...
!
...TH...
CLENCH
THEN...

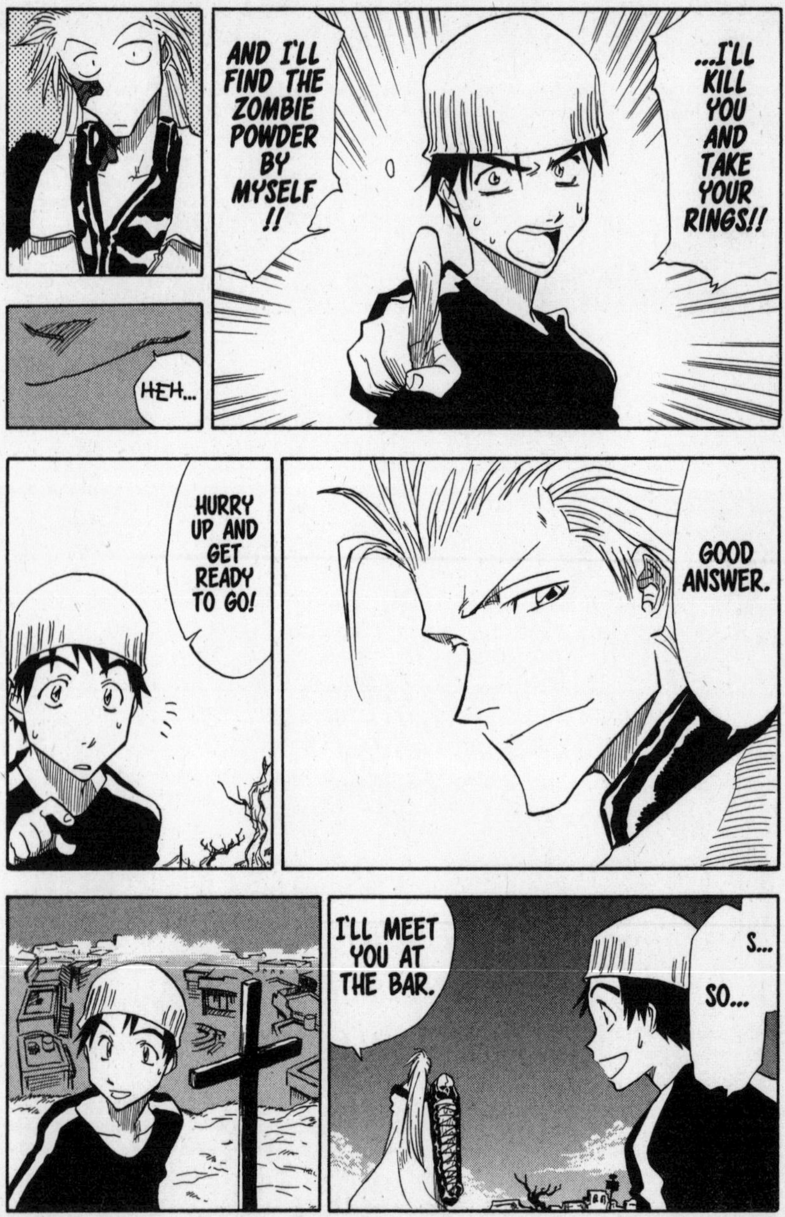
...I'LL KILL YOU AND TAKE YOUR RINGS!!
AND I'LL FIND THE ZOMBIE POWDER BY MYSELF!!
HEH...
GOOD ANSWER.
HURRY UP AND GET READY TO GO!
S...
SO...
I'LL MEET YOU AT THE BAR.

READ THIS WAY

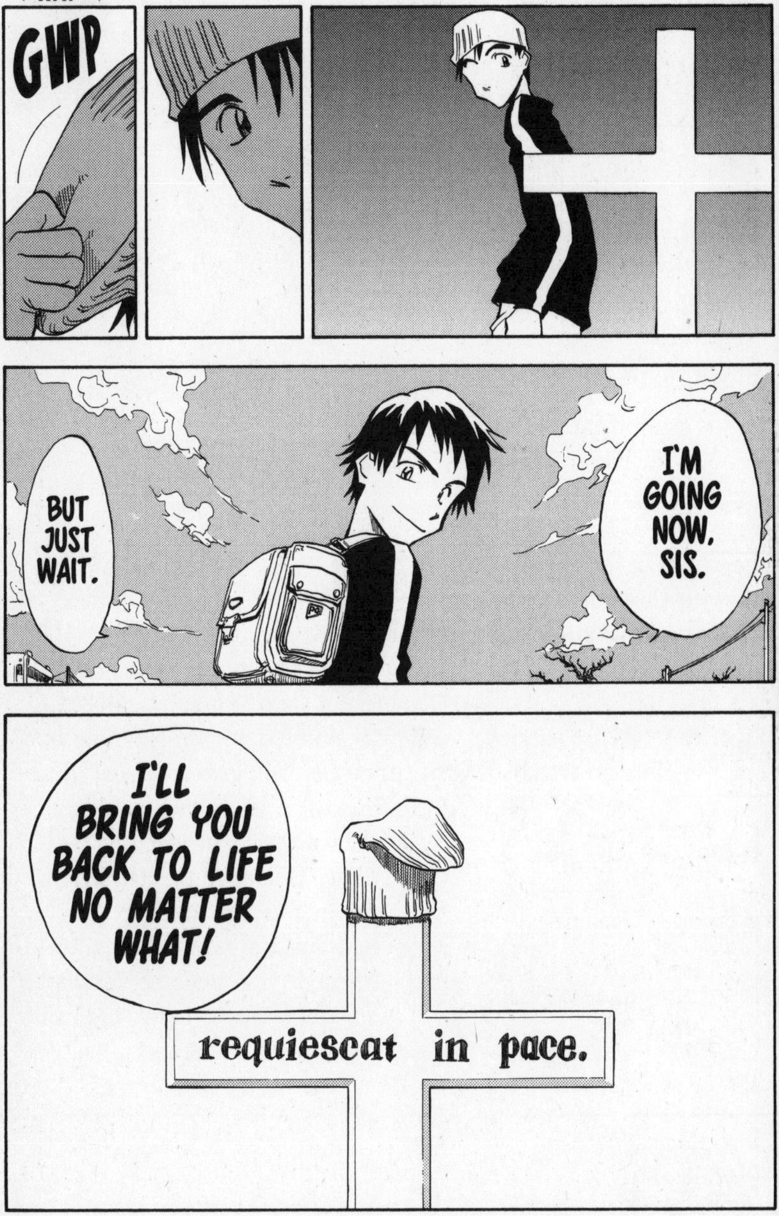
GWP
I'M GOING NOW, SIS.
BUT JUST WAIT.
I'LL BRING YOU BACK TO LIFE NO MATTER WHAT!
requiescat in pace.

B-side NAKED MONKEYS 1.

Gamma Akutabi
芥火ガンマ

Height : 190.2cm
Weight : 102kg
Date of Birth : November 28
Age : 22
Blood Type : AO

In this section I'd like to answer some of the more common questions that the readers have about the characters, as well as their taste in food. Let's start off with Gamma. At 102 kg (224 pounds), he's surprisingly

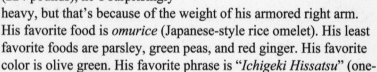

heavy, but that's because of the weight of his armored right arm. His favorite food is *omurice* (Japanese-style rice omelet). His least favorite foods are parsley, green peas, and red ginger. His favorite color is olive green. His favorite phrase is "*Ichigeki Hissatsu*" (one-

hit kill). I guess that's about it. By the way, his hair is really hard to draw. I changed the hairstyle from my first design to make it easier to draw...but now I think the old hairstyle was easier to draw after all. But he looks better in this new hairstyle so I guess it's fine.

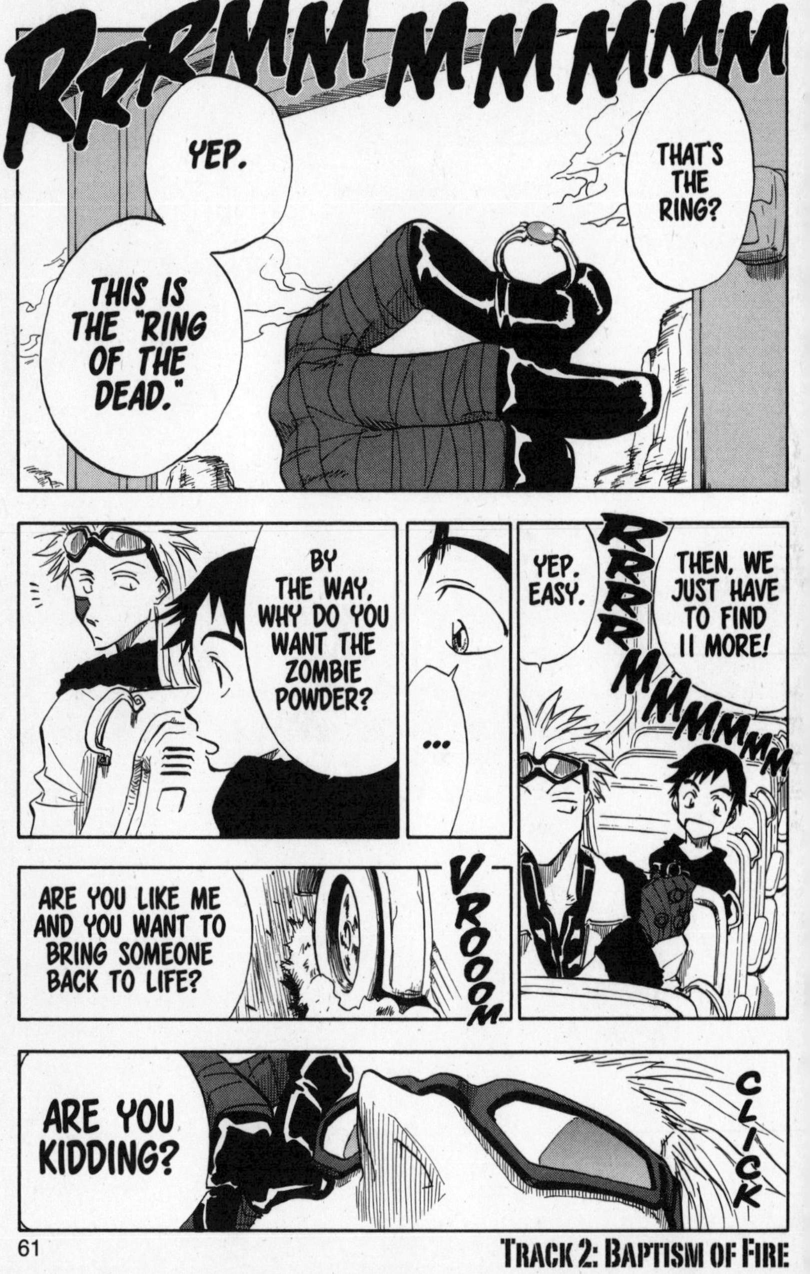
RRRMM MMMMMM
THAT'S THE RING?
YEP.
THIS IS THE "RING OF THE DEAD."
THEN, WE JUST HAVE TO FIND 11 MORE!
RRRRMMMMMMM
YEP. EASY.
...
BY THE WAY, WHY DO YOU WANT THE ZOMBIE POWDER?
VROOOOM
ARE YOU LIKE ME AND YOU WANT TO BRING SOMEONE BACK TO LIFE?
CLICK
ARE YOU KIDDING?

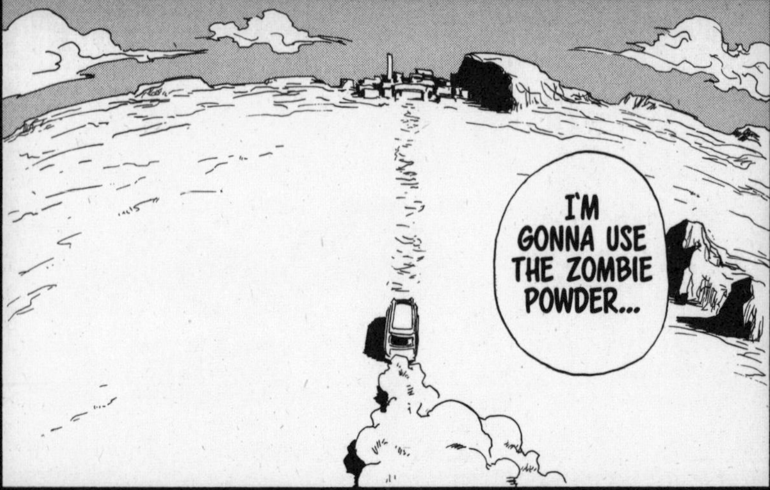
I'M GONNA USE THE ZOMBIE POWDER...

TRACK 2:
BAPTISM OF FIRE

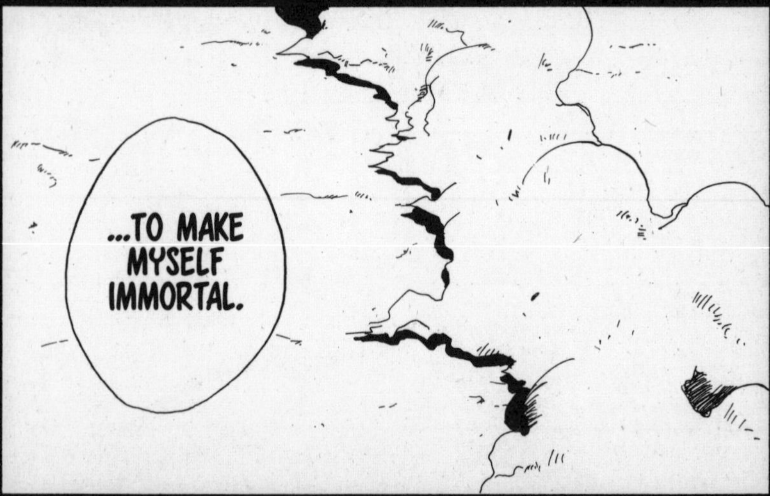
...TO MAKE MYSELF IMMORTAL.

READ THIS WAY

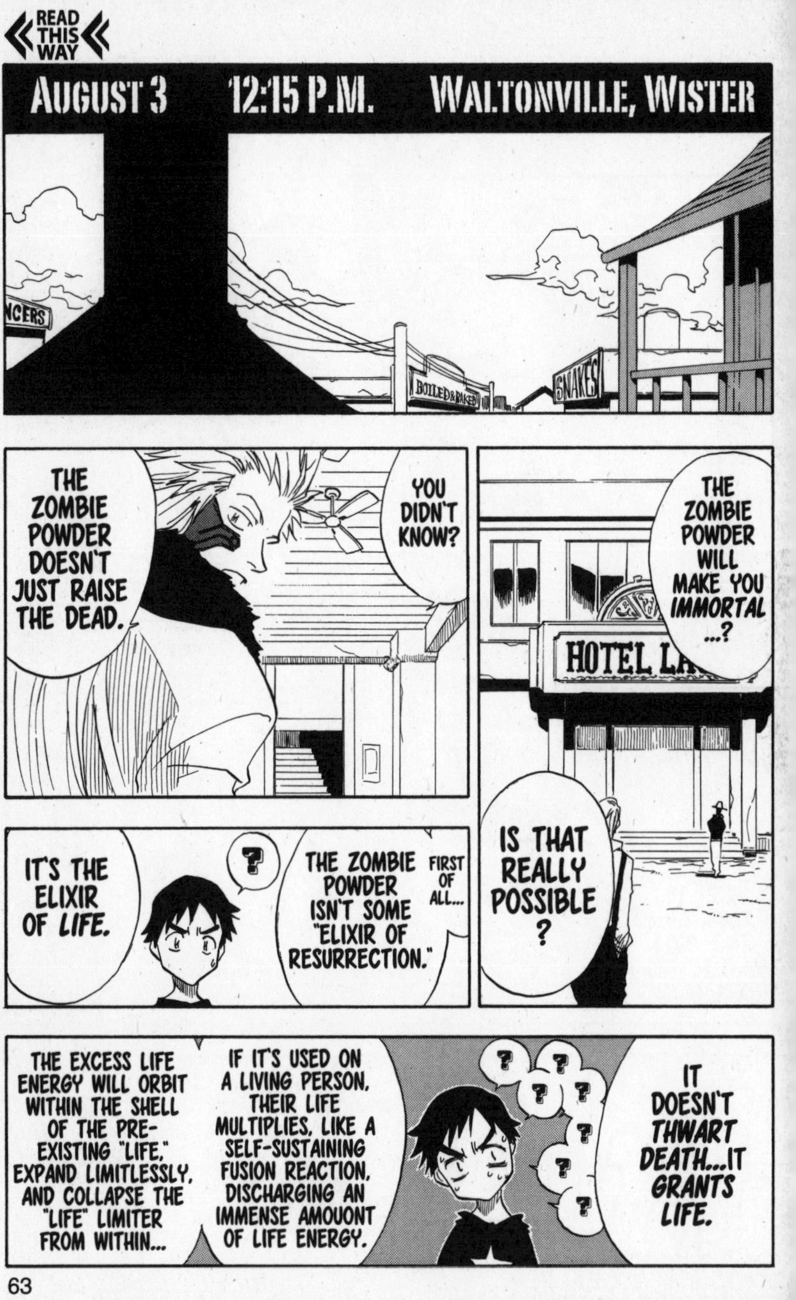
AUGUST 3 12:15 P.M. WALTONVILLE, WISTER
NCERS
BOILED & BAKED
SNAKES
THE ZOMBIE POWDER WILL MAKE YOU IMMORTAL ...?
HOTEL
IS THAT REALLY POSSIBLE?
YOU DIDN'T KNOW?
THE ZOMBIE POWDER DOESN'T JUST RAISE THE DEAD.
FIRST OF ALL...
THE ZOMBIE POWDER ISN'T SOME "ELIXIR OF RESURRECTION."
?
IT'S THE ELIXIR OF LIFE.
IT DOESN'T THWART DEATH...IT GRANTS LIFE.
? ? ? ? ? ? ?
IF IT'S USED ON A LIVING PERSON, THEIR LIFE MULTIPLIES, LIKE A SELF-SUSTAINING FUSION REACTION, DISCHARGING AN IMMENSE AMOUONT OF LIFE ENERGY.
THE EXCESS LIFE ENERGY WILL ORBIT WITHIN THE SHELL OF THE PRE-EXISTING "LIFE," EXPAND LIMITLESSLY, AND COLLAPSE THE "LIFE" LIMITER FROM WITHIN...

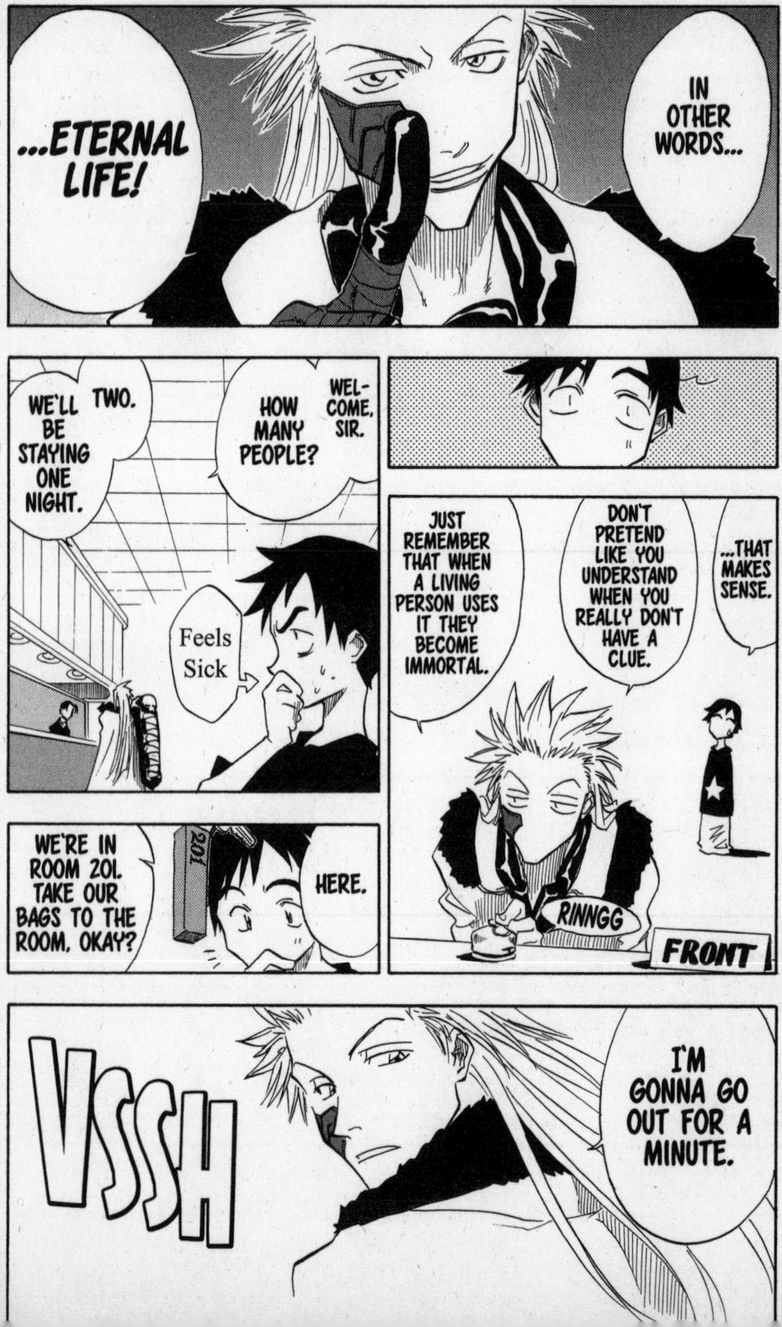
IN OTHER WORDS...
...ETERNAL LIFE!
...THAT MAKES SENSE.
DON'T PRETEND LIKE YOU UNDERSTAND WHEN YOU REALLY DON'T HAVE A CLUE.
JUST REMEMBER THAT WHEN A LIVING PERSON USES IT THEY BECOME IMMORTAL.
RINNGG
FRONT
WEL-COME, SIR.
HOW MANY PEOPLE?
TWO.
WE'LL BE STAYING ONE NIGHT.
Feels Sick
201
HERE.
WE'RE IN ROOM 201. TAKE OUR BAGS TO THE ROOM, OKAY?
I'M GONNA GO OUT FOR A MINUTE.
VSSH

READ THIS WAY

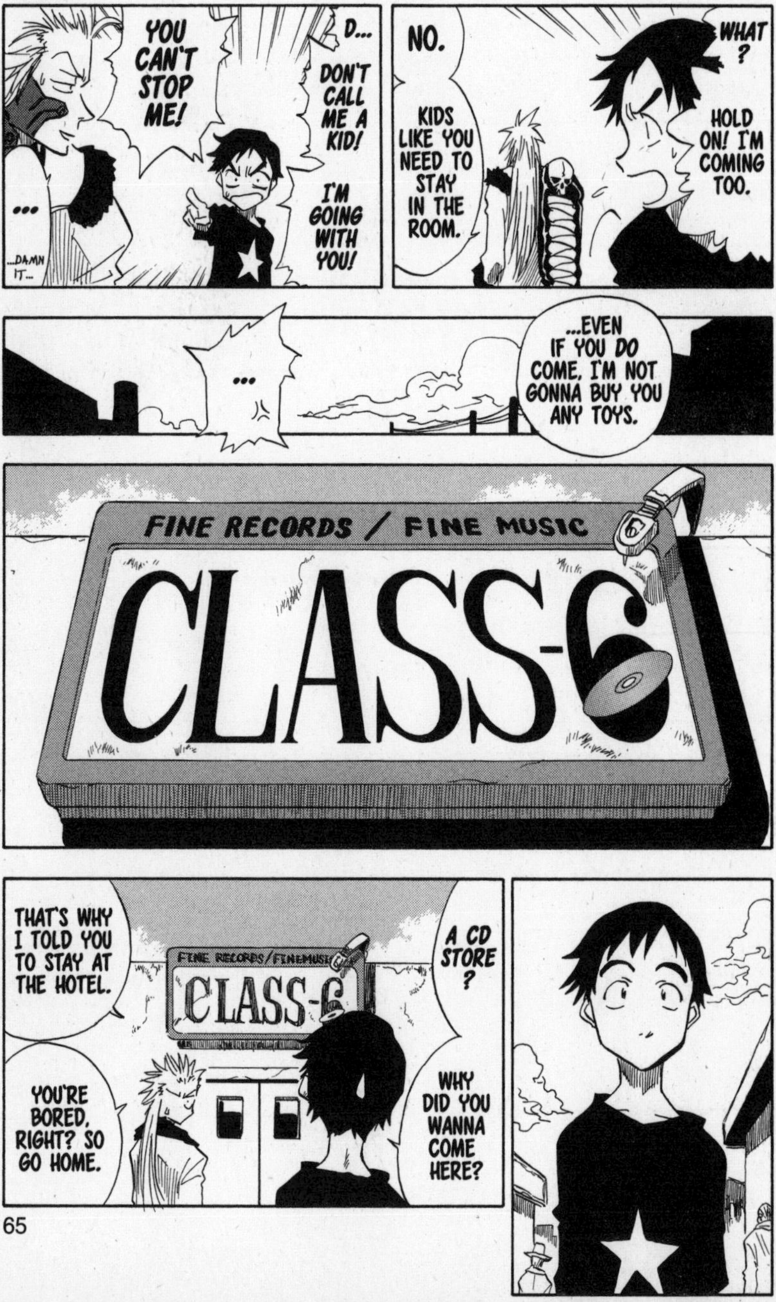
WHAT?
HOLD ON! I'M COMING TOO.
NO.
KIDS LIKE YOU NEED TO STAY IN THE ROOM.
D...
DON'T CALL ME A KID!
I'M GOING WITH YOU!
YOU CAN'T STOP ME!
...
...DAMN IT...
...EVEN IF YOU DO COME, I'M NOT GONNA BUY YOU ANY TOYS.
...
FINE RECORDS / FINE MUSIC
CLASS-6
A CD STORE?
WHY DID YOU WANNA COME HERE?
FINE RECORDS/FINEMUSIC
CLASS-6
THAT'S WHY I TOLD YOU TO STAY AT THE HOTEL.
YOU'RE BORED, RIGHT? SO GO HOME.

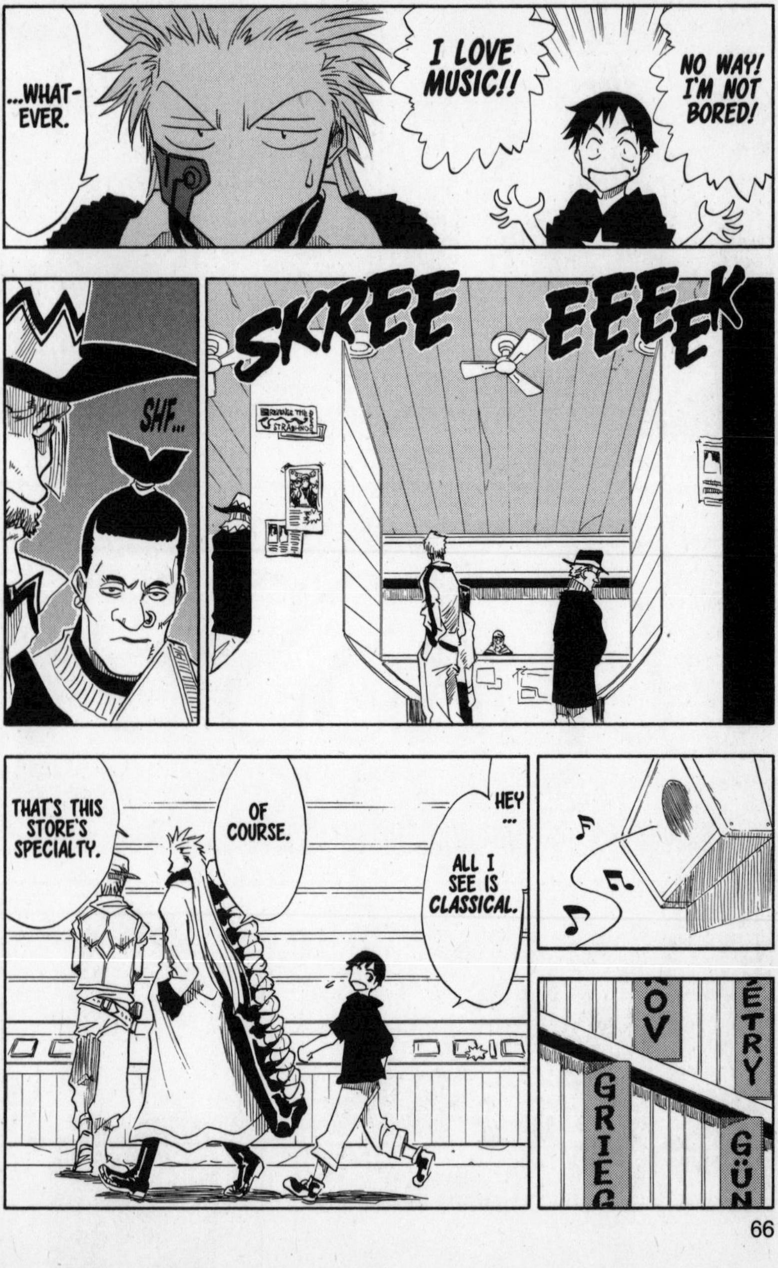
NO WAY! I'M NOT BORED!
I LOVE MUSIC!!
...WHAT-EVER.
SKREEEEEEK
SHF...
NOV
ÉTRY
GRIEG
GÜN
HEY... ALL I SEE IS CLASSICAL.
OF COURSE.
THAT'S THIS STORE'S SPECIALTY.

READ THIS WAY

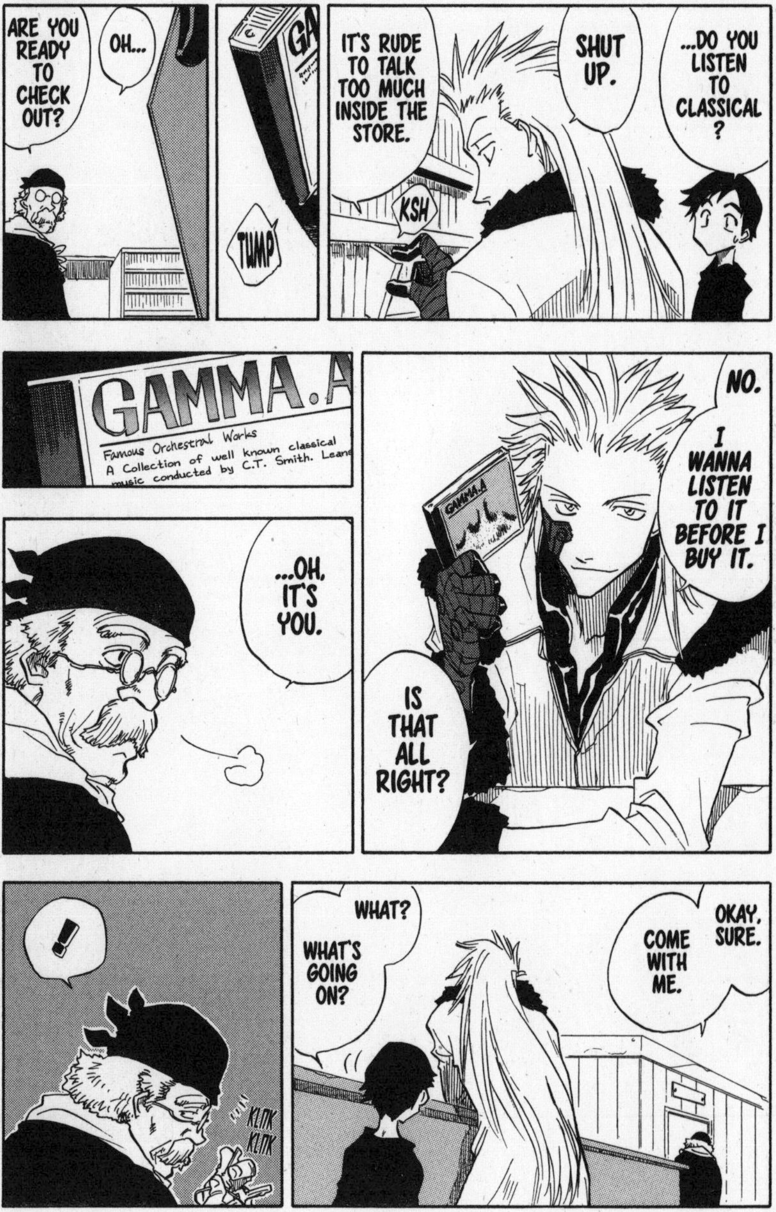
...DO YOU LISTEN TO CLASSICAL?
SHUT UP.
IT'S RUDE TO TALK TOO MUCH INSIDE THE STORE.
KSH
TUMP
OH...
ARE YOU READY TO CHECK OUT?
NO.
I WANNA LISTEN TO IT BEFORE I BUY IT.
GAMMA.A
IS THAT ALL RIGHT?
GAMMA.A
Famous Orchestral Works
A Collection of well known classical
music conducted by C.T. Smith.
...OH, IT'S YOU.
OKAY, SURE.
COME WITH ME.
WHAT?
WHAT'S GOING ON?
!
KLINK KLINK

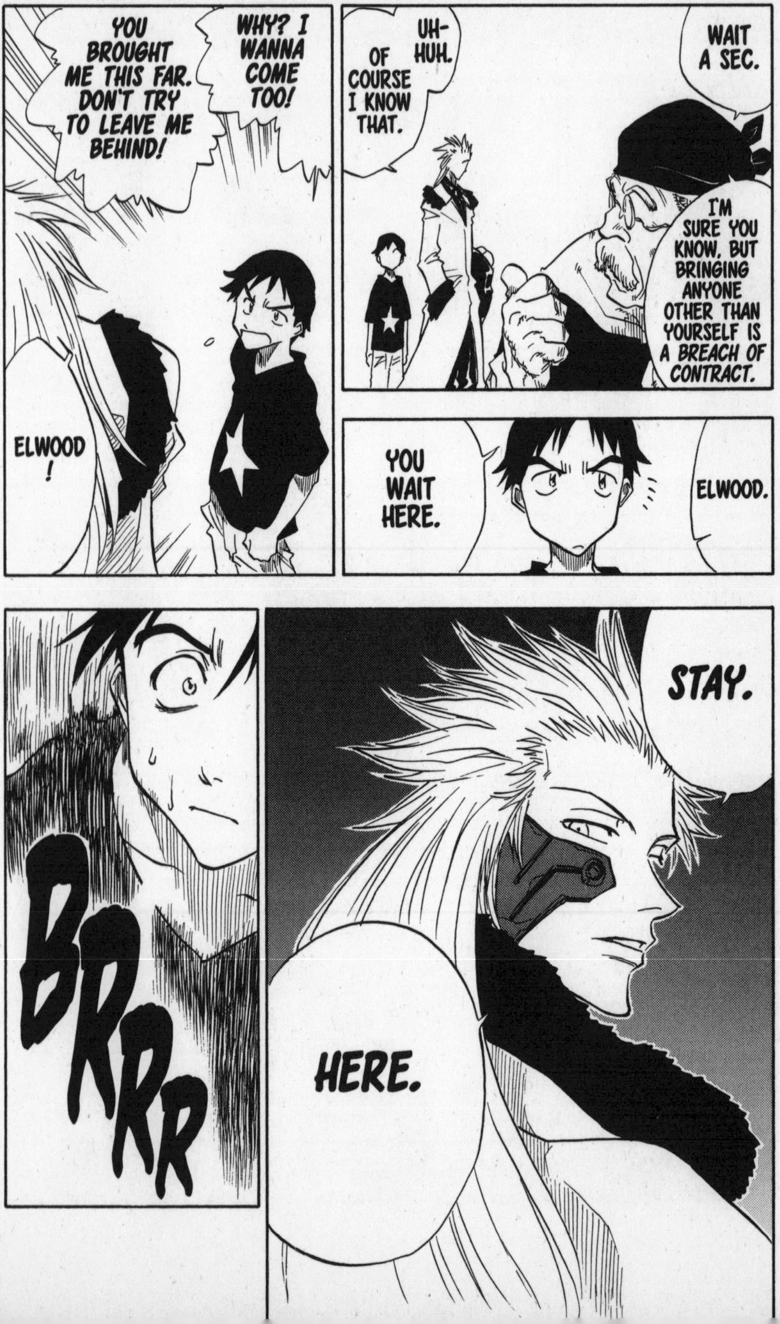
WAIT A SEC.
I'M SURE YOU KNOW, BUT BRINGING ANYONE OTHER THAN YOURSELF IS A BREACH OF CONTRACT.
UH-HUH.
OF COURSE I KNOW THAT.
ELWOOD.
YOU WAIT HERE.
WHY? I WANNA COME TOO!
YOU BROUGHT ME THIS FAR. DON'T TRY TO LEAVE ME BEHIND!
ELWOOD!
STAY.
HERE.
BRRR

READ THIS WAY

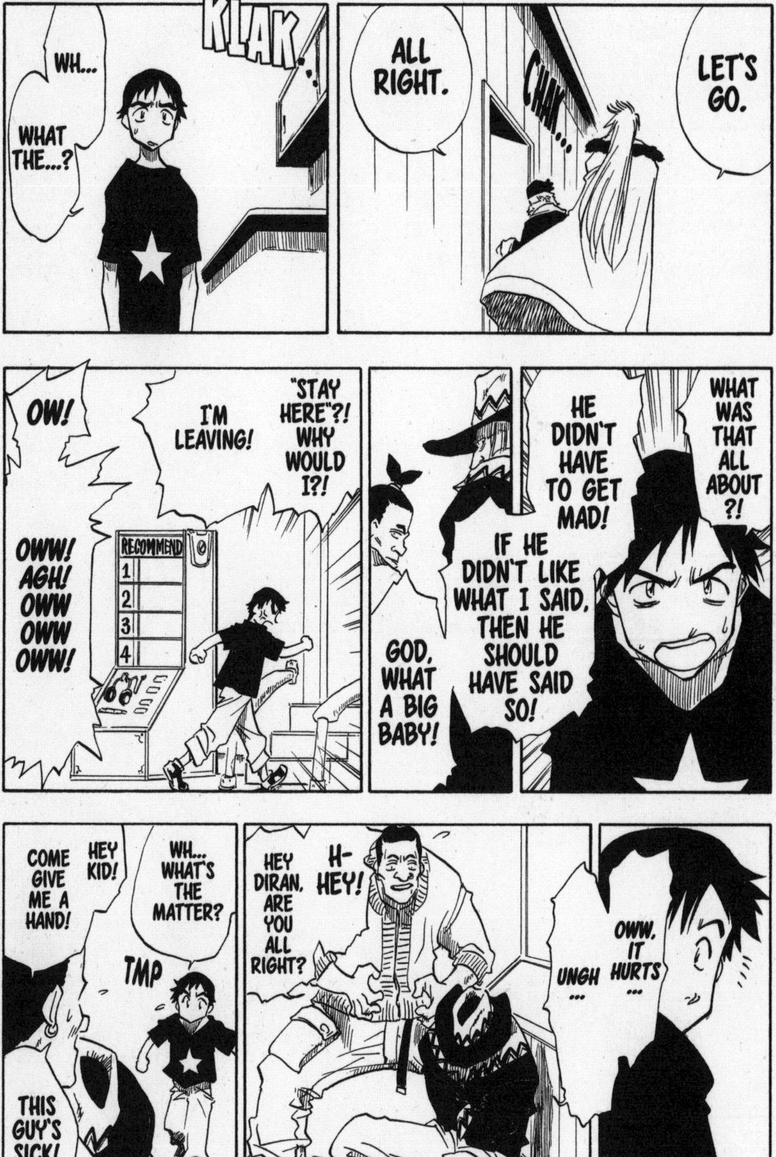
LET'S GO.
CHAK...
ALL RIGHT.
KLAK...
WH...
WHAT THE...?
WHAT WAS THAT ALL ABOUT?!
HE DIDN'T HAVE TO GET MAD!
IF HE DIDN'T LIKE WHAT I SAID, THEN HE SHOULD HAVE SAID SO!
GOD, WHAT A BIG BABY!
"STAY HERE"?! WHY WOULD I?!
I'M LEAVING!
OW!
OWW! AGH! OWW OWW OWW!
RECOMMEND
1
2
3
4
OWW, IT HURTS...
UNGH...
H- HEY!
HEY DIRAN, ARE YOU ALL RIGHT?
WH... WHAT'S THE MATTER?
TMP
HEY KID!
COME GIVE ME A HAND!
THIS GUY'S SICK!

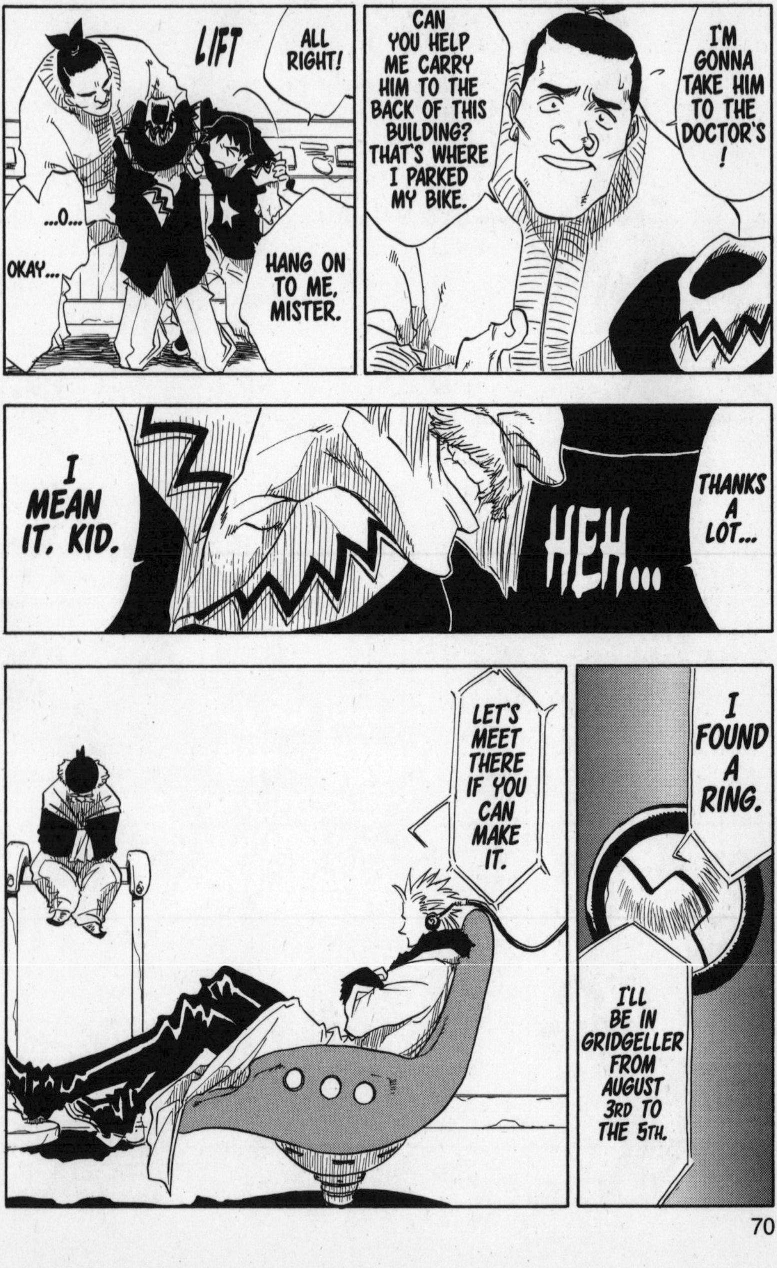
I'M GONNA TAKE HIM TO THE DOCTOR'S!
CAN YOU HELP ME CARRY HIM TO THE BACK OF THIS BUILDING? THAT'S WHERE I PARKED MY BIKE.
ALL RIGHT!
LIFT
HANG ON TO ME, MISTER.
...O... OKAY...
THANKS A LOT...
HEH...
I MEAN IT, KID.
I FOUND A RING.
I'LL BE IN GRIDGELLER FROM AUGUST 3RD TO THE 5TH.
LET'S MEET THERE IF YOU CAN MAKE IT.

READ THIS WAY

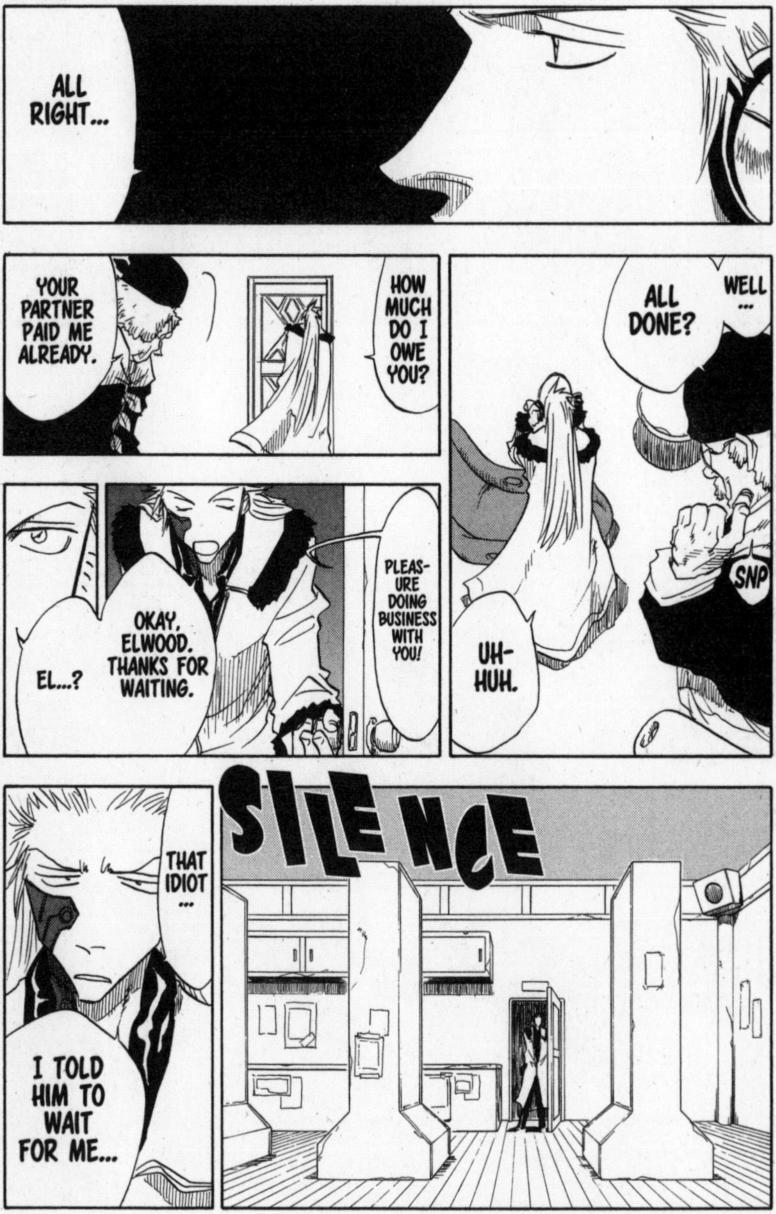

ALL RIGHT...
ALL DONE?
WELL...
SNP
UH-HUH.
HOW MUCH DO I OWE YOU?
YOUR PARTNER PAID ME ALREADY.
PLEAS-URE DOING BUSINESS WITH YOU!
OKAY, ELWOOD. THANKS FOR WAITING.
EL...?
SILENCE
THAT IDIOT...
I TOLD HIM TO WAIT FOR ME...

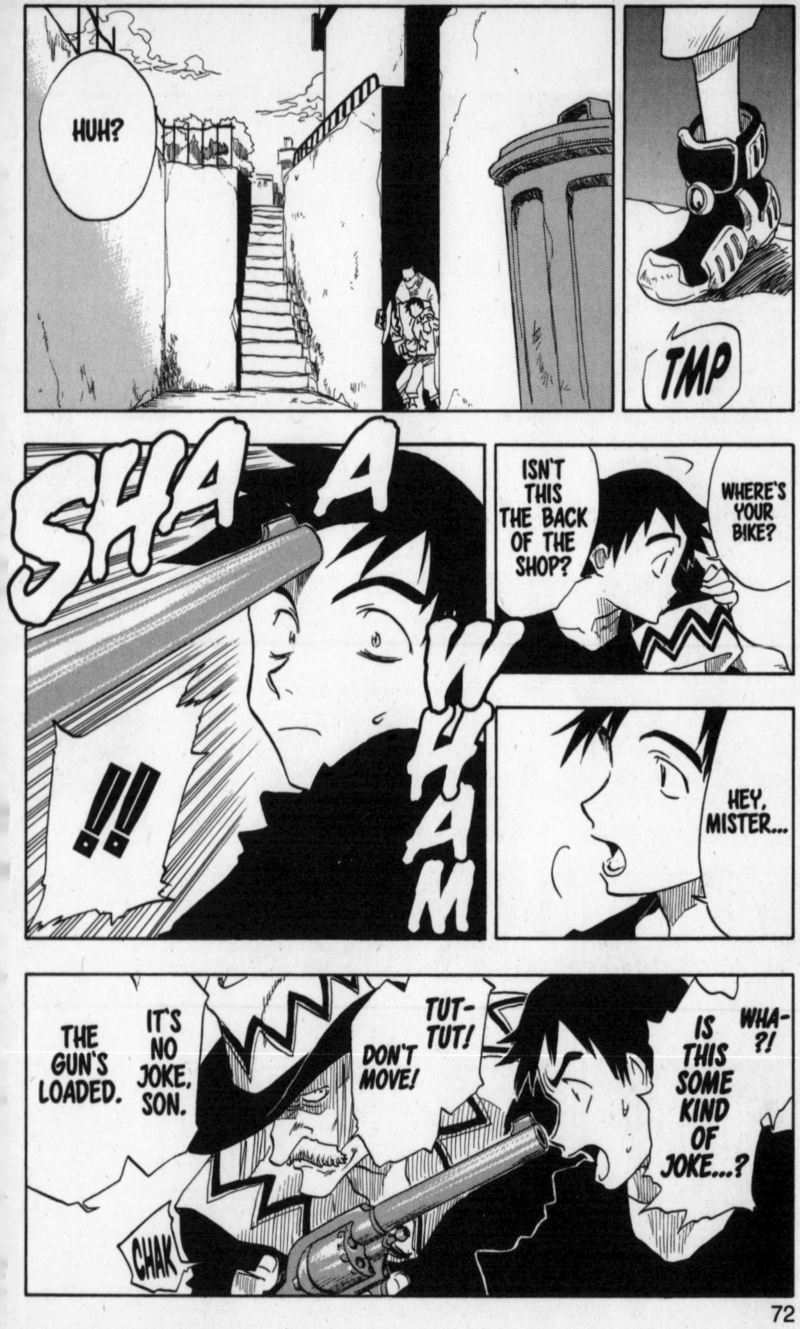
TMP
HUH?
WHERE'S YOUR BIKE?
ISN'T THIS THE BACK OF THE SHOP?
HEY, MISTER...
SHA A
WHAM
!!
WHA-?!
IS THIS SOME KIND OF JOKE...?
TUT-TUT!
DON'T MOVE!
IT'S NO JOKE, SON.
THE GUN'S LOADED.
CHAK

READ THIS WAY

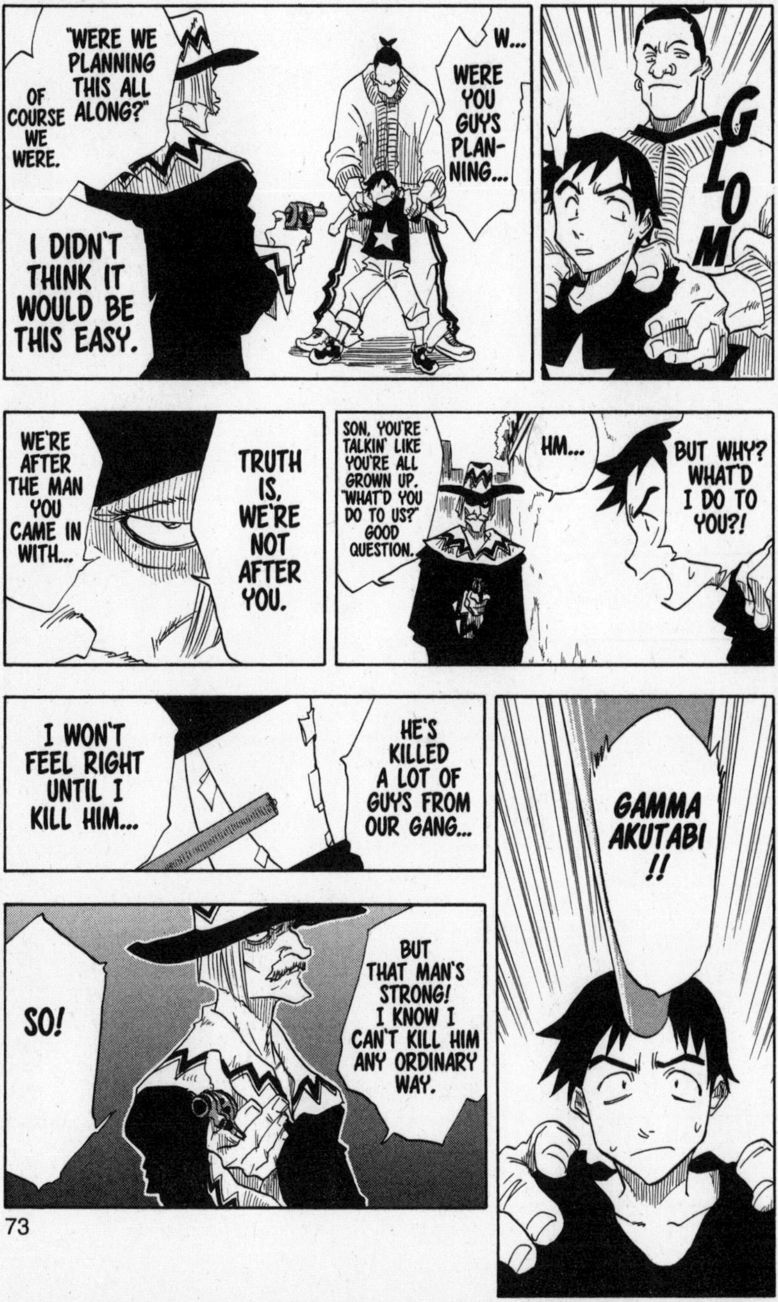
GLOM
W... WERE YOU GUYS PLANNING...
"WERE WE PLANNING THIS ALL ALONG?"
OF COURSE WE WERE.
I DIDN'T THINK IT WOULD BE THIS EASY.
BUT WHY? WHAT'D I DO TO YOU?!
HM...
SON, YOU'RE TALKIN' LIKE YOU'RE ALL GROWN UP. "WHAT'D YOU DO TO US?" GOOD QUESTION.
TRUTH IS, WE'RE NOT AFTER YOU.
WE'RE AFTER THE MAN YOU CAME IN WITH...
GAMMA AKUTABI !!
HE'S KILLED A LOT OF GUYS FROM OUR GANG...
I WON'T FEEL RIGHT UNTIL I KILL HIM...
BUT THAT MAN'S STRONG! I KNOW I CAN'T KILL HIM ANY ORDINARY WAY.
SO!

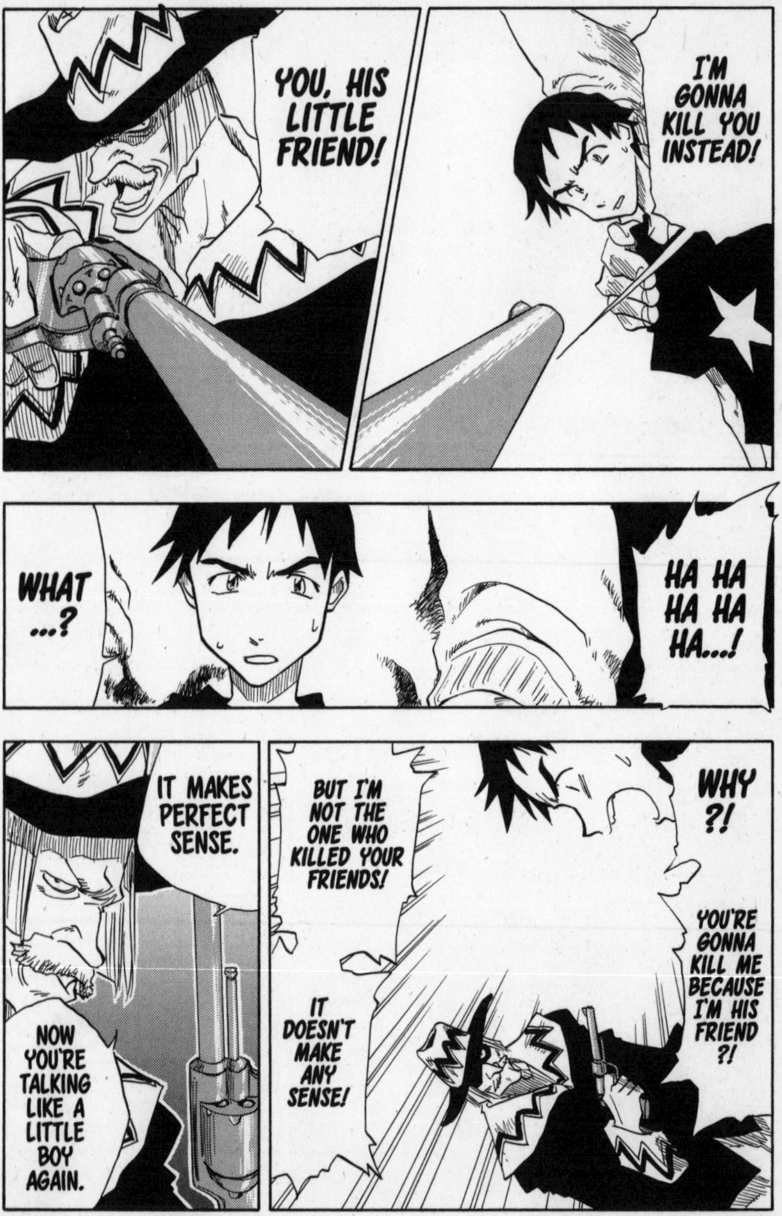
I'M GONNA KILL YOU INSTEAD!
YOU, HIS LITTLE FRIEND!
HA HA HA HA HA...!
WHAT ...?
WHY ?!
YOU'RE GONNA KILL ME BECAUSE I'M HIS FRIEND ?!
BUT I'M NOT THE ONE WHO KILLED YOUR FRIENDS!
IT DOESN'T MAKE ANY SENSE!
IT MAKES PERFECT SENSE.
NOW YOU'RE TALKING LIKE A LITTLE BOY AGAIN.

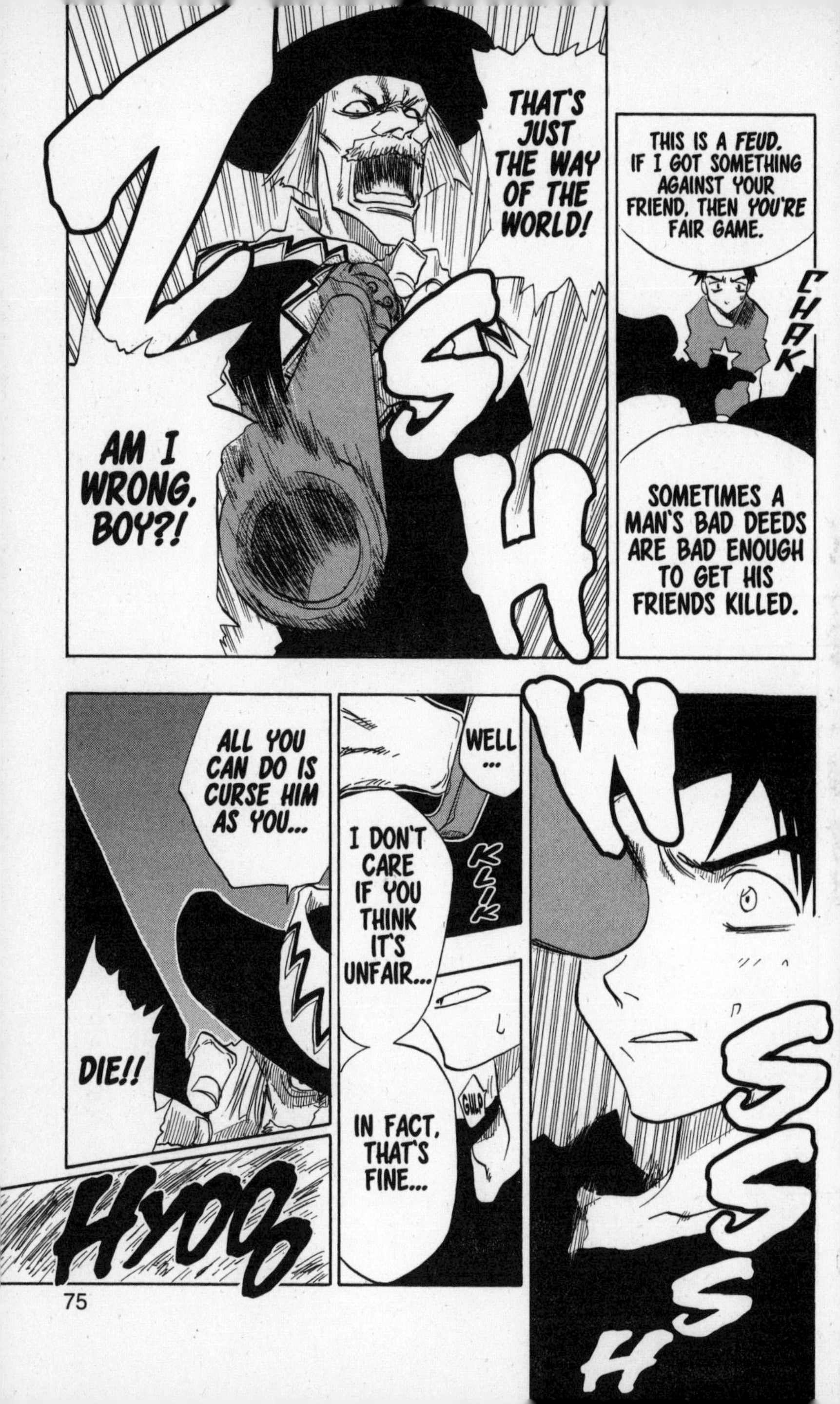
THIS IS A FEUD. IF I GOT SOMETHING AGAINST YOUR FRIEND, THEN YOU'RE FAIR GAME.
CHAK
SOMETIMES A MAN'S BAD DEEDS ARE BAD ENOUGH TO GET HIS FRIENDS KILLED.
THAT'S JUST THE WAY OF THE WORLD!
AM I WRONG, BOY?!
WELL...
I DON'T CARE IF YOU THINK IT'S UNFAIR...
KLIK
GULP
IN FACT, THAT'S FINE...
ALL YOU CAN DO IS CURSE HIM AS YOU...
DIE!!
HYOO

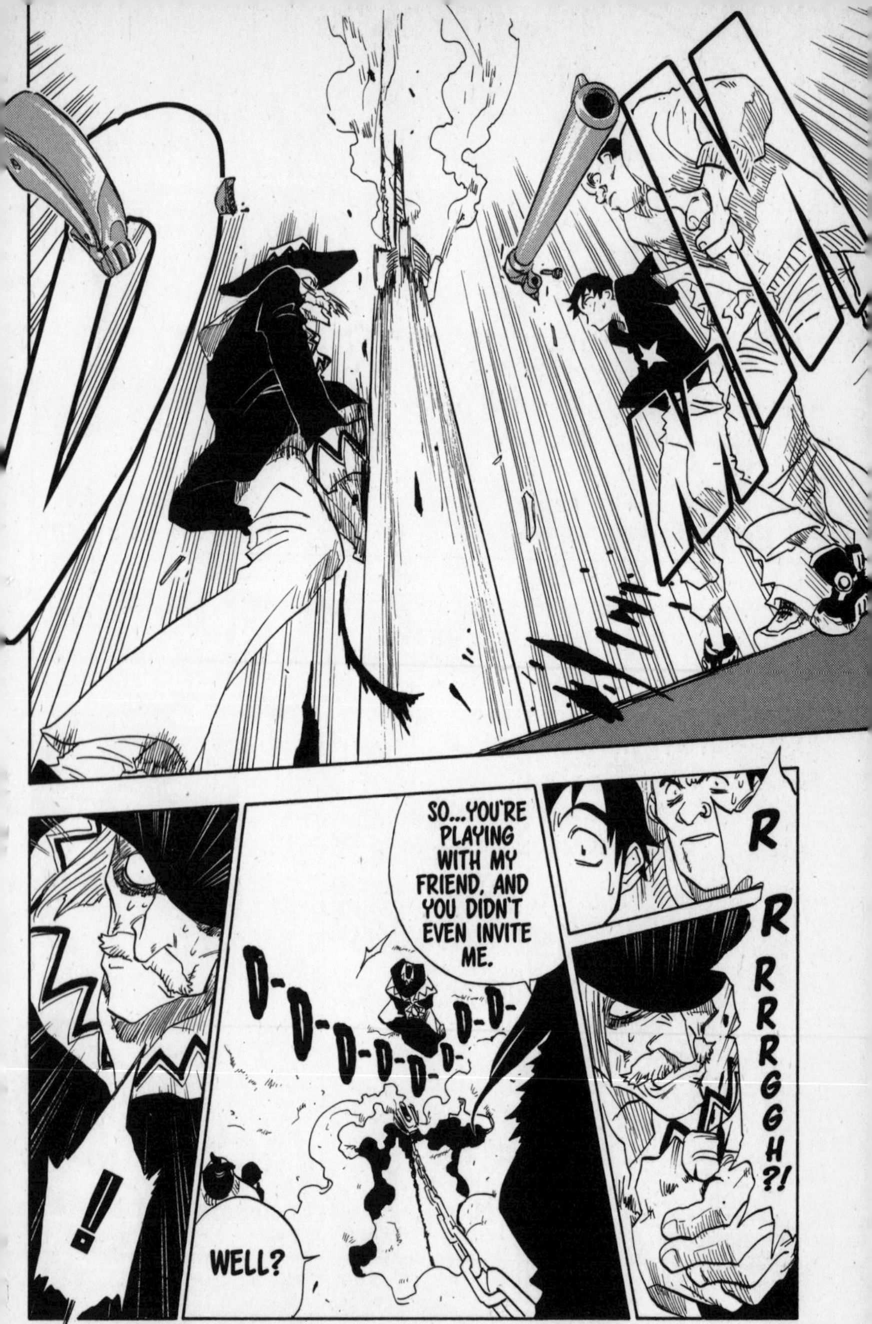
RRRRRRGGGH?!
SO...YOU'RE PLAYING WITH MY FRIEND, AND YOU DIDN'T EVEN INVITE ME.
D-D-D-D-D-D-D-D-D-
WELL?
!

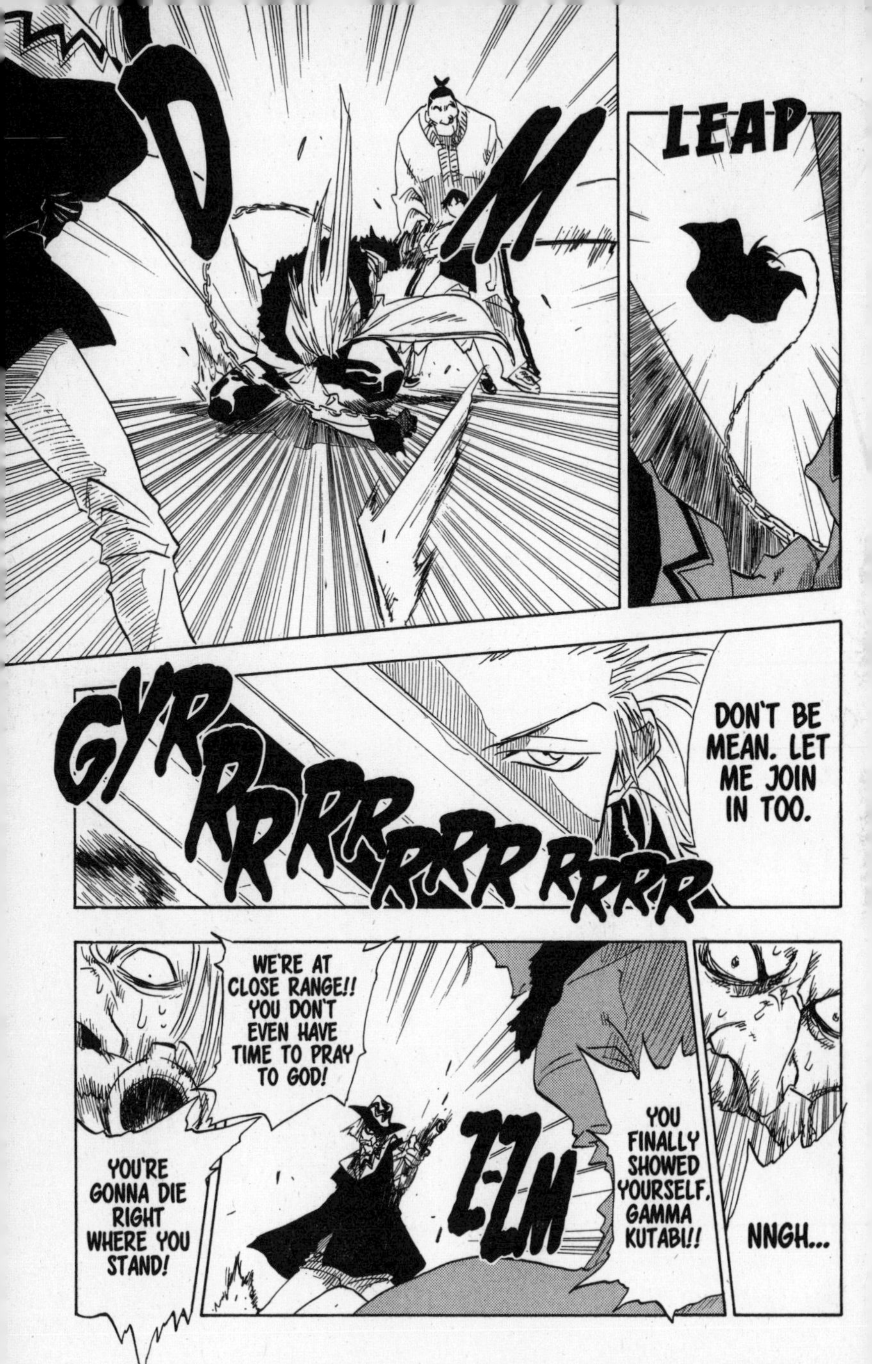
LEAP
DON'T BE MEAN. LET ME JOIN IN TOO.
GYRRRRRRRRRRRR
NNGH...
YOU FINALLY SHOWED YOURSELF, GAMMA KUTABI!!
WE'RE AT CLOSE RANGE!! YOU DON'T EVEN HAVE TIME TO PRAY TO GOD!
YOU'RE GONNA DIE RIGHT WHERE YOU STAND!

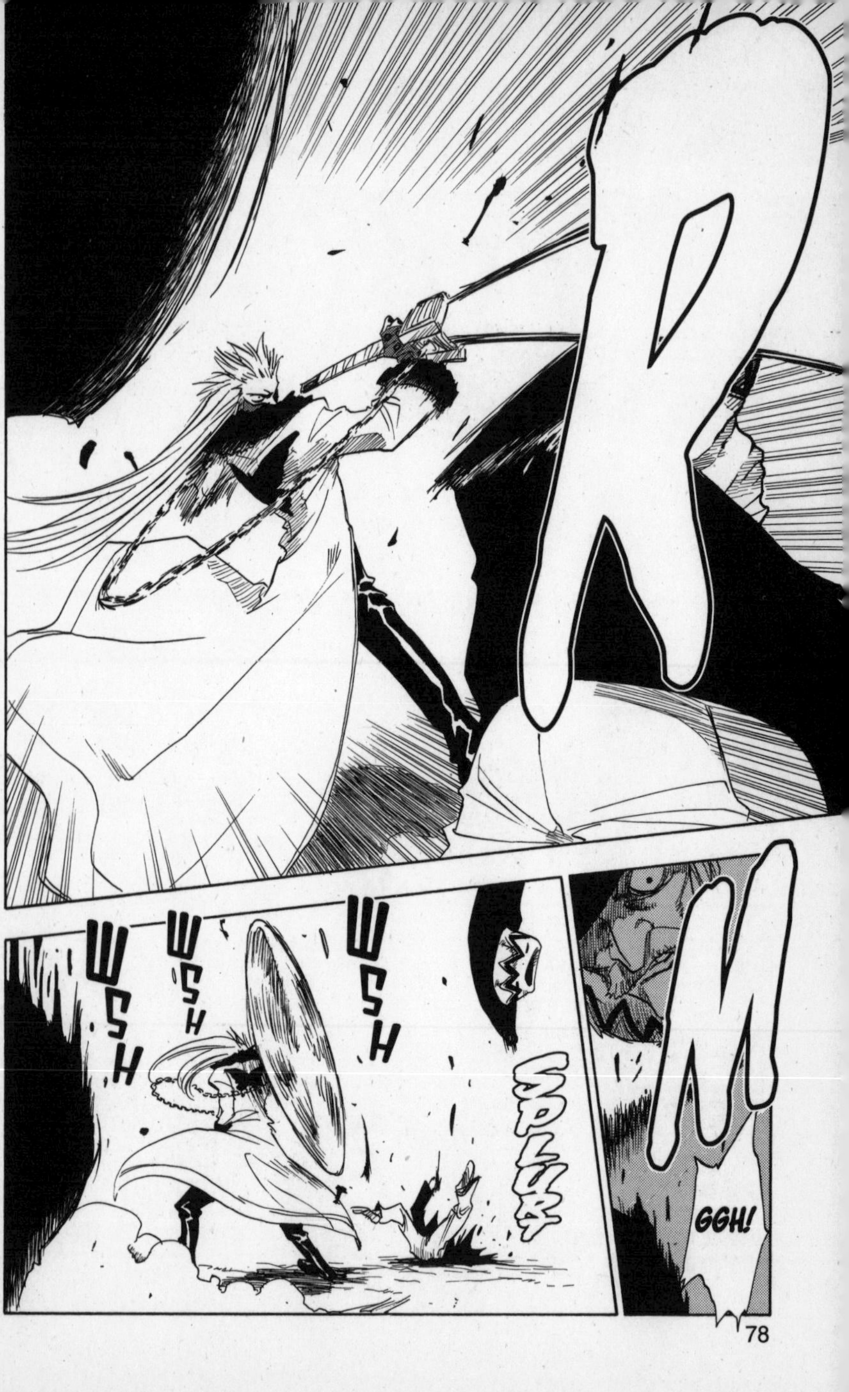
GGH!
WSH
WSH
WSH

READ THIS WAY

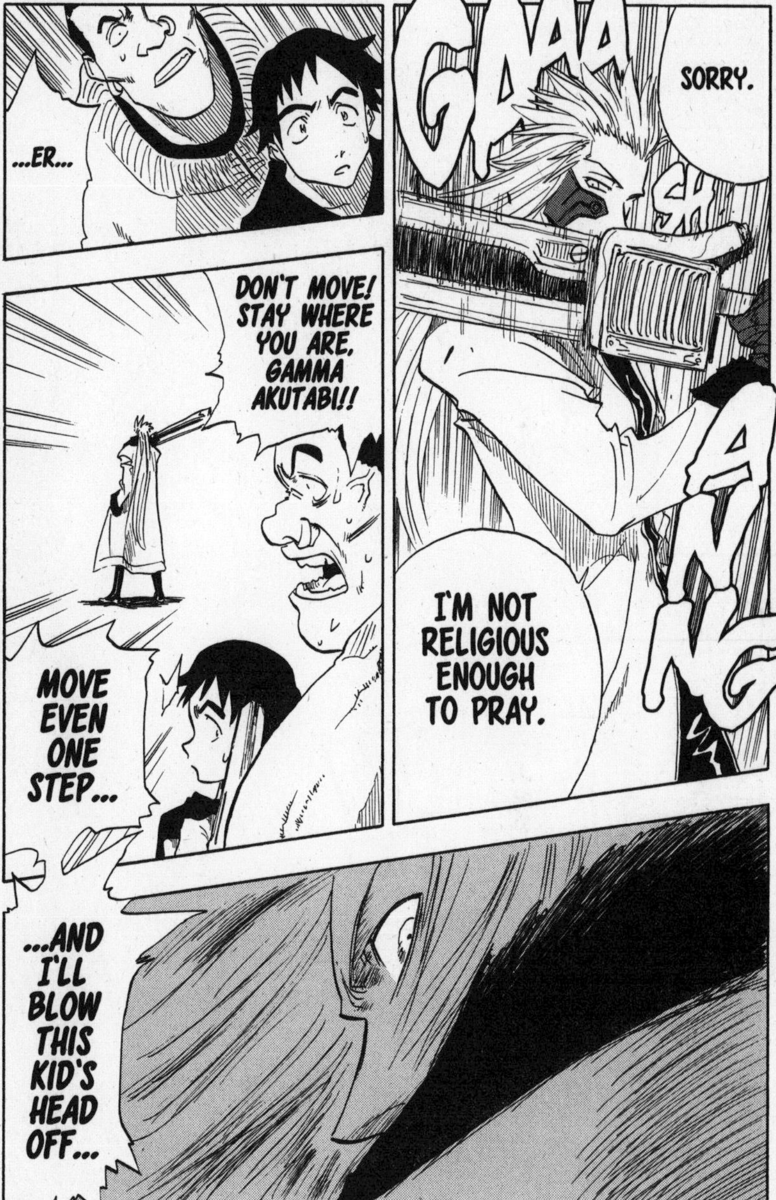
GAAA
SORRY.
I'M NOT RELIGIOUS ENOUGH TO PRAY.
...ER...
DON'T MOVE! STAY WHERE YOU ARE, GAMMA AKUTABI!!
MOVE EVEN ONE STEP...
...AND I'LL BLOW THIS KID'S HEAD OFF...

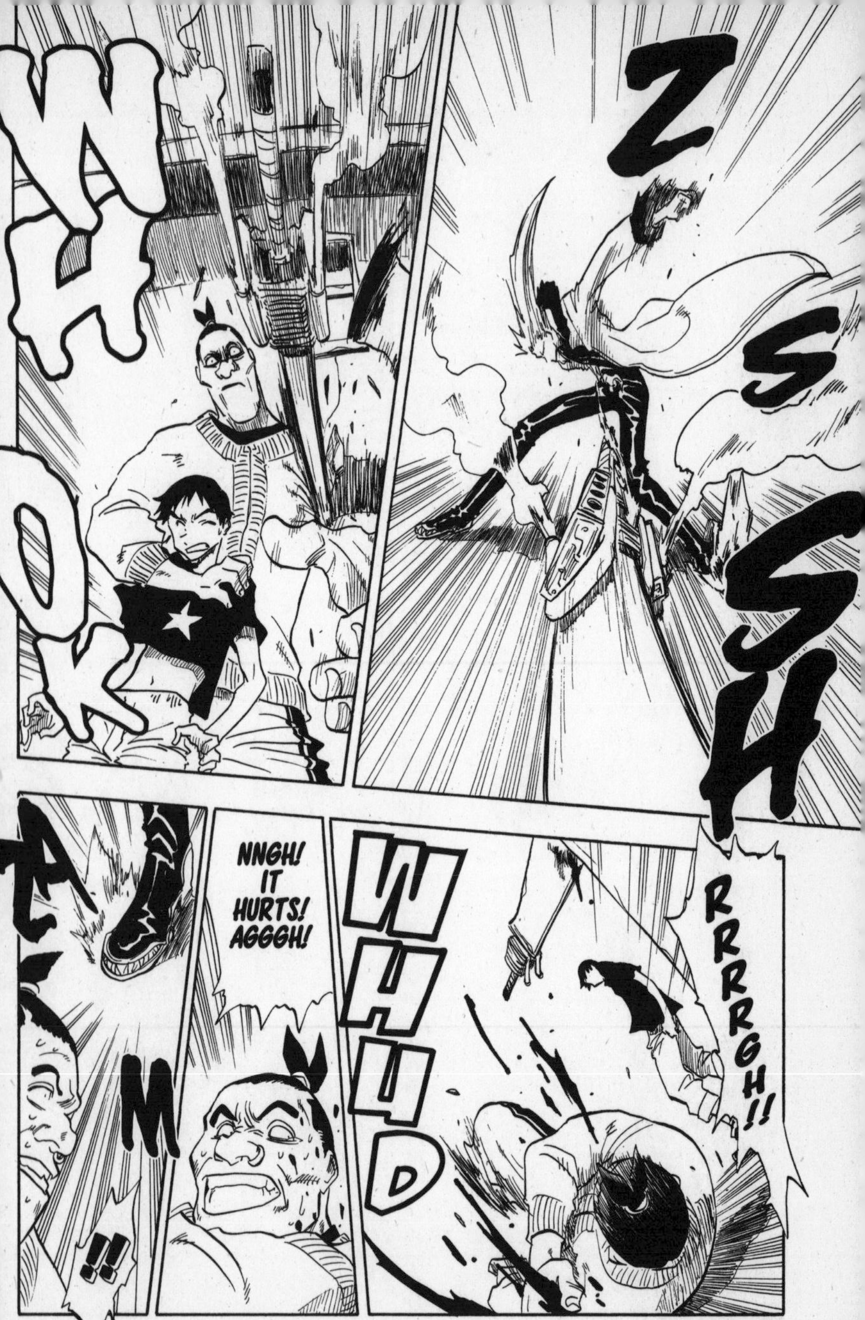
ZSSH
RRRRGH!!
WHUD
NNGH! IT HURTS! AGGGH!

READ THIS WAY

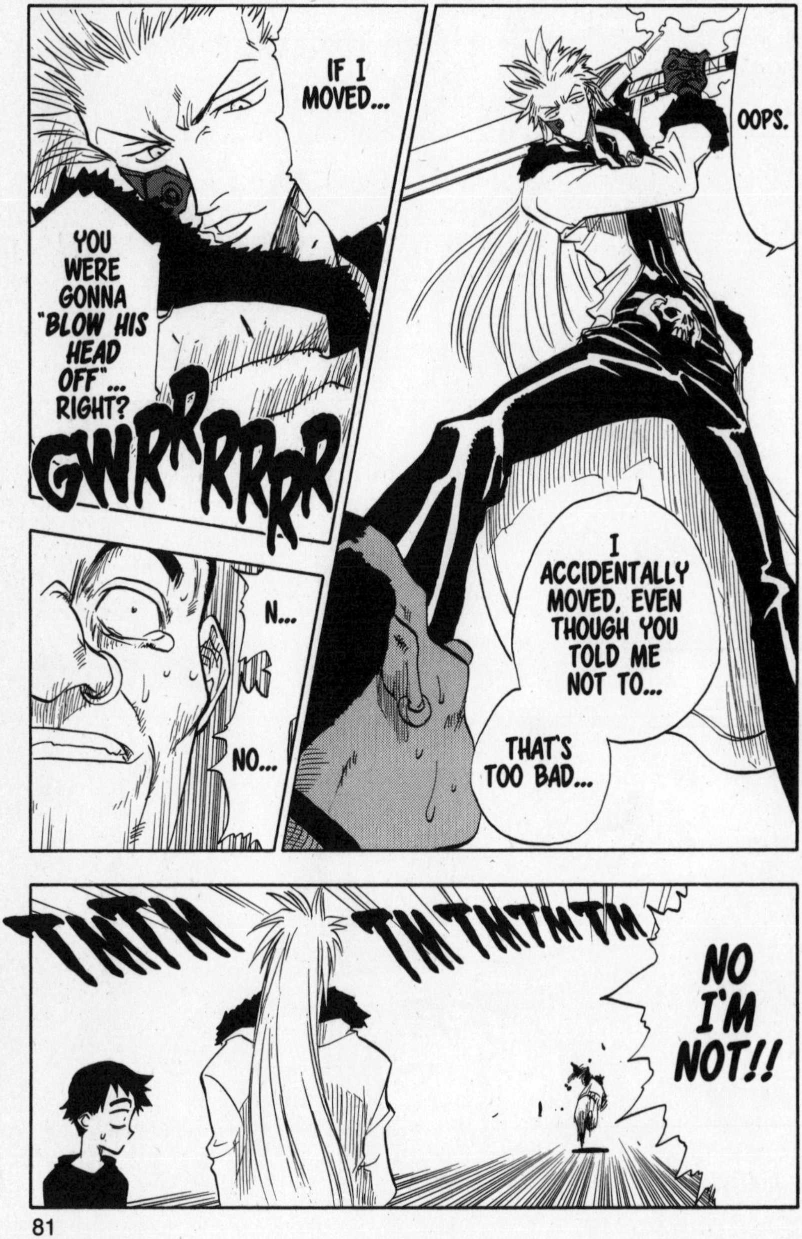
OOPS.
I ACCIDENTALLY MOVED, EVEN THOUGH YOU TOLD ME NOT TO...
THAT'S TOO BAD...
IF I MOVED...
YOU WERE GONNA "BLOW HIS HEAD OFF"... RIGHT?
GWRRRRRR
N...
NO...
NO I'M NOT!!
TM TMTMTMTM
TMTM

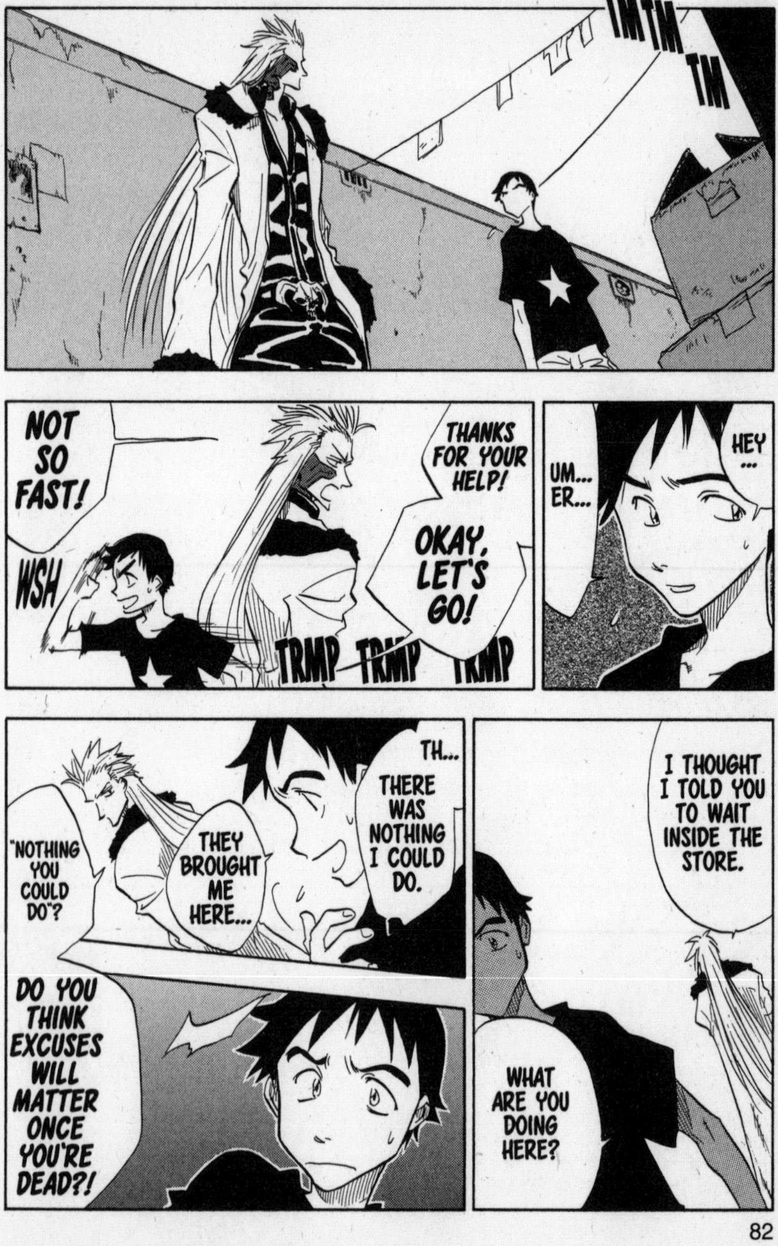
TM TM TM
HEY...
UM... ER...
THANKS FOR YOUR HELP!
OKAY, LET'S GO!
TRMP TRMP TRMP
NOT SO FAST!
WSH
I THOUGHT I TOLD YOU TO WAIT INSIDE THE STORE.
WHAT ARE YOU DOING HERE?
TH...
THERE WAS NOTHING I COULD DO.
THEY BROUGHT ME HERE...
"NOTHING YOU COULD DO"?
DO YOU THINK EXCUSES WILL MATTER ONCE YOU'RE DEAD?!

READ THIS WAY

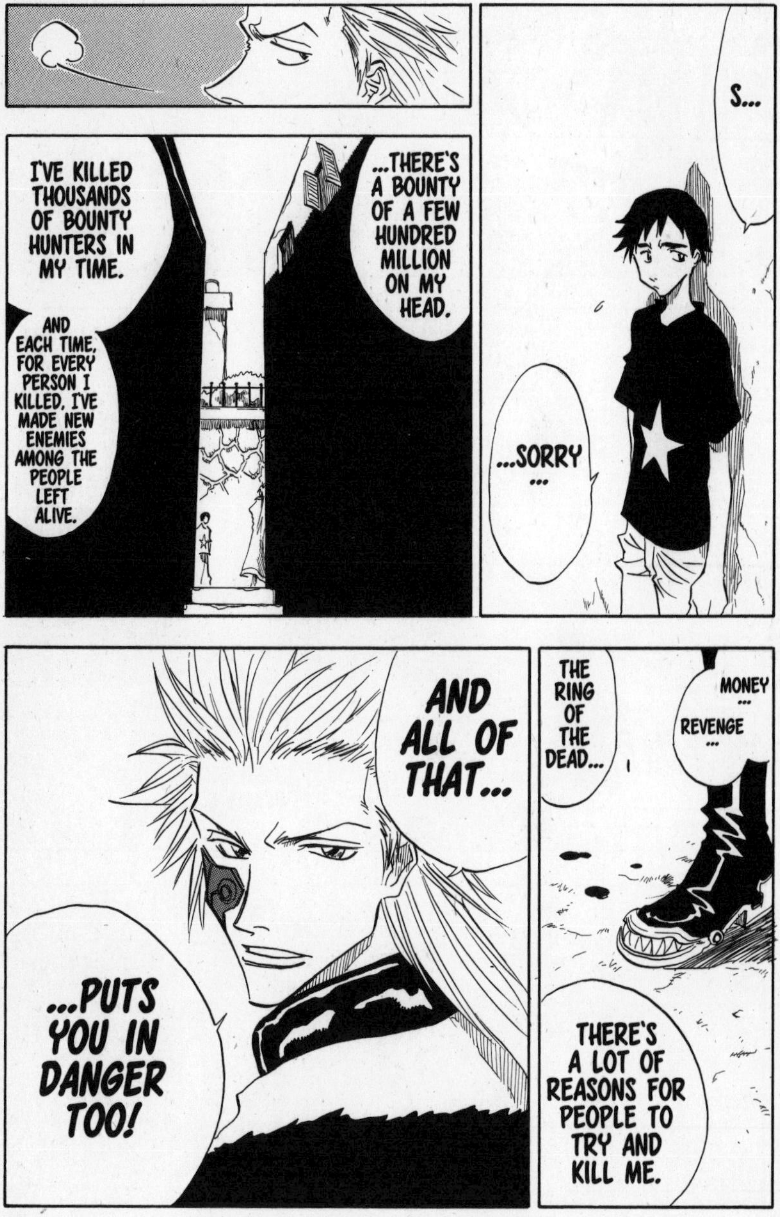

S...
...SORRY ...
...THERE'S A BOUNTY OF A FEW HUNDRED MILLION ON MY HEAD.
I'VE KILLED THOUSANDS OF BOUNTY HUNTERS IN MY TIME.
AND EACH TIME, FOR EVERY PERSON I KILLED, I'VE MADE NEW ENEMIES AMONG THE PEOPLE LEFT ALIVE.
MONEY ...
REVENGE ...
THE RING OF THE DEAD...
THERE'S A LOT OF REASONS FOR PEOPLE TO TRY AND KILL ME.
AND ALL OF THAT...
...PUTS YOU IN DANGER TOO!

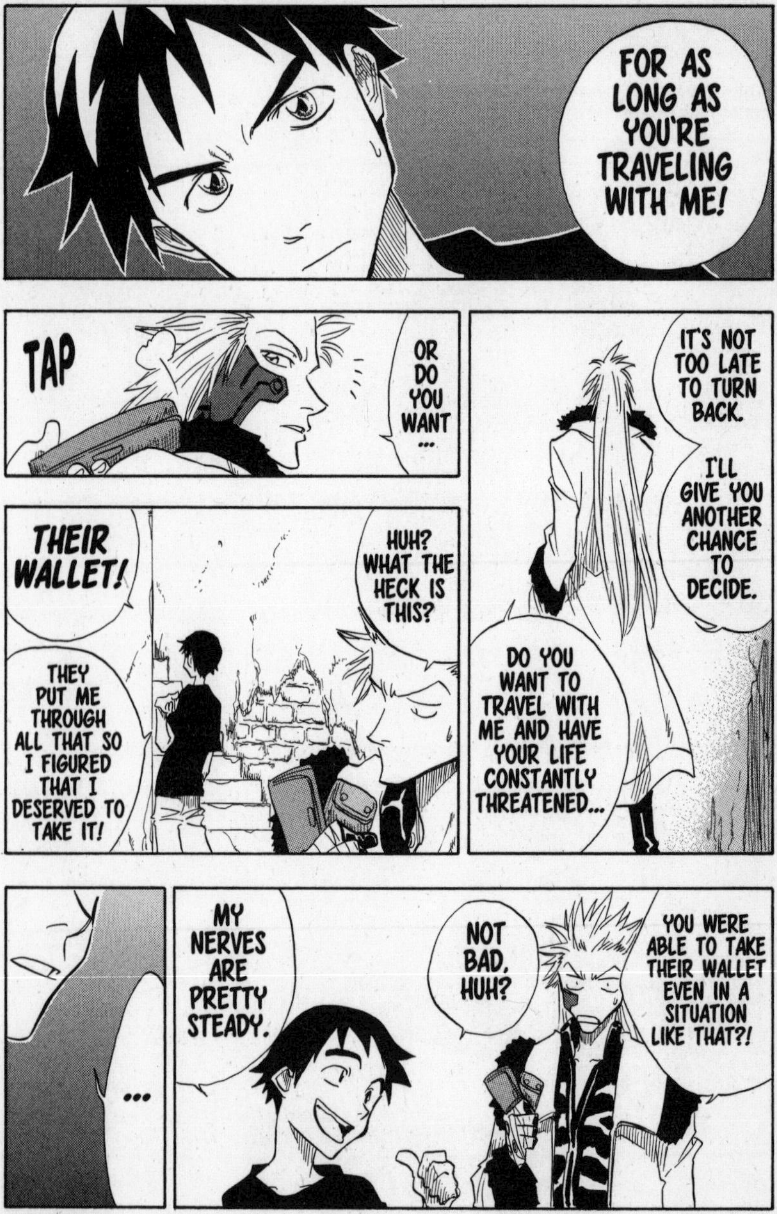
FOR AS LONG AS YOU'RE TRAVELING WITH ME!
IT'S NOT TOO LATE TO TURN BACK.
I'LL GIVE YOU ANOTHER CHANCE TO DECIDE.
DO YOU WANT TO TRAVEL WITH ME AND HAVE YOUR LIFE CONSTANTLY THREATENED...
OR DO YOU WANT...
TAP
HUH? WHAT THE HECK IS THIS?
THEIR WALLET!
THEY PUT ME THROUGH ALL THAT SO I FIGURED THAT I DESERVED TO TAKE IT!
YOU WERE ABLE TO TAKE THEIR WALLET EVEN IN A SITUATION LIKE THAT?!
NOT BAD, HUH?
MY NERVES ARE PRETTY STEADY.
...

READ THIS WAY

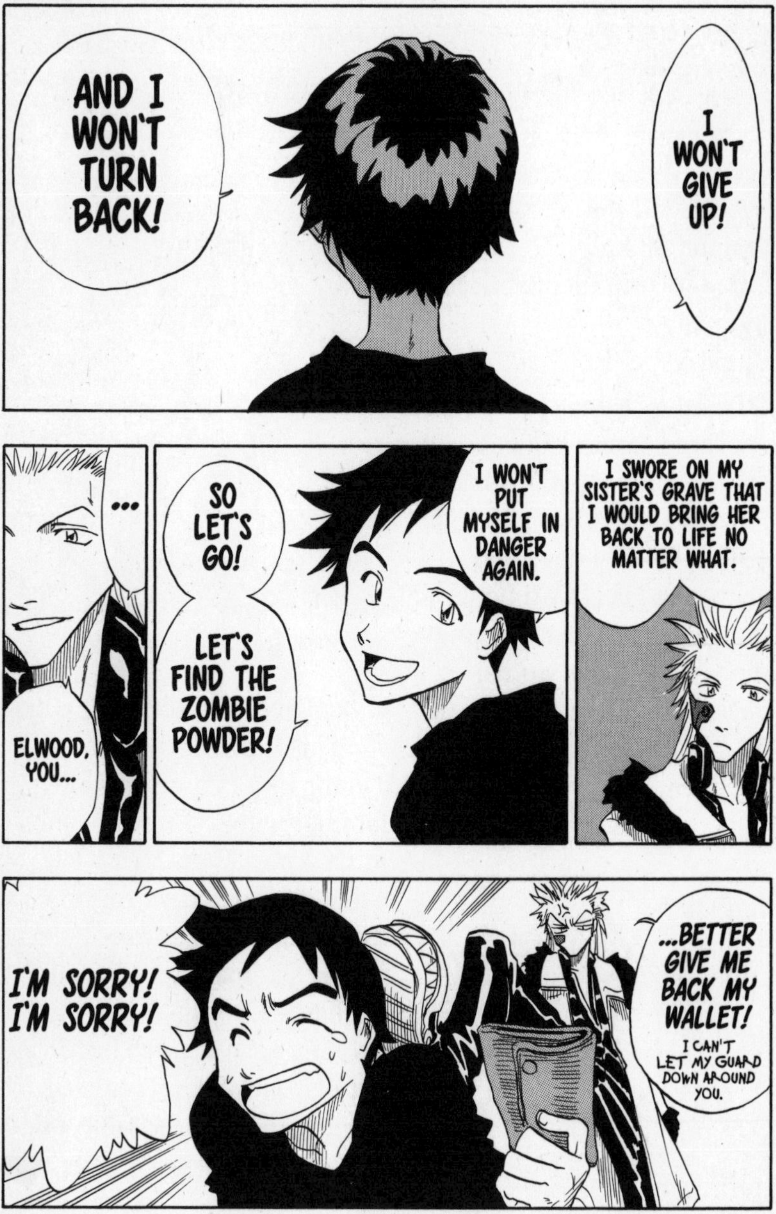
I WON'T GIVE UP!
AND I WON'T TURN BACK!
I SWORE ON MY SISTER'S GRAVE THAT I WOULD BRING HER BACK TO LIFE NO MATTER WHAT.
I WON'T PUT MYSELF IN DANGER AGAIN.
SO LET'S GO!
LET'S FIND THE ZOMBIE POWDER!
...
ELWOOD, YOU...
...BETTER GIVE ME BACK MY WALLET!
I CAN'T LET MY GUARD DOWN AROUND YOU.
I'M SORRY! I'M SORRY!

B-side NAKED MONKEYS 2.

John Elwood Shepherd
ジョン・エルウッド・シェパード

Height: 151 cm
Weight: 38 kg
Date Of Birth: September 10
Age: 13
Blood Type: BO

Of all the characters who've appeared so far, Elwood is probably the most levelheaded. He took care of his sick older sister, did the houschold chores and is almost better than necessary at managing money. (In other words, he's cheap.) He likes all kinds of food, which is also something that he's proud of. By the way, "Elwood" is the name of the president of an American record company. (Those that are

familiar with CCM magazine might know about him.) The name was so perfect for him that I just had to borrow it. The star mark on Elwood's clothes is the logo for a clothing maker called "Big Fat Star Jack" that specializes in inexpensive heavy-duty clothing. It's his favorite brand.

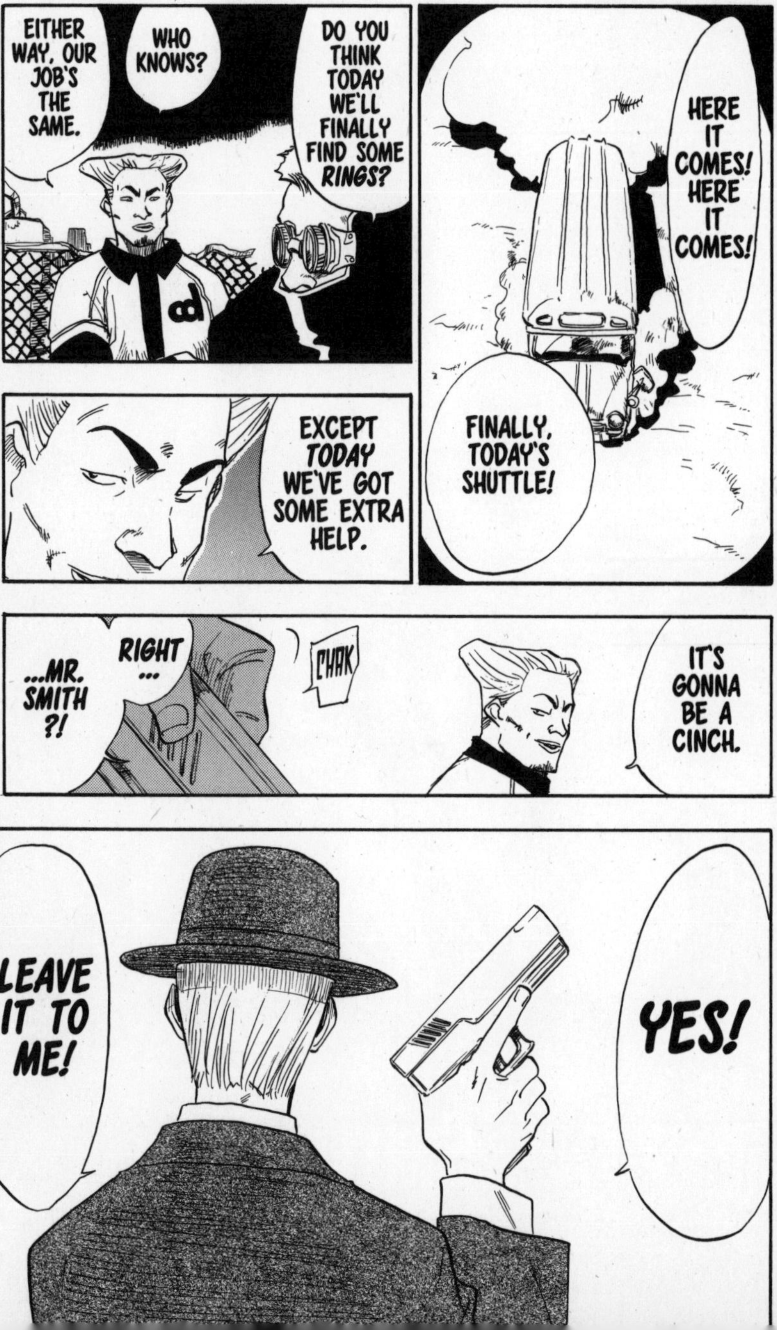
HERE IT COMES! HERE IT COMES!
FINALLY, TODAY'S SHUTTLE!
DO YOU THINK TODAY WE'LL FINALLY FIND SOME *RINGS*?
WHO KNOWS?
EITHER WAY, OUR JOB'S THE SAME.
EXCEPT *TODAY* WE'VE GOT SOME EXTRA HELP.
IT'S GONNA BE A CINCH.
CHAK
RIGHT...
...MR. SMITH?!
YES!
LEAVE IT TO ME!

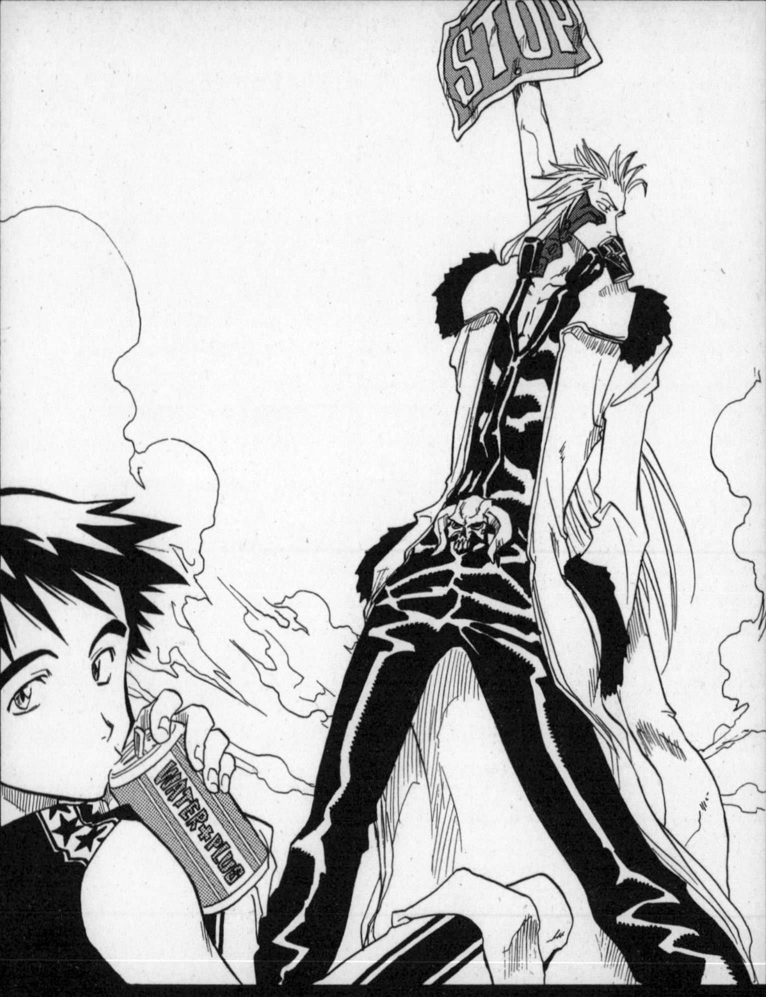
STOP
WATER+PLUG

TRACK 3:

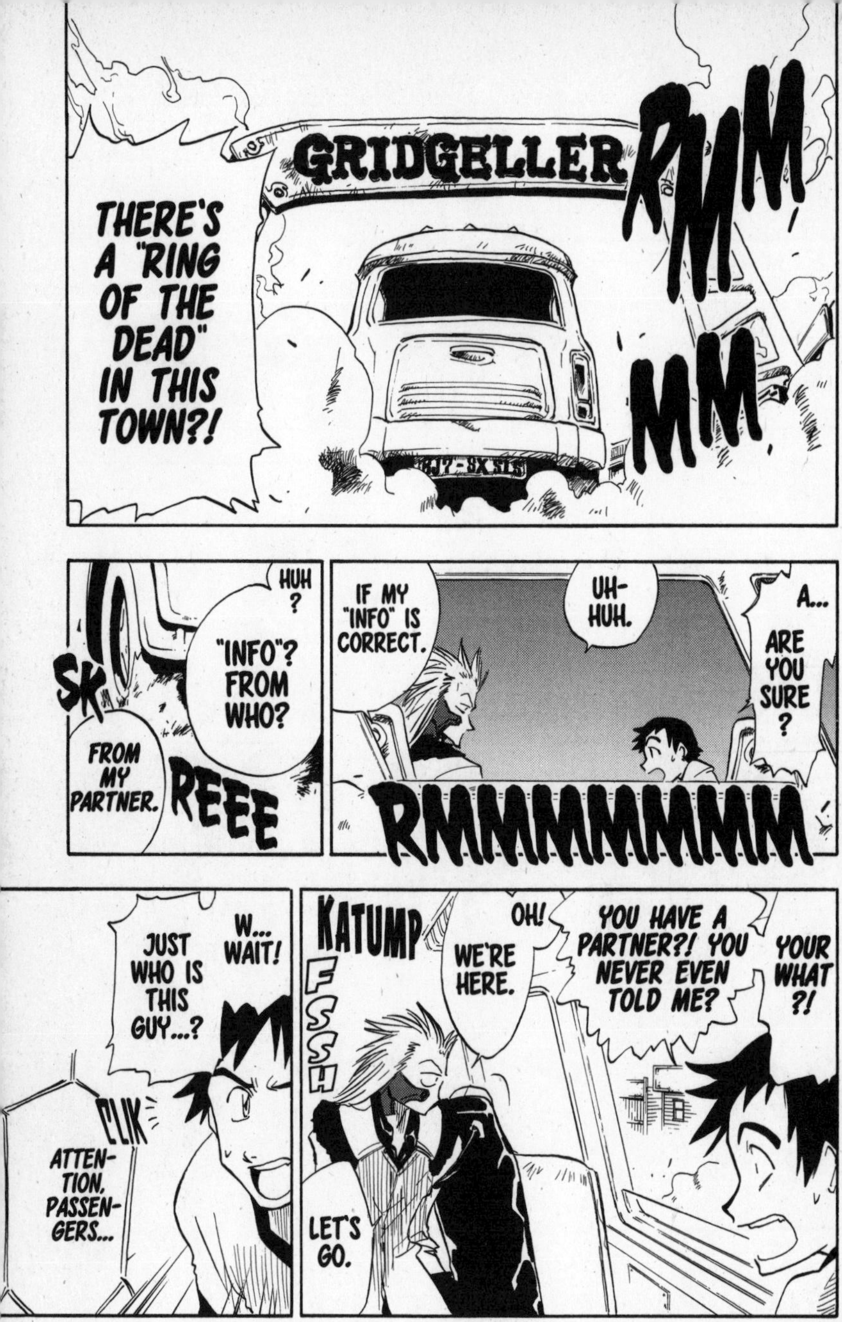
GRIDGELLER
THERE'S A "RING OF THE DEAD" IN THIS TOWN?!
RMM
MM
A... ARE YOU SURE?
UH-HUH.
IF MY "INFO" IS CORRECT.
RMMMMMMMM
HUH?
"INFO"? FROM WHO?
SK
FROM MY PARTNER.
REEE
YOUR WHAT?!
YOU HAVE A PARTNER?! YOU NEVER EVEN TOLD ME?
OH!
WE'RE HERE.
KATUMP
FSSH
LET'S GO.
W... WAIT!
JUST WHO IS THIS GUY...?
CLIK
ATTEN-TION, PASSEN-GERS...

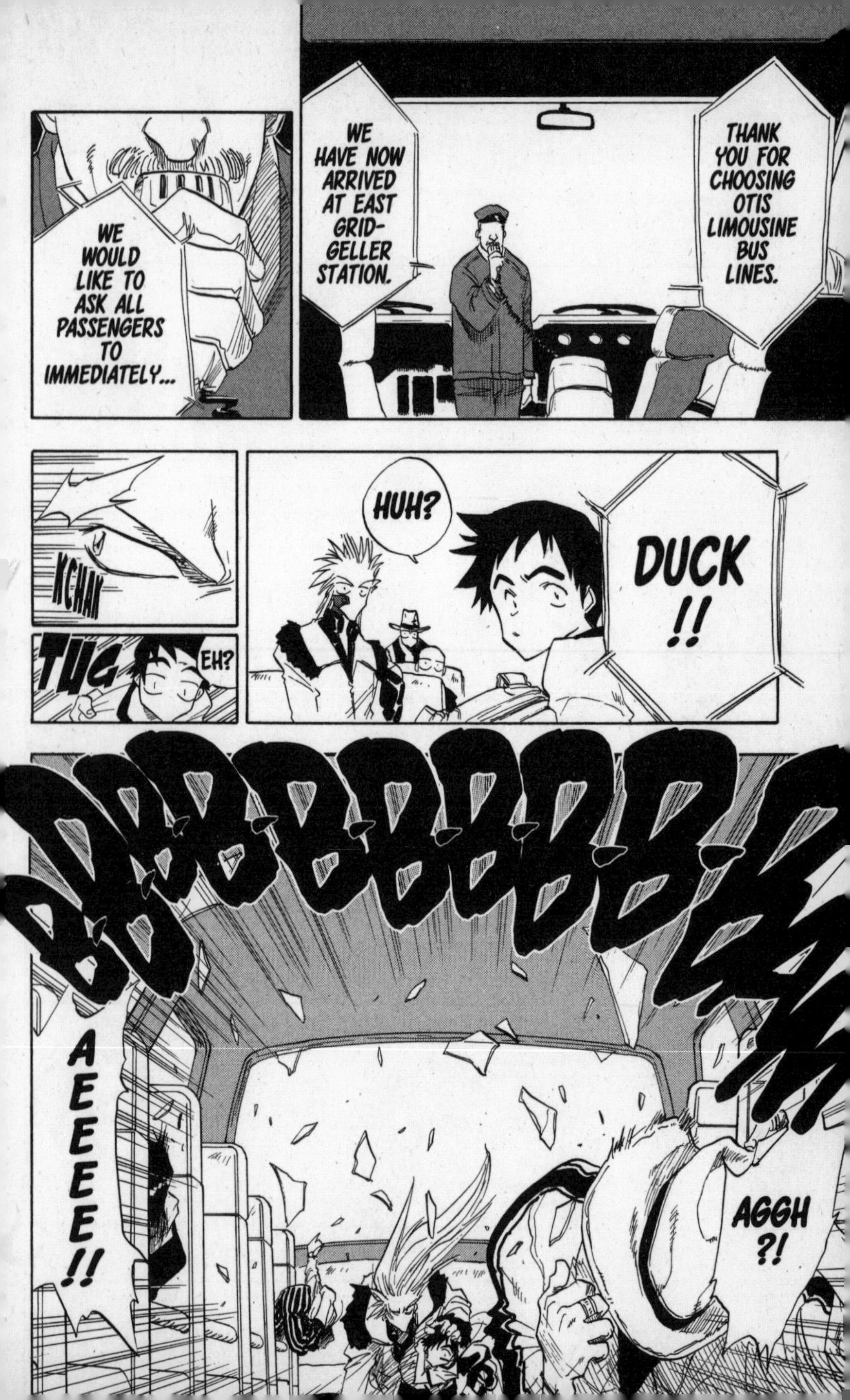
THANK YOU FOR CHOOSING OTIS LIMOUSINE BUS LINES.
WE HAVE NOW ARRIVED AT EAST GRID-GELLER STATION.
WE WOULD LIKE TO ASK ALL PASSENGERS TO IMMEDIATELY...
DUCK!!
HUH?
KCHAK
EH?
TUG
AGGH?!
AEEEEE!!

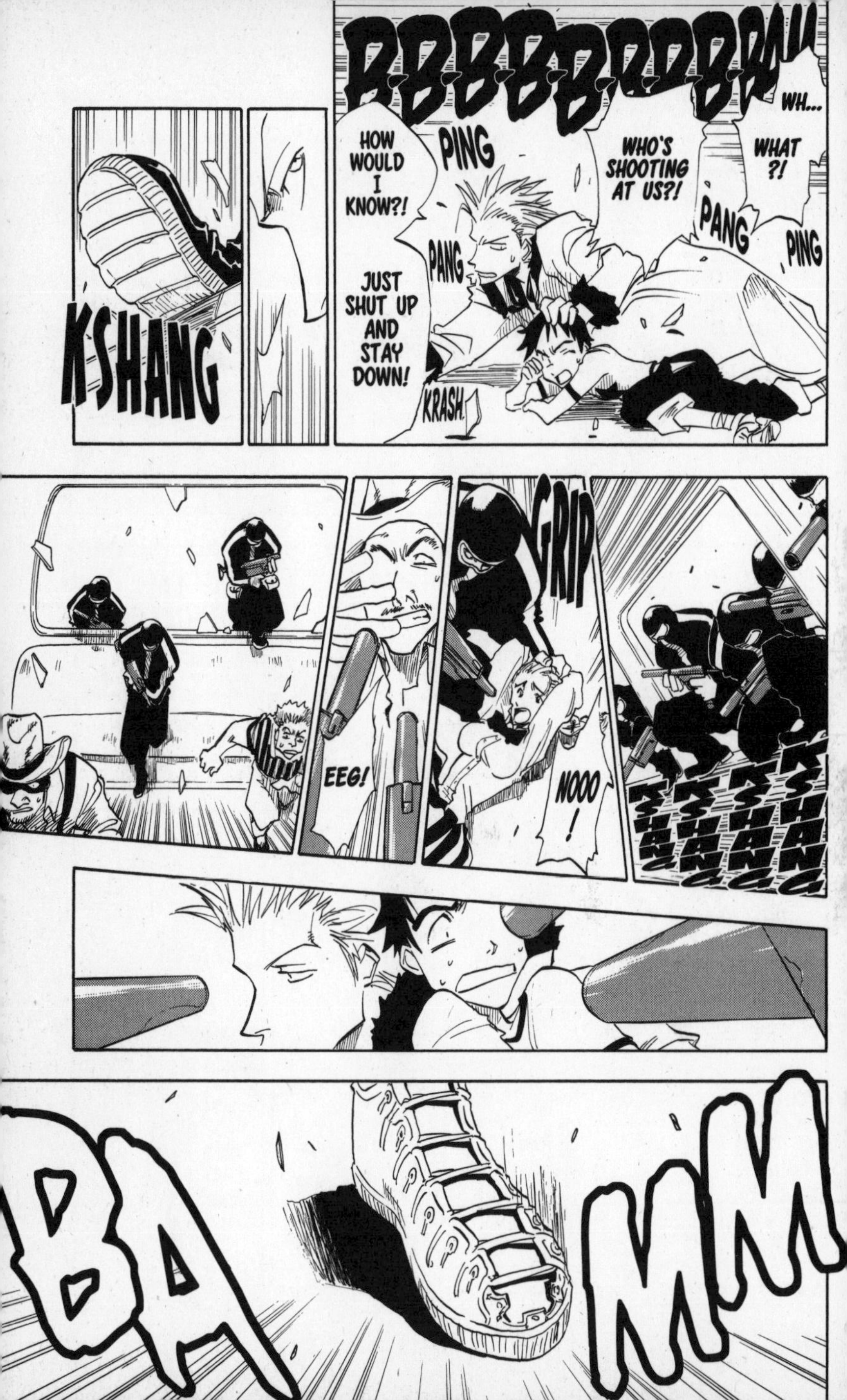
BBBBBDDBBA!!
WH...
WHAT ?!
WHO'S SHOOTING AT US?!
PING
PANG
PING
PANG
HOW WOULD I KNOW?!
JUST SHUT UP AND STAY DOWN!
KRASH
KSHANG
KSHANG
KSHANG
KSHANG
KSHANG
GRIP
NOOO!
EEG!
BAMM

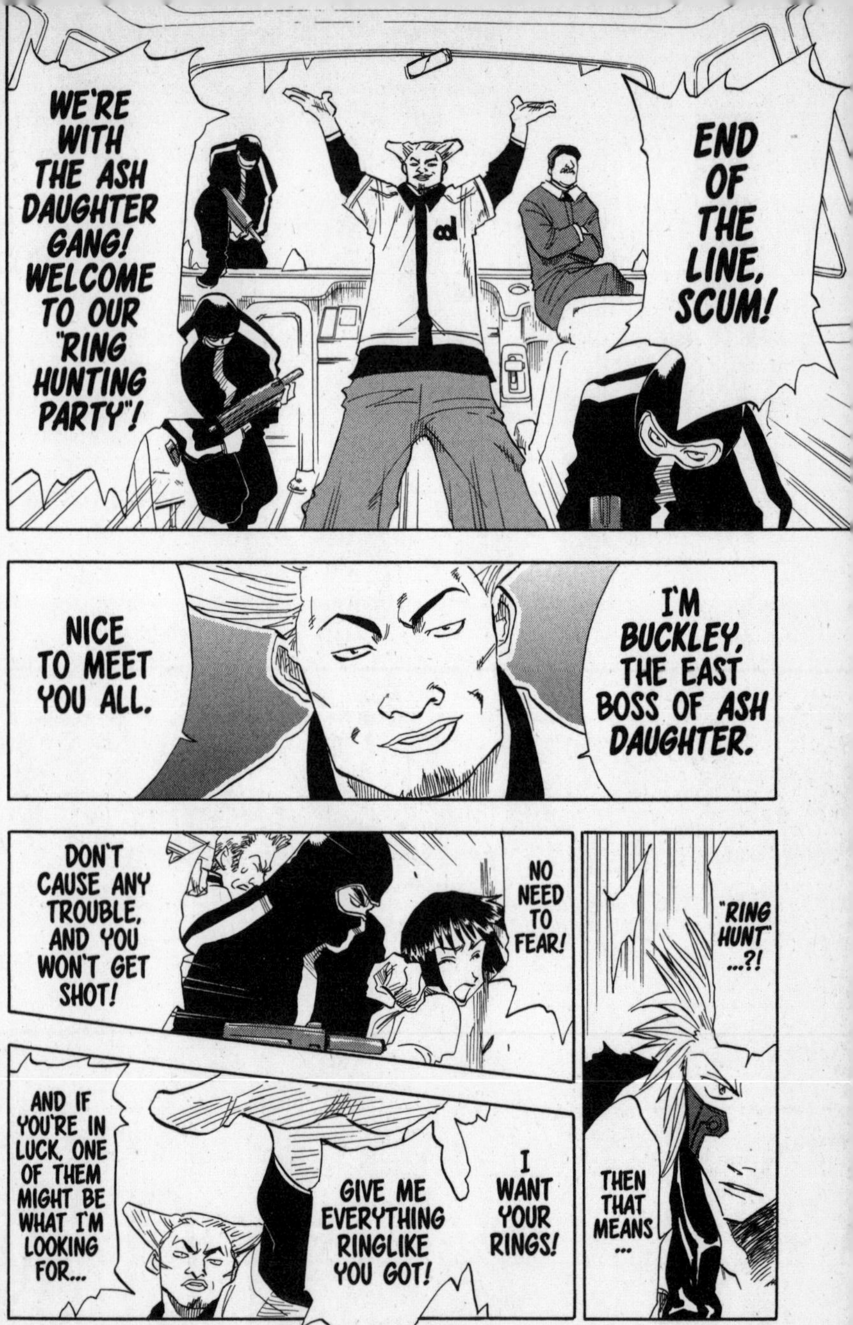
END OF THE LINE, SCUM!
WE'RE WITH THE ASH DAUGHTER GANG! WELCOME TO OUR "RING HUNTING PARTY"!
I'M BUCKLEY, THE EAST BOSS OF ASH DAUGHTER.
NICE TO MEET YOU ALL.
"RING HUNT" ...?!
THEN THAT MEANS...
NO NEED TO FEAR!
DON'T CAUSE ANY TROUBLE, AND YOU WON'T GET SHOT!
I WANT YOUR RINGS!
GIVE ME EVERYTHING RINGLIKE YOU GOT!
AND IF YOU'RE IN LUCK, ONE OF THEM MIGHT BE WHAT I'M LOOKING FOR...

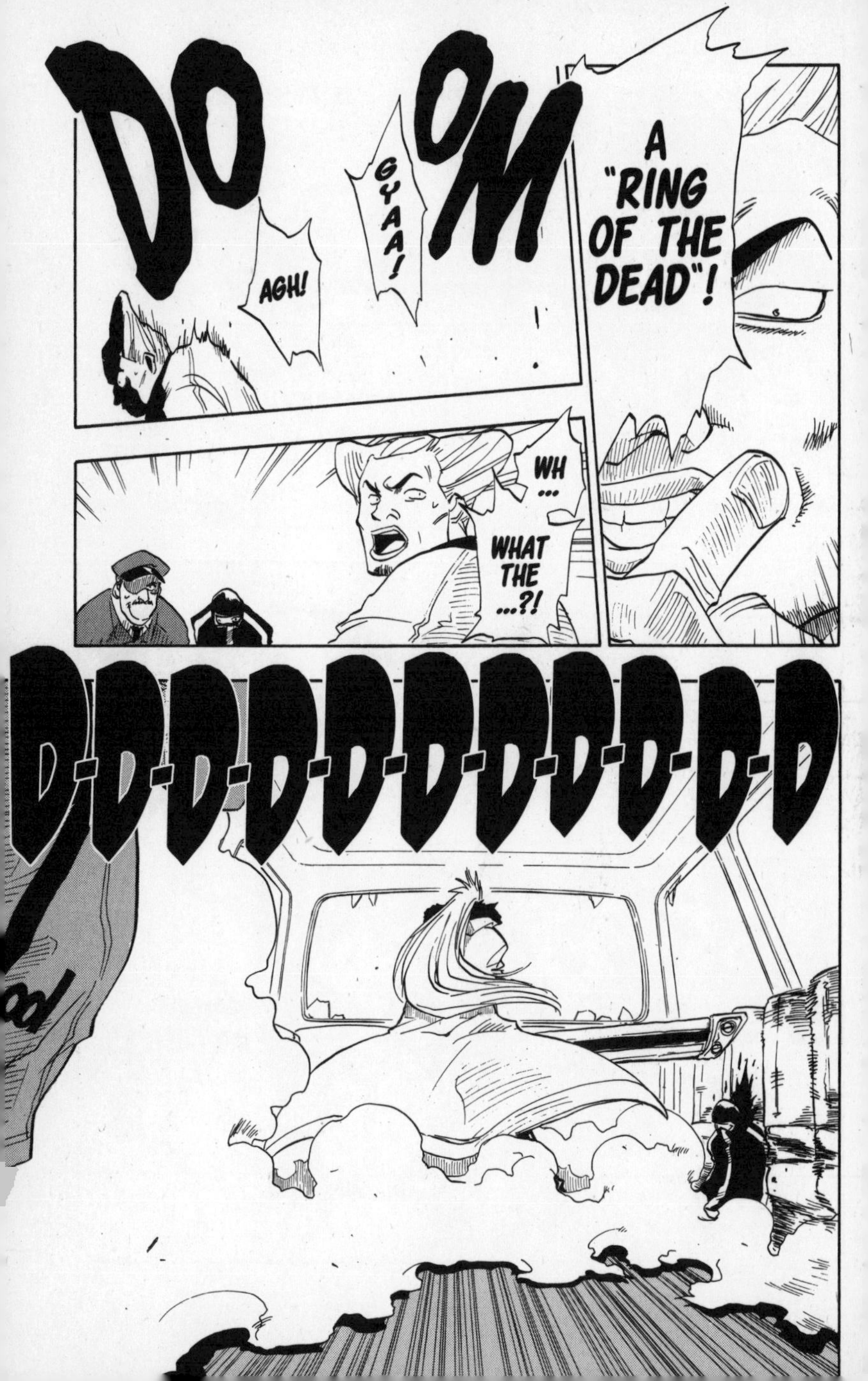
A "RING OF THE DEAD"!
DOOM
GYAAA!
AGH!
WH...
WHAT THE...?!
D-D-D-D-D-D-D-D-D-D-D

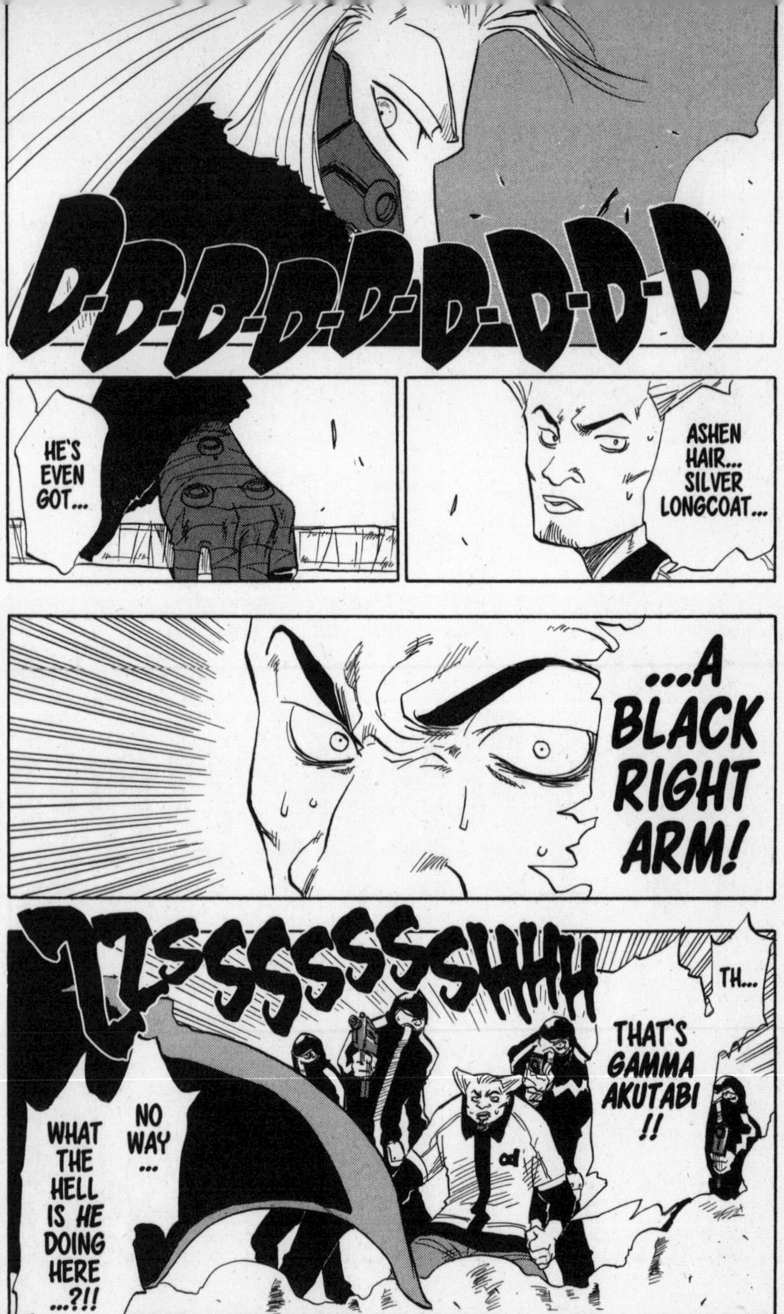
D-D-D-D-D-D-D-D-D-D
ASHEN HAIR... SILVER LONGCOAT...
HE'S EVEN GOT...
...A BLACK RIGHT ARM!
ZZSSSSSSSHHH
TH...
THAT'S GAMMA AKUTABI!!
NO WAY...
WHAT THE HELL IS HE DOING HERE...?!!

READ THIS WAY

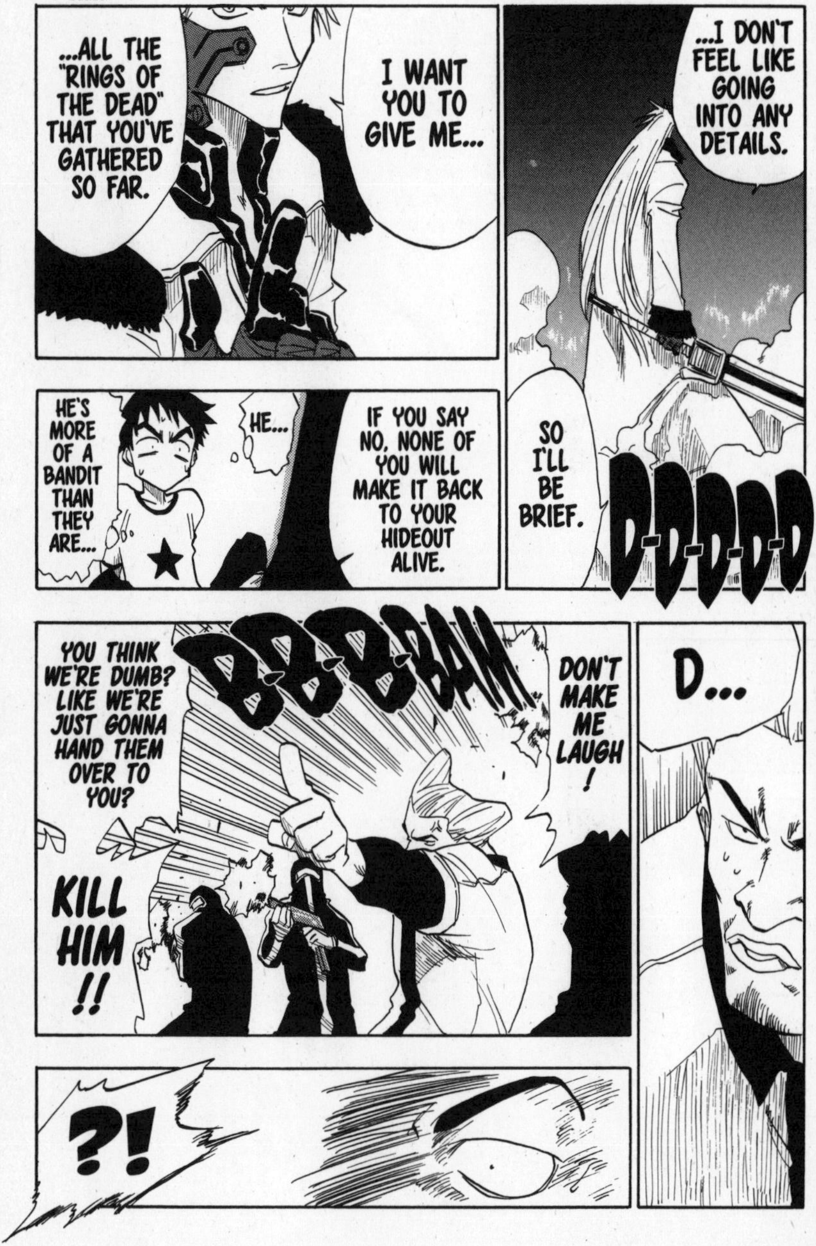
...I DON'T FEEL LIKE GOING INTO ANY DETAILS.
SO I'LL BE BRIEF.
D-D-D-D-D-D
I WANT YOU TO GIVE ME...
...ALL THE "RINGS OF THE DEAD" THAT YOU'VE GATHERED SO FAR.
IF YOU SAY NO, NONE OF YOU WILL MAKE IT BACK TO YOUR HIDEOUT ALIVE.
HE...
HE'S MORE OF A BANDIT THAN THEY ARE...
D...
DON'T MAKE ME LAUGH!
YOU THINK WE'RE DUMB? LIKE WE'RE JUST GONNA HAND THEM OVER TO YOU?
BBBBBAM
KILL HIM!!
?!

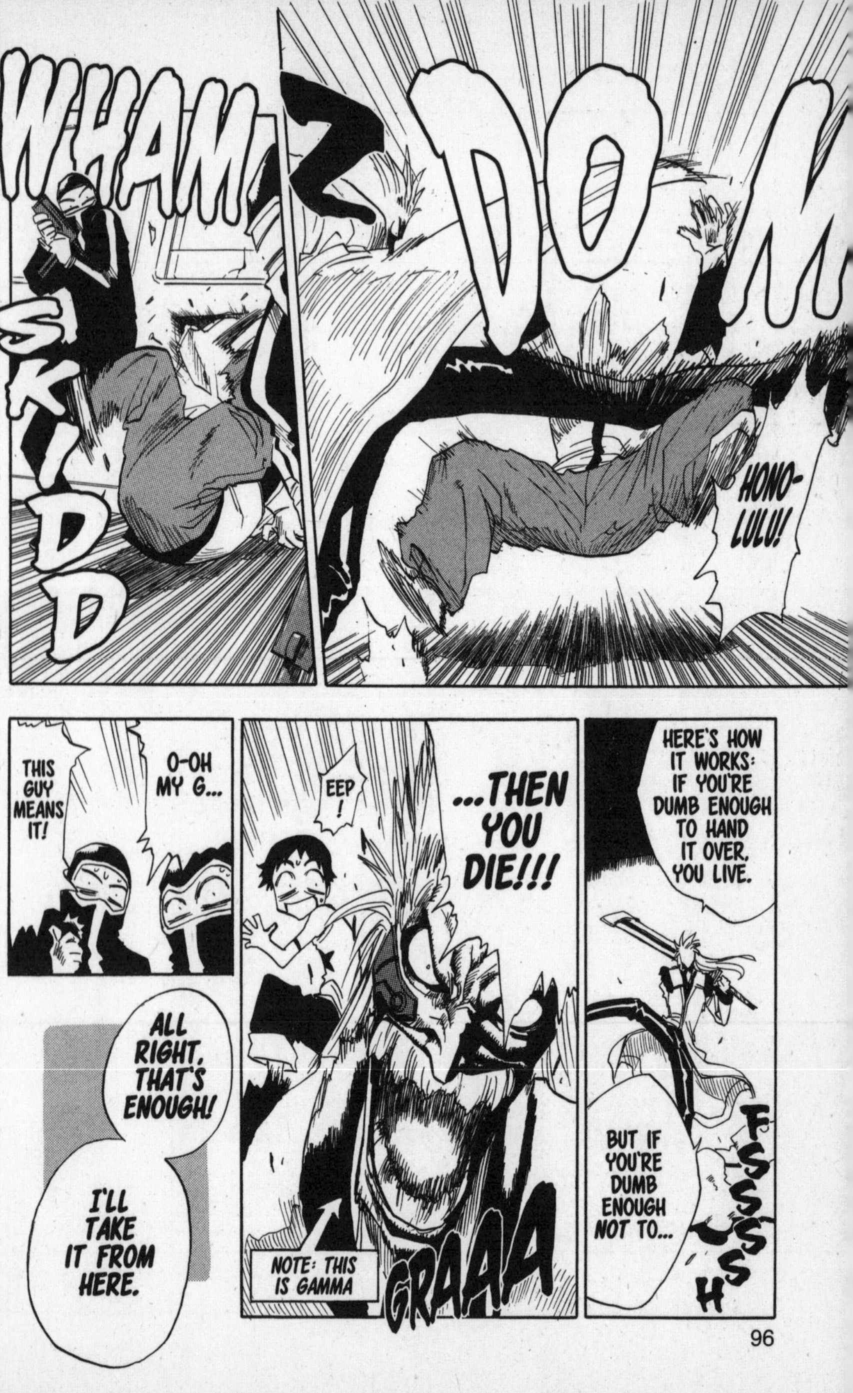
DOM
HONO-LULU!
WHAM
SKIDD
HERE'S HOW IT WORKS: IF YOU'RE DUMB ENOUGH TO HAND IT OVER, YOU LIVE.
BUT IF YOU'RE DUMB ENOUGH NOT TO...
FSSSSH
EEP!
...THEN YOU DIE!!!
NOTE: THIS IS GAMMA
GRAAA
O-OH MY G...
THIS GUY MEANS IT!
ALL RIGHT, THAT'S ENOUGH!
I'LL TAKE IT FROM HERE.

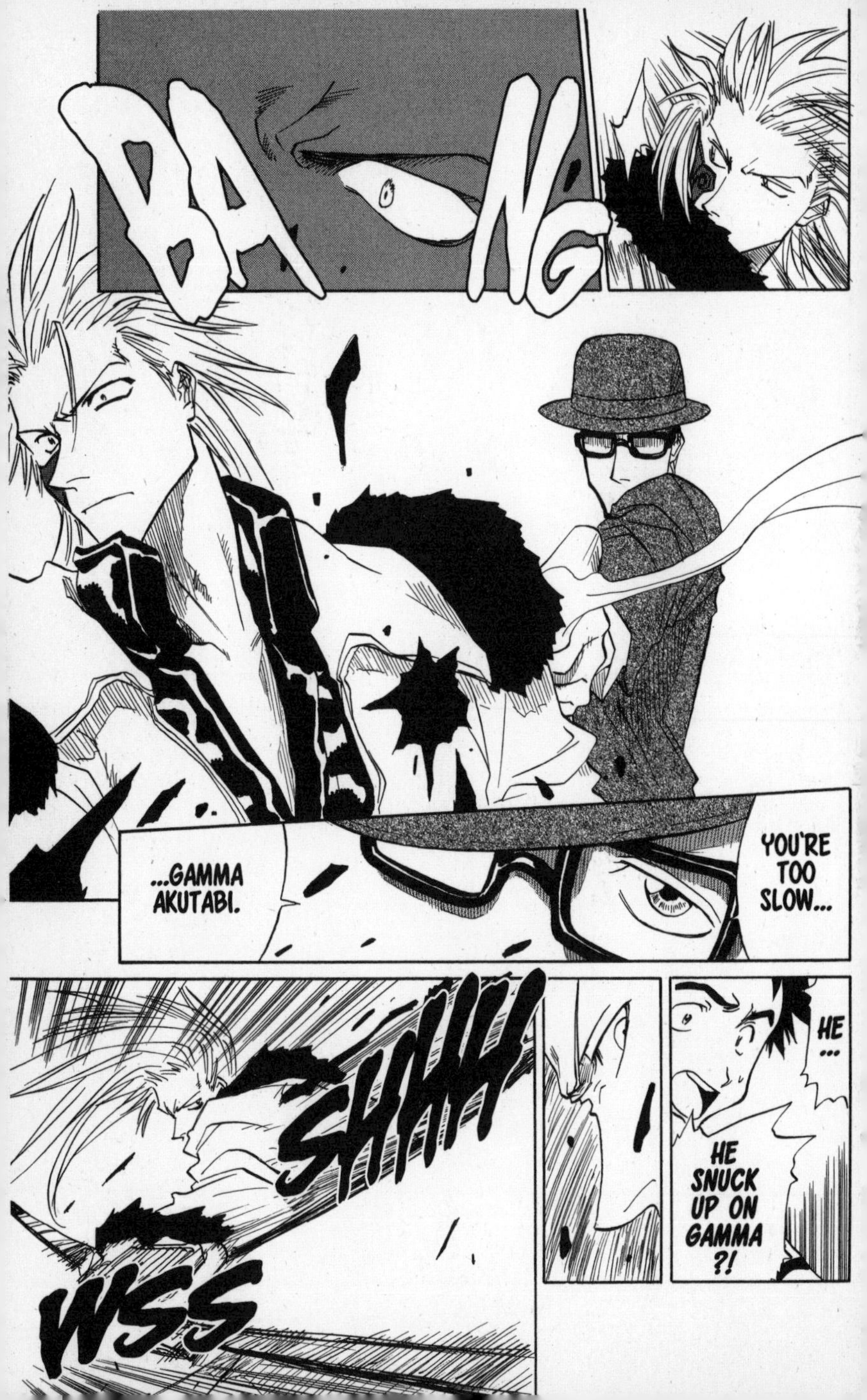
BANG
YOU'RE TOO SLOW...
...GAMMA AKUTABI.
HE ...
HE SNUCK UP ON GAMMA ?!
SHHH
WSS

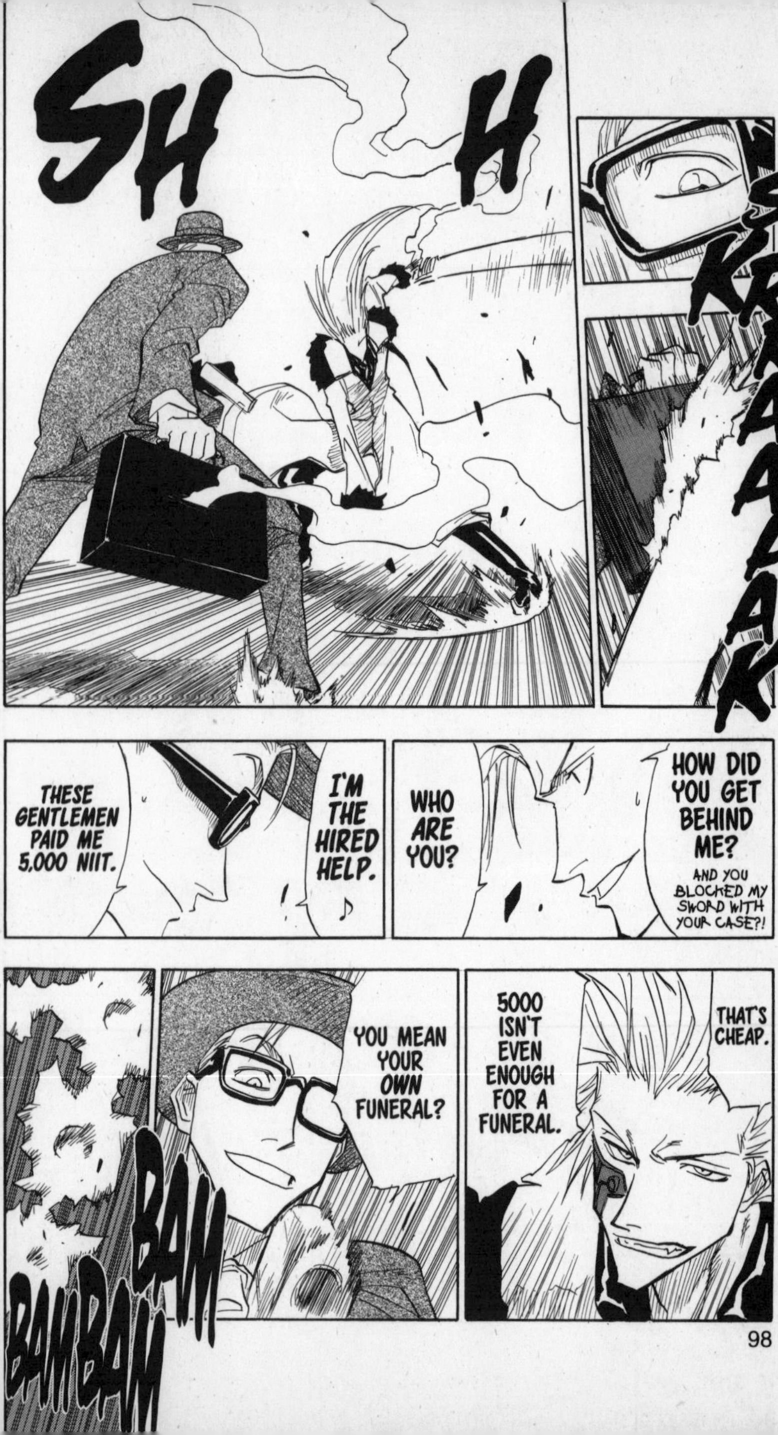
SKRAAAAK
SH
H
HOW DID YOU GET BEHIND ME?
AND YOU BLOCKED MY SWORD WITH YOUR CASE?!
WHO ARE YOU?
I'M THE HIRED HELP.
THESE GENTLEMEN PAID ME 5,000 NIIT.
THAT'S CHEAP.
5000 ISN'T EVEN ENOUGH FOR A FUNERAL.
YOU MEAN YOUR OWN FUNERAL?
BAM
BAM BAM

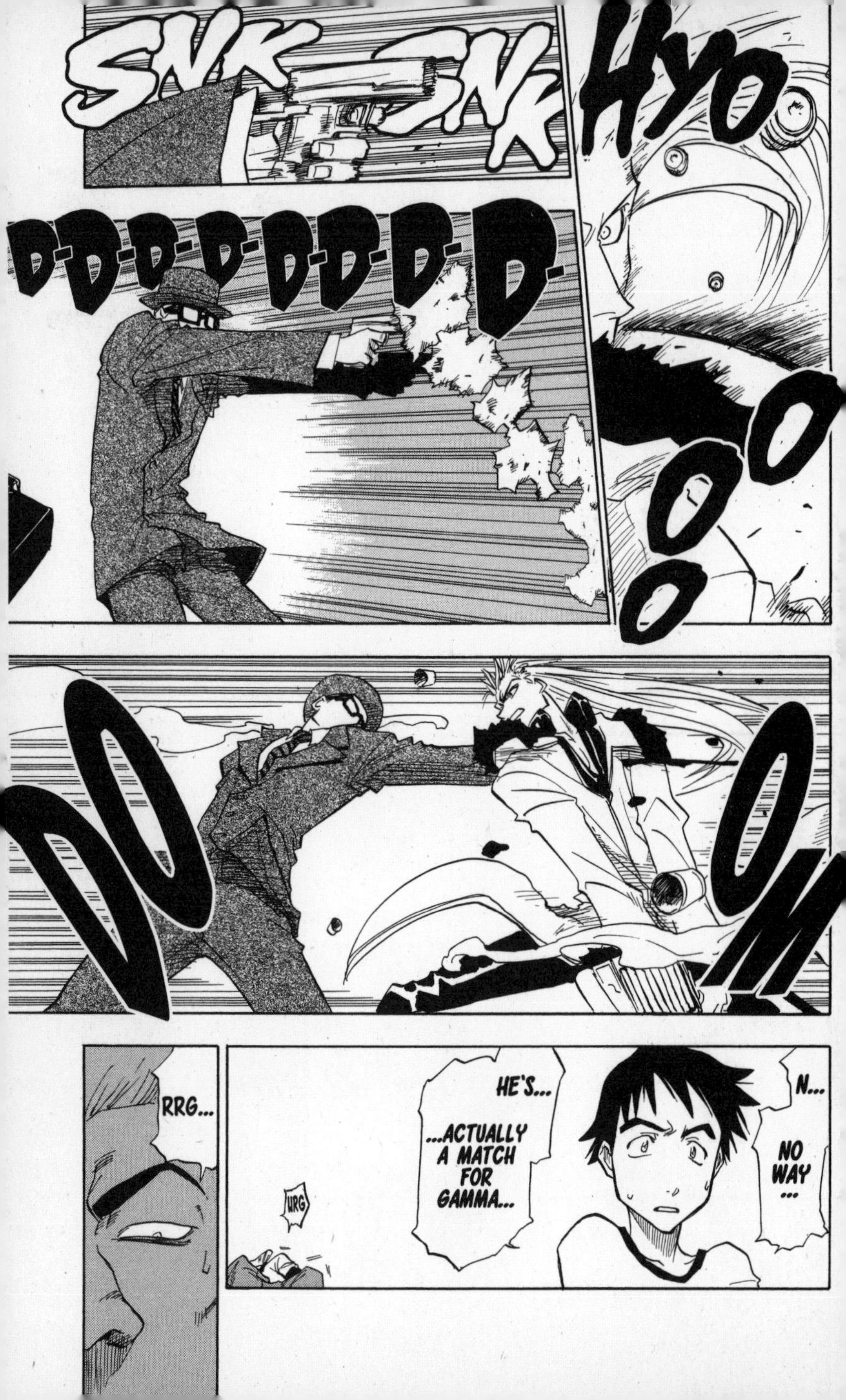
HYOOOO
SNK SNK
D-D-D-D-D-D-D-D-
DOOM
N...
NO WAY...
HE'S...
...ACTUALLY A MATCH FOR GAMMA...
URG
RRG...

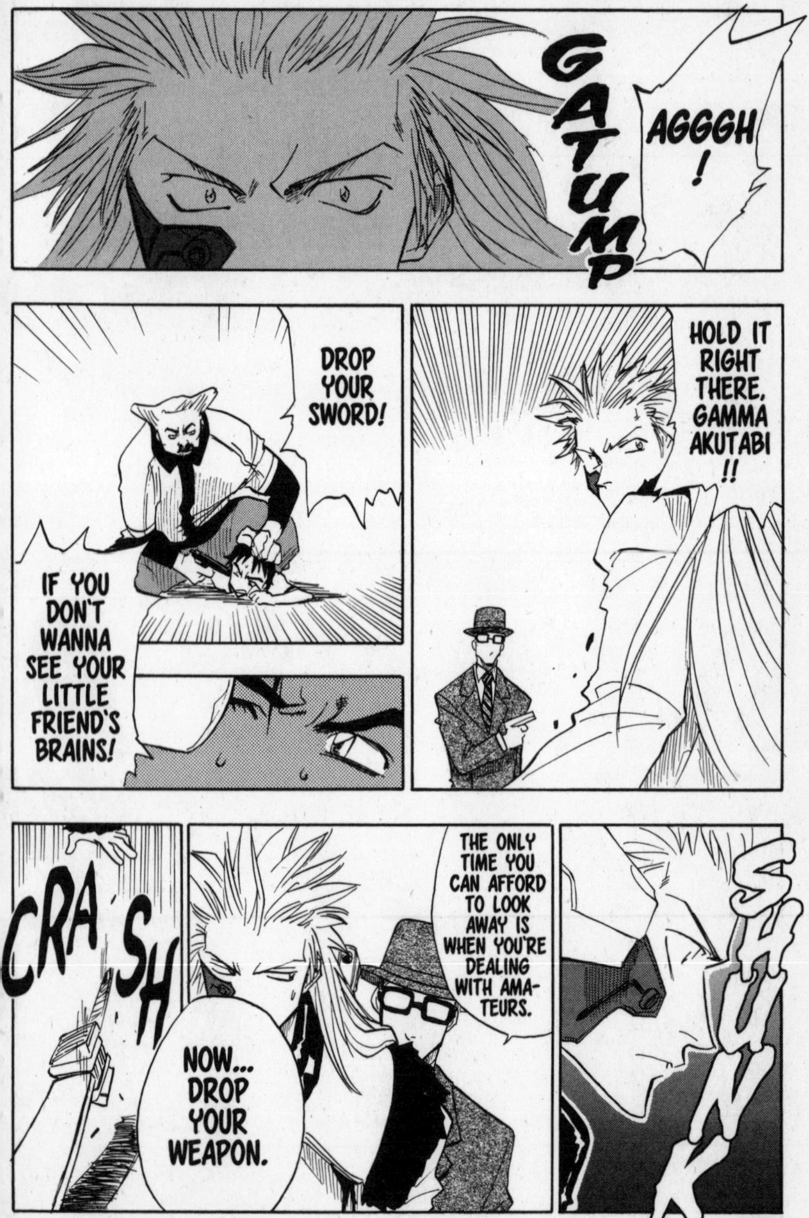
AGGGH!
GATUMP
HOLD IT RIGHT THERE, GAMMA AKUTABI!!
DROP YOUR SWORD!
IF YOU DON'T WANNA SEE YOUR LITTLE FRIEND'S BRAINS!
SHUNK
THE ONLY TIME YOU CAN AFFORD TO LOOK AWAY IS WHEN YOU'RE DEALING WITH AMA-TEURS.
NOW... DROP YOUR WEAPON.
CRASH

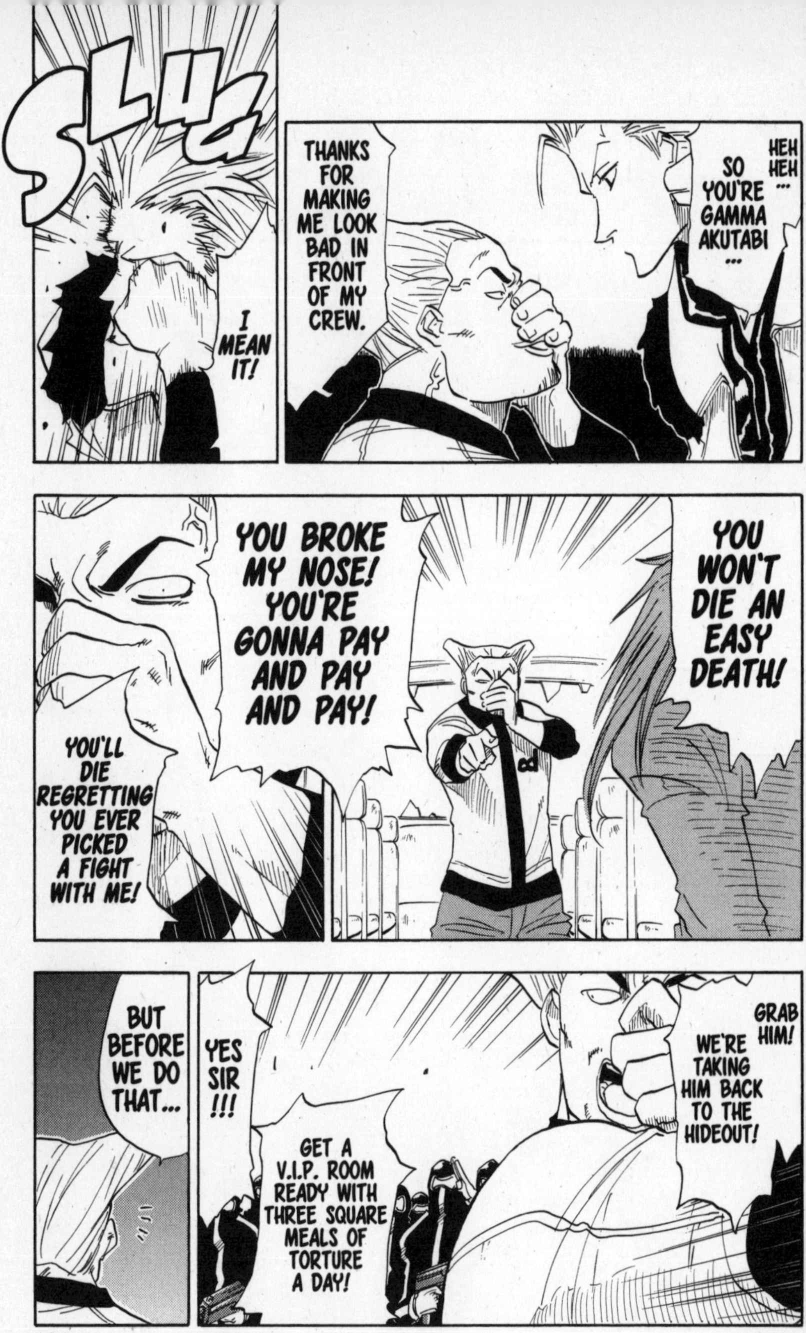
HEH HEH...
SO YOU'RE GAMMA AKUTABI...
THANKS FOR MAKING ME LOOK BAD IN FRONT OF MY CREW.
SLUG
I MEAN IT!
YOU WON'T DIE AN EASY DEATH!
YOU BROKE MY NOSE! YOU'RE GONNA PAY AND PAY AND PAY!
YOU'LL DIE REGRETTING YOU EVER PICKED A FIGHT WITH ME!
GRAB HIM!
WE'RE TAKING HIM BACK TO THE HIDEOUT!
GET A V.I.P. ROOM READY WITH THREE SQUARE MEALS OF TORTURE A DAY!
YES SIR!!!
BUT BEFORE WE DO THAT...

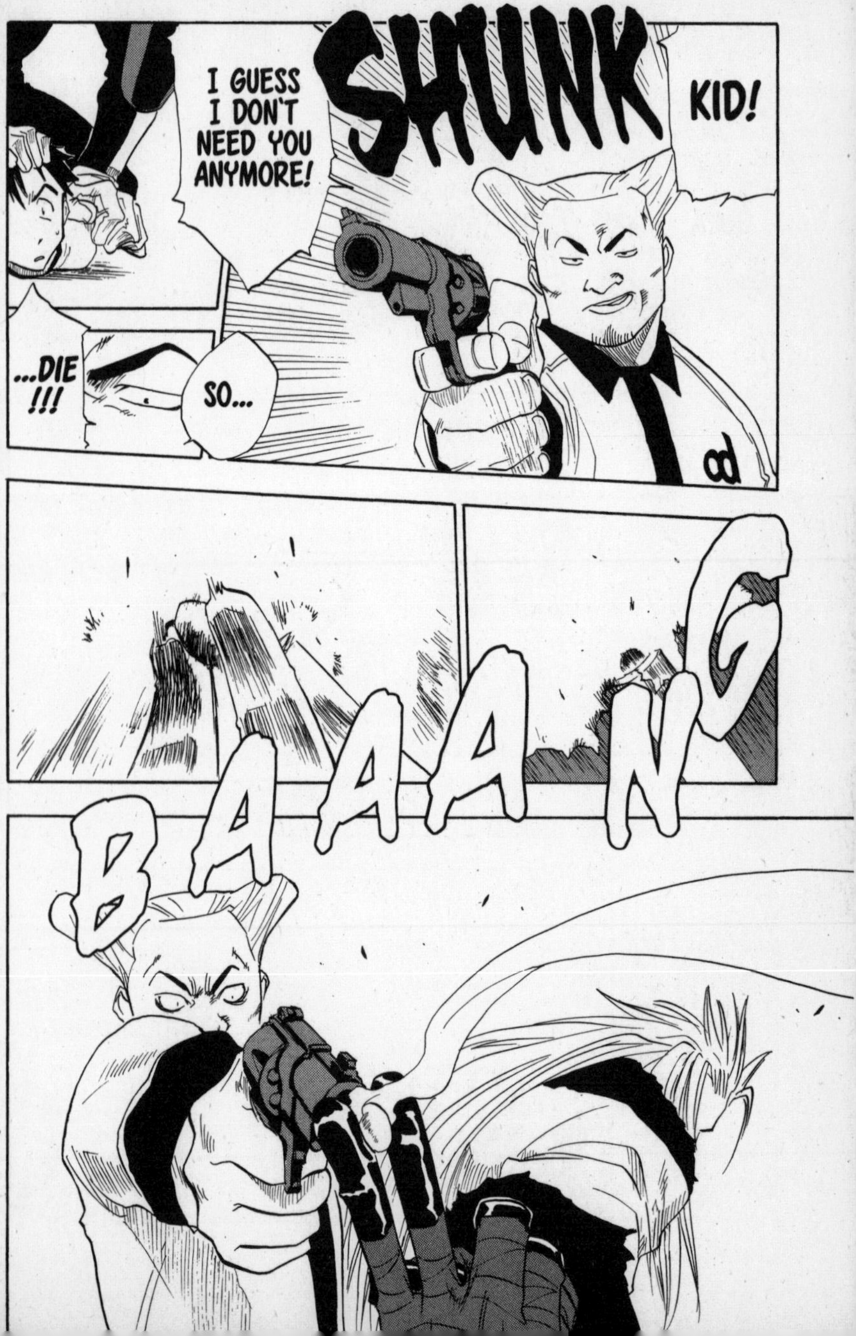
KID!
SHUNK
I GUESS I DON'T NEED YOU ANYMORE!
SO...
...DIE !!!
BAAANG

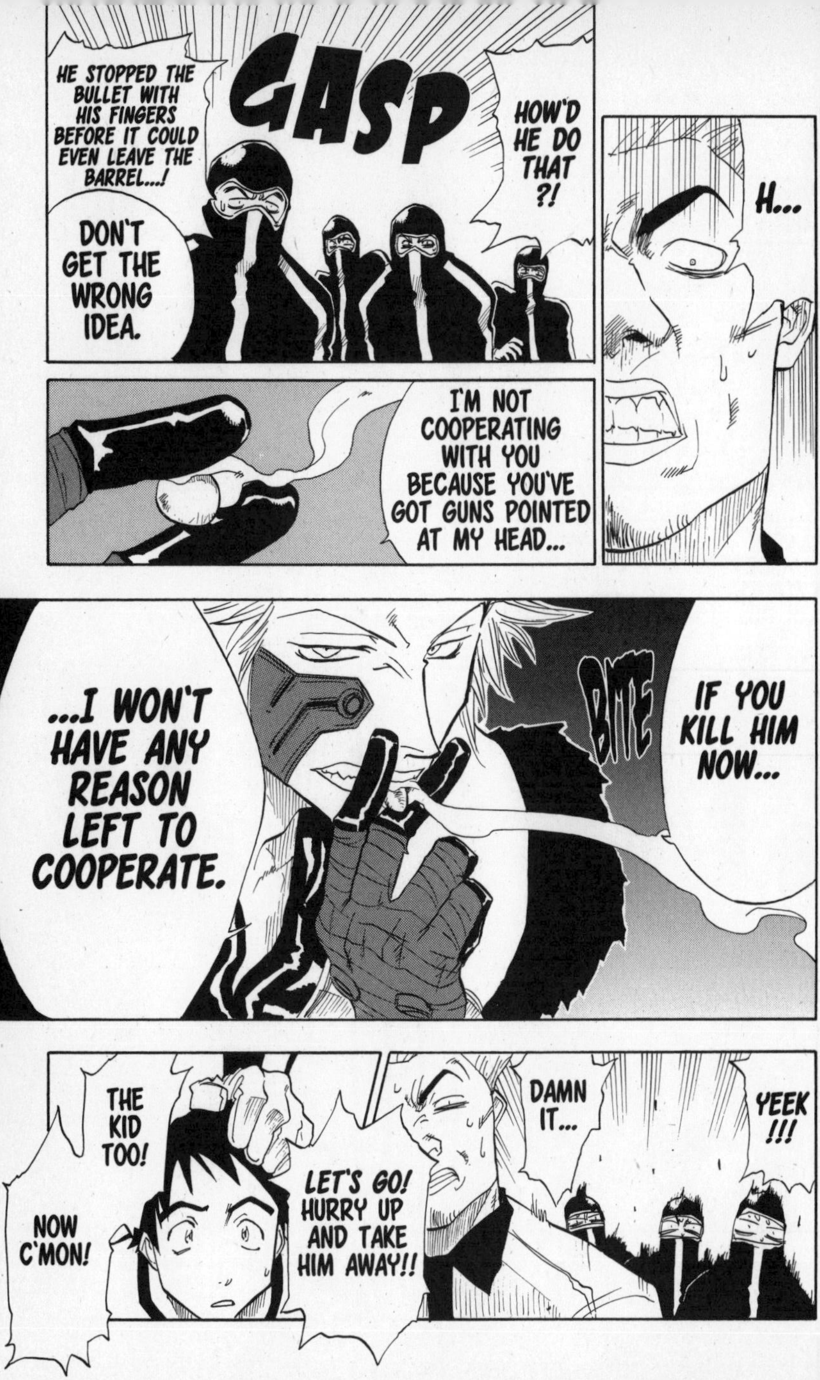
H...
HOW'D HE DO THAT?!
GASP
HE STOPPED THE BULLET WITH HIS FINGERS BEFORE IT COULD EVEN LEAVE THE BARREL...!
DON'T GET THE WRONG IDEA.
I'M NOT COOPERATING WITH YOU BECAUSE YOU'VE GOT GUNS POINTED AT MY HEAD...
IF YOU KILL HIM NOW...
BITE
...I WON'T HAVE ANY REASON LEFT TO COOPERATE.
YEEK!!!
DAMN IT...
LET'S GO! HURRY UP AND TAKE HIM AWAY!!
THE KID TOO!
NOW C'MON!

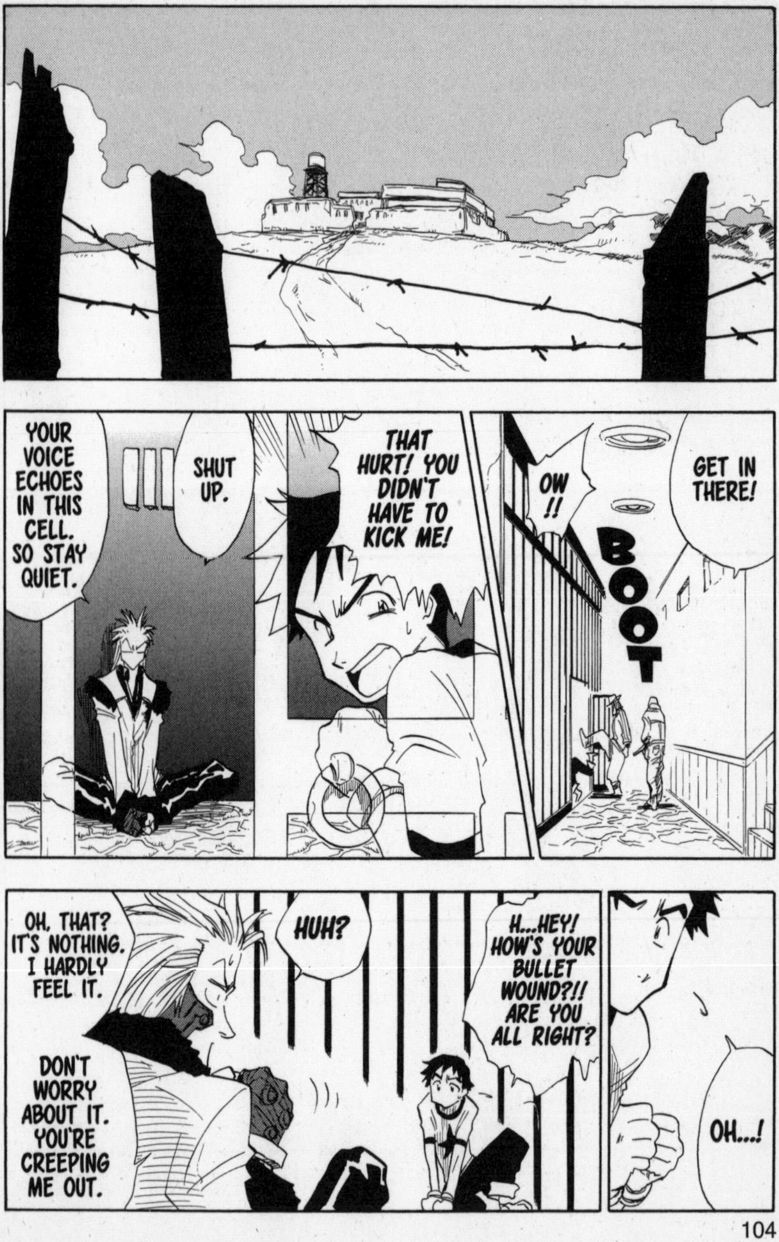
GET IN THERE!
BOOT
OW !!
THAT HURT! YOU DIDN'T HAVE TO KICK ME!
SHUT UP.
YOUR VOICE ECHOES IN THIS CELL. SO STAY QUIET.
OH...!
H...HEY! HOW'S YOUR BULLET WOUND?!! ARE YOU ALL RIGHT?
HUH?
OH, THAT? IT'S NOTHING. I HARDLY FEEL IT.
DON'T WORRY ABOUT IT. YOU'RE CREEPING ME OUT.

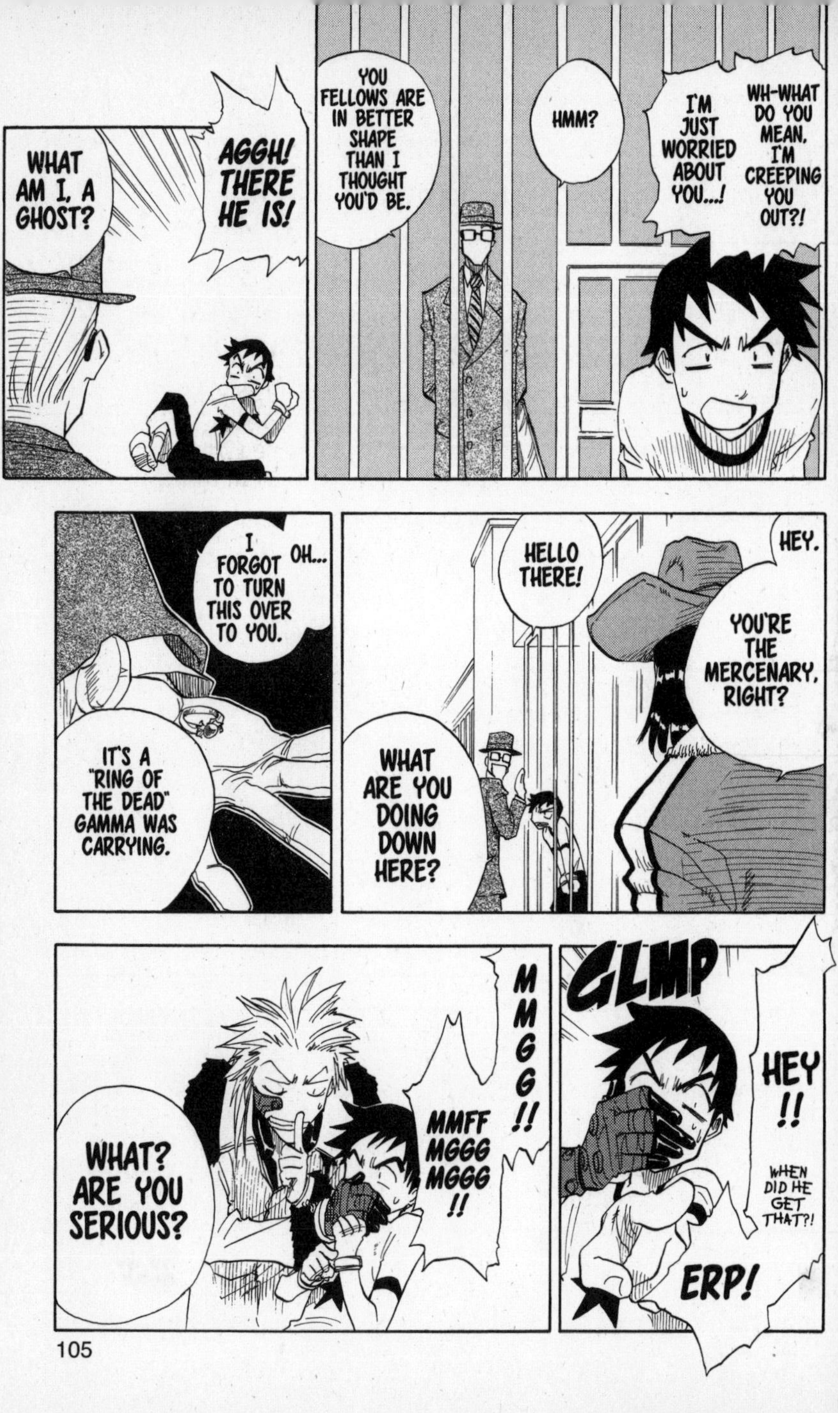
WH-WHAT DO YOU MEAN, I'M CREEPING YOU OUT?!
I'M JUST WORRIED ABOUT YOU...!
HMM?
YOU FELLOWS ARE IN BETTER SHAPE THAN I THOUGHT YOU'D BE.
AGGH! THERE HE IS!
WHAT AM I, A GHOST?
HEY.
YOU'RE THE MERCENARY, RIGHT?
HELLO THERE!
WHAT ARE YOU DOING DOWN HERE?
OH...
I FORGOT TO TURN THIS OVER TO YOU.
IT'S A "RING OF THE DEAD" GAMMA WAS CARRYING.
GLMP
HEY!!
WHEN DID HE GET THAT?!
ERP!
MMGG!!
MMFF MGGG MGGG!!
WHAT? ARE YOU SERIOUS?

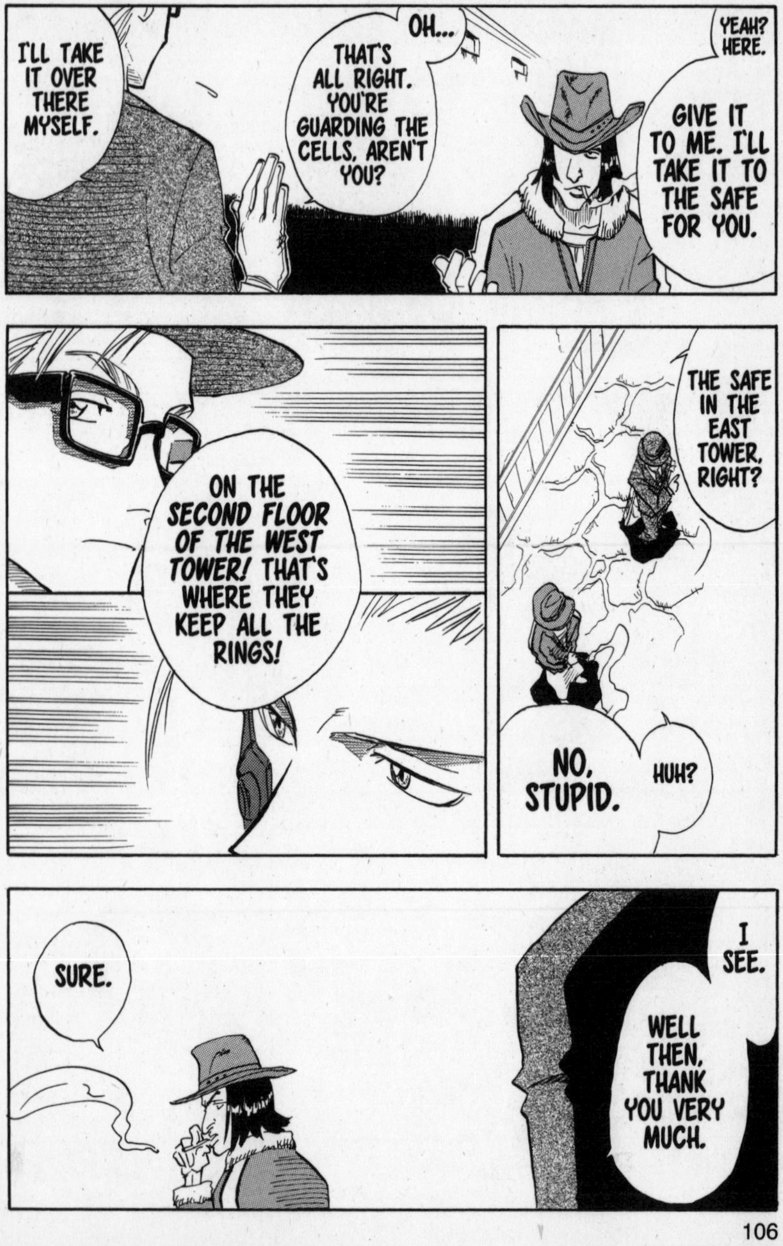
YEAH? HERE.
GIVE IT TO ME. I'LL TAKE IT TO THE SAFE FOR YOU.
OH...
THAT'S ALL RIGHT. YOU'RE GUARDING THE CELLS, AREN'T YOU?
I'LL TAKE IT OVER THERE MYSELF.
THE SAFE IN THE EAST TOWER, RIGHT?
HUH?
NO, STUPID.
ON THE SECOND FLOOR OF THE WEST TOWER! THAT'S WHERE THEY KEEP ALL THE RINGS!
I SEE.
WELL THEN, THANK YOU VERY MUCH.
SURE.

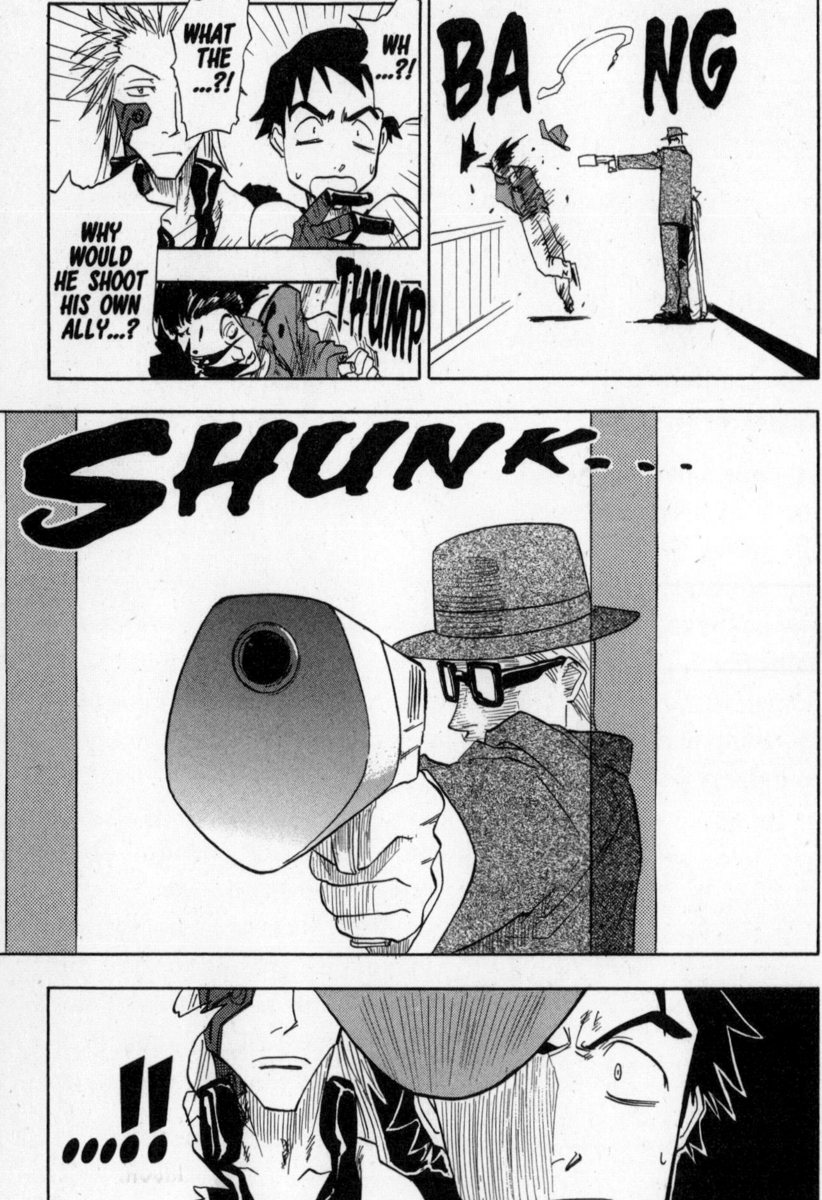
BA NG
WH ...?!
WHAT THE ...?!
THUMP
WHY WOULD HE SHOOT HIS OWN ALLY...?
SHUNK...
....!!

B-side NAKED MONKEYS 3.

C.T.Smith
C.T.スミス

Height：175cm
Weight：65kg
Date of Birth：September 25
Age：unknown
Blood Type：AB

Gamma's partner, he is the most mysterious member of the group. With his suit, hat and suitcase, some readers say he looks like a salesman. Personally, I was imagining someone more along the lines of a London banker. He doesn't have any particular skill that stands out above the rest, but he's extremely good at everything he does. (I envy him.) When asked about some of his likes and dislikes he said, "I like cinnamon tea and jelly beans. I don't really have any dislikes." By the way, because he holds his gun in his left hand most of the time, people tend to think that he's left handed, but actually he's the only ambidextrous member of the group.

Track 4:
Shakin' Edges & Smokin' Barrels

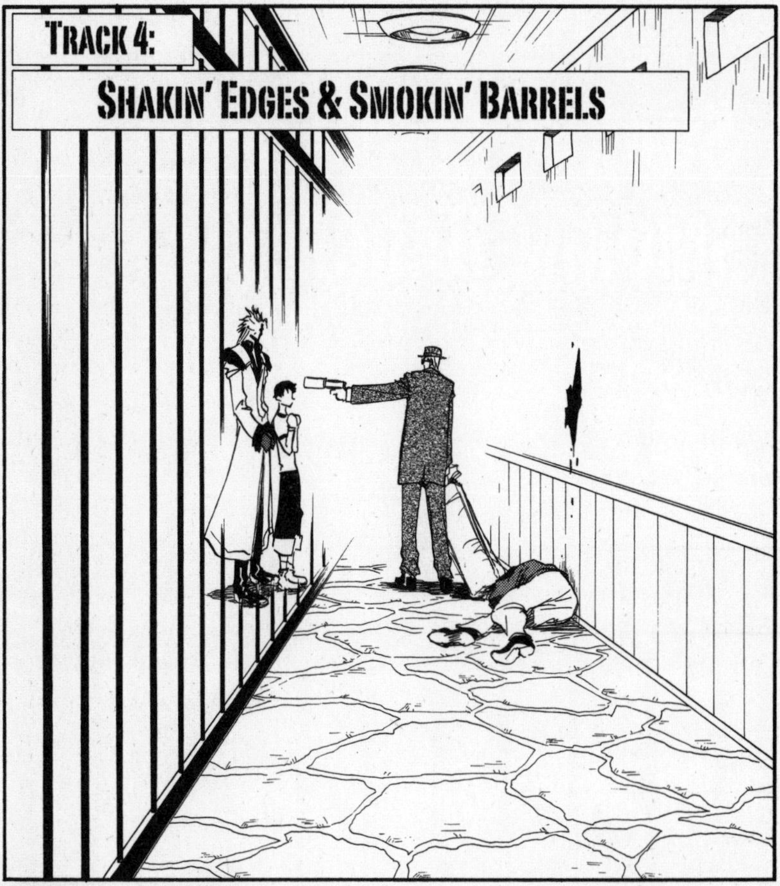

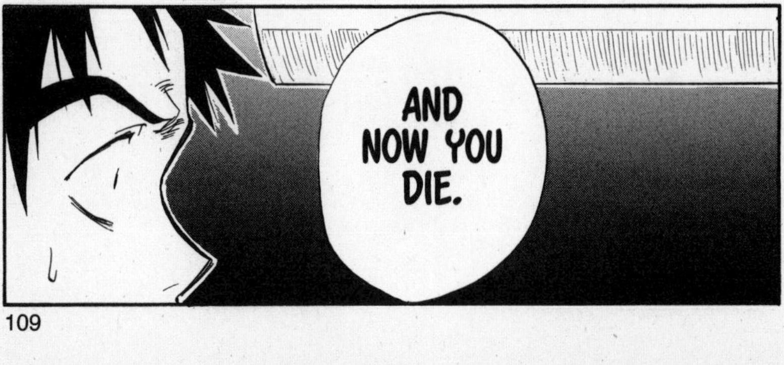
AND NOW YOU DIE.

TRACK 4:
SHAKIN' EDGES &
SMOKIN' BARRELS

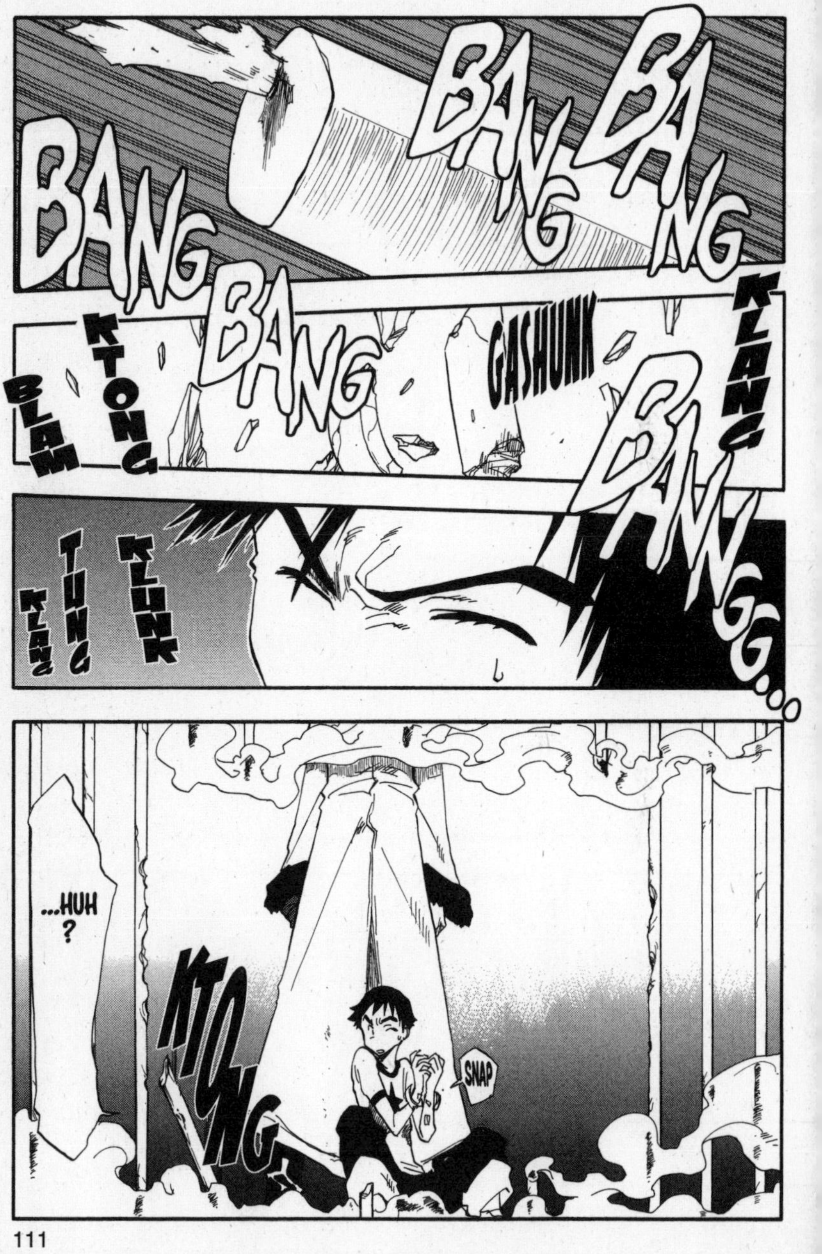
BANG
BANG
BANG
BANG
KLANG
GASHUNK
KTONG
BLAM
BANNGG...
KLUNK
TUNG
KLANG
SNAP
KTONG
...HUH?

JUST KIDDING! ♪

WHY ARE...THE HANDCUFFS AND CELL BARS...?

WH...

WHY...?

NOW THAT YOU'VE HAD A GOOD SCARE, LET'S GET OUT OF HERE AND BE ON OUR WAY!

WELL THEN!

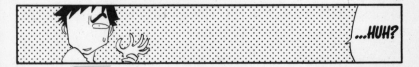

...HUH?

HE'S OUR ENEMY, RIGHT?

WHY ARE WE TEAMING UP WITH HIM?

W...

WAIT A SEC!

GRAB

SOUNDS GOOD.

GET UP, ELWOOD!

LET'S GO!

READ THIS WAY

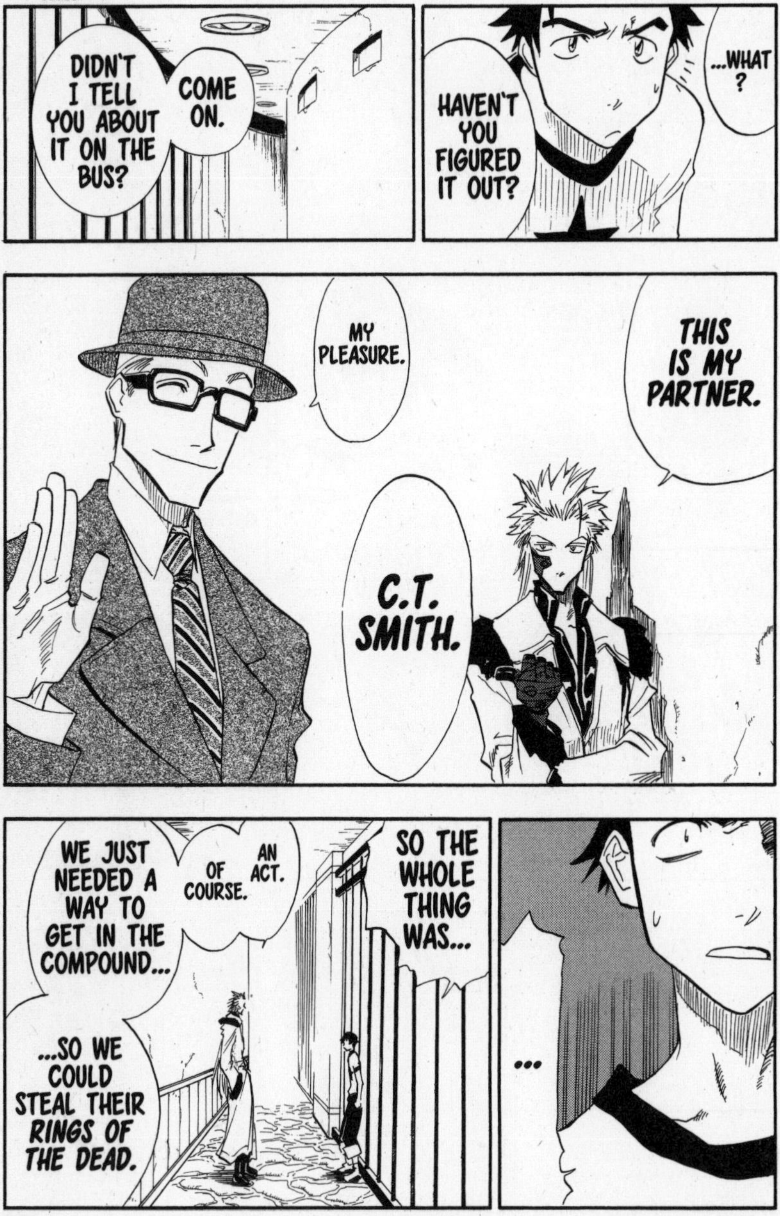

...WHAT?
HAVEN'T YOU FIGURED IT OUT?
COME ON.
DIDN'T I TELL YOU ABOUT IT ON THE BUS?
THIS IS MY PARTNER.
MY PLEASURE.
C.T. SMITH.
...
SO THE WHOLE THING WAS...
AN ACT.
OF COURSE.
WE JUST NEEDED A WAY TO GET IN THE COMPOUND...
...SO WE COULD STEAL THEIR RINGS OF THE DEAD.

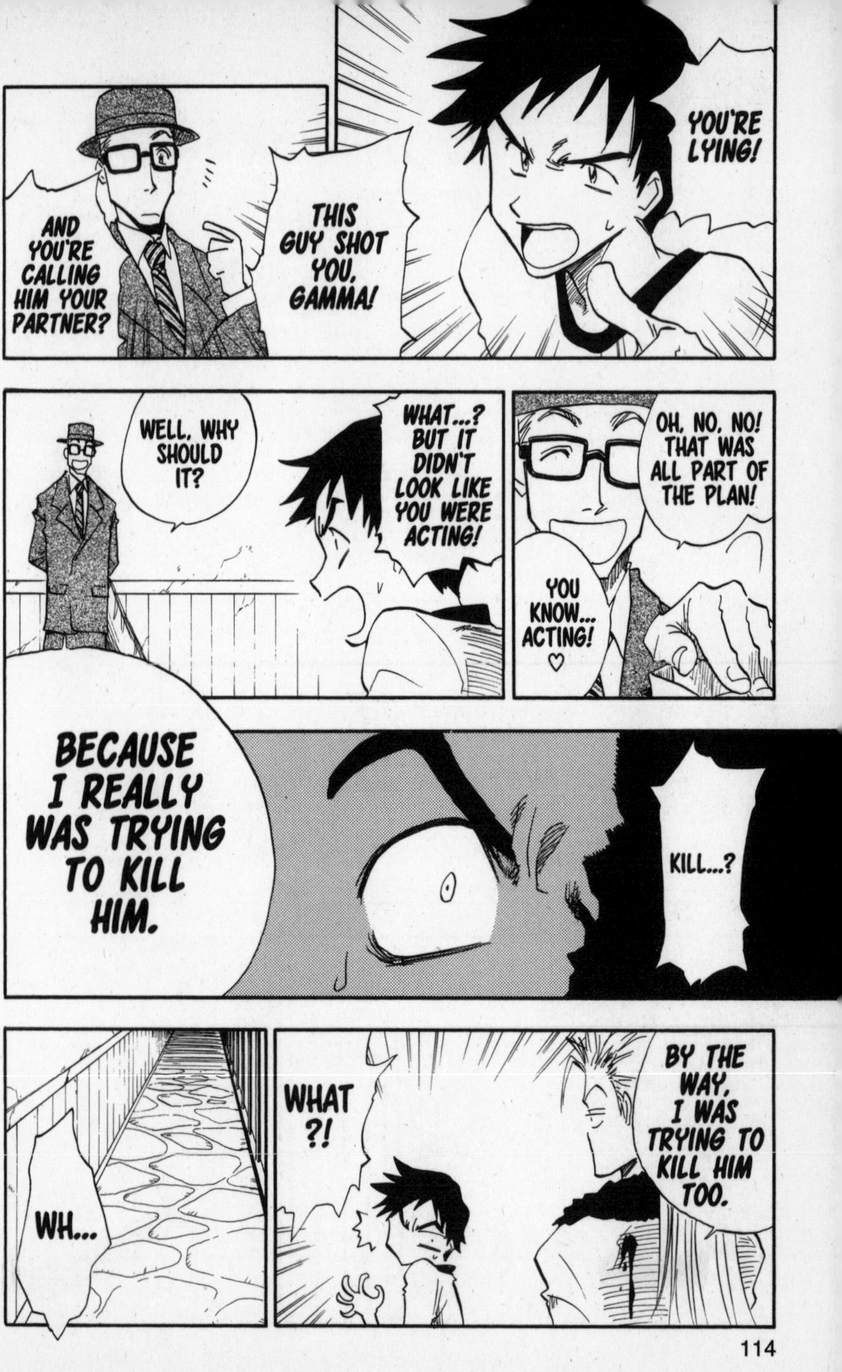
YOU'RE LYING!
THIS GUY SHOT YOU, GAMMA!
AND YOU'RE CALLING HIM YOUR PARTNER?
OH, NO, NO! THAT WAS ALL PART OF THE PLAN!
YOU KNOW... ACTING! ♡
WHAT...? BUT IT DIDN'T LOOK LIKE YOU WERE ACTING!
WELL, WHY SHOULD IT?
BECAUSE I REALLY WAS TRYING TO KILL HIM.
KILL...?
BY THE WAY, I WAS TRYING TO KILL HIM TOO.
WHAT?!
WH...

READ THIS WAY

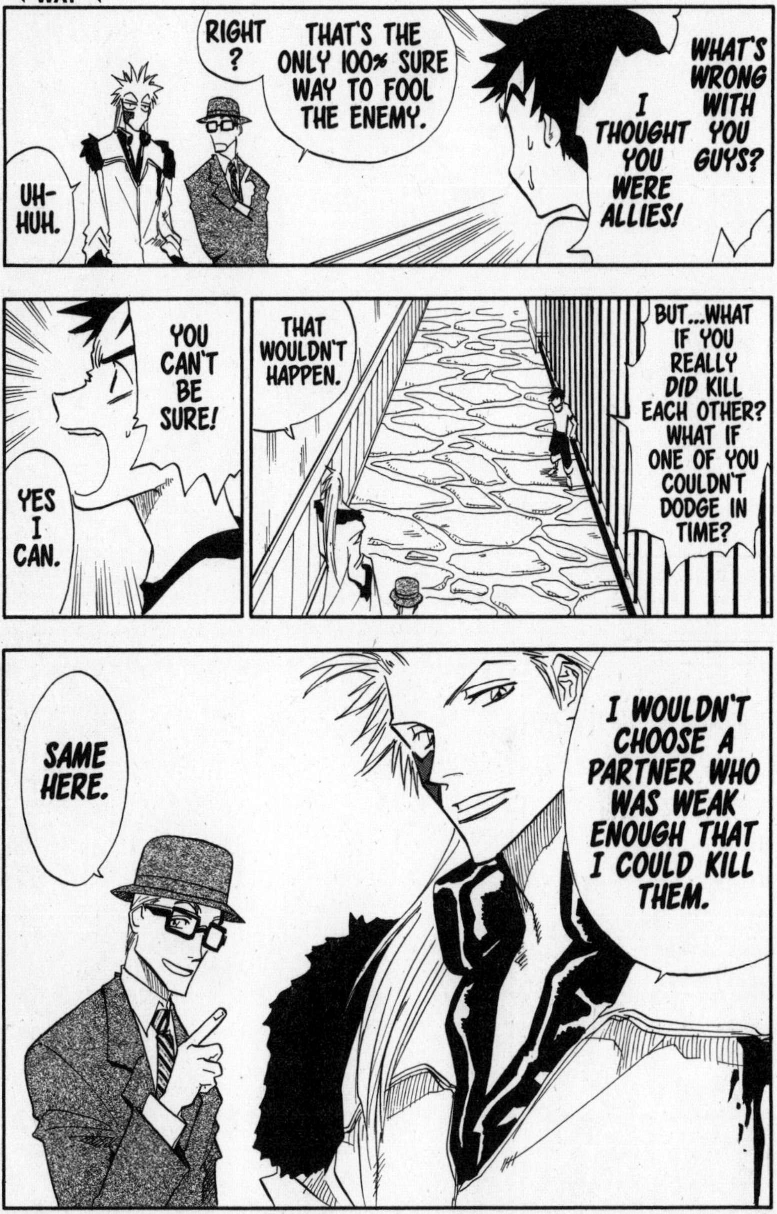
WHAT'S WRONG WITH YOU GUYS?
I THOUGHT YOU WERE ALLIES!
THAT'S THE ONLY 100% SURE WAY TO FOOL THE ENEMY.
RIGHT?
UH-HUH.
BUT...WHAT IF YOU REALLY DID KILL EACH OTHER? WHAT IF ONE OF YOU COULDN'T DODGE IN TIME?
THAT WOULDN'T HAPPEN.
YOU CAN'T BE SURE!
YES I CAN.
I WOULDN'T CHOOSE A PARTNER WHO WAS WEAK ENOUGH THAT I COULD KILL THEM.
SAME HERE.

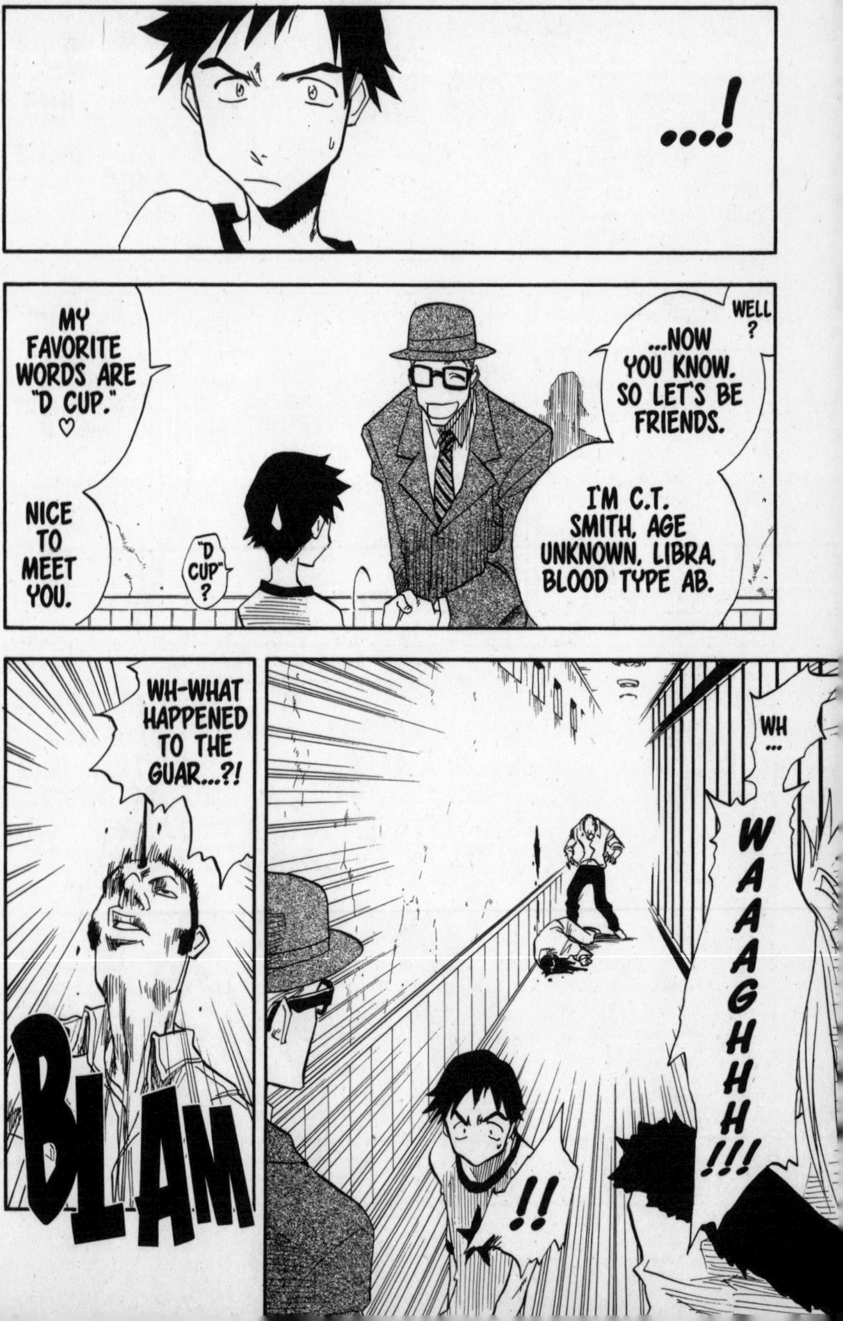
...!
WELL?
...NOW YOU KNOW. SO LET'S BE FRIENDS.
I'M C.T. SMITH, AGE UNKNOWN, LIBRA, BLOOD TYPE AB.
"D CUP"?
MY FAVORITE WORDS ARE "D CUP." ♡
NICE TO MEET YOU.
WH...
WAAAAGHHHH!!!
!!
WH-WHAT HAPPENED TO THE GUAR...?!
BLAM

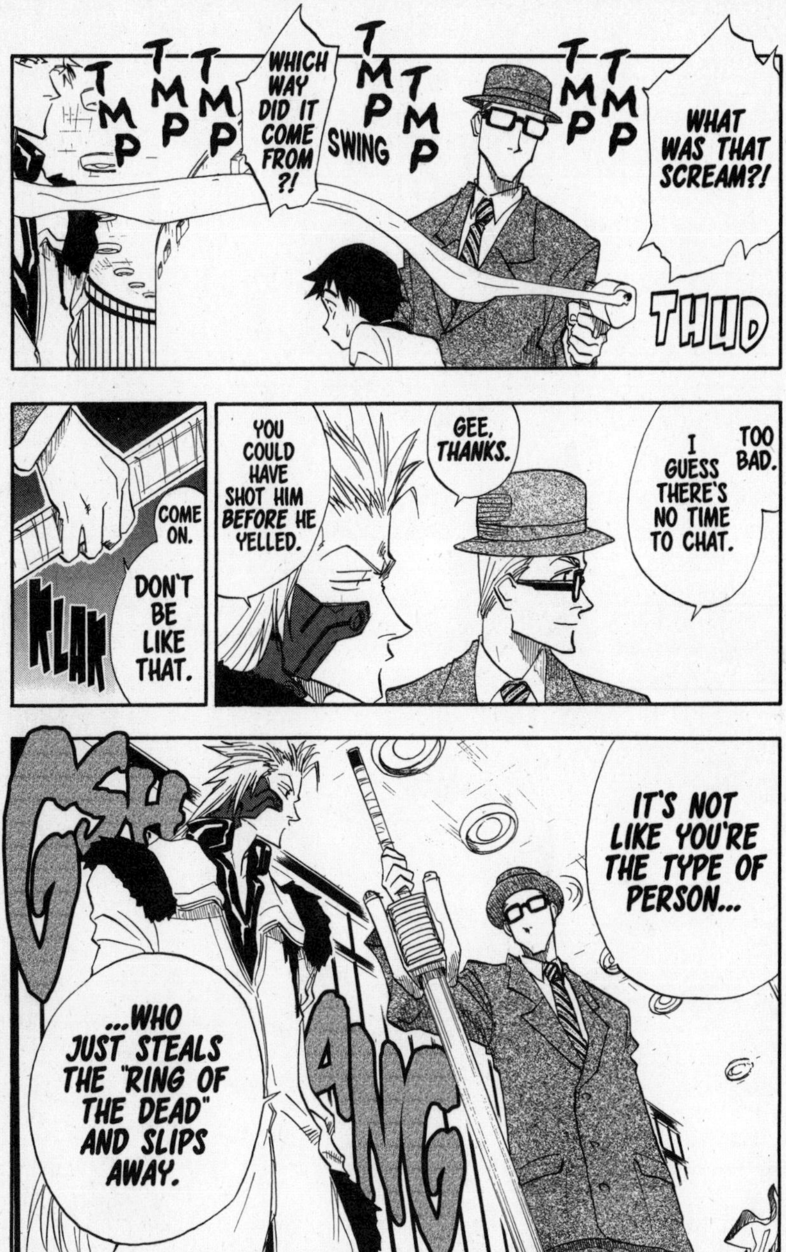
WHAT WAS THAT SCREAM?!
TMP TMP
THUD
TMP
SWING
TMP
WHICH WAY DID IT COME FROM?!
TMP TMP TMP
TOO BAD.
I GUESS THERE'S NO TIME TO CHAT.
GEE, THANKS.
YOU COULD HAVE SHOT HIM BEFORE HE YELLED.
COME ON.
DON'T BE LIKE THAT.
KLAK
IT'S NOT LIKE YOU'RE THE TYPE OF PERSON...
...WHO JUST STEALS THE "RING OF THE DEAD" AND SLIPS AWAY.
GSH

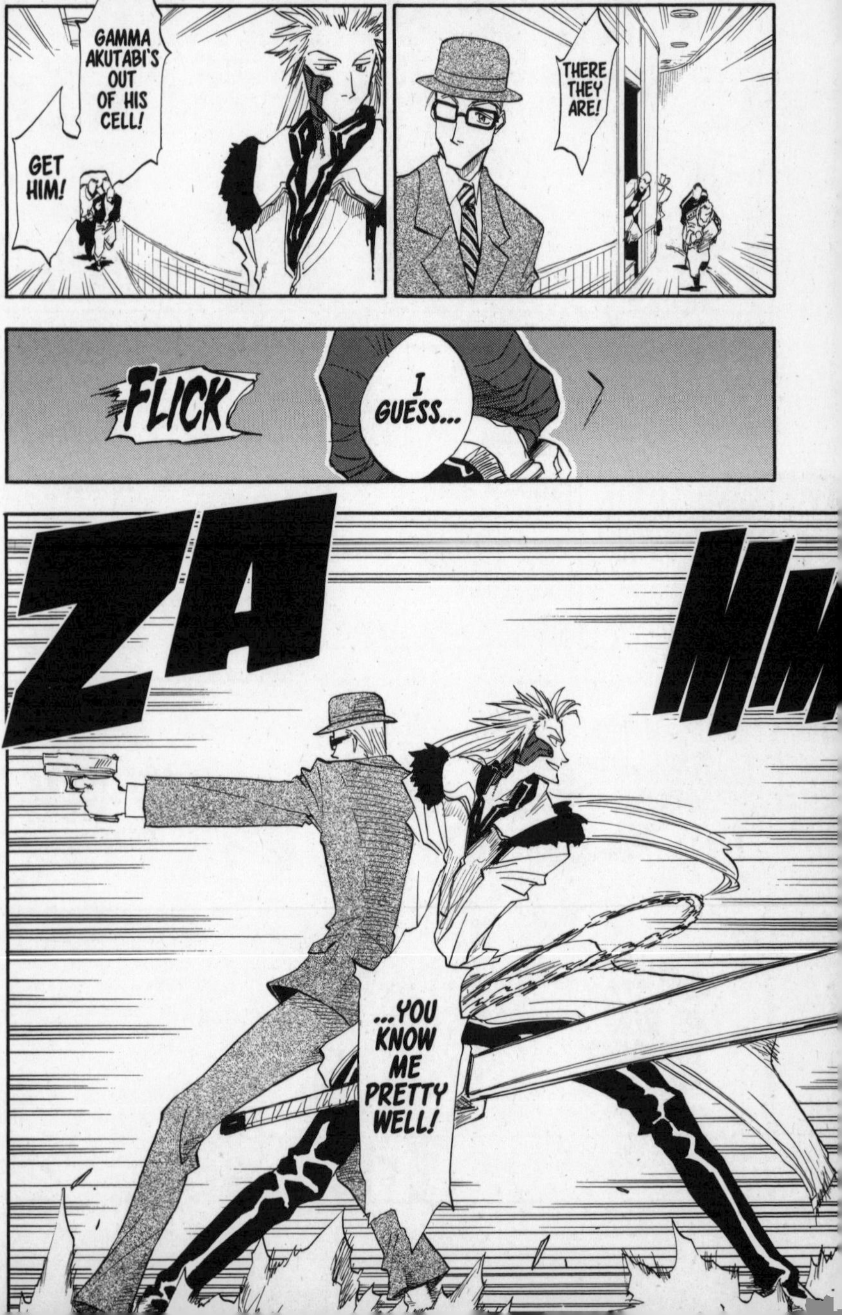
THERE THEY ARE!
GAMMA AKUTABI'S OUT OF HIS CELL!
GET HIM!
I GUESS...
FLICK
ZA
HM
...YOU KNOW ME PRETTY WELL!

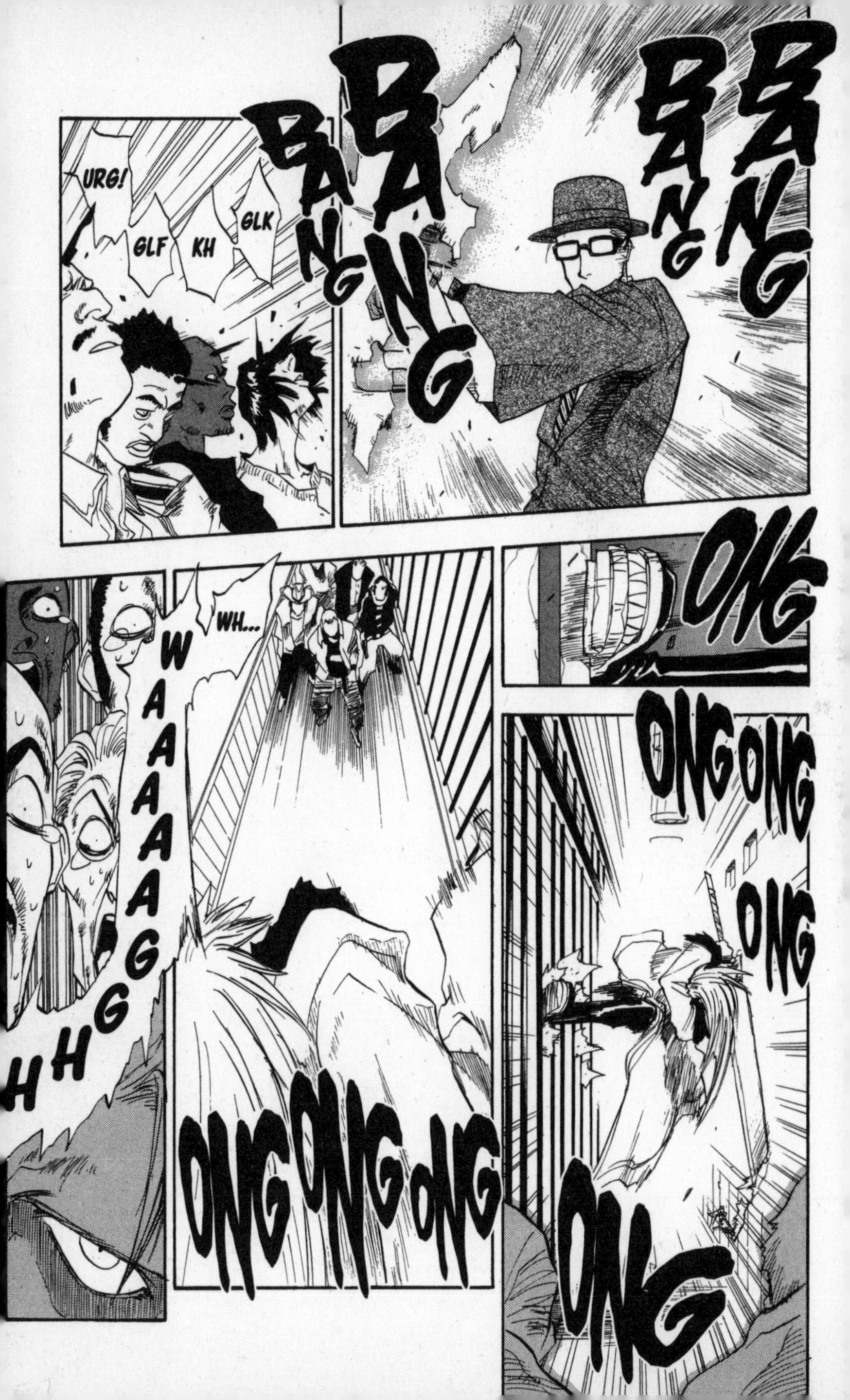
BANG
BANG
BANG
BANG
GLK
KH
GLF
URG!
ONG
ONG ONG
ONG
ONG
WH...
ONG ONG ONG ONG
WAAAAAAGHHH

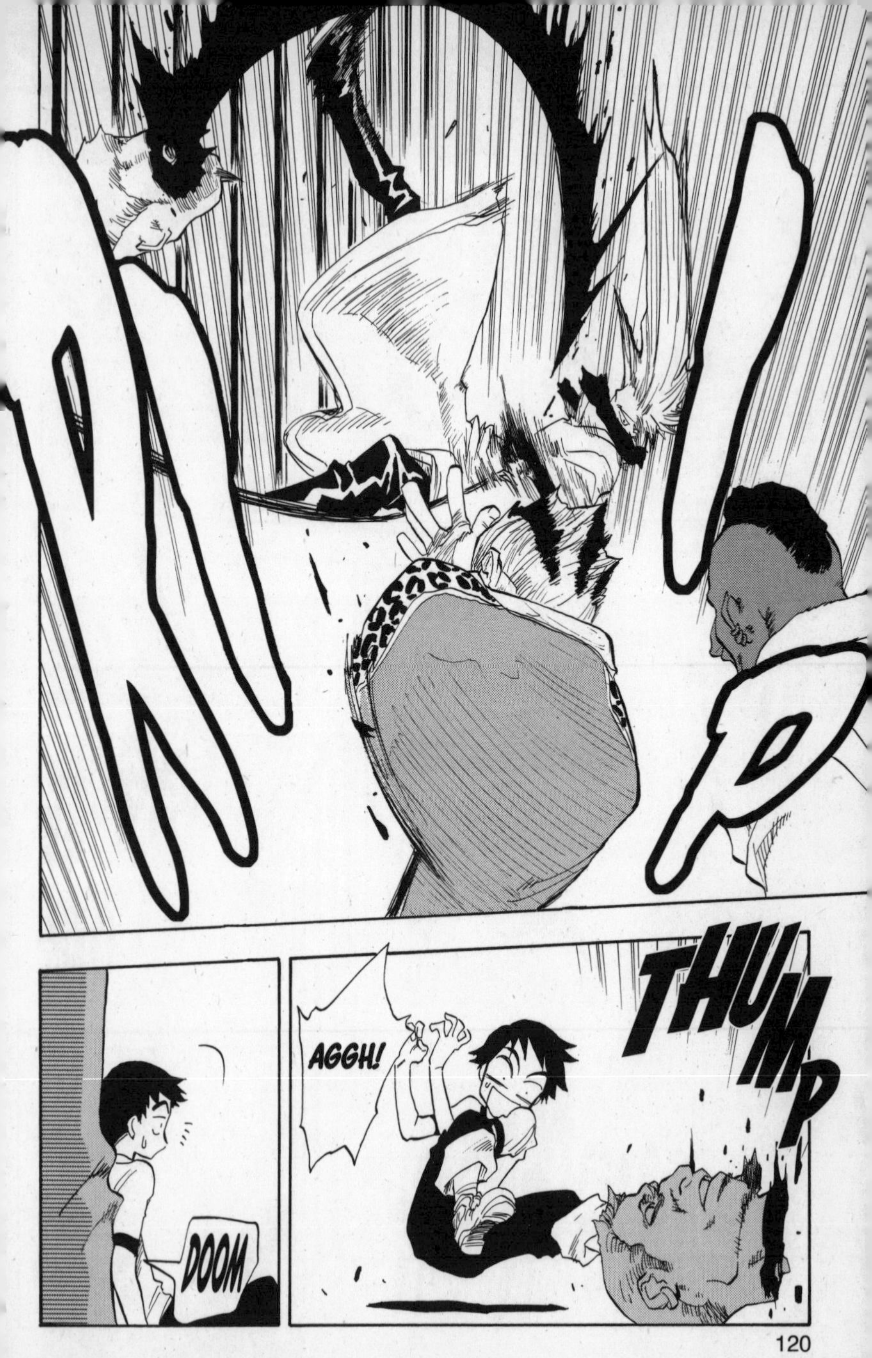
THUMP
AGGH!
DOOM

NEE HEE

LOOOOOOOOM

HE LOOKS FOR HIS THROWING KNIFE.

HE REMEMBERS THAT THEY TOOK THE KNIVES FROM HIM WHEN THEY BROUGHT HIM TO THE CELL.

SMITH !!

KI SHAKKN

THIS KID HAD THESE KNIVES ON HIM.

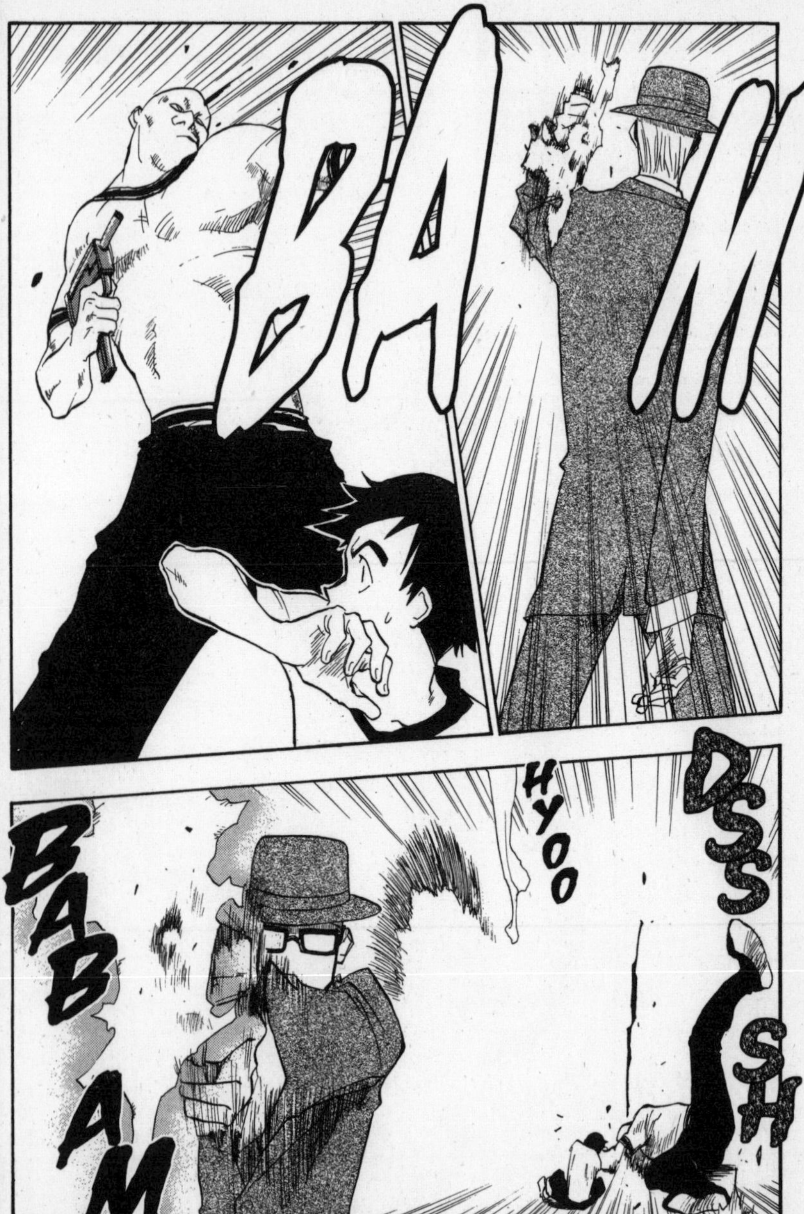
BAM
DSSSH
HYOO
BABAM

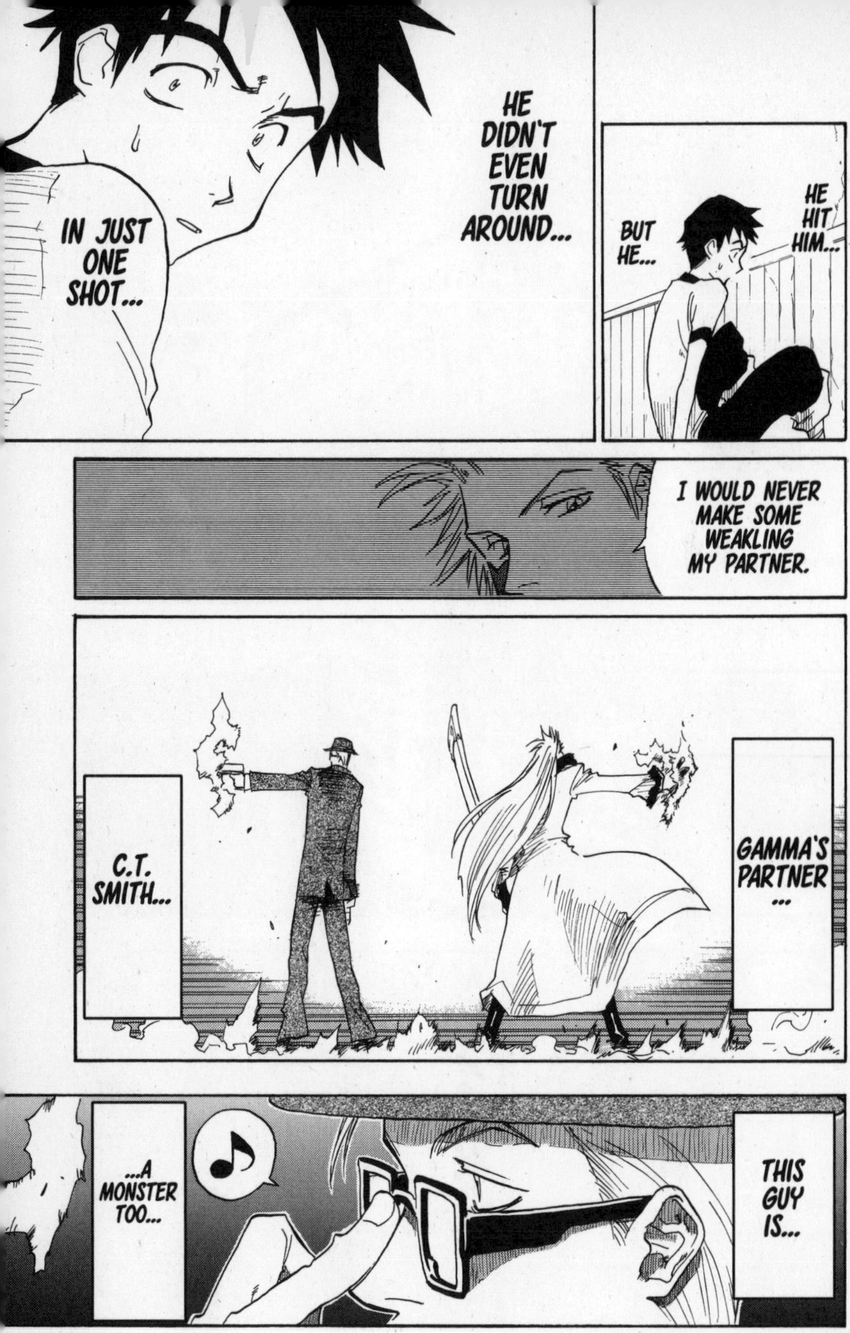
HE HIT HIM...
BUT HE...
HE DIDN'T EVEN TURN AROUND...
IN JUST ONE SHOT...
I WOULD NEVER MAKE SOME WEAKLING MY PARTNER.
GAMMA'S PARTNER ...
C.T. SMITH...
THIS GUY IS...
♪
...A MONSTER TOO...

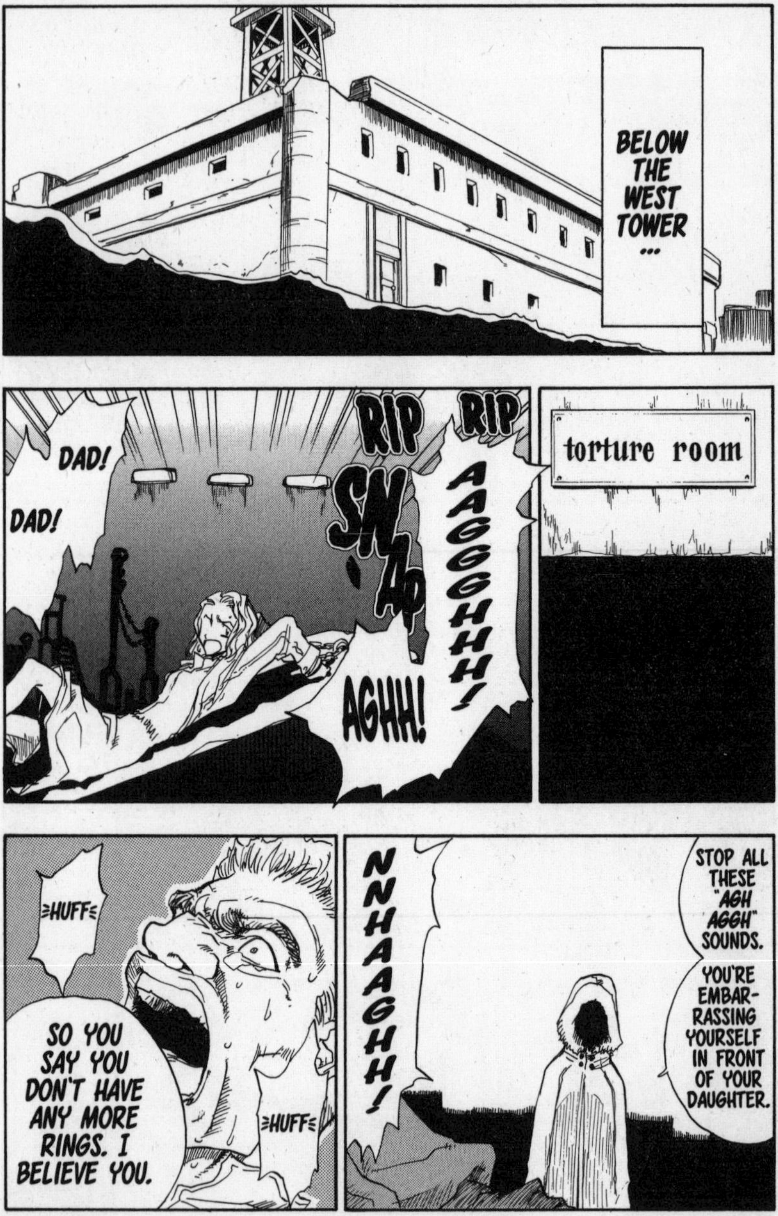
BELOW THE WEST TOWER ...
torture room
RIP
RIP
SNAP
AAGGGHHH!
AGHH!
DAD!
DAD!
STOP ALL THESE "AGH AGGH" SOUNDS.
YOU'RE EMBARRASSING YOURSELF IN FRONT OF YOUR DAUGHTER.
NNHAAAGHH!
HUFF
SO YOU SAY YOU DON'T HAVE ANY MORE RINGS. I BELIEVE YOU.
HUFF

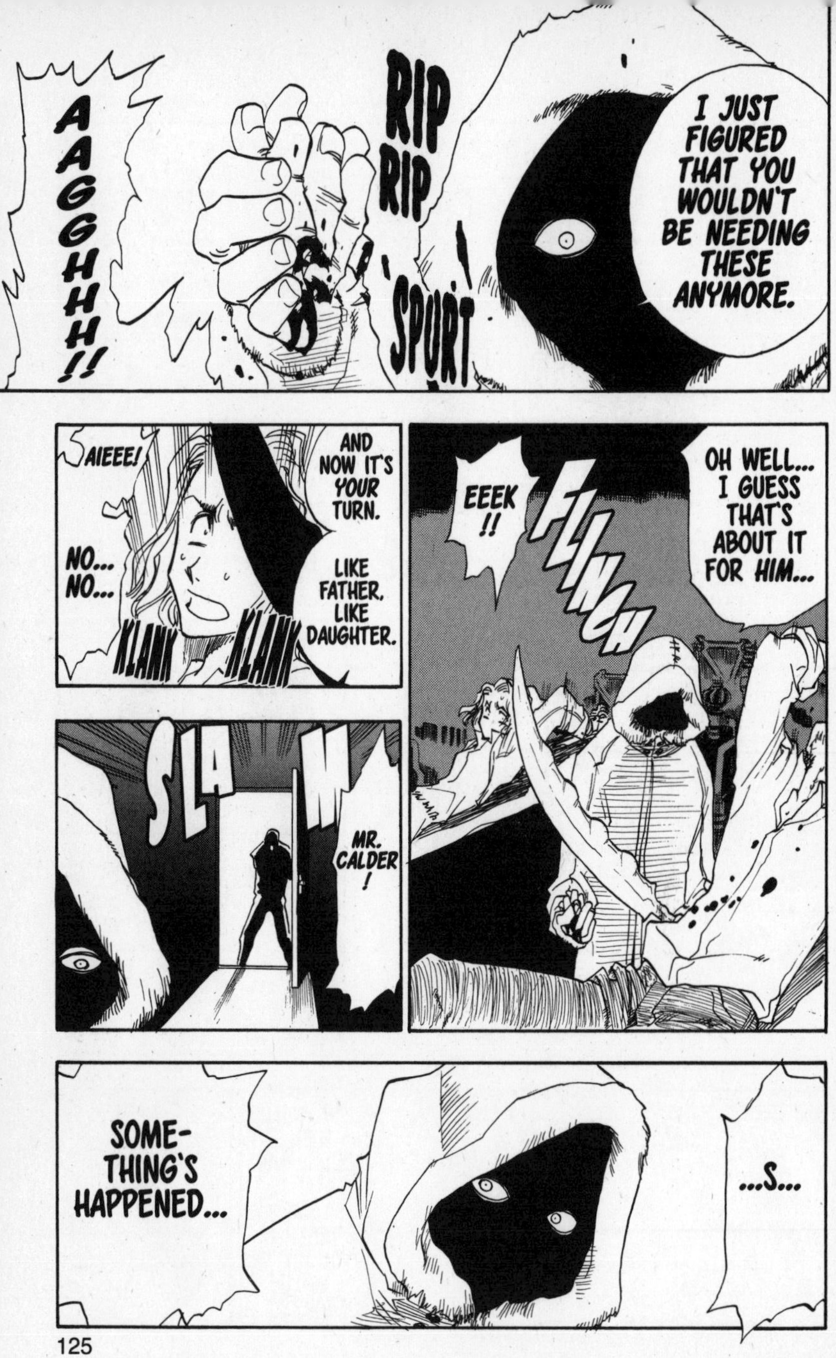

I JUST FIGURED THAT YOU WOULDN'T BE NEEDING THESE ANYMORE.
RIP RIP
SPURT
AAGGHHHH!!
OH WELL... I GUESS THAT'S ABOUT IT FOR HIM...
FLINCH
EEEK!!
AND NOW IT'S YOUR TURN.
LIKE FATHER, LIKE DAUGHTER.
AIEEE!
NO... NO...
KLANK KLANK
SLAM
MR. CALDER!
...S...
SOME-THING'S HAPPENED...

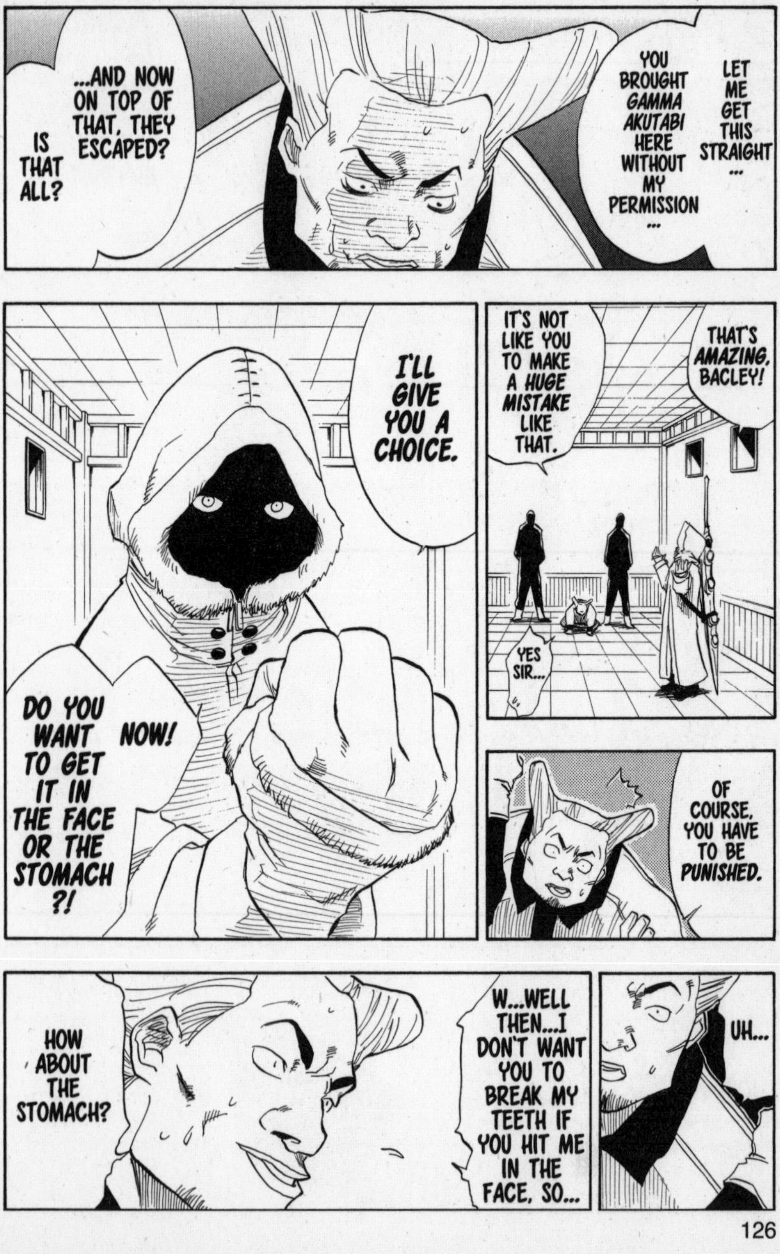
LET ME GET THIS STRAIGHT...
YOU BROUGHT GAMMA AKUTABI HERE WITHOUT MY PERMISSION...
...AND NOW ON TOP OF THAT, THEY ESCAPED?
IS THAT ALL?
THAT'S AMAZING, BACLEY!
IT'S NOT LIKE YOU TO MAKE A HUGE MISTAKE LIKE THAT.
YES SIR...
OF COURSE, YOU HAVE TO BE PUNISHED.
I'LL GIVE YOU A CHOICE.
NOW!
DO YOU WANT TO GET IT IN THE FACE OR THE STOMACH?!
UH...
W...WELL THEN...I DON'T WANT YOU TO BREAK MY TEETH IF YOU HIT ME IN THE FACE, SO...
HOW ABOUT THE STOMACH?

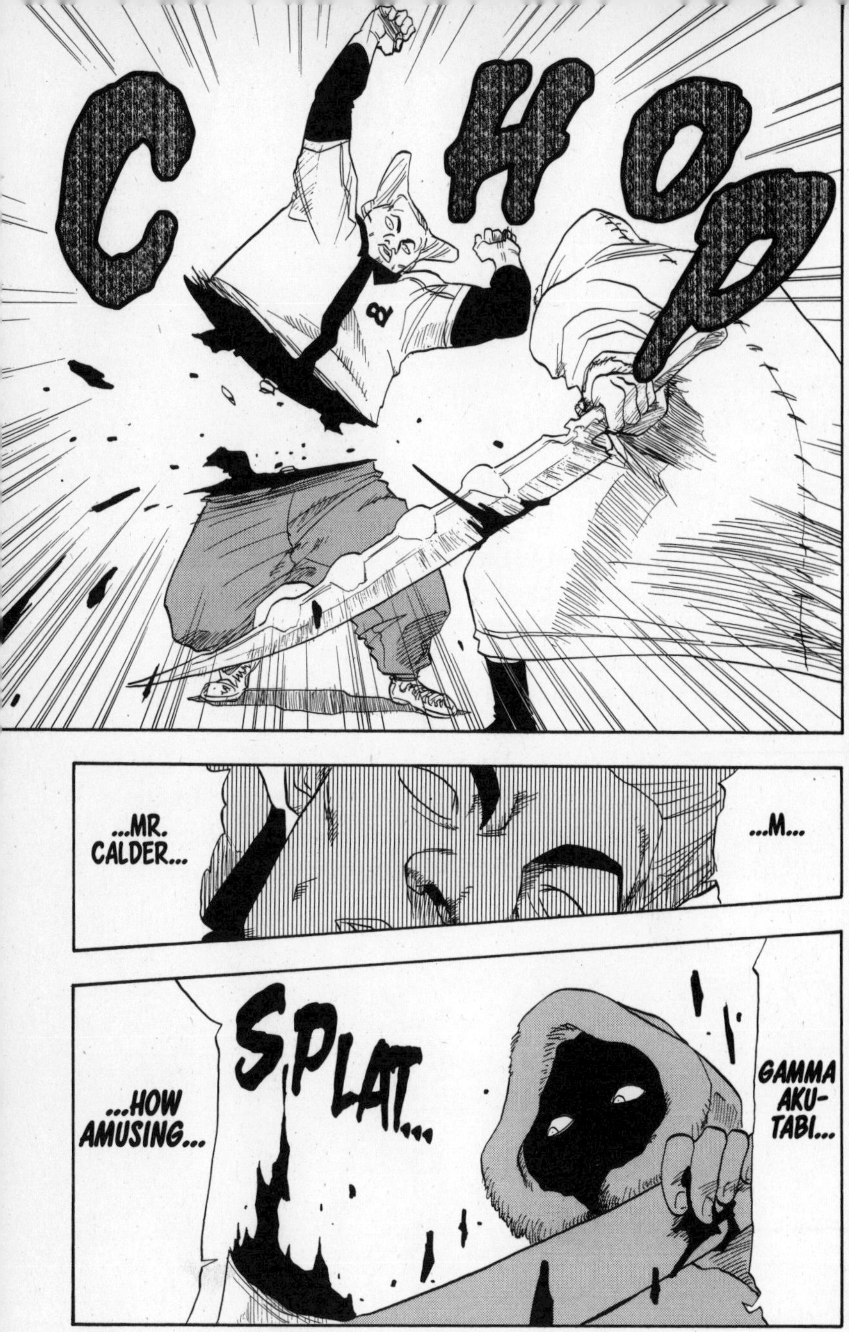
CHOP
...M...
...MR. CALDER...
GAMMA AKUTABI...
SPLAT...
...HOW AMUSING...

B-side NAKED MONKEYS 4.

Sheryl Ann Shepherd
シェリル・アン・シェパード

Height: 160.3 cm
Weight: 43 kg
Date of Birth: September 11
Age: 20
Blood Type: O

Elwood's older sister. On the surface she appears to have it together because she's calm, gentle, and educated…but actually she doesn't think too deeply about things and doesn't dwell on small details. She's also gullible and she isn't very good with financial matters. Her favorite foods are cream stew and meatloaf. Her dislikes include eggplant and mental arithmetic. She's also sensitive to cold weather.

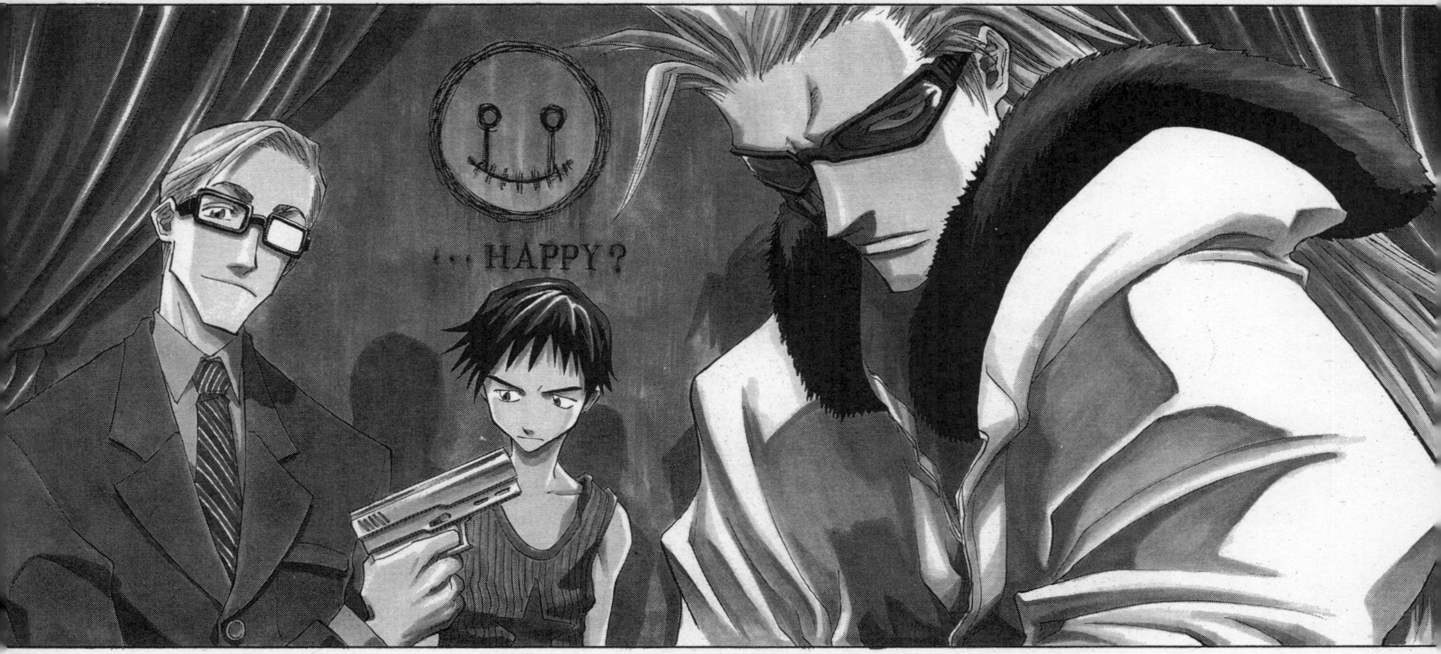
...HAPPY?

Track 5: Face Behind the Mask

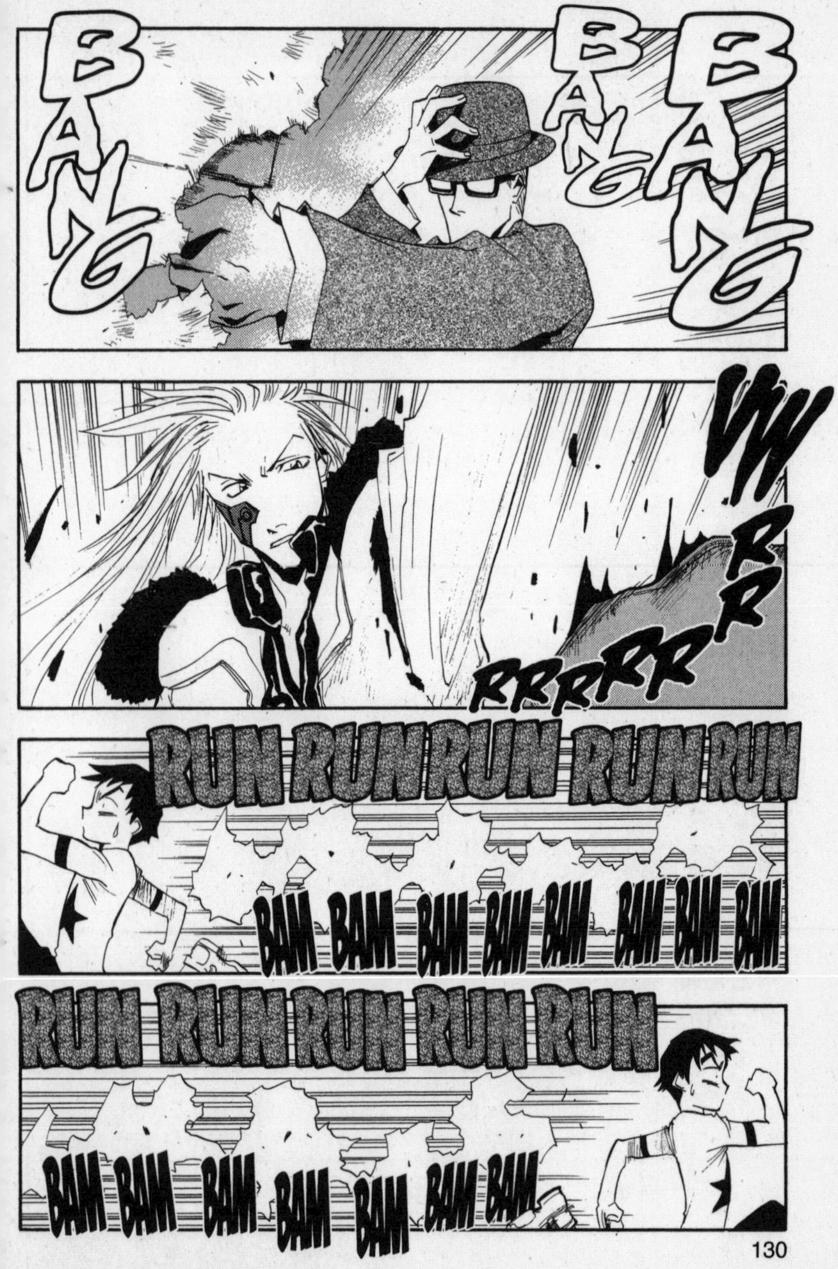
BANG
BANG
BANG
VWRRRRRRRRR
RUN RUN RUN RUN RUN
BAM BAM BAM BAM BAM BAM BAM BAM
RUN RUN RUN RUN RUN
BAM BAM BAM BAM BAM BAM BAM

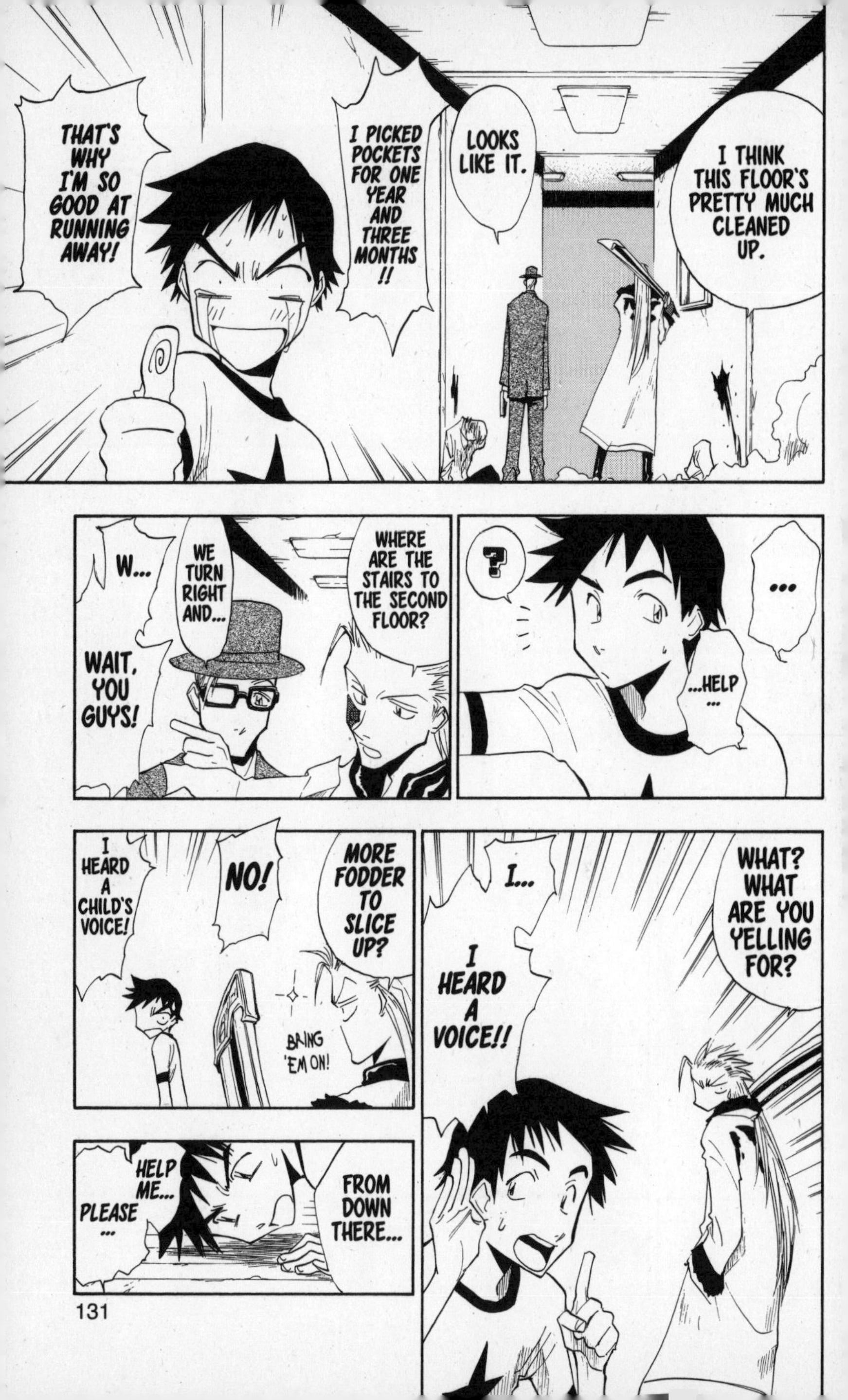
I THINK THIS FLOOR'S PRETTY MUCH CLEANED UP.
LOOKS LIKE IT.
I PICKED POCKETS FOR ONE YEAR AND THREE MONTHS!!
THAT'S WHY I'M SO GOOD AT RUNNING AWAY!
...
?
...HELP ...
WHERE ARE THE STAIRS TO THE SECOND FLOOR?
WE TURN RIGHT AND...
W...
WAIT, YOU GUYS!
WHAT? WHAT ARE YOU YELLING FOR?
I...
I HEARD A VOICE!!
MORE FODDER TO SLICE UP?
NO!
I HEARD A CHILD'S VOICE!
BRING 'EM ON!
FROM DOWN THERE...
HELP ME... PLEASE ...

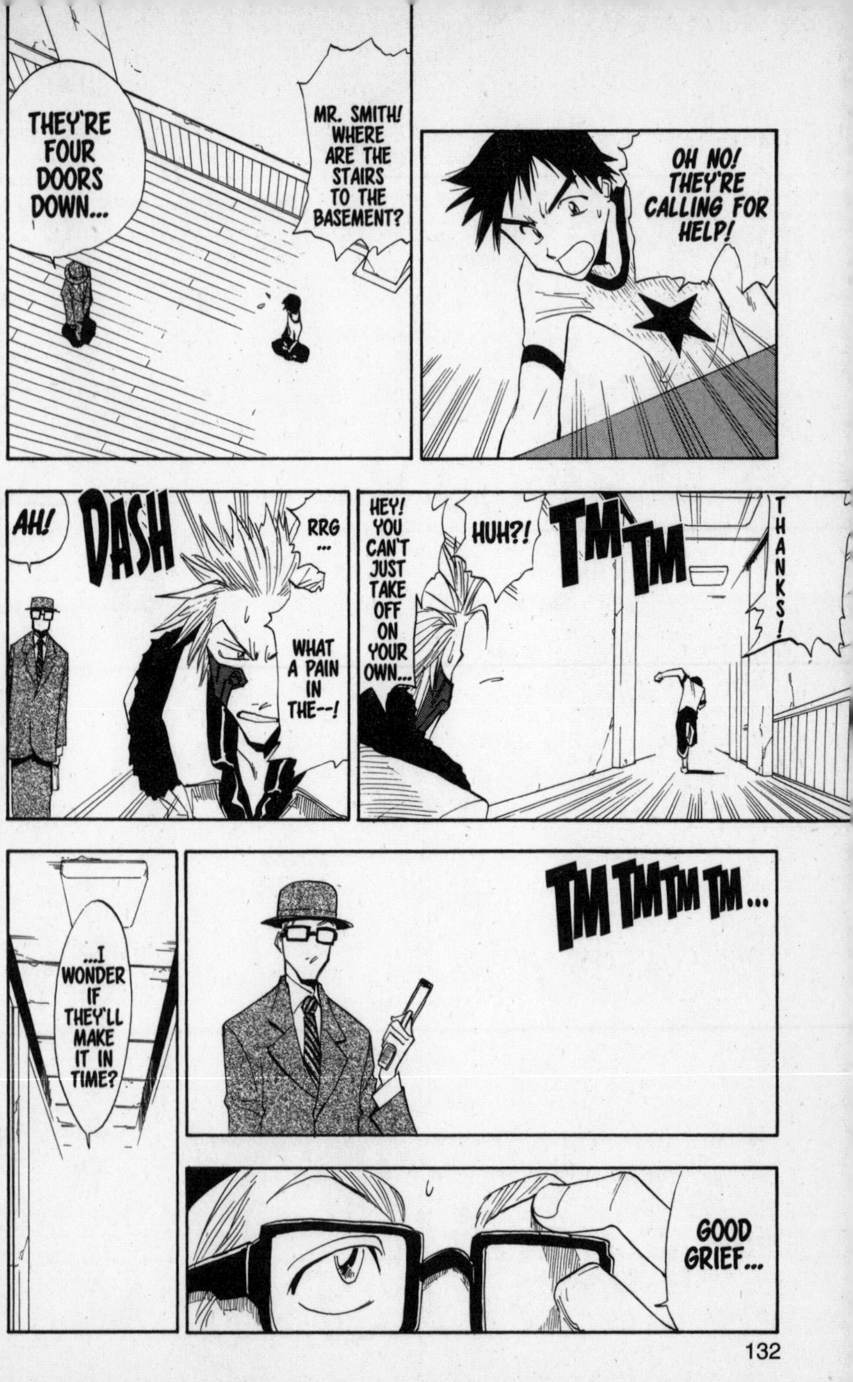
OH NO! THEY'RE CALLING FOR HELP!
MR. SMITH! WHERE ARE THE STAIRS TO THE BASEMENT?
THEY'RE FOUR DOORS DOWN...
THANKS!
TM TM
HUH?!
HEY! YOU CAN'T JUST TAKE OFF ON YOUR OWN...
RRG...
WHAT A PAIN IN THE--!
DASH
AH!
TM TM TM TM...
GOOD GRIEF...
...I WONDER IF THEY'LL MAKE IT IN TIME?

READ THIS WAY

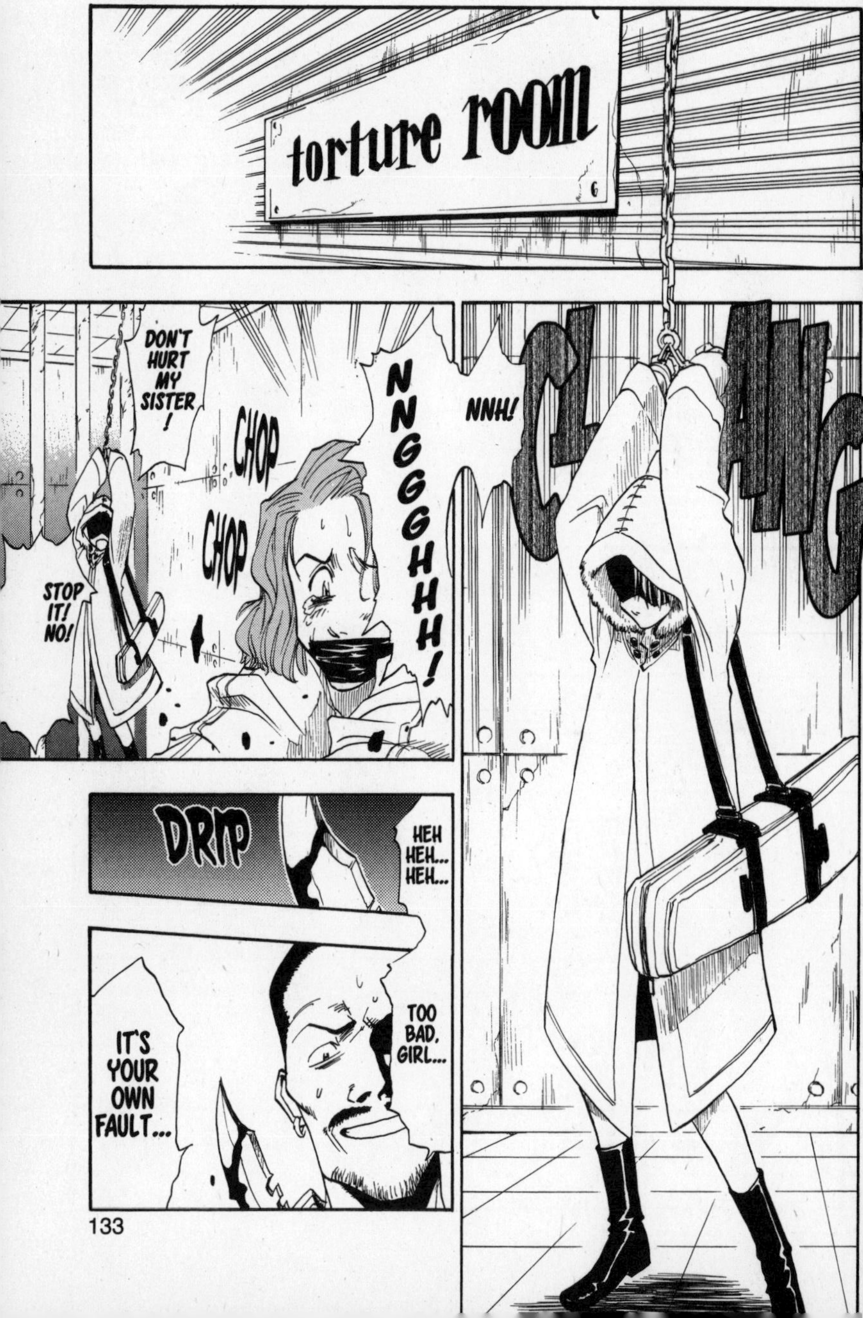
torture room
NNH!
CLANG
NNGGGHHH!
CHOP
CHOP
DON'T HURT MY SISTER!
STOP IT! NO!
HEH HEH... HEH...
DRIP
TOO BAD, GIRL...
IT'S YOUR OWN FAULT...

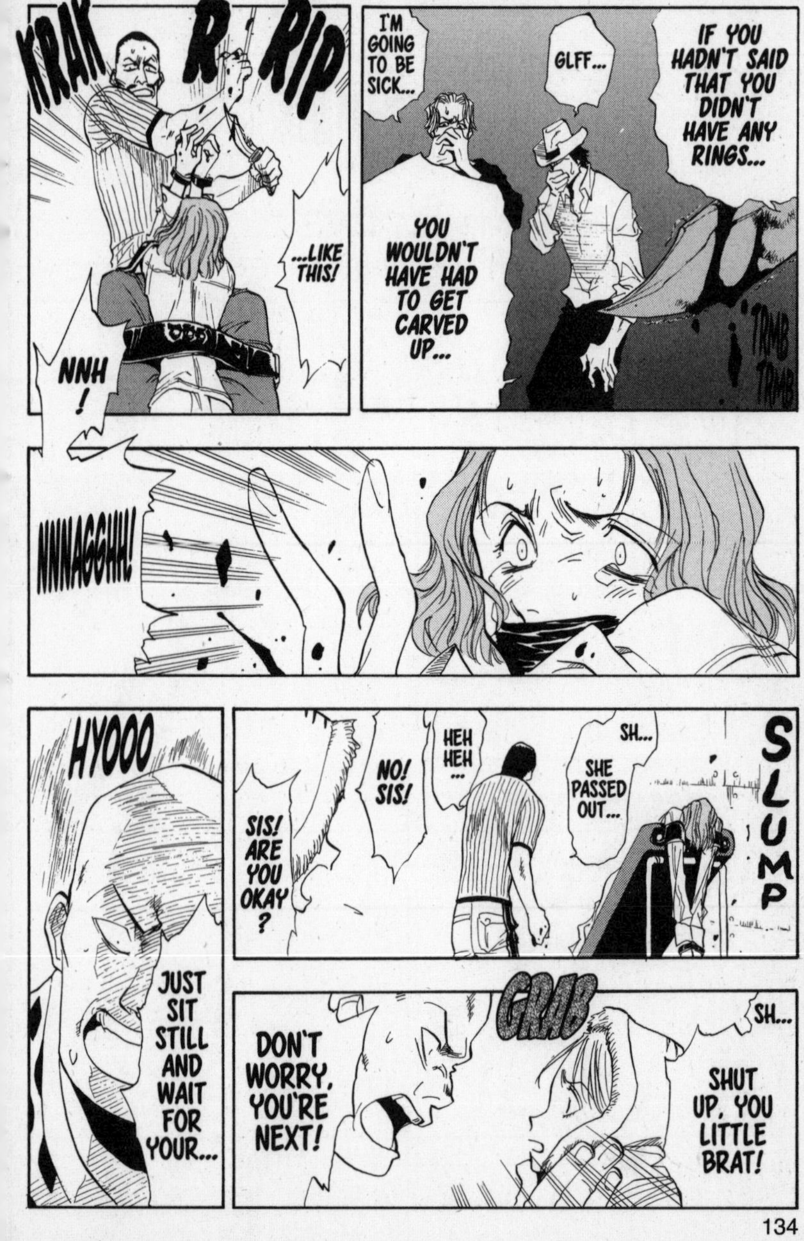
IF YOU HADN'T SAID THAT YOU DIDN'T HAVE ANY RINGS...
GLFF...
I'M GOING TO BE SICK...
YOU WOULDN'T HAVE HAD TO GET CARVED UP...
TRMB TRMB
RIP
R
KRAK
...LIKE THIS!
NNH!
NNNAGGHH!
SLUMP
SH...
SHE PASSED OUT...
HEH HEH...
NO! SIS!
SIS! ARE YOU OKAY?
SH...
SHUT UP, YOU LITTLE BRAT!
GRAB
DON'T WORRY, YOU'RE NEXT!
HYOOO
JUST SIT STILL AND WAIT FOR YOUR...

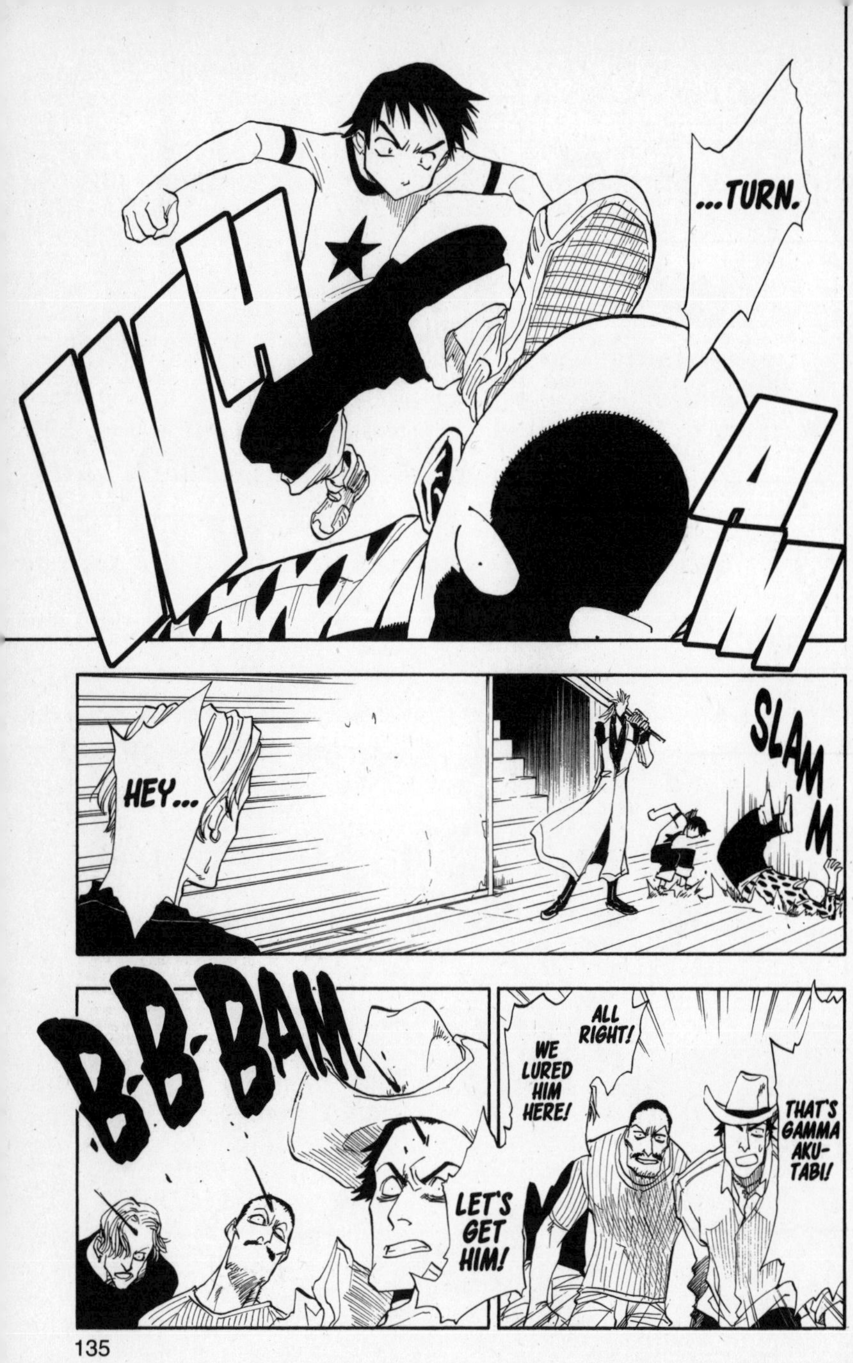
...TURN.
WHAM
SLAMM
HEY...
THAT'S GAMMA AKU-TABI!
ALL RIGHT!
WE LURED HIM HERE!
B-B-BAM
LET'S GET HIM!

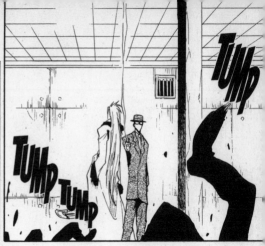

TUMP

TUMP TUMP TUMP

"PLAN," EH...?

TOO LATE NOW.

I WONDER IF THAT WAS ALL THERE WAS TO IT?

TH...

THANKS!

IT CAME OFF!

SHF

SHF

SLAM

DASH

ARE YOU ALL RIGHT?

YOU'VE REALLY BEEN THROUGH A LOT...

READ THIS WAY

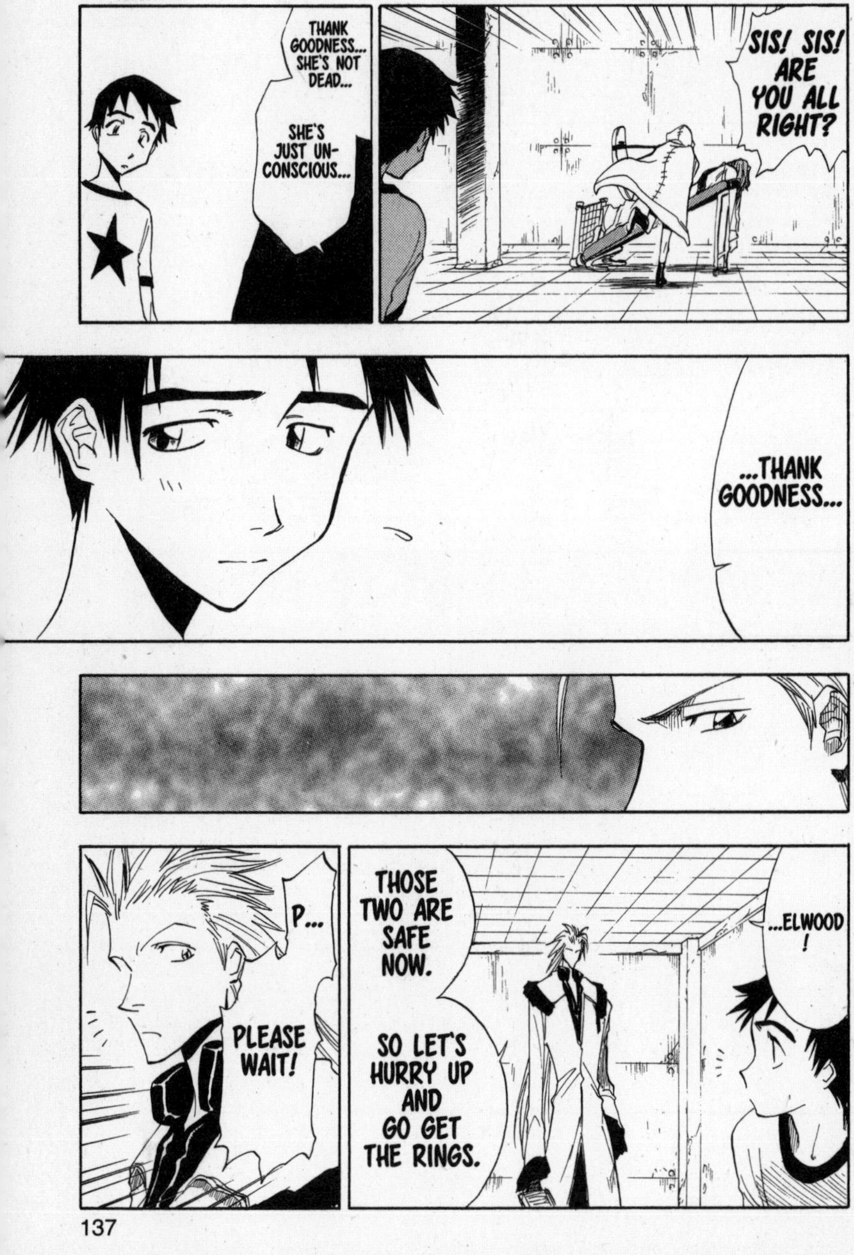

SIS! SIS! ARE YOU ALL RIGHT?
THANK GOODNESS... SHE'S NOT DEAD...
SHE'S JUST UN-CONSCIOUS...
...THANK GOODNESS...
...ELWOOD!
THOSE TWO ARE SAFE NOW.
SO LET'S HURRY UP AND GO GET THE RINGS.
P...
PLEASE WAIT!

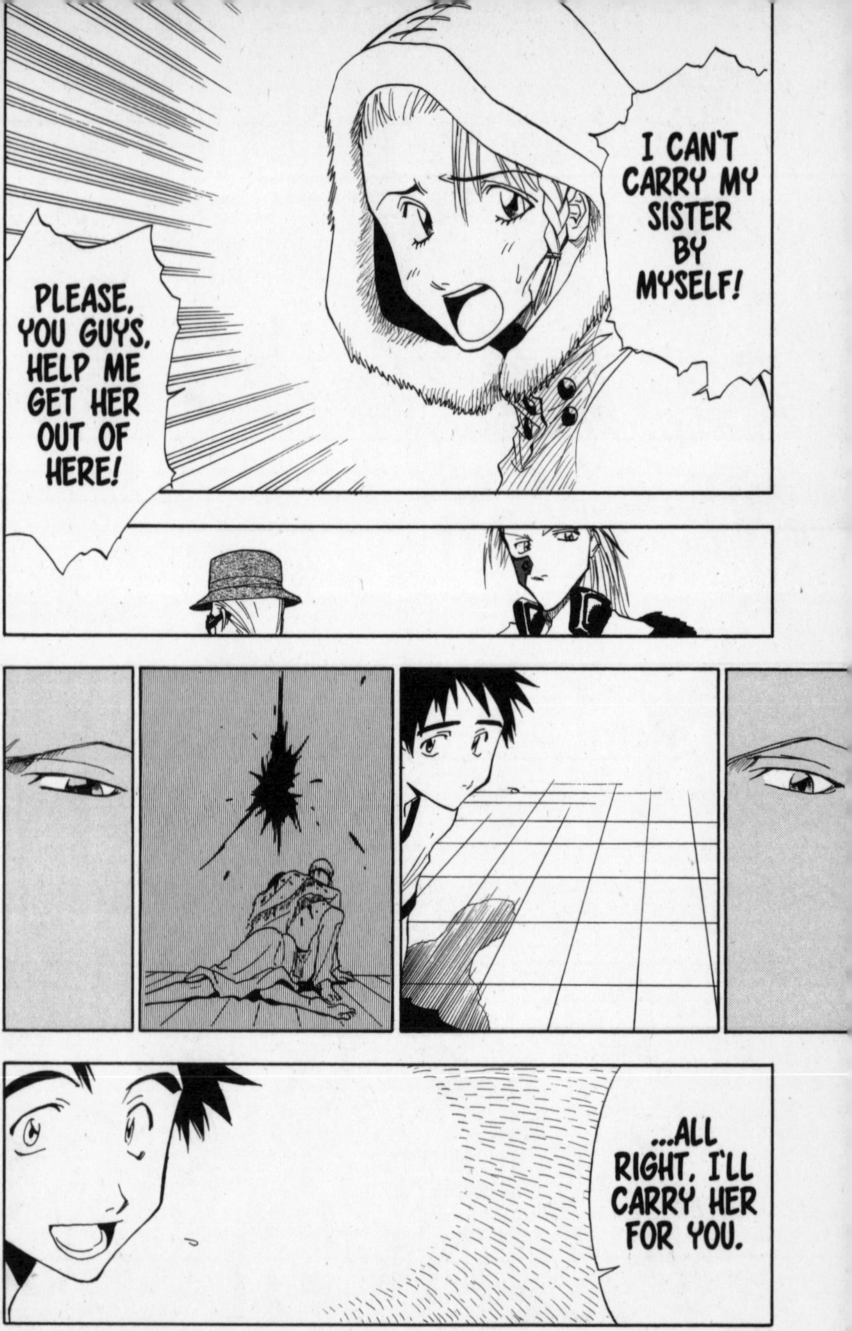
I CAN'T CARRY MY SISTER BY MYSELF!
PLEASE, YOU GUYS, HELP ME GET HER OUT OF HERE!
...ALL RIGHT, I'LL CARRY HER FOR YOU.

READ THIS WAY

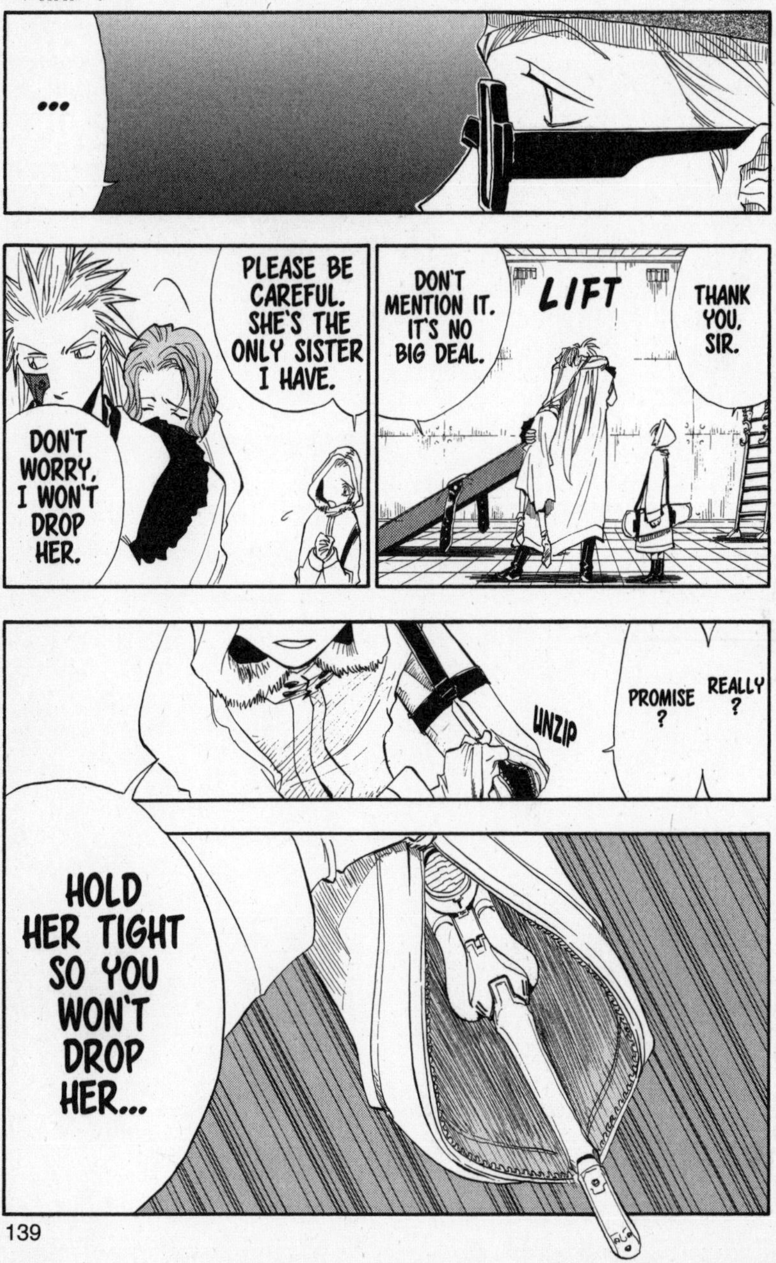
...
THANK YOU, SIR.
LIFT
DON'T MENTION IT. IT'S NO BIG DEAL.
PLEASE BE CAREFUL. SHE'S THE ONLY SISTER I HAVE.
DON'T WORRY, I WON'T DROP HER.
REALLY?
PROMISE?
UNZIP
HOLD HER TIGHT SO YOU WON'T DROP HER...

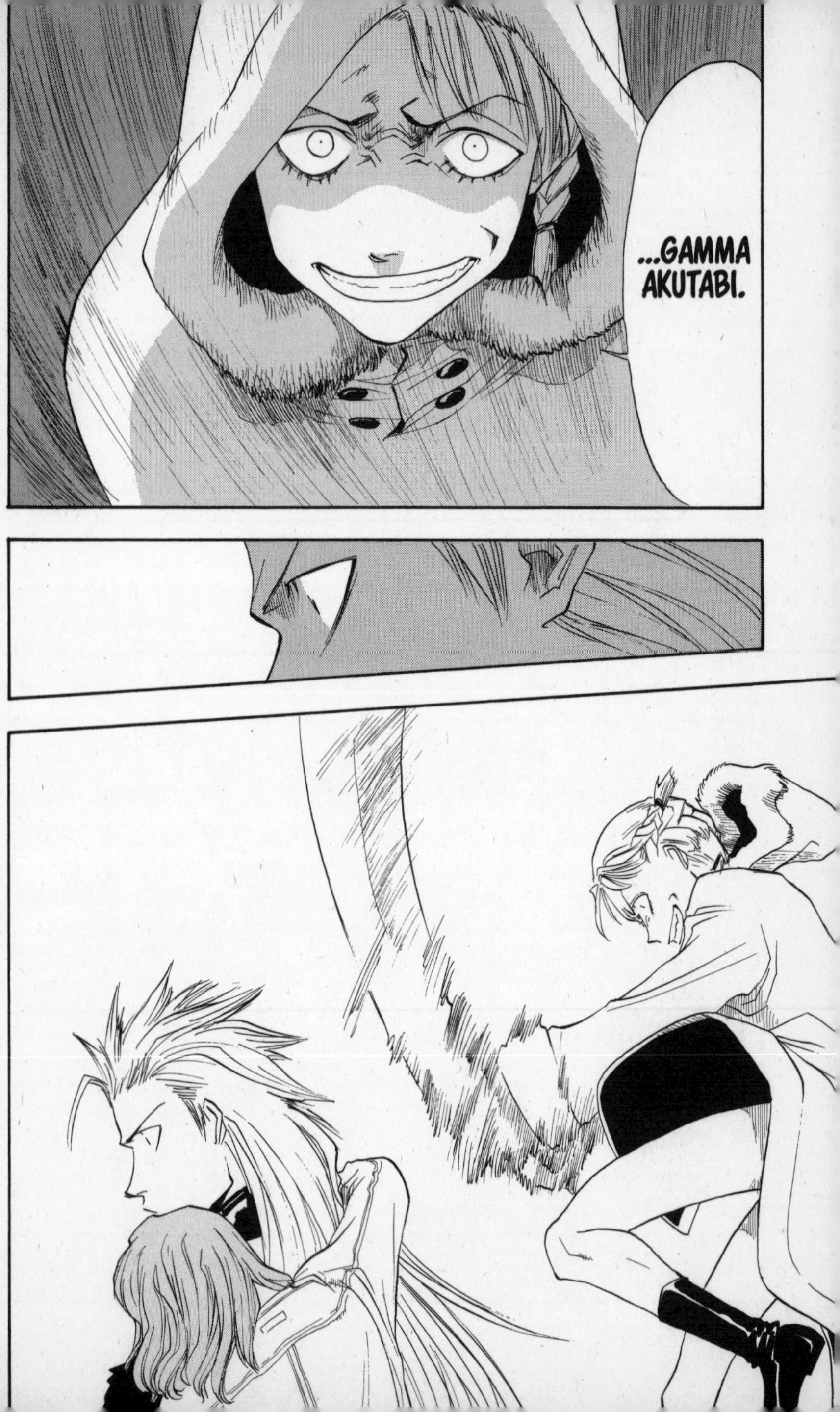
...GAMMA AKUTABI.

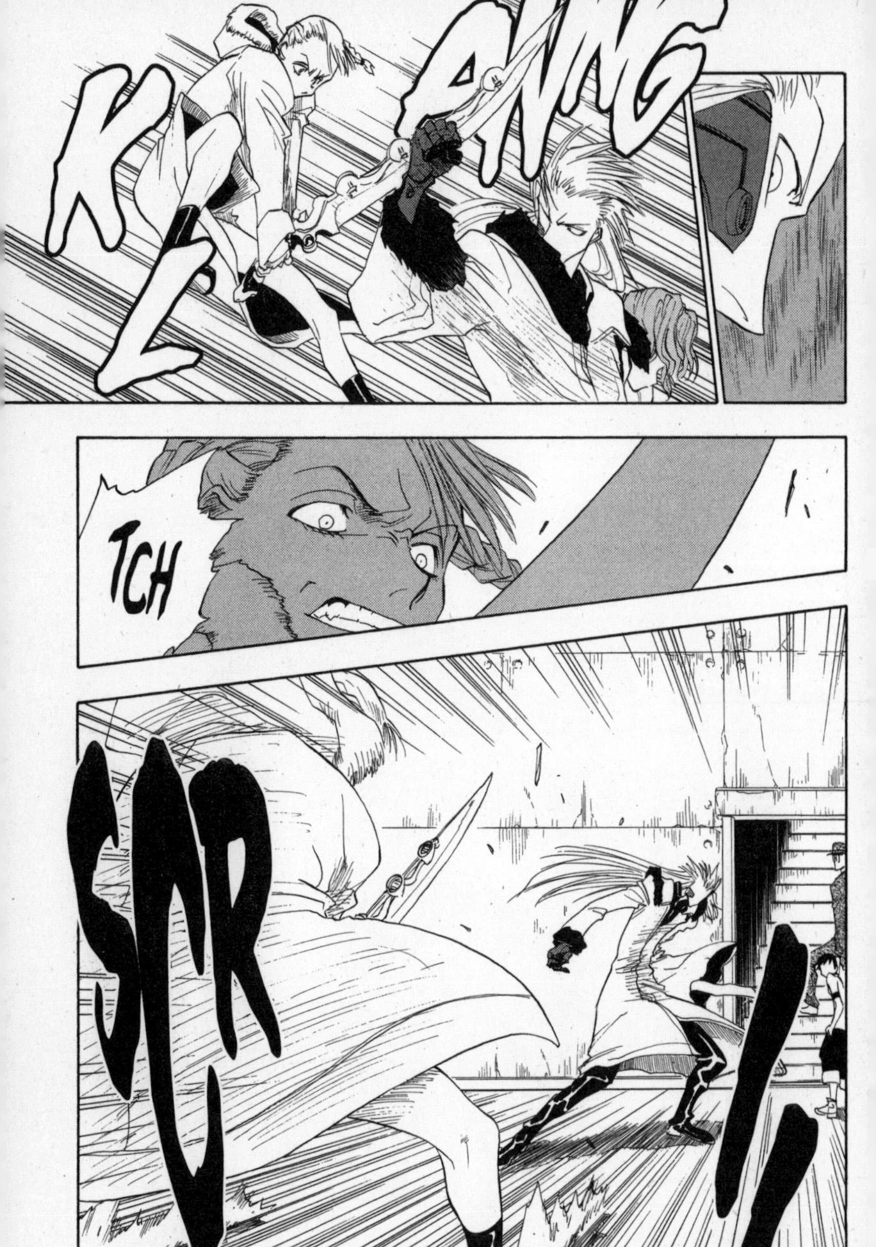
KLANG
TCH
SCR

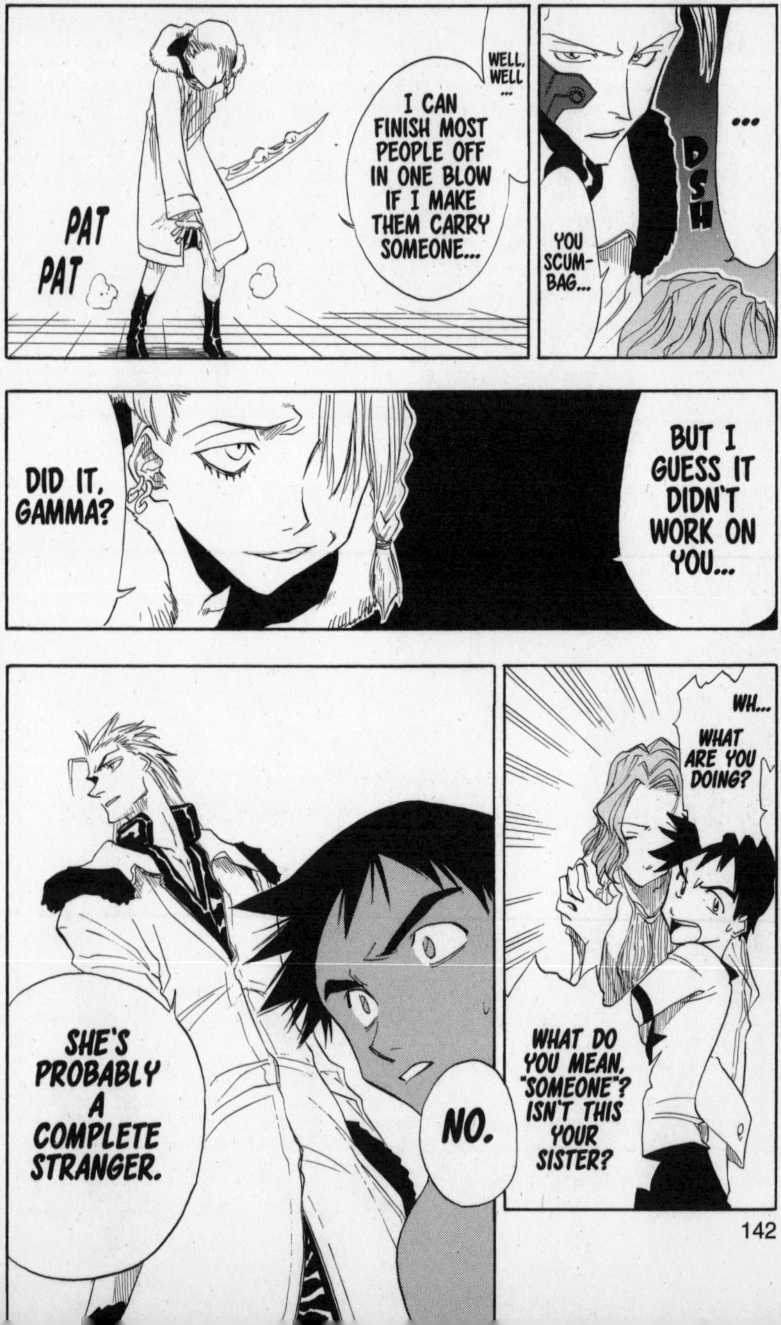
...
DSH
YOU SCUM-BAG...
WELL, WELL ...
I CAN FINISH MOST PEOPLE OFF IN ONE BLOW IF I MAKE THEM CARRY SOMEONE...
PAT PAT
BUT I GUESS IT DIDN'T WORK ON YOU...
DID IT, GAMMA?
WH...
WHAT ARE YOU DOING?
WHAT DO YOU MEAN, "SOMEONE"? ISN'T THIS YOUR SISTER?
NO.
SHE'S PROBABLY A COMPLETE STRANGER.

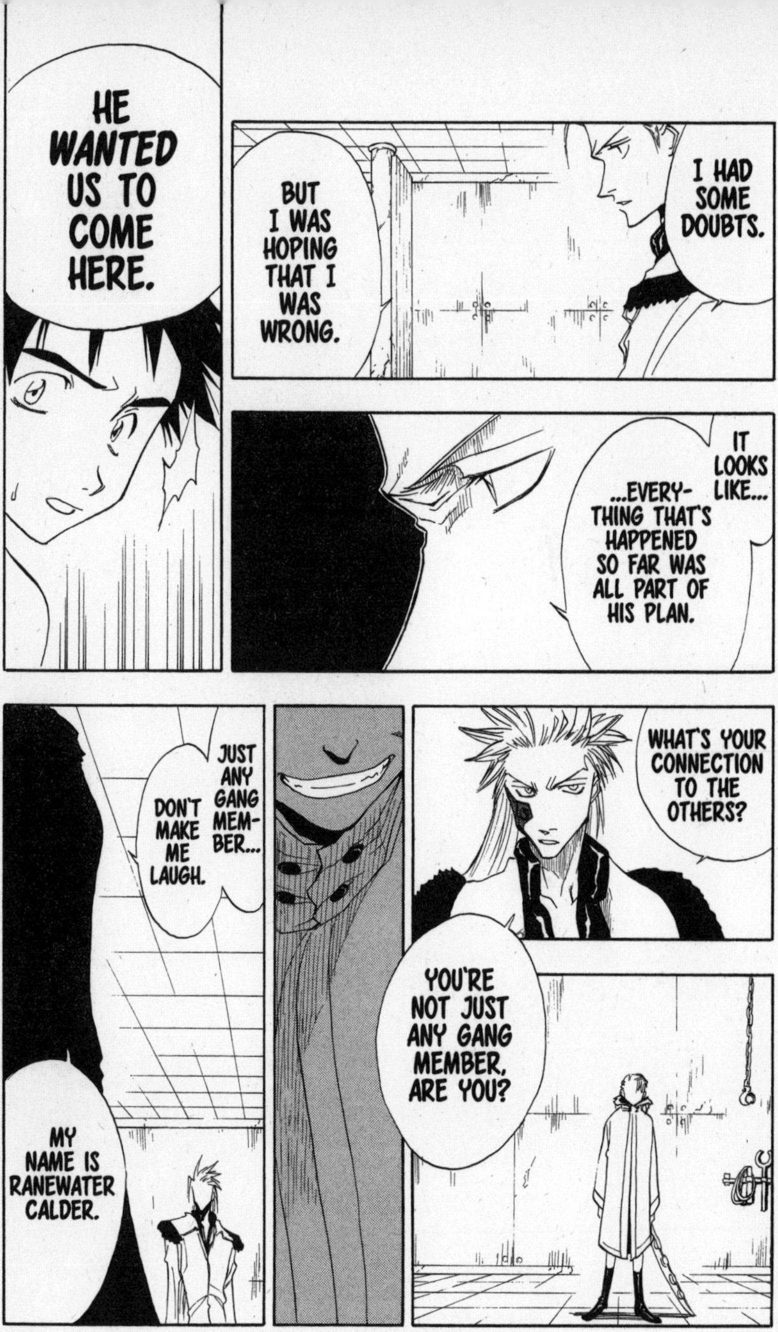
I HAD SOME DOUBTS.
BUT I WAS HOPING THAT I WAS WRONG.
IT LOOKS LIKE...
...EVERY-THING THAT'S HAPPENED SO FAR WAS ALL PART OF HIS PLAN.
HE WANTED US TO COME HERE.
WHAT'S YOUR CONNECTION TO THE OTHERS?
YOU'RE NOT JUST ANY GANG MEMBER, ARE YOU?
JUST ANY GANG MEM-BER...
DON'T MAKE ME LAUGH.
MY NAME IS RANEWATER CALDER.

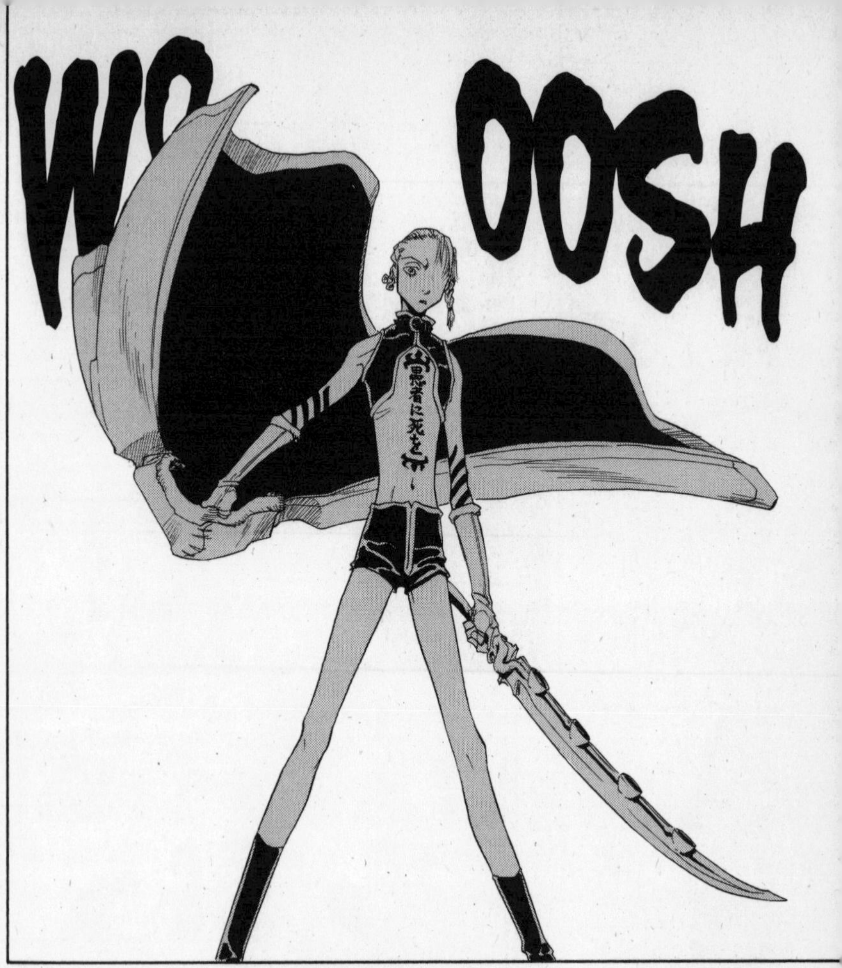
WO OOSH
愚者に死を

*TATTOO=DEATH TO FOOLS

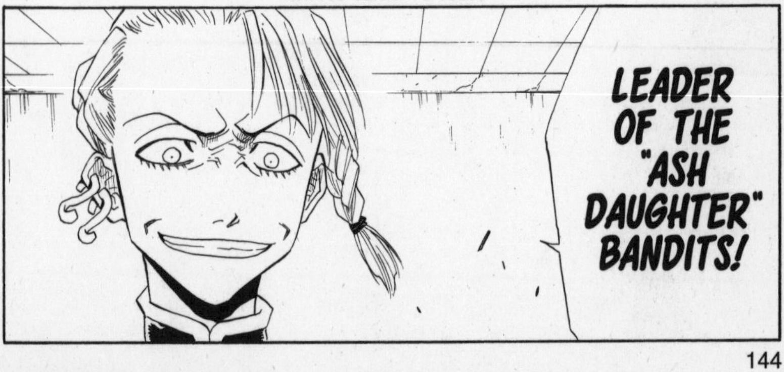
LEADER OF THE "ASH DAUGHTER" BANDITS!

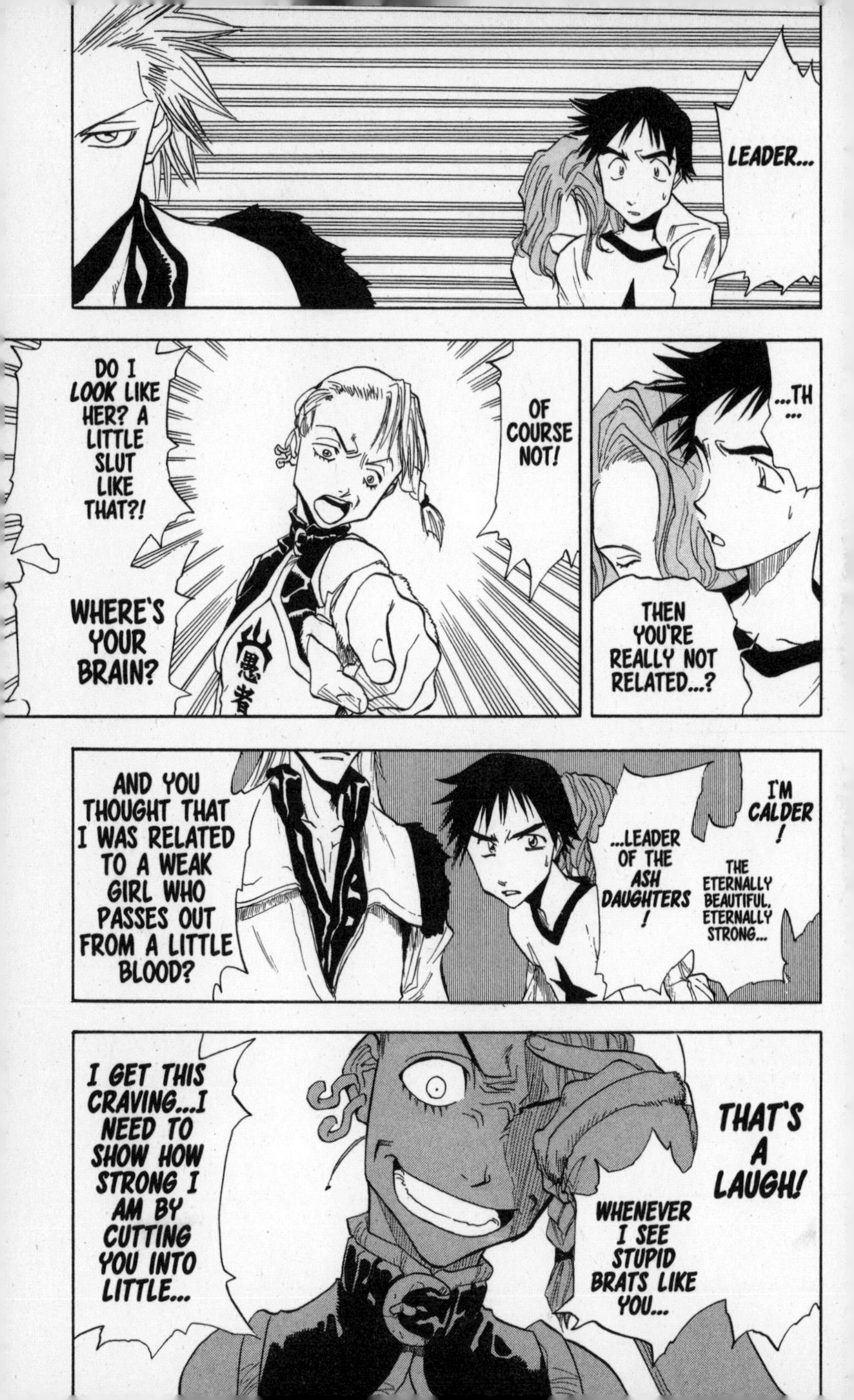
LEADER...
...TH ...
THEN YOU'RE REALLY NOT RELATED...?
OF COURSE NOT!
DO I LOOK LIKE HER? A LITTLE SLUT LIKE THAT?!
WHERE'S YOUR BRAIN?
I'M CALDER!
THE ETERNALLY BEAUTIFUL, ETERNALLY STRONG...
...LEADER OF THE ASH DAUGHTERS!
AND YOU THOUGHT THAT I WAS RELATED TO A WEAK GIRL WHO PASSES OUT FROM A LITTLE BLOOD?
THAT'S A LAUGH!
WHENEVER I SEE STUPID BRATS LIKE YOU...
I GET THIS CRAVING...I NEED TO SHOW HOW STRONG I AM BY CUTTING YOU INTO LITTLE...

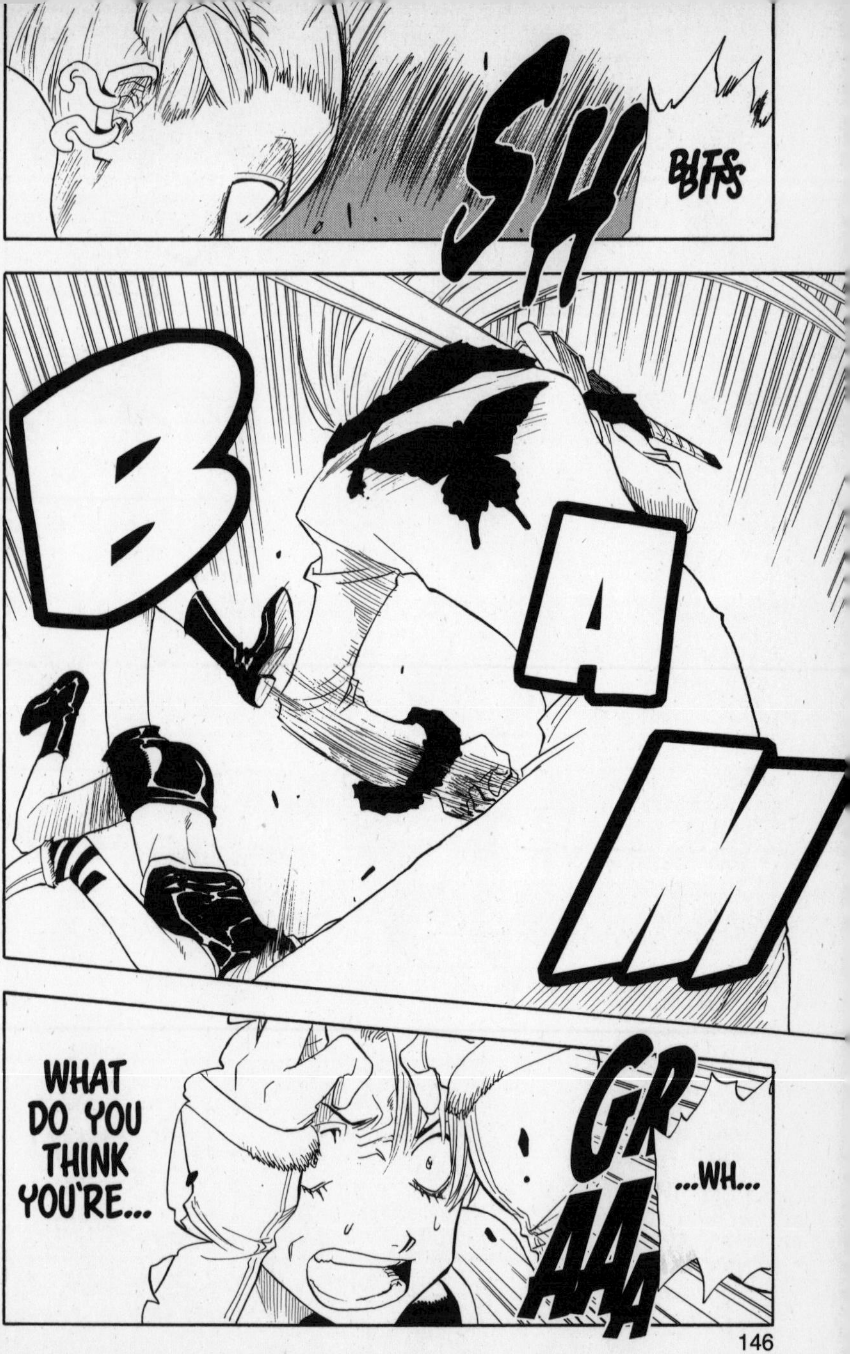
SH
BITS BITS
BAM
GRAAAA
...WH...
WHAT DO YOU THINK YOU'RE...

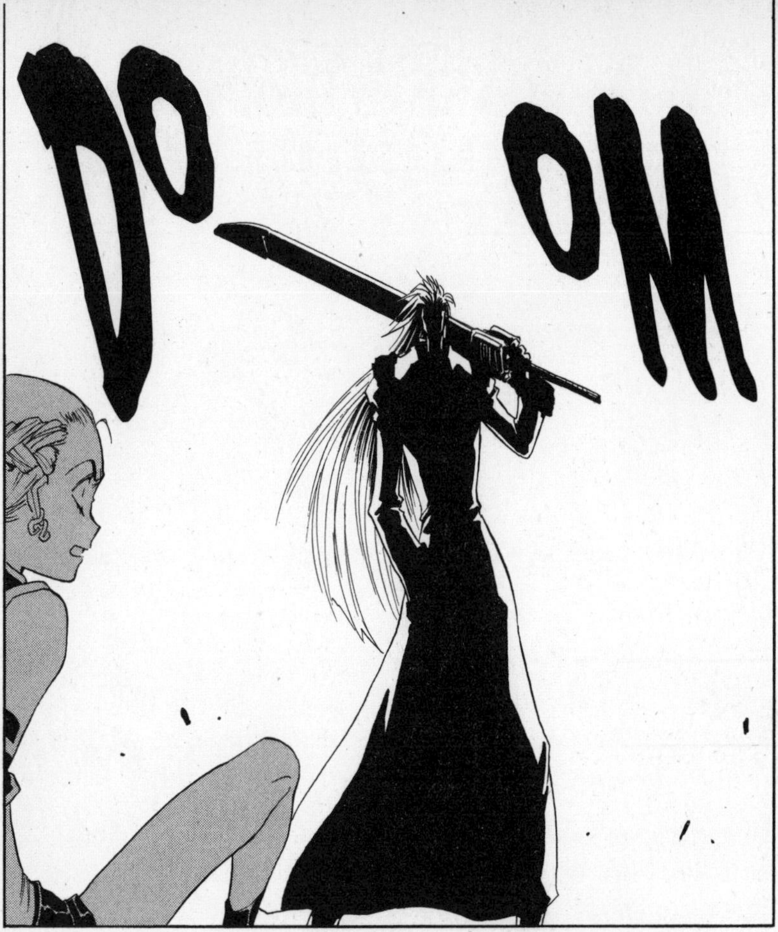
DO OM

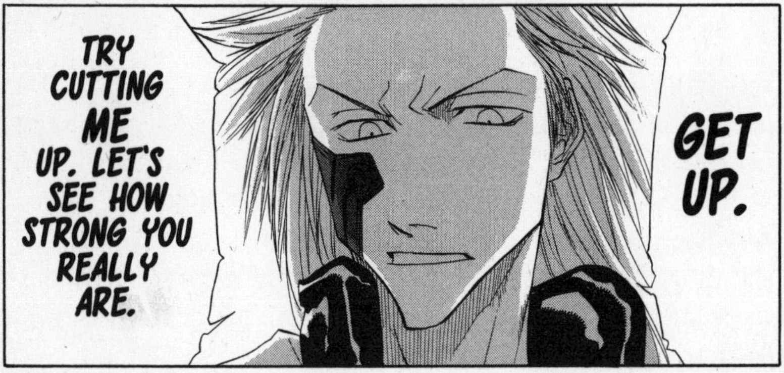
GET UP.
TRY CUTTING ME UP. LET'S SEE HOW STRONG YOU REALLY ARE.

NAKED MONKEYS DEMO Version

Gamma Original Concept Sketch

This is the very first version of Gamma. The overall image isn't very different from now but his coat and hairstyle are a little different. His sword was not a chainsaw like the one he has now; instead the entire sword would vibrate when the engine was started. It was a somewhat perverted weapon.

You may be able to guess from his overall look that Gamma's initial concept was that of a "samurai." At that stage the comic was called *Samurai Drive* and not only were there no Rings of the Dead, it wasn't even a Western. The only thing that the story had in common with the final version is that Gamma has a huge bounty on his head. After that, a lot of stuff happened and I ended up with the Western theme, but that's a different story altogether.

Tite Kubo

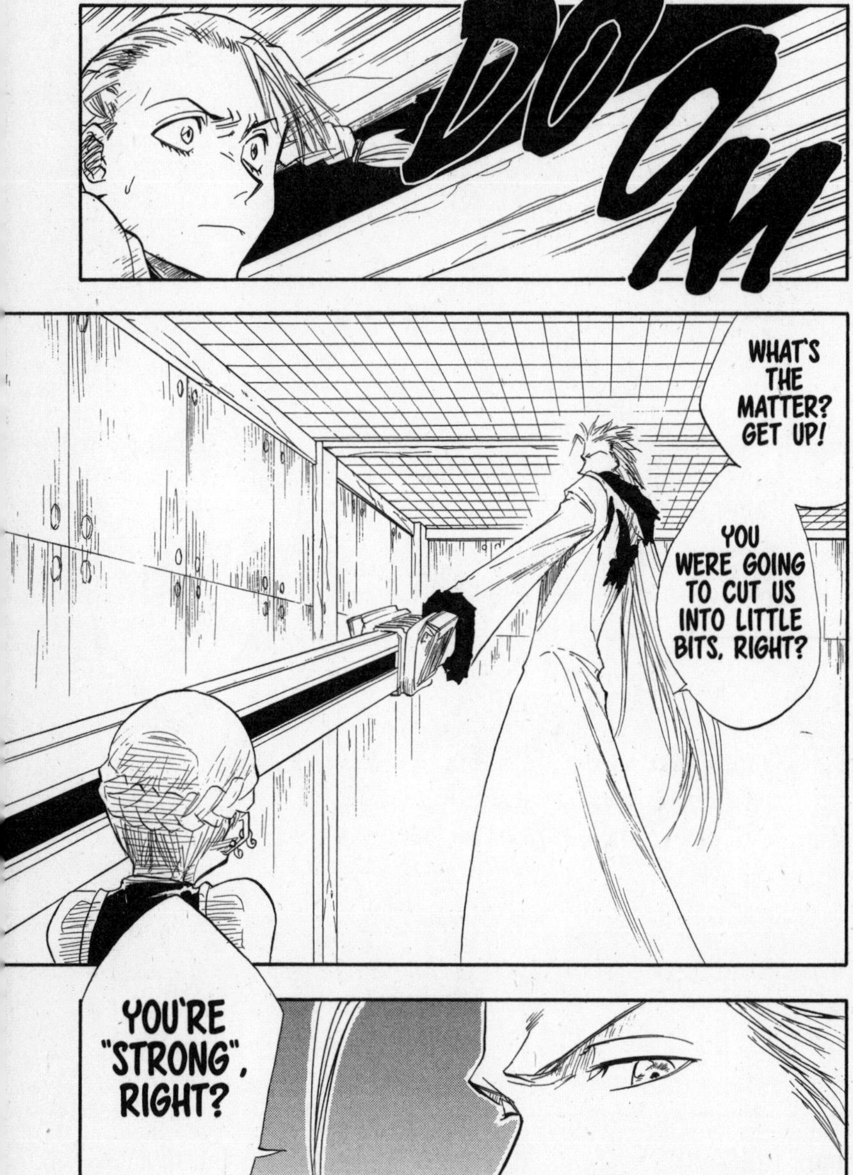
DOOM
WHAT'S THE MATTER? GET UP!
YOU WERE GOING TO CUT US INTO LITTLE BITS, RIGHT?
YOU'RE "STRONG", RIGHT?

Track 6: Deceiving Jet Joe

TRACK 6:
DECEIVING JET JOE

READ THIS WAY

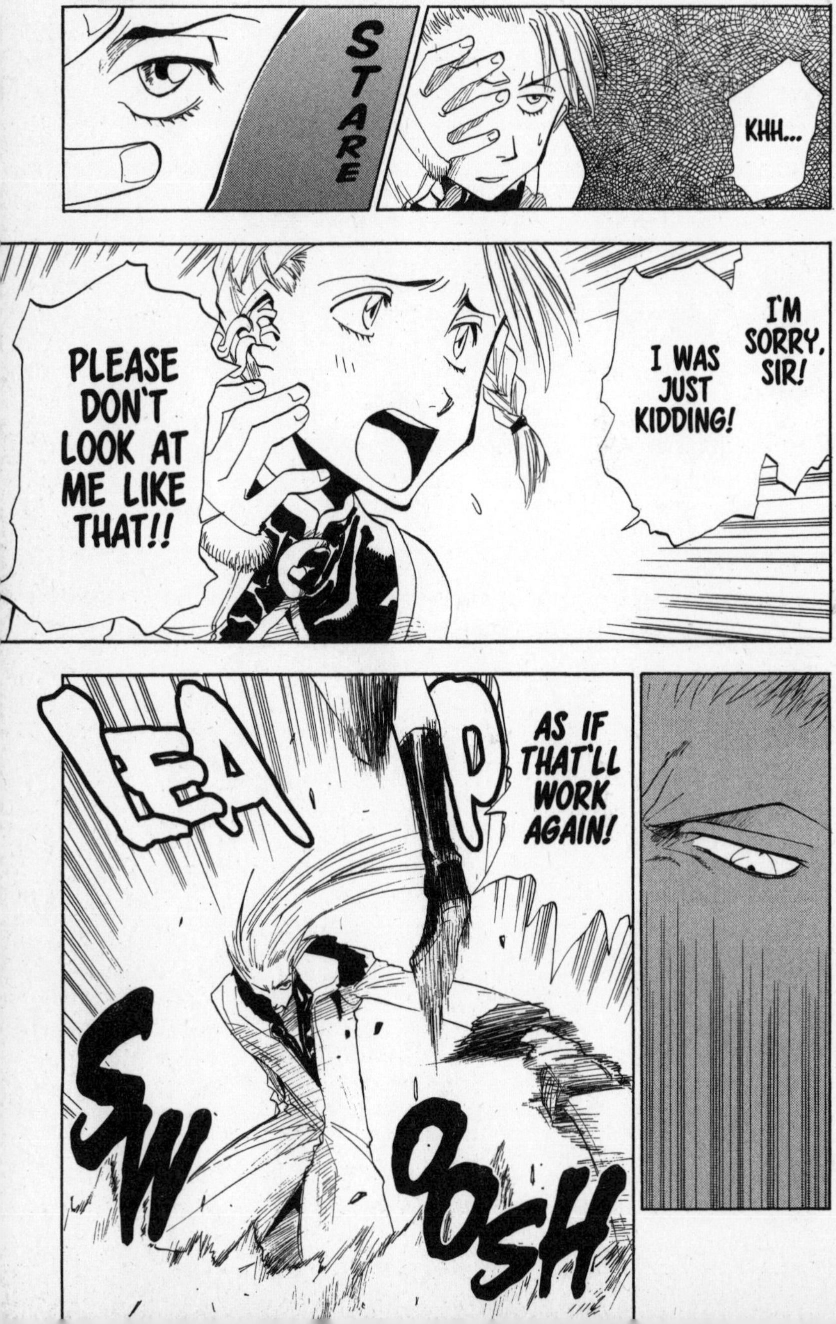
KHH...
STARE
I'M SORRY, SIR!
I WAS JUST KIDDING!
PLEASE DON'T LOOK AT ME LIKE THAT!!
LEAP
AS IF THAT'LL WORK AGAIN!
SWOOSH

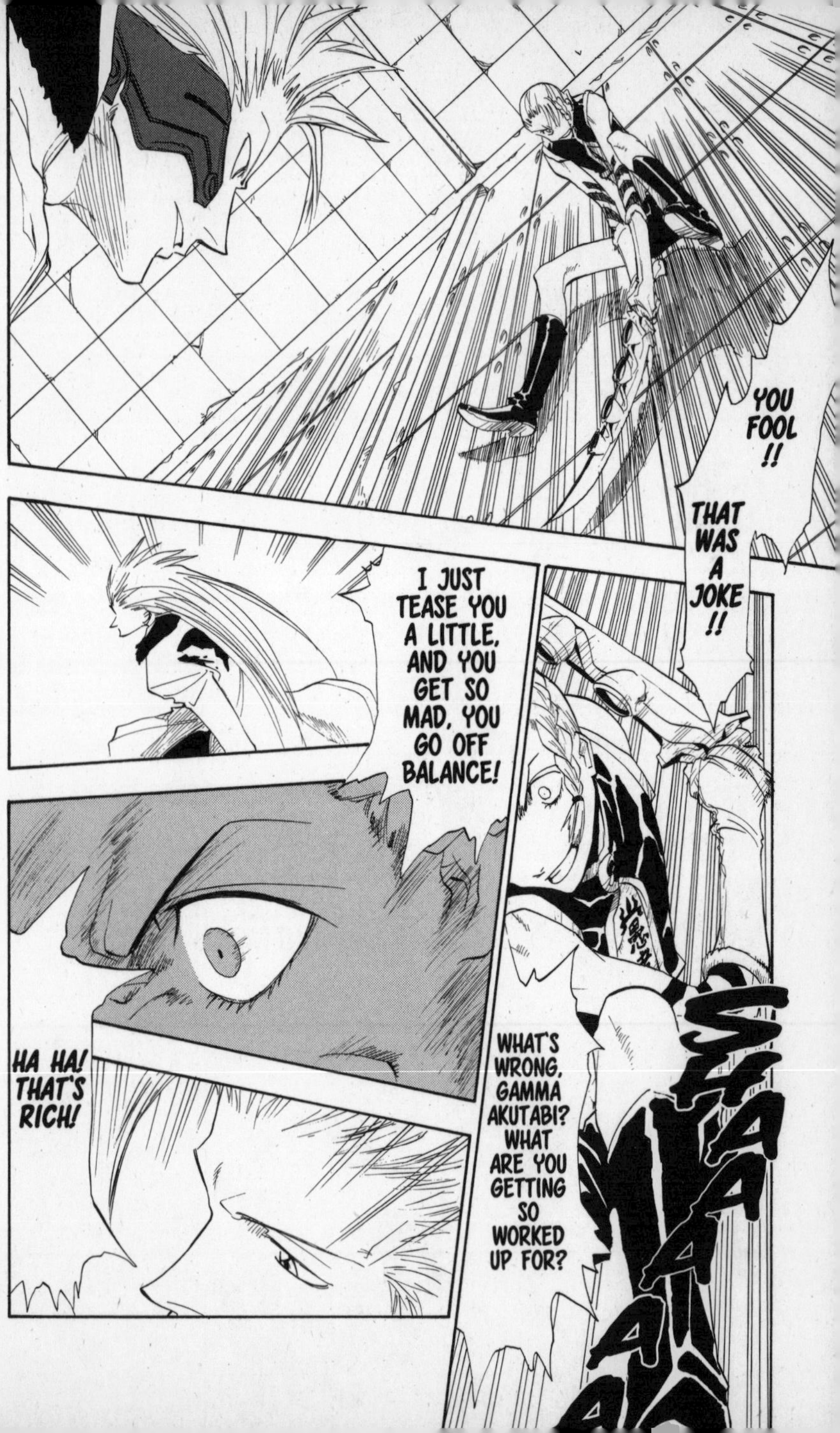
YOU FOOL!!
THAT WAS A JOKE!!
I JUST TEASE YOU A LITTLE, AND YOU GET SO MAD, YOU GO OFF BALANCE!
WHAT'S WRONG, GAMMA AKUTABI? WHAT ARE YOU GETTING SO WORKED UP FOR?
HA HA! THAT'S RICH!

READ THIS WAY

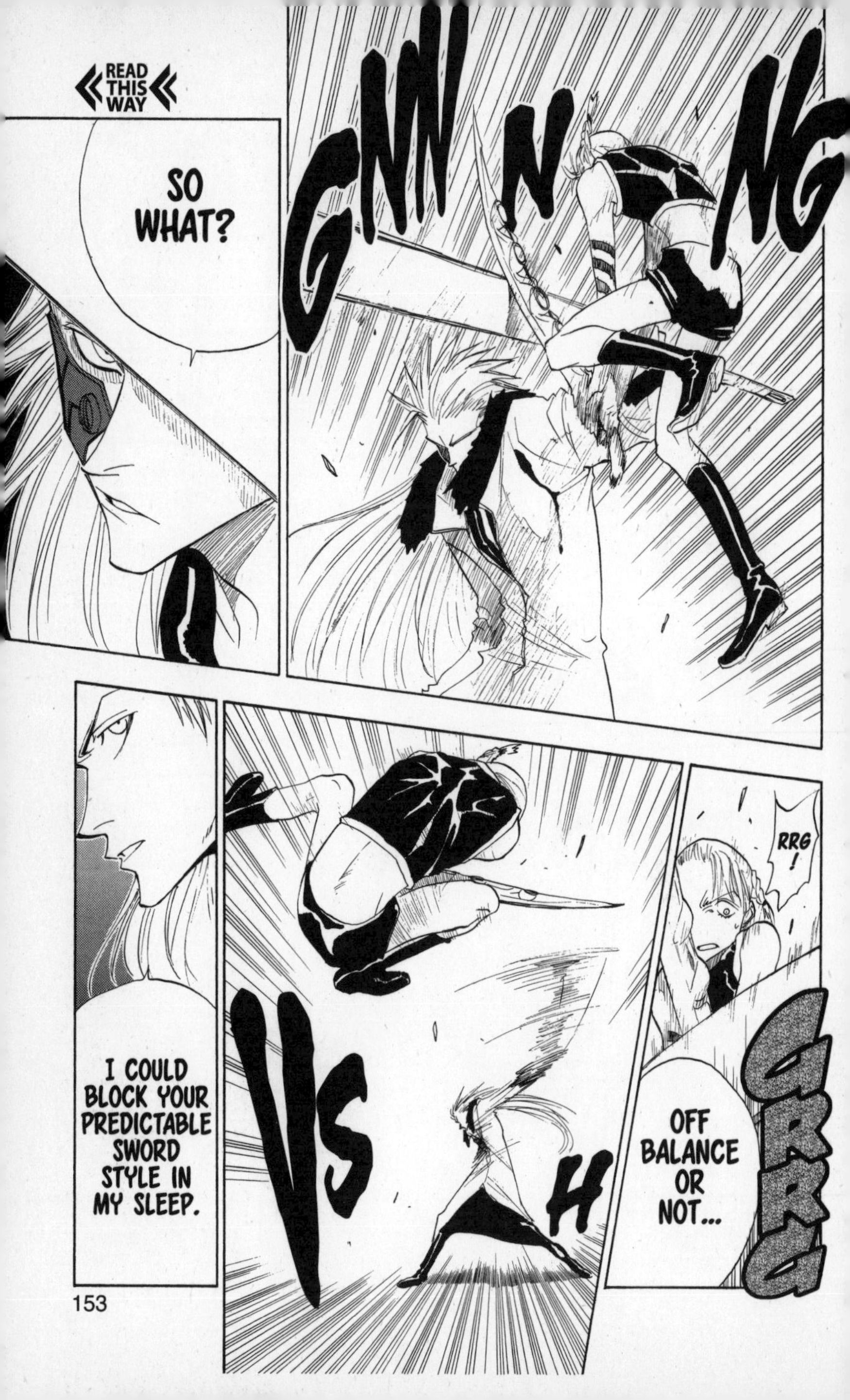

GNN N NG
SO WHAT?
RRG!
OFF BALANCE OR NOT...
GRRG
VSH
I COULD BLOCK YOUR PREDICTABLE SWORD STYLE IN MY SLEEP.

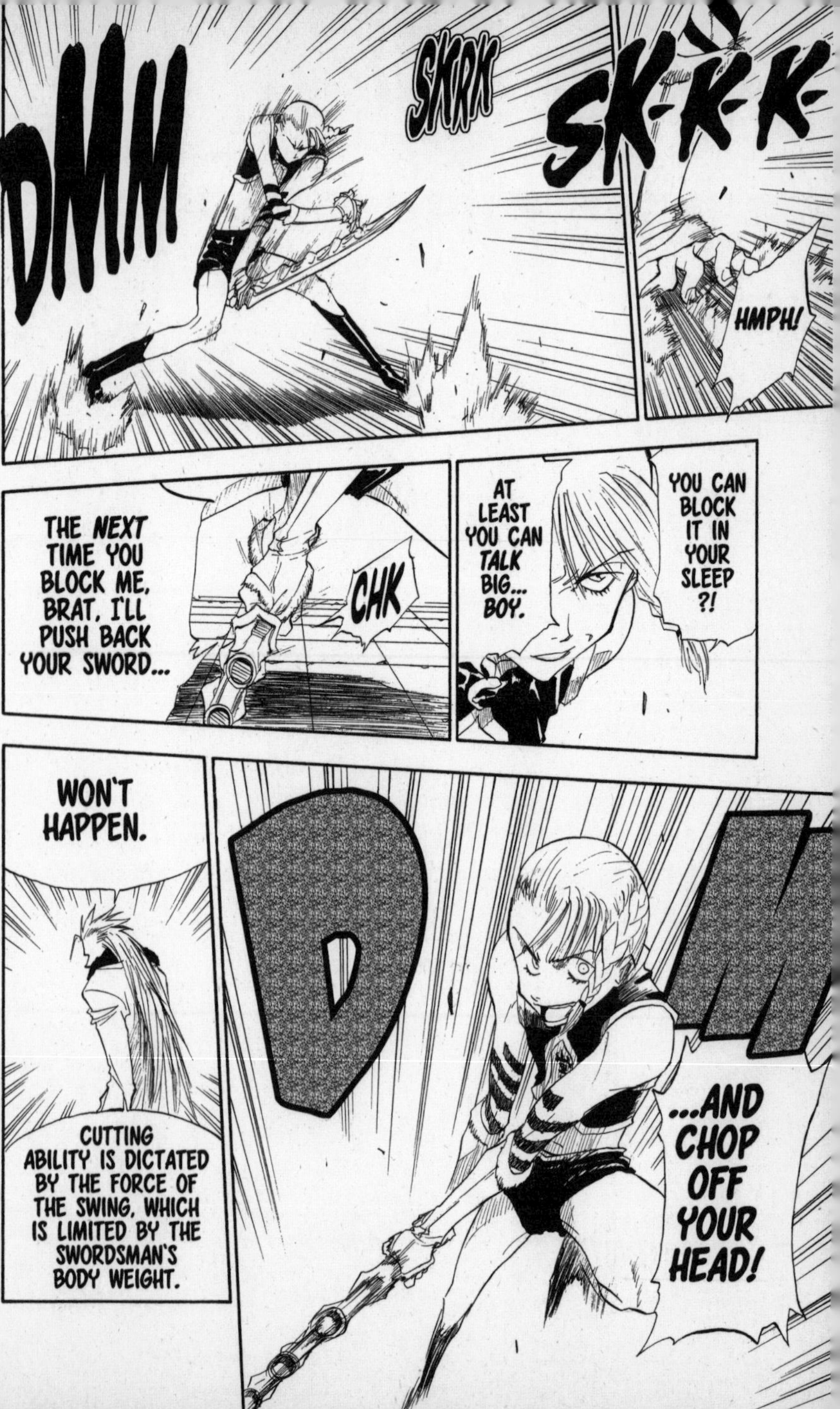

SK-K-K
HMPH!
SKRK
DMM
YOU CAN BLOCK IT IN YOUR SLEEP?!
AT LEAST YOU CAN TALK BIG... BOY.
THE NEXT TIME YOU BLOCK ME, BRAT, I'LL PUSH BACK YOUR SWORD...
CHK
DM
...AND CHOP OFF YOUR HEAD!
WON'T HAPPEN.
CUTTING ABILITY IS DICTATED BY THE FORCE OF THE SWING, WHICH IS LIMITED BY THE SWORDSMAN'S BODY WEIGHT.

READ THIS WAY

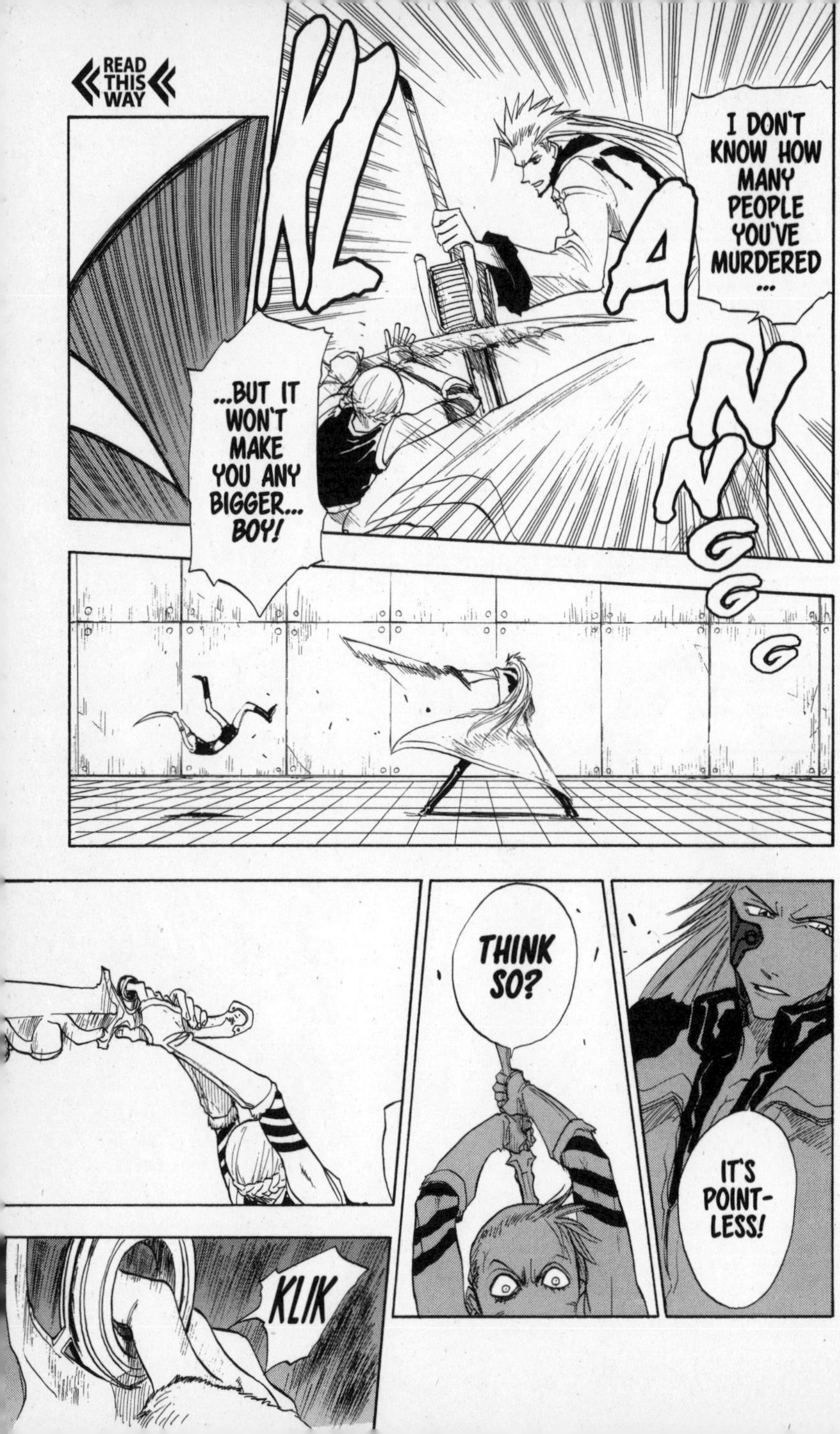
I DON'T KNOW HOW MANY PEOPLE YOU'VE MURDERED ...
KLANNGGGG
...BUT IT WON'T MAKE YOU ANY BIGGER... BOY!
IT'S POINT-LESS!
THINK SO?
KLIK

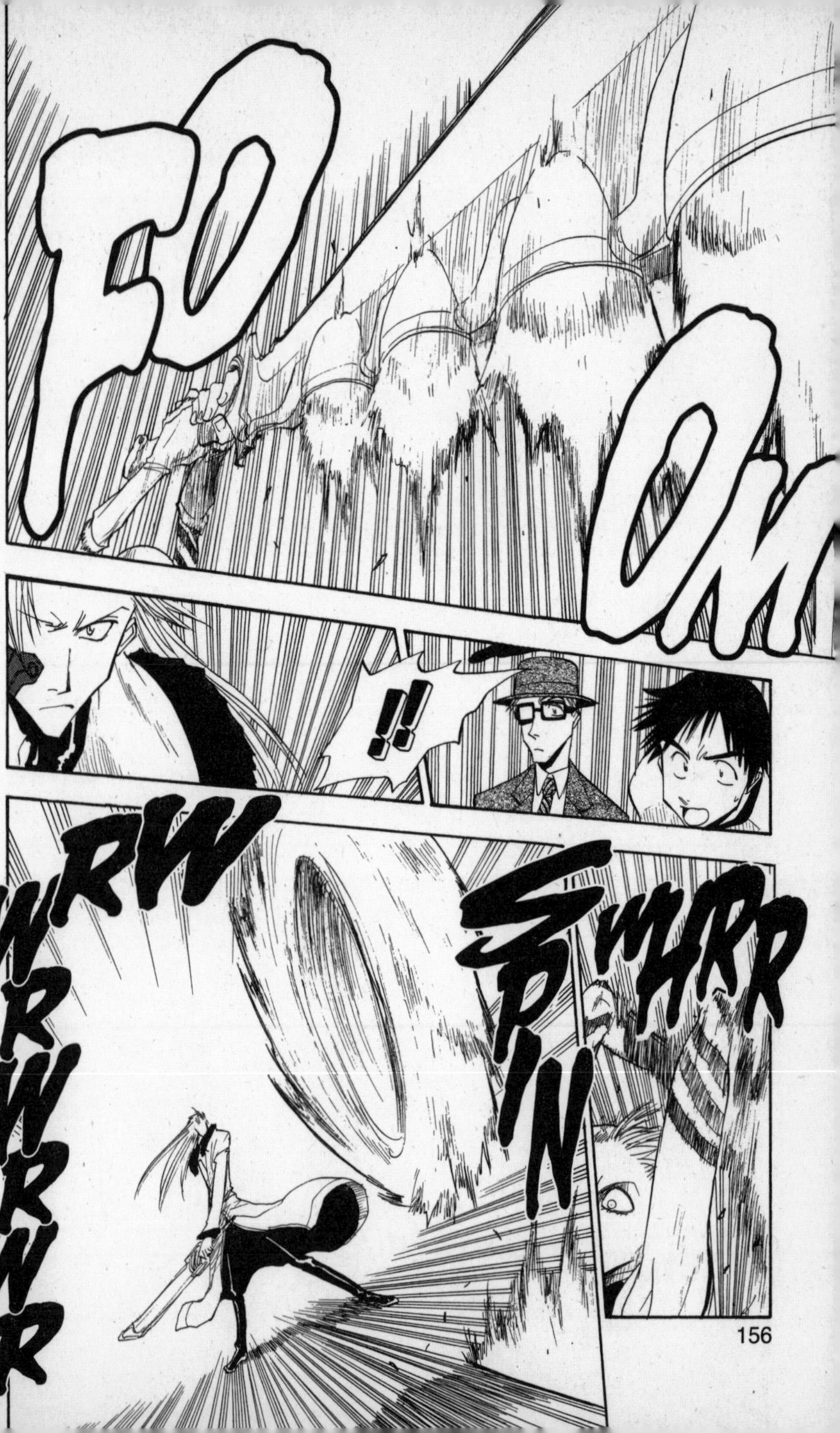
FOOM
!!
SWHRR
SPIN
WRWRWRWRWR

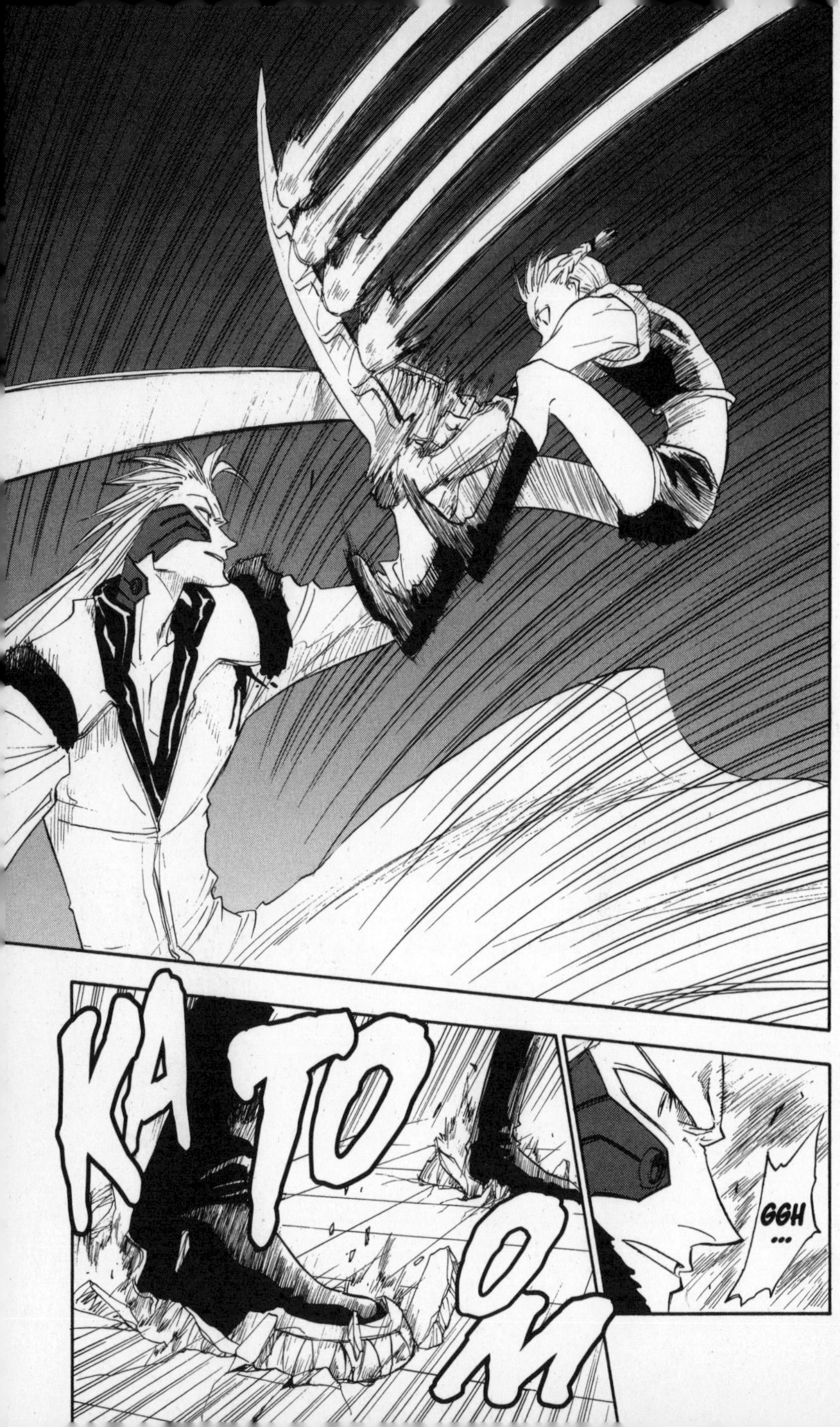
GGH...
KATOOM

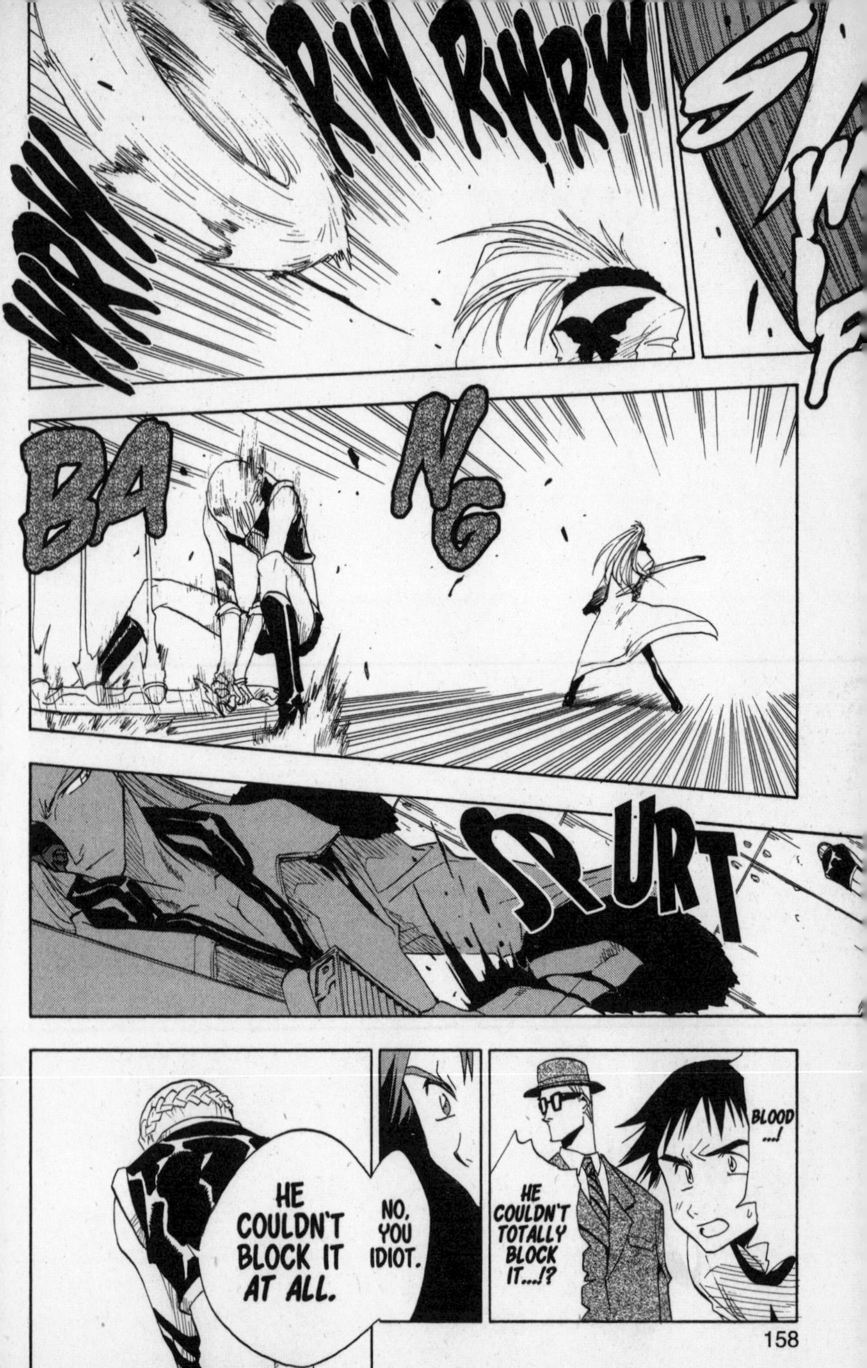
BANG
SPURT
BLOOD ...!
HE COULDN'T TOTALLY BLOCK IT...!?
NO, YOU IDIOT.
HE COULDN'T BLOCK IT AT ALL.

READ THIS WAY

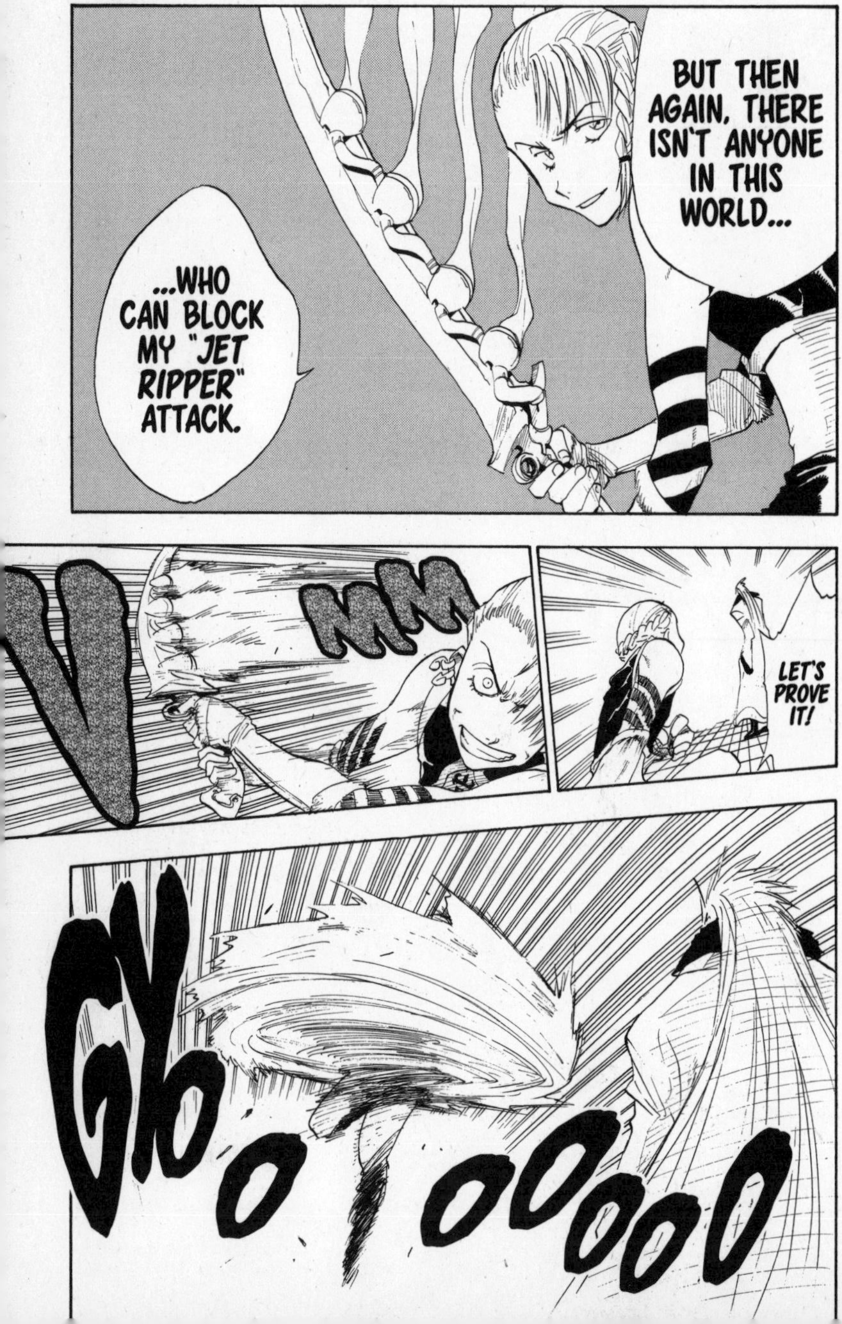
BUT THEN AGAIN, THERE ISN'T ANYONE IN THIS WORLD...
...WHO CAN BLOCK MY "JET RIPPER" ATTACK.
LET'S PROVE IT!
VMM
GOOOOOOOO

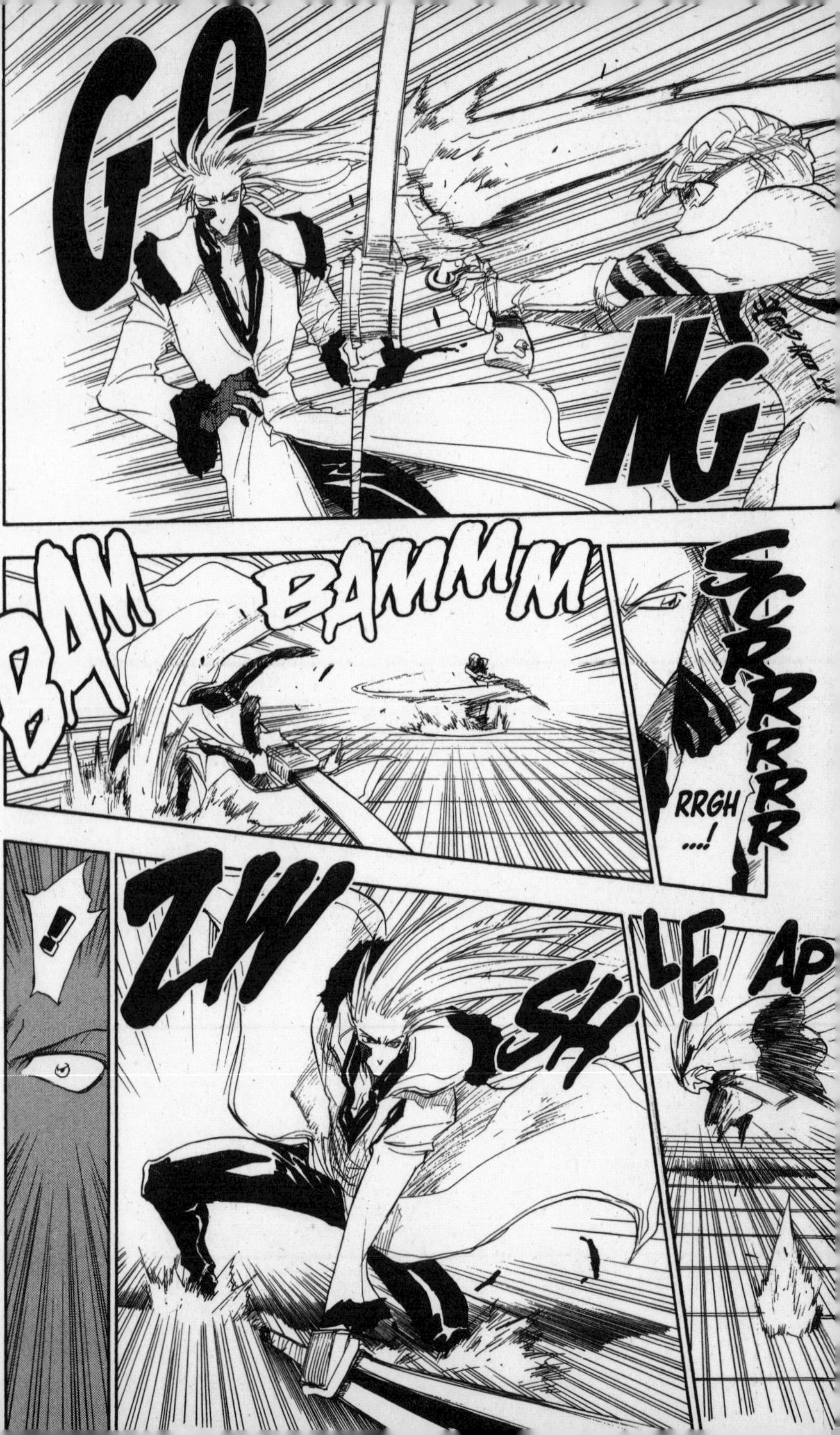
GONG
SCRRRRR
RRGH ...!
BAM
BAMMM
LEAP
ZWSH
!

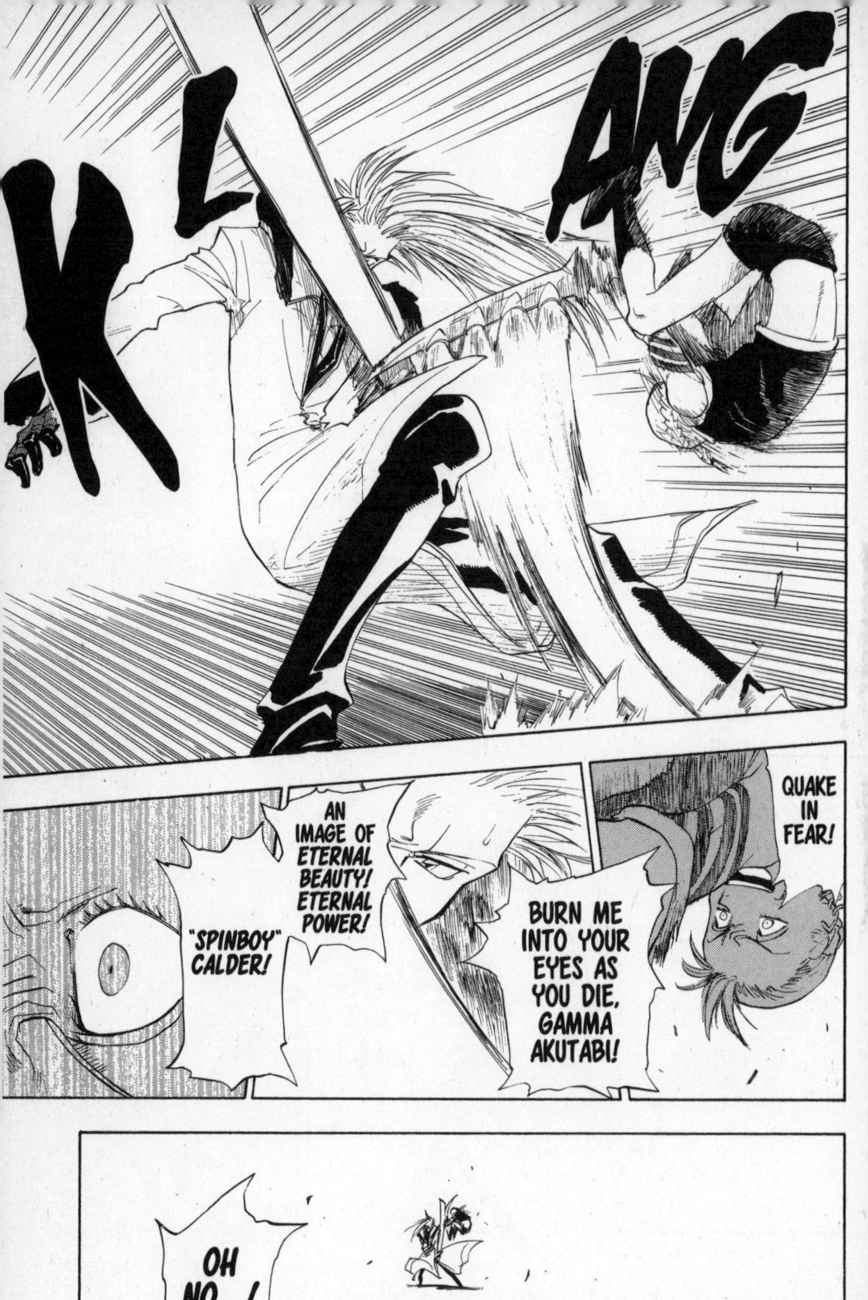
KLANG
QUAKE IN FEAR!
BURN ME INTO YOUR EYES AS YOU DIE, GAMMA AKUTABI!
AN IMAGE OF ETERNAL BEAUTY! ETERNAL POWER!
"SPINBOY" CALDER!
OH NO...!

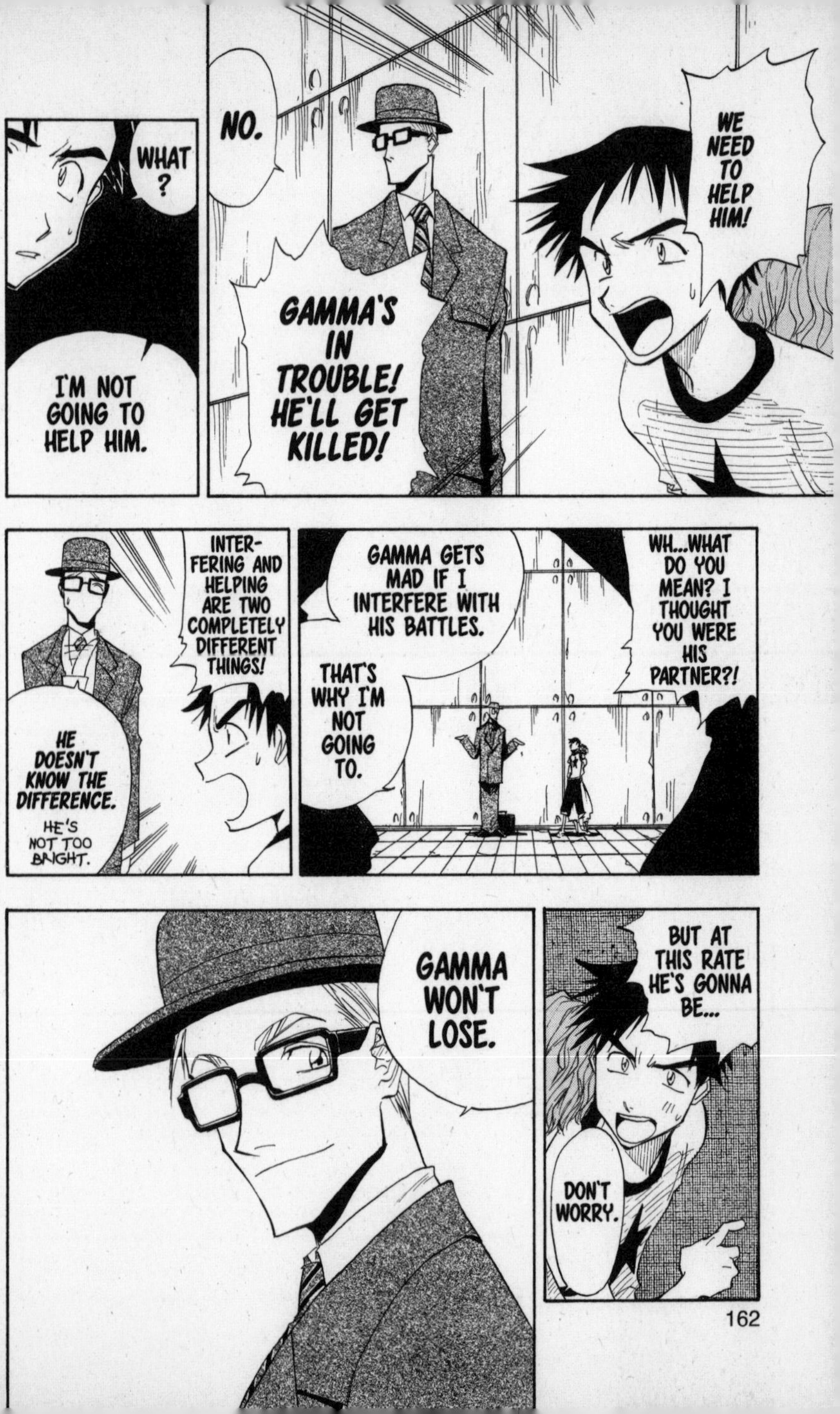

WE NEED TO HELP HIM!
NO.
GAMMA'S IN TROUBLE! HE'LL GET KILLED!
WHAT?
I'M NOT GOING TO HELP HIM.
WH...WHAT DO YOU MEAN? I THOUGHT YOU WERE HIS PARTNER?!
GAMMA GETS MAD IF I INTERFERE WITH HIS BATTLES.
THAT'S WHY I'M NOT GOING TO.
INTER-FERING AND HELPING ARE TWO COMPLETELY DIFFERENT THINGS!
HE DOESN'T KNOW THE DIFFERENCE.
HE'S NOT TOO BRIGHT.
BUT AT THIS RATE HE'S GONNA BE...
DON'T WORRY.
GAMMA WON'T LOSE.

READ THIS WAY

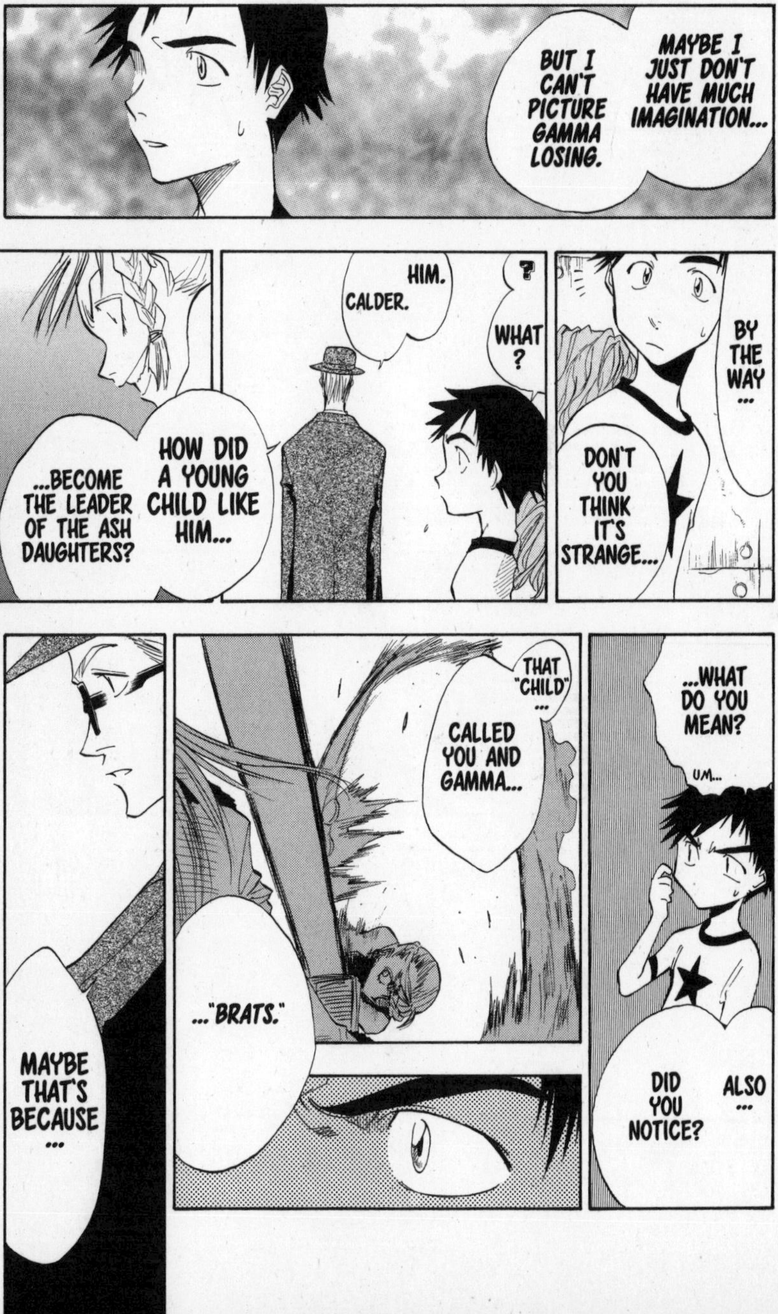
MAYBE I JUST DON'T HAVE MUCH IMAGINATION...
BUT I CAN'T PICTURE GAMMA LOSING.
BY THE WAY...
DON'T YOU THINK IT'S STRANGE...
?
WHAT?
HIM. CALDER.
HOW DID A YOUNG CHILD LIKE HIM...
...BECOME THE LEADER OF THE ASH DAUGHTERS?
...WHAT DO YOU MEAN?
UM...
ALSO...
DID YOU NOTICE?
THAT "CHILD"...
CALLED YOU AND GAMMA...
..."BRATS."
MAYBE THAT'S BECAUSE...

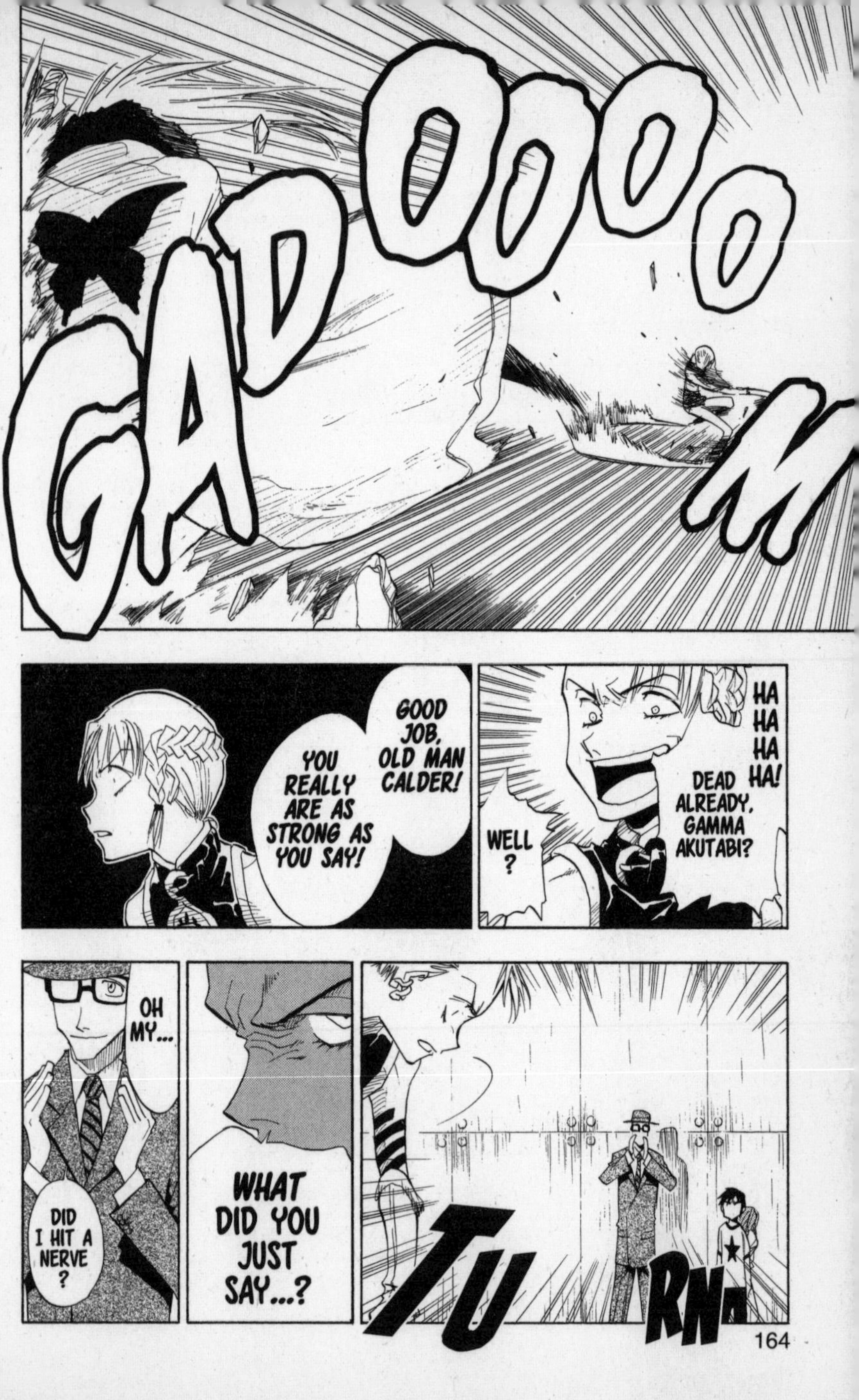
GADOOOOOM
HA HA HA HA!
DEAD ALREADY, GAMMA AKUTABI?
WELL ?
GOOD JOB, OLD MAN CALDER!
YOU REALLY ARE AS STRONG AS YOU SAY!
TURN
WHAT DID YOU JUST SAY...?
OH MY...
DID I HIT A NERVE ?

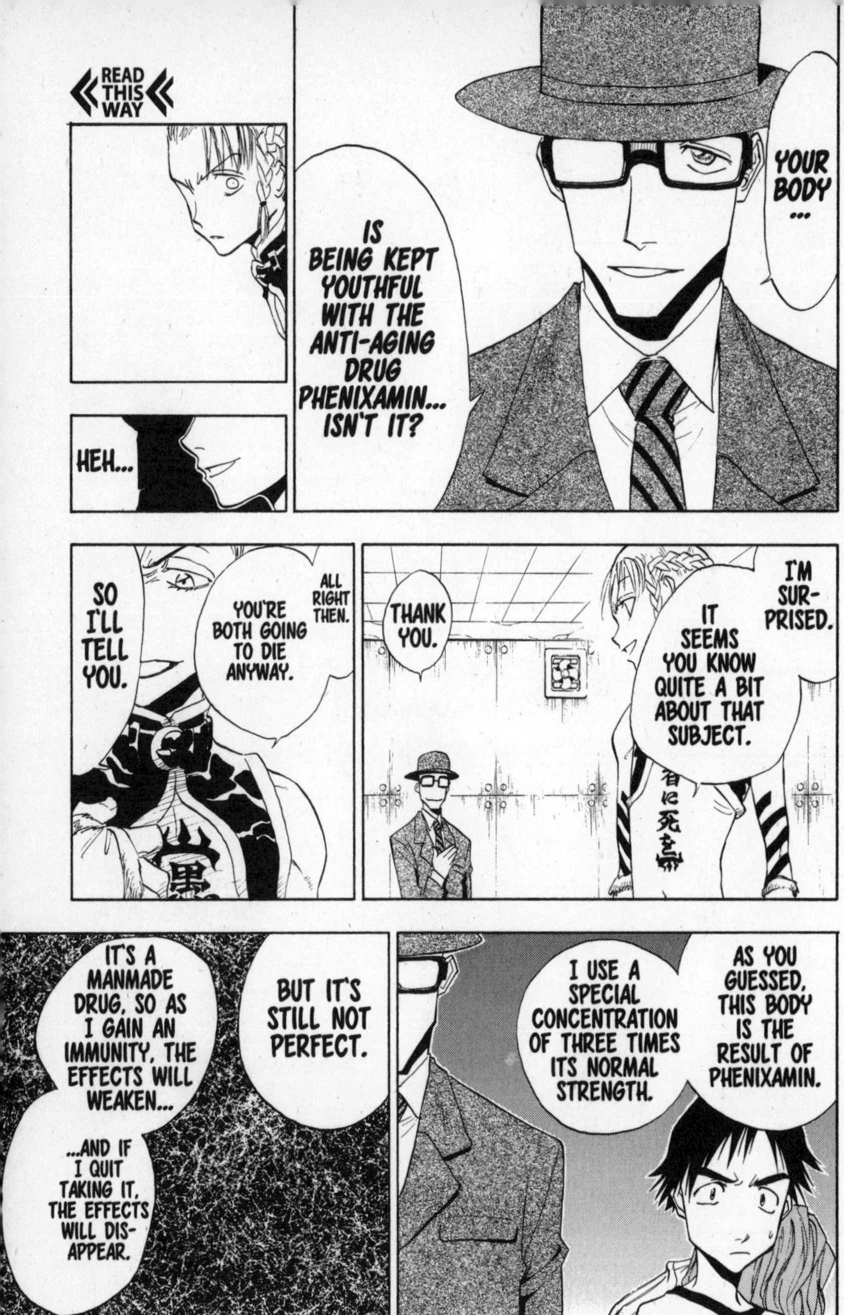
READ THIS WAY
YOUR BODY...
IS BEING KEPT YOUTHFUL WITH THE ANTI-AGING DRUG PHENIXAMIN... ISN'T IT?
HEH...
I'M SURPRISED.
IT SEEMS YOU KNOW QUITE A BIT ABOUT THAT SUBJECT.
THANK YOU.
ALL RIGHT THEN.
YOU'RE BOTH GOING TO DIE ANYWAY.
SO I'LL TELL YOU.
AS YOU GUESSED, THIS BODY IS THE RESULT OF PHENIXAMIN.
I USE A SPECIAL CONCENTRATION OF THREE TIMES ITS NORMAL STRENGTH.
BUT IT'S STILL NOT PERFECT.
IT'S A MANMADE DRUG, SO AS I GAIN AN IMMUNITY, THE EFFECTS WILL WEAKEN...
...AND IF I QUIT TAKING IT, THE EFFECTS WILL DISAPPEAR.

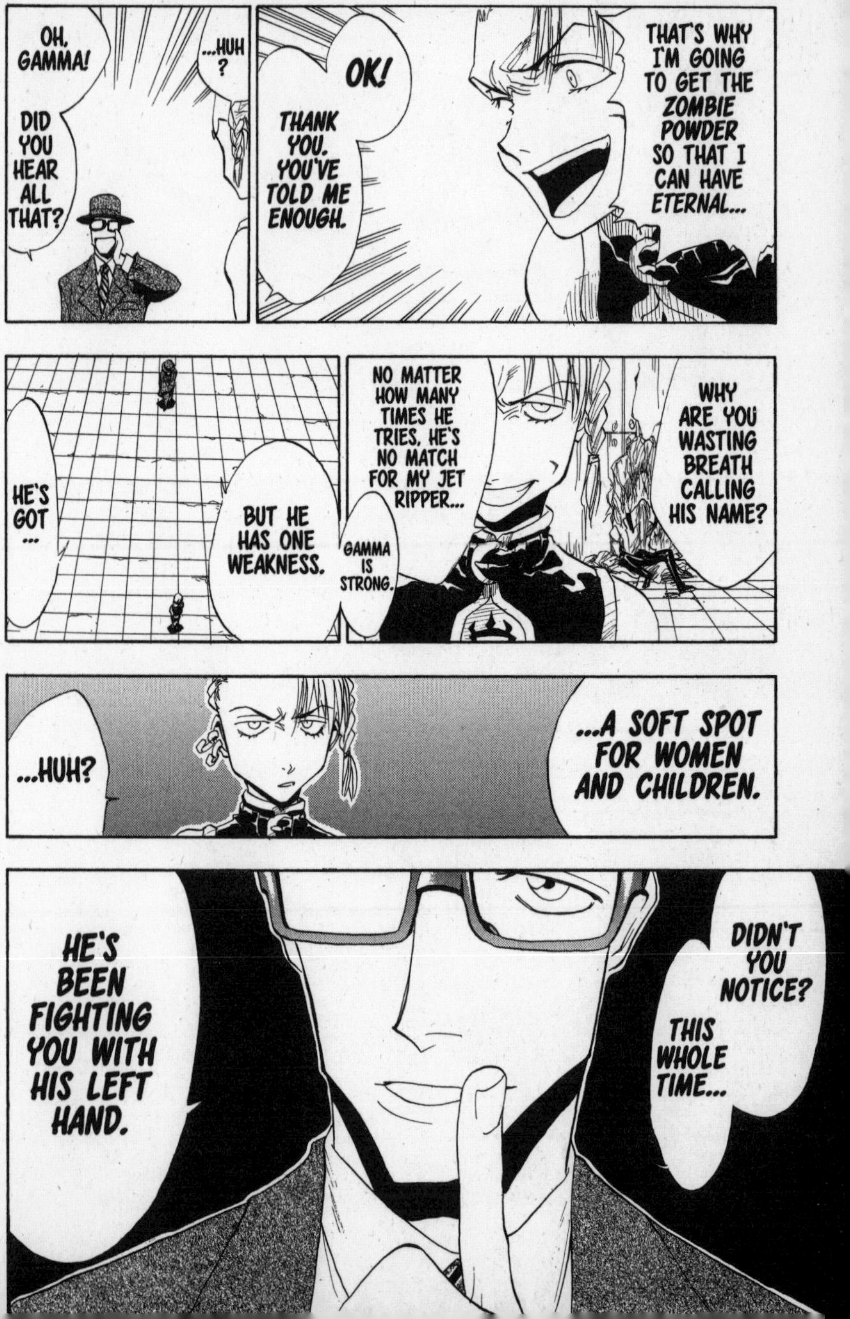
THAT'S WHY I'M GOING TO GET THE ZOMBIE POWDER SO THAT I CAN HAVE ETERNAL...
OK!
THANK YOU. YOU'VE TOLD ME ENOUGH.
...HUH?
OH, GAMMA!
DID YOU HEAR ALL THAT?
WHY ARE YOU WASTING BREATH CALLING HIS NAME?
NO MATTER HOW MANY TIMES HE TRIES, HE'S NO MATCH FOR MY JET RIPPER...
GAMMA IS STRONG.
BUT HE HAS ONE WEAKNESS.
HE'S GOT ...
...A SOFT SPOT FOR WOMEN AND CHILDREN.
...HUH?
DIDN'T YOU NOTICE?
THIS WHOLE TIME...
HE'S BEEN FIGHTING YOU WITH HIS LEFT HAND.

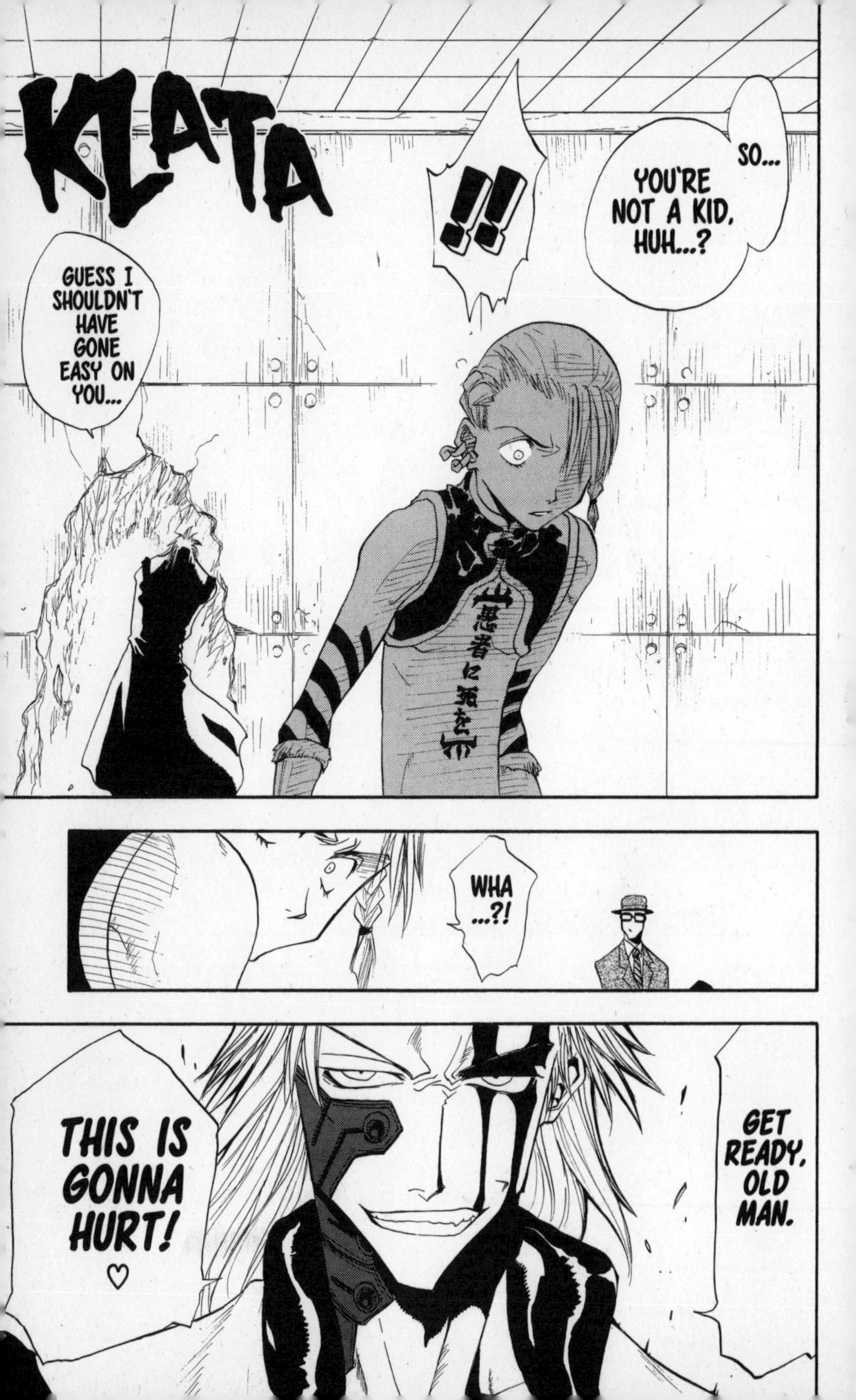
SO... YOU'RE NOT A KID, HUH...?
!!
KLATA
GUESS I SHOULDN'T HAVE GONE EASY ON YOU...
愚者に死を
WHA...?!
GET READY, OLD MAN.
THIS IS GONNA HURT! ♡

B-side NAKED MONKEYS 5.

Ranewater Calder
レーンウォーター・キャルダー

Height: 158 cm.
Weight: 43 kg.
Date of Birth: March 4
Age: Unknown
Blood Type: BB

Calder, an extreme narcissist, has passionate fans among some of the female readers. I got a lot of requests from readers who wanted to see him with his hair down, so I decided to draw him like that.

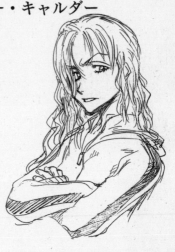

Kuāng Jonathan Bacley
鄺・ジョナサン・バックリィ

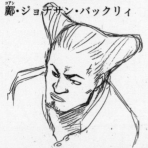

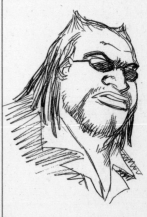

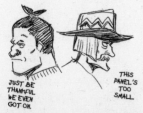

JUST BE THANKFUL WE EVEN GOT ON.
THIS PANEL'S TOO SMALL

Daniel Rubeck & Diran Tobin
ダニエル・ルーベック&ディラン・トービン

There weren't too many requests to see these guys, but I felt bad for them since they died right away so I decided to at least reveal their full names. I really like Bacley's hairstyle.

Mujata Colvin Kinqro
ムジャータ・コルヴィン・キンクロ

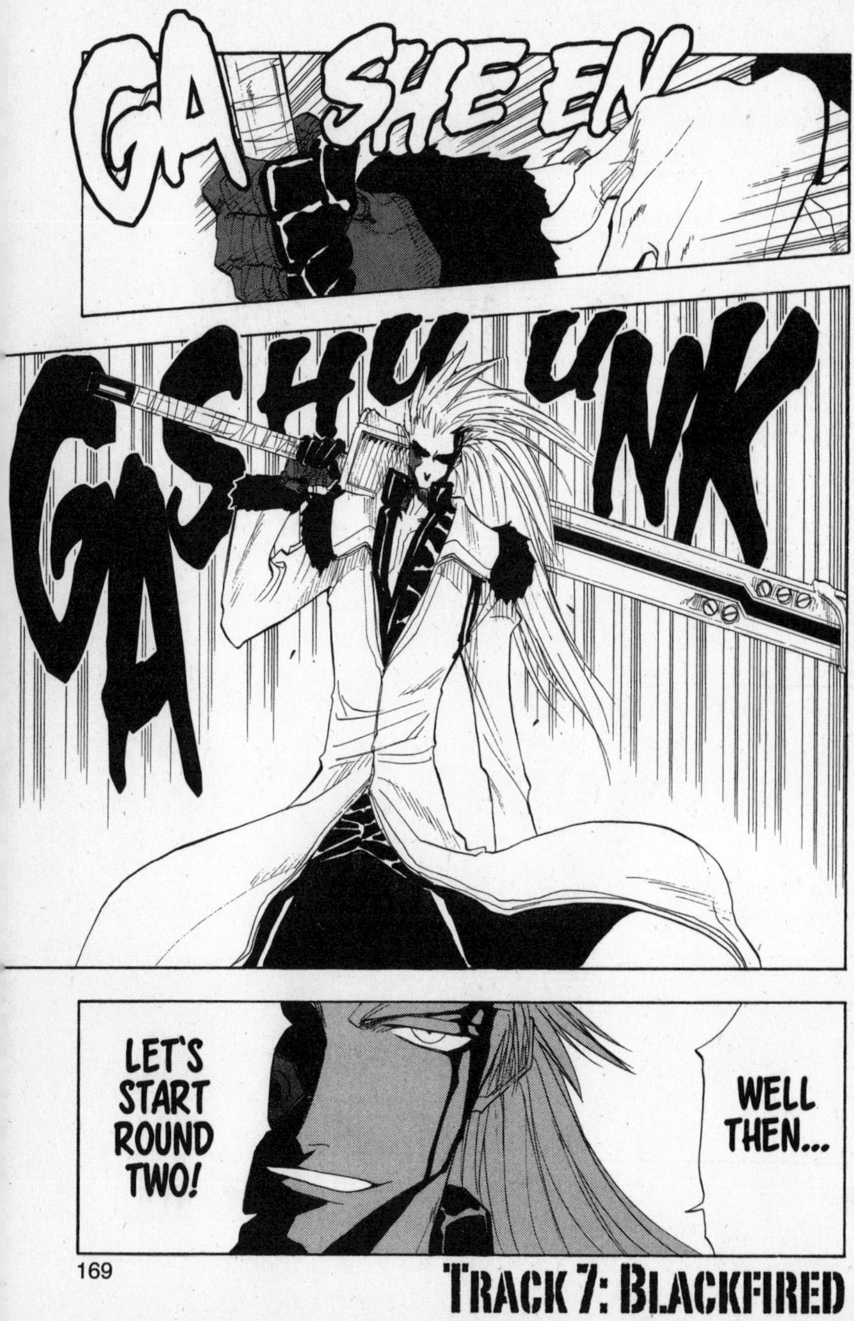
GA SHE EN
GASHU UNK
WELL THEN...
LET'S START ROUND TWO!

TRACK 7: BLACKFIRED

TRACK 7:
BLACKFIRED

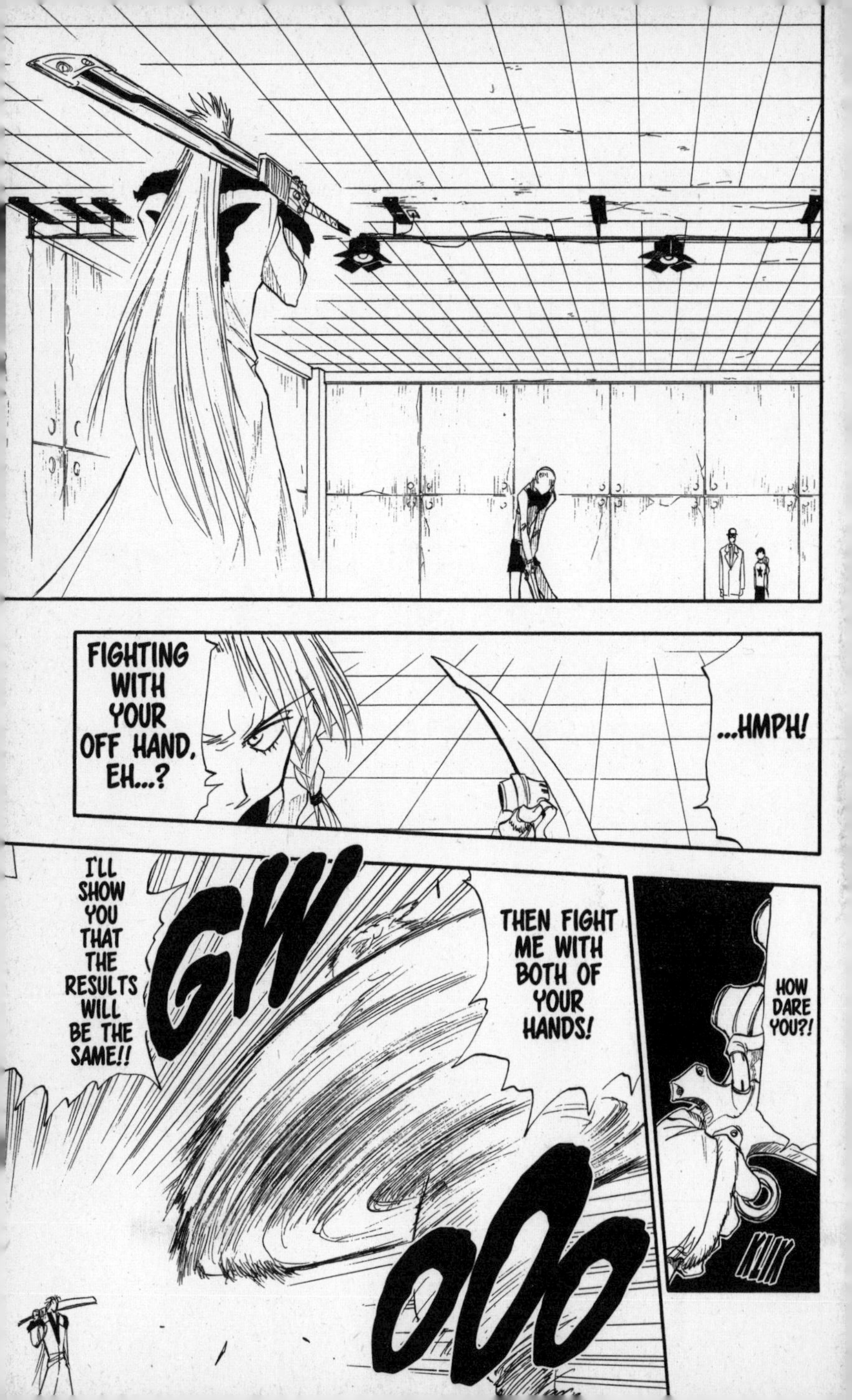
...HMPH!
FIGHTING WITH YOUR OFF HAND, EH...?
HOW DARE YOU?!
KLIK
THEN FIGHT ME WITH BOTH OF YOUR HANDS!
I'LL SHOW YOU THAT THE RESULTS WILL BE THE SAME!!
GWOOO

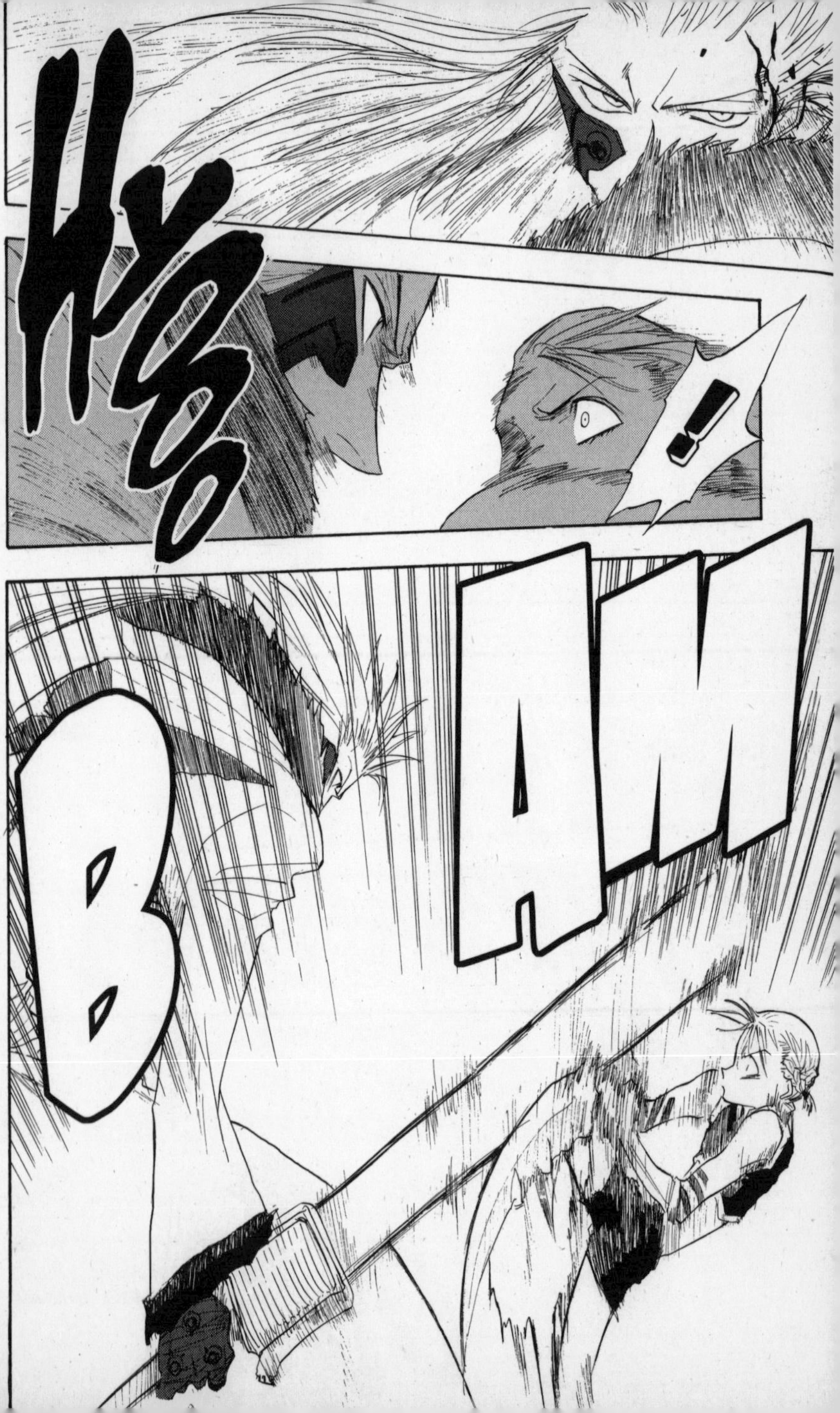
!
BAM

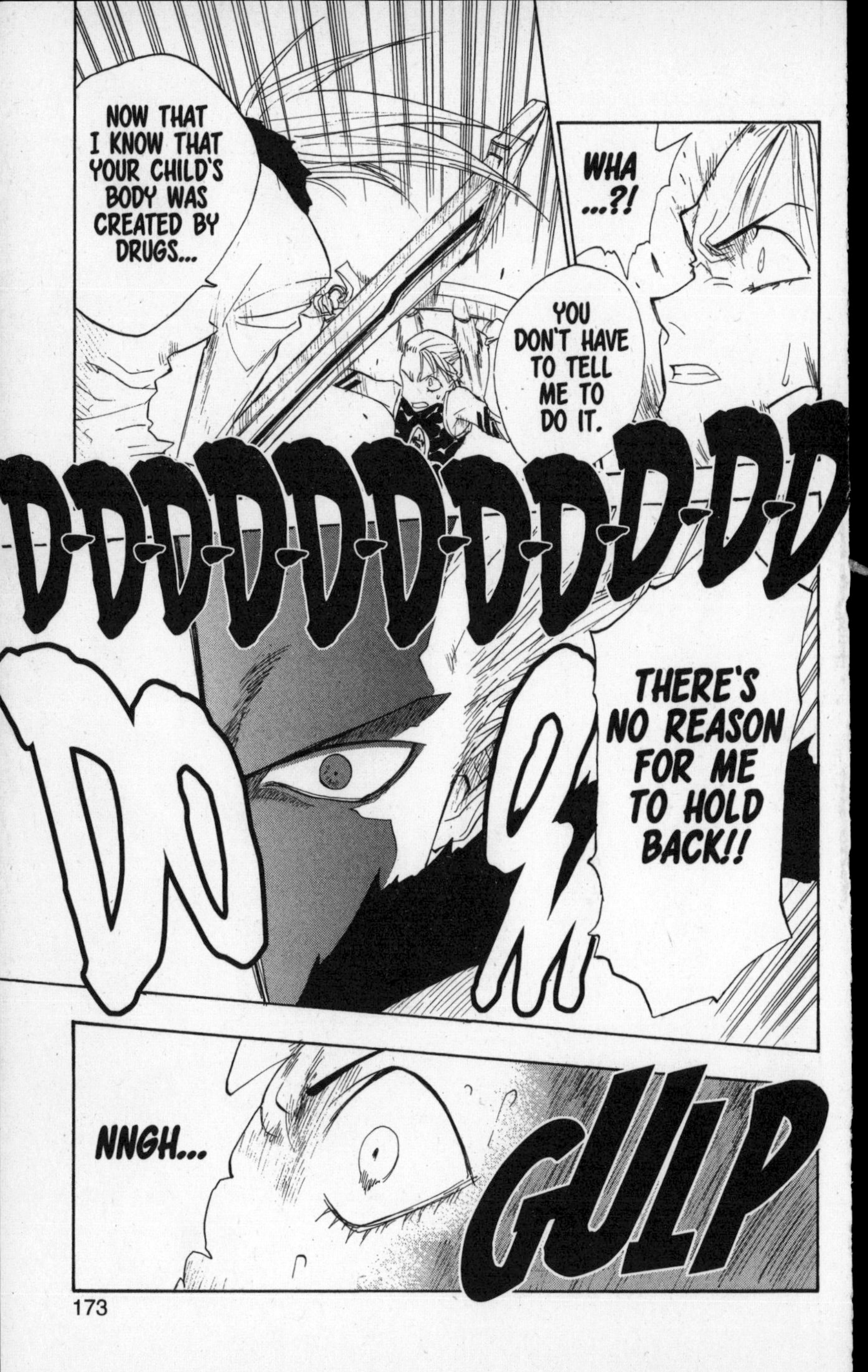
WHA ...?!
YOU DON'T HAVE TO TELL ME TO DO IT.
NOW THAT I KNOW THAT YOUR CHILD'S BODY WAS CREATED BY DRUGS...
D-D-D-D-D-D-D-D-D-D-D-D-D
THERE'S NO REASON FOR ME TO HOLD BACK!!
GULP
NNGH...

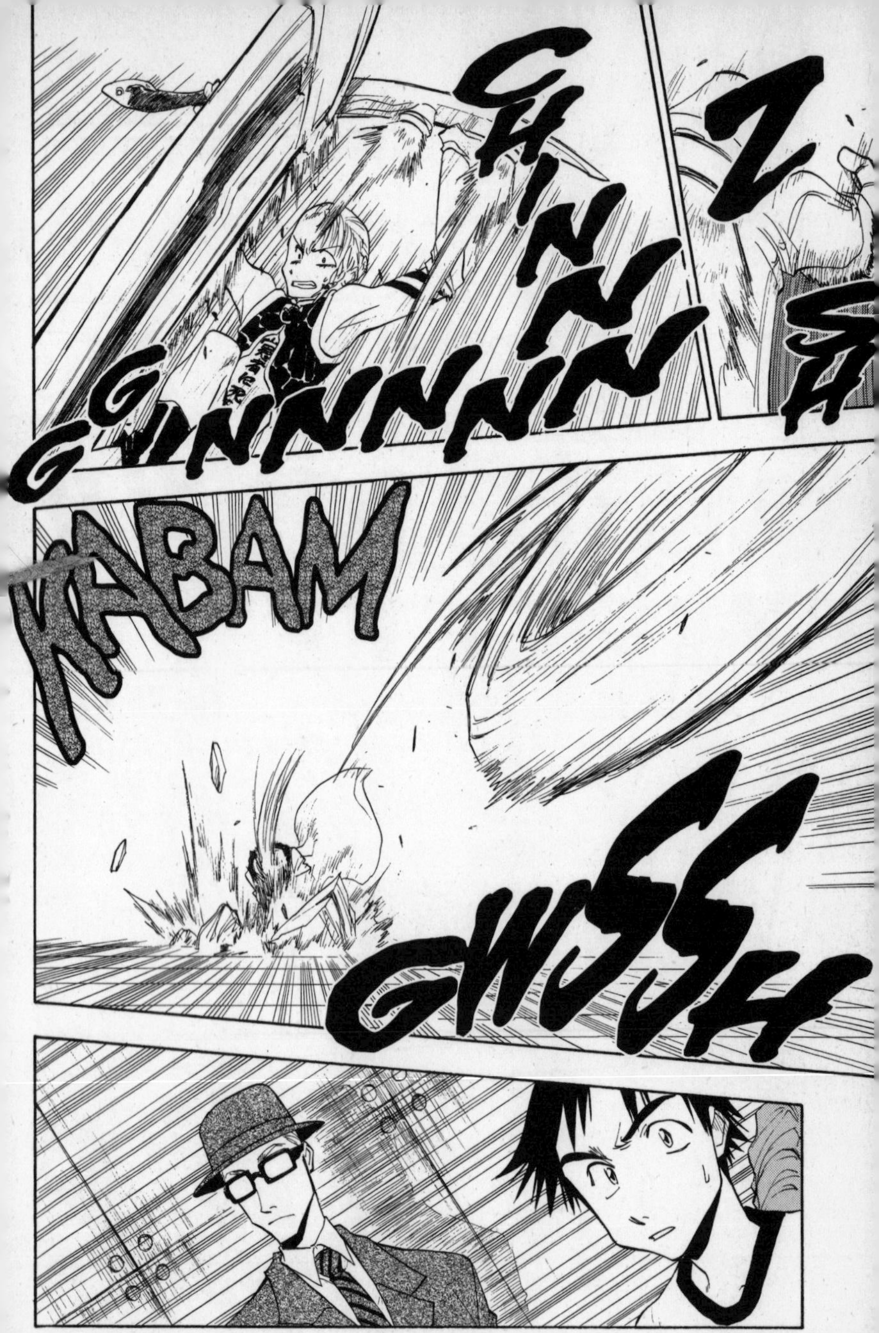
KABAM

READ THIS WAY

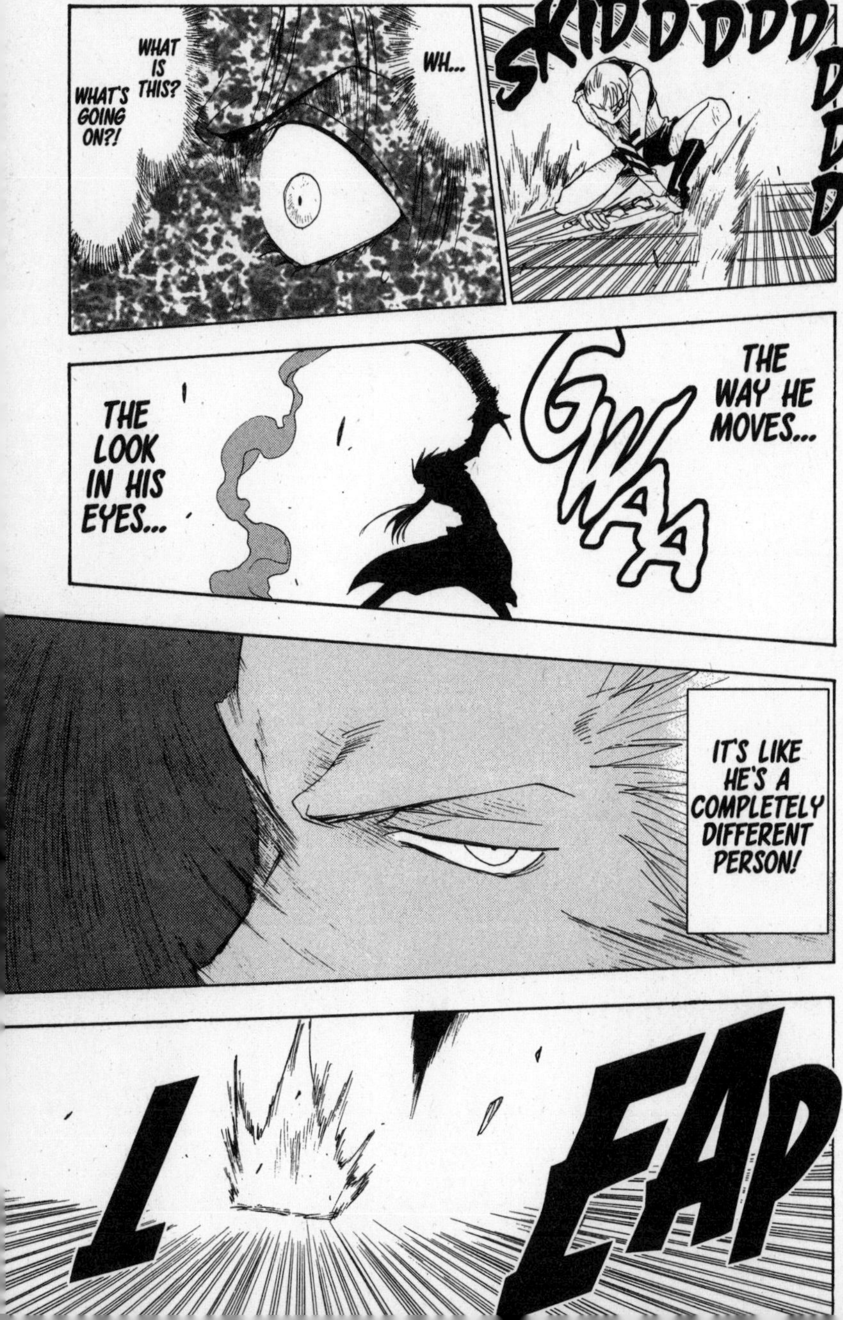
SKIDDDDDDDDD
WH...
WHAT IS THIS?
WHAT'S GOING ON?!
THE WAY HE MOVES...
GWAAA
THE LOOK IN HIS EYES...
IT'S LIKE HE'S A COMPLETELY DIFFERENT PERSON!
LEAP

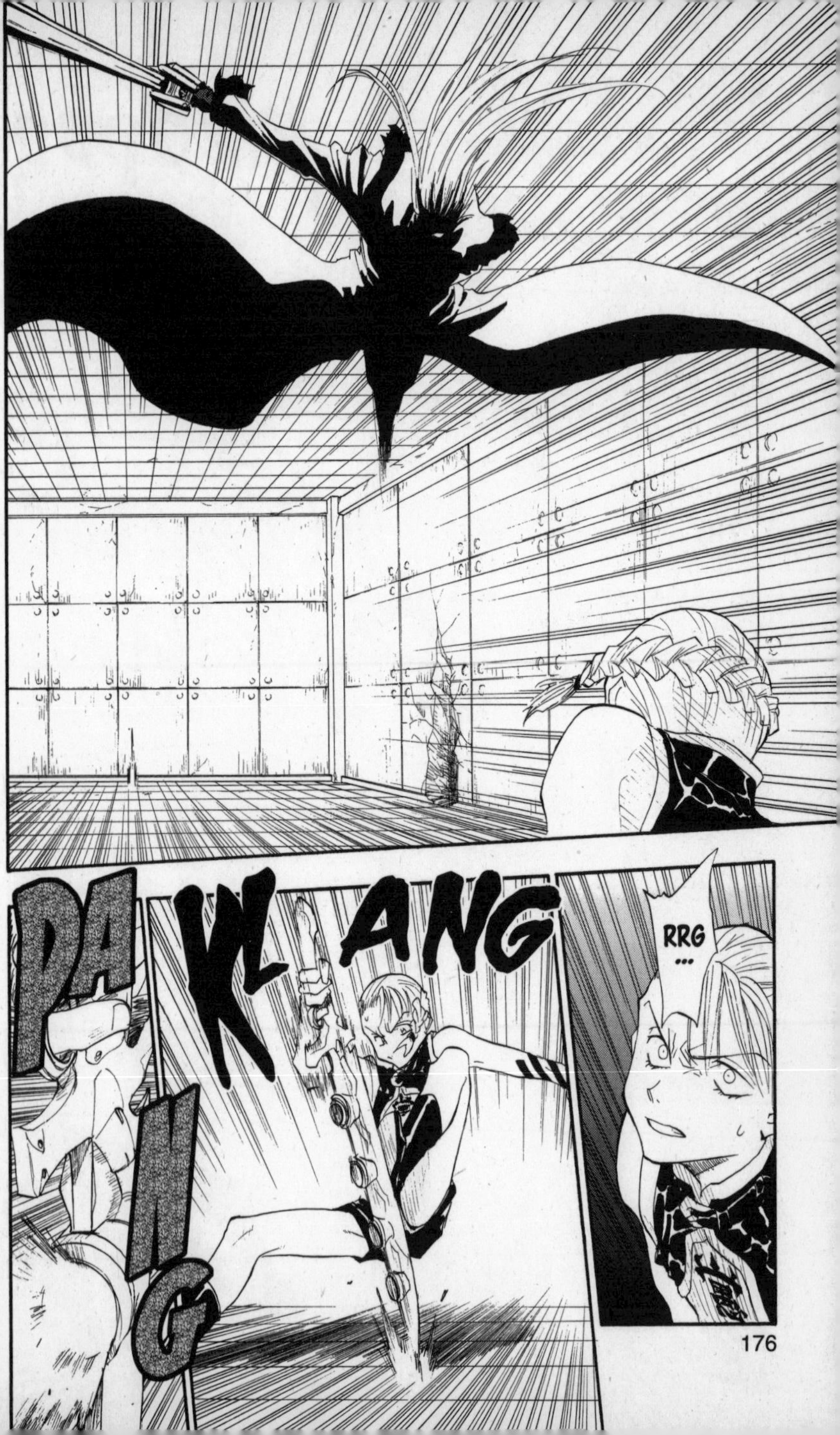
RRG ...
KLANG
PANG

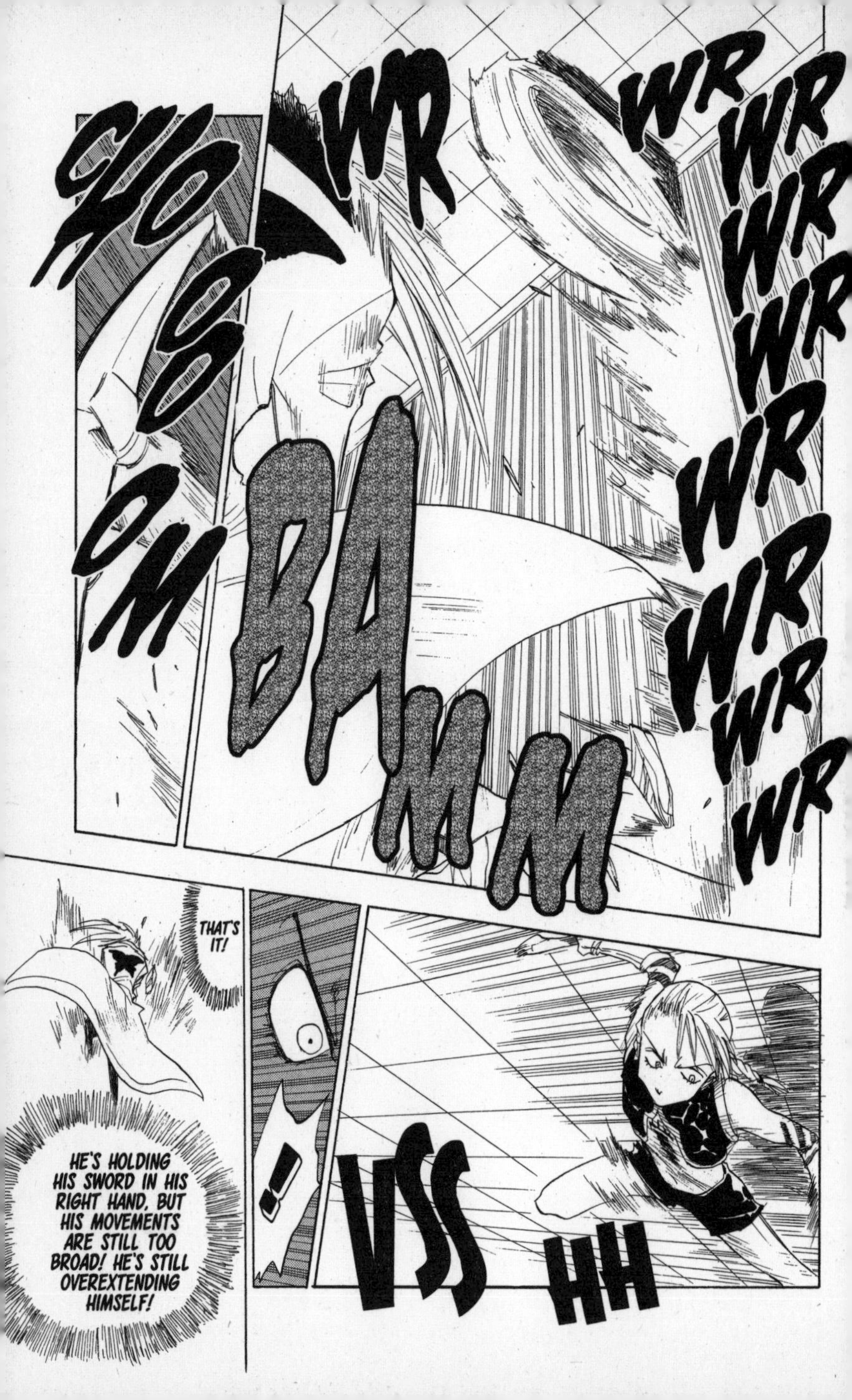
WR WR WR WR WR WR WR WR WR WR WR WR
BAMM
VSSHH
!
THAT'S IT!
HE'S HOLDING HIS SWORD IN HIS RIGHT HAND, BUT HIS MOVEMENTS ARE STILL TOO BROAD! HE'S STILL OVEREXTENDING HIMSELF!

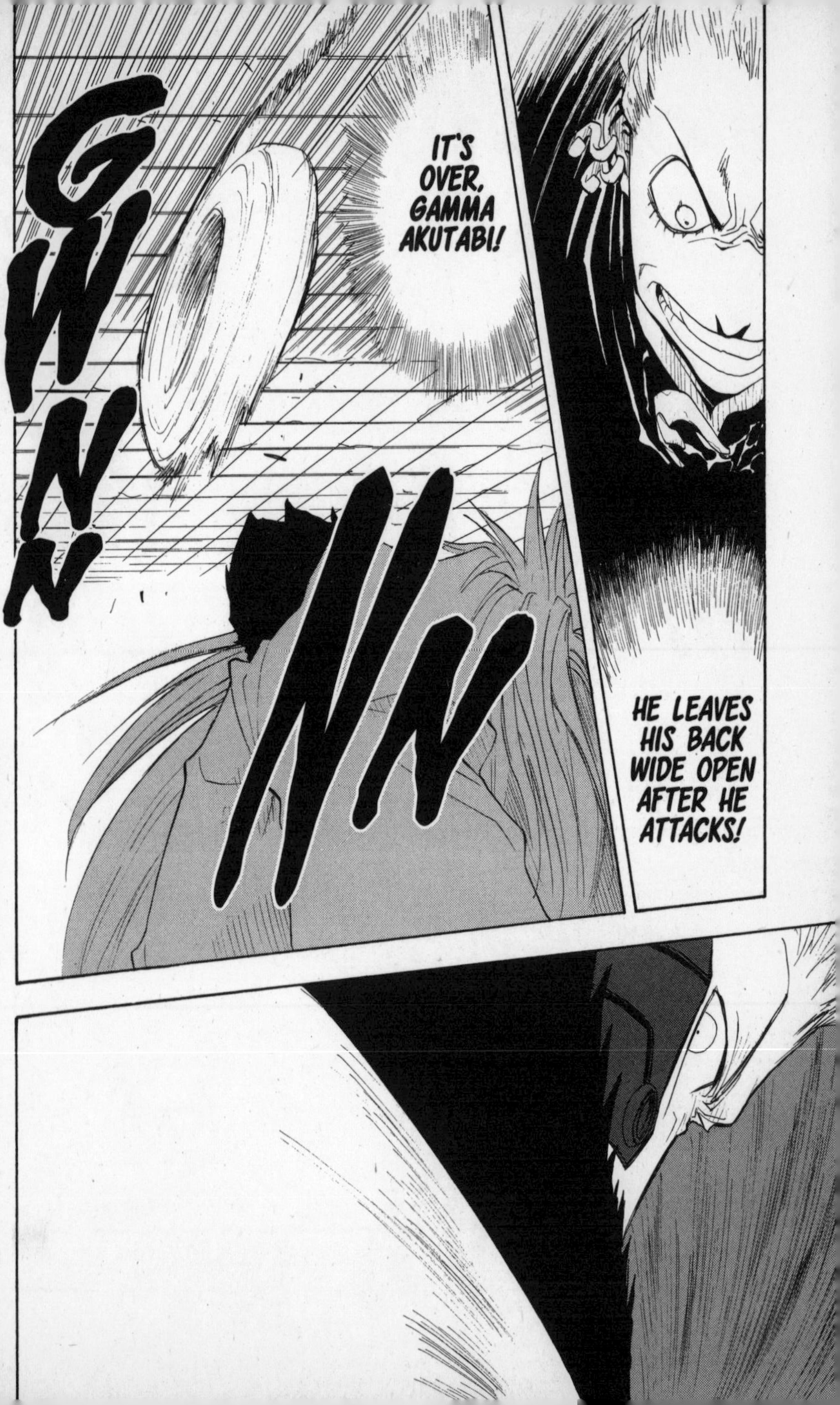
HE LEAVES HIS BACK WIDE OPEN AFTER HE ATTACKS!
IT'S OVER, GAMMA AKUTABI!
GWNNN
NN

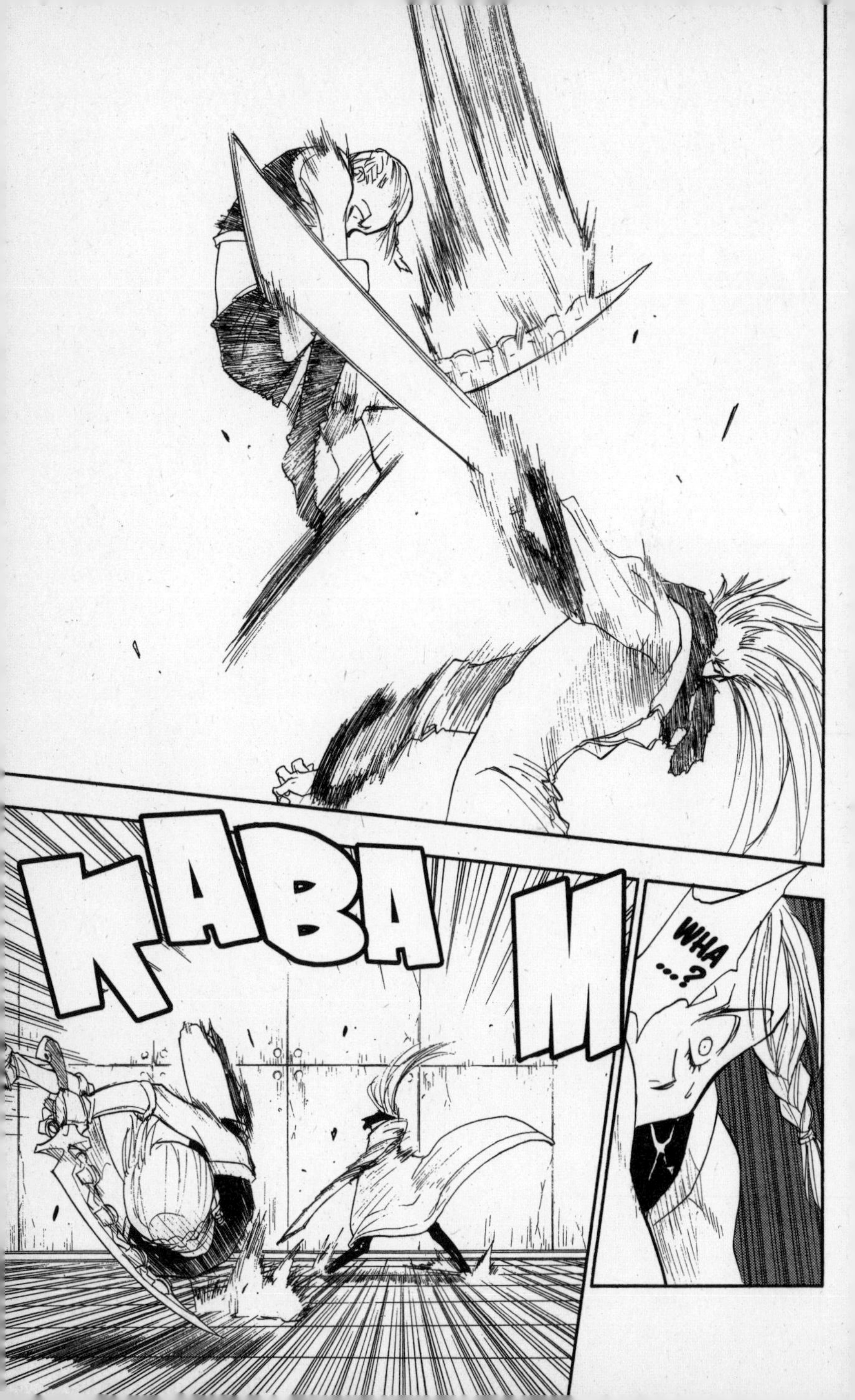
KABAM
WHA ...?

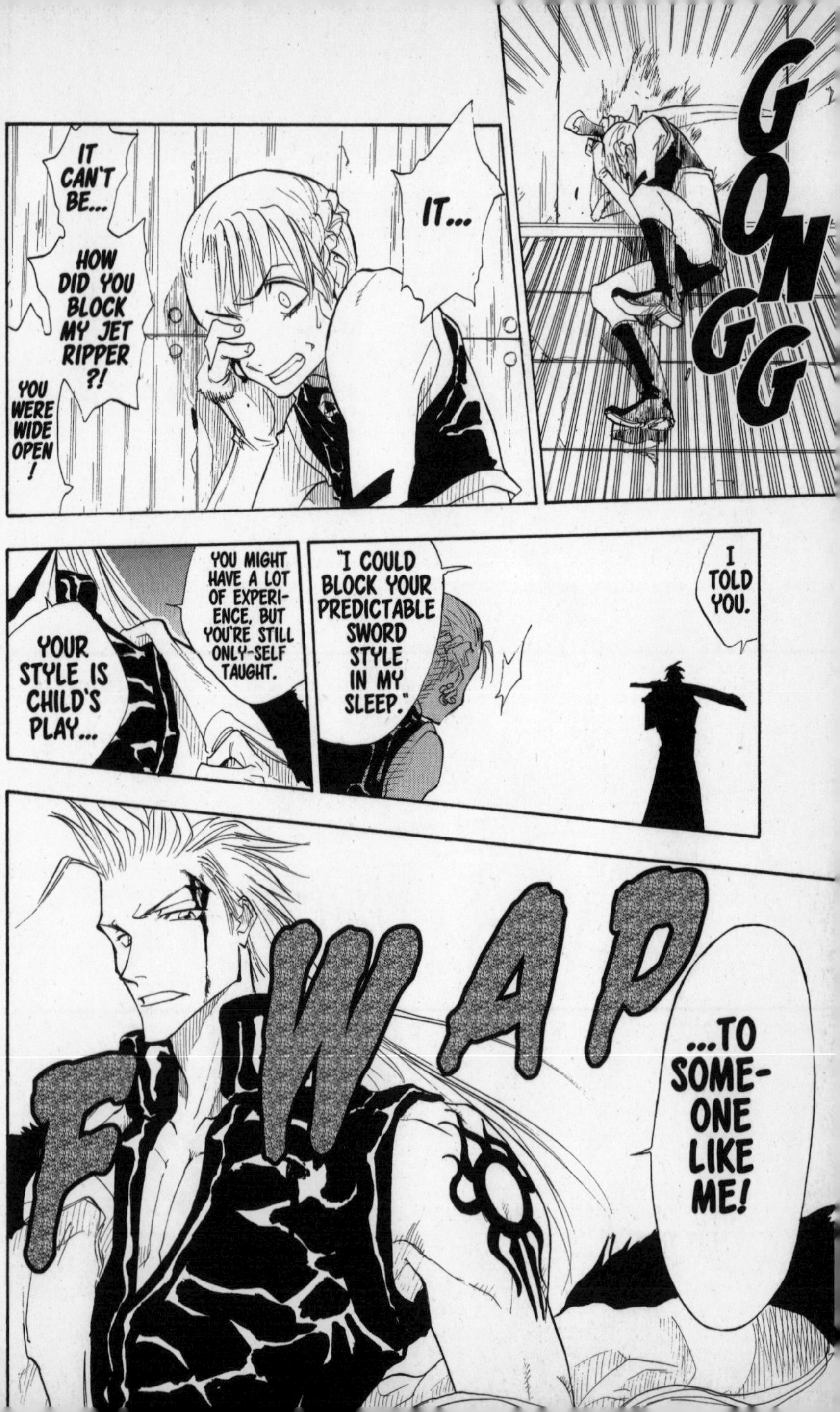
GONGG
IT...
IT CAN'T BE...
HOW DID YOU BLOCK MY JET RIPPER?!
YOU WERE WIDE OPEN!
I TOLD YOU.
"I COULD BLOCK YOUR PREDICTABLE SWORD STYLE IN MY SLEEP."
YOU MIGHT HAVE A LOT OF EXPERIENCE, BUT YOU'RE STILL ONLY-SELF TAUGHT.
YOUR STYLE IS CHILD'S PLAY...
FWAP
...TO SOMEONE LIKE ME!

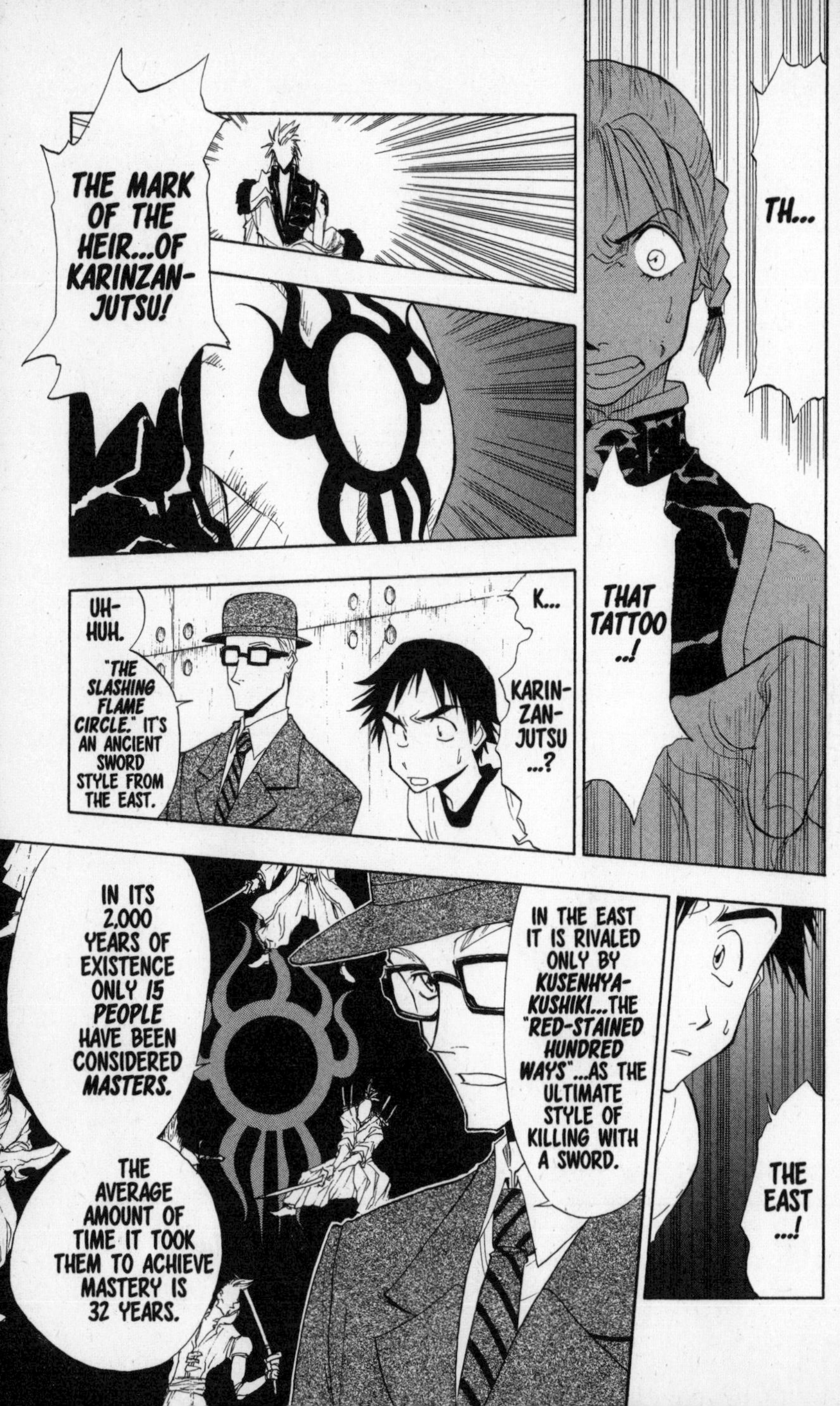
TH...
THAT TATTOO ...!
THE MARK OF THE HEIR...OF KARINZAN-JUTSU!
K...
KARIN-ZAN-JUTSU ...?
UH-HUH.
"THE SLASHING FLAME CIRCLE." IT'S AN ANCIENT SWORD STYLE FROM THE EAST.
THE EAST ...!
IN THE EAST IT IS RIVALED ONLY BY KUSENHYA-KUSHIKI...THE "RED-STAINED HUNDRED WAYS"...AS THE ULTIMATE STYLE OF KILLING WITH A SWORD.
IN ITS 2,000 YEARS OF EXISTENCE ONLY 15 PEOPLE HAVE BEEN CONSIDERED MASTERS.
THE AVERAGE AMOUNT OF TIME IT TOOK THEM TO ACHIEVE MASTERY IS 32 YEARS.

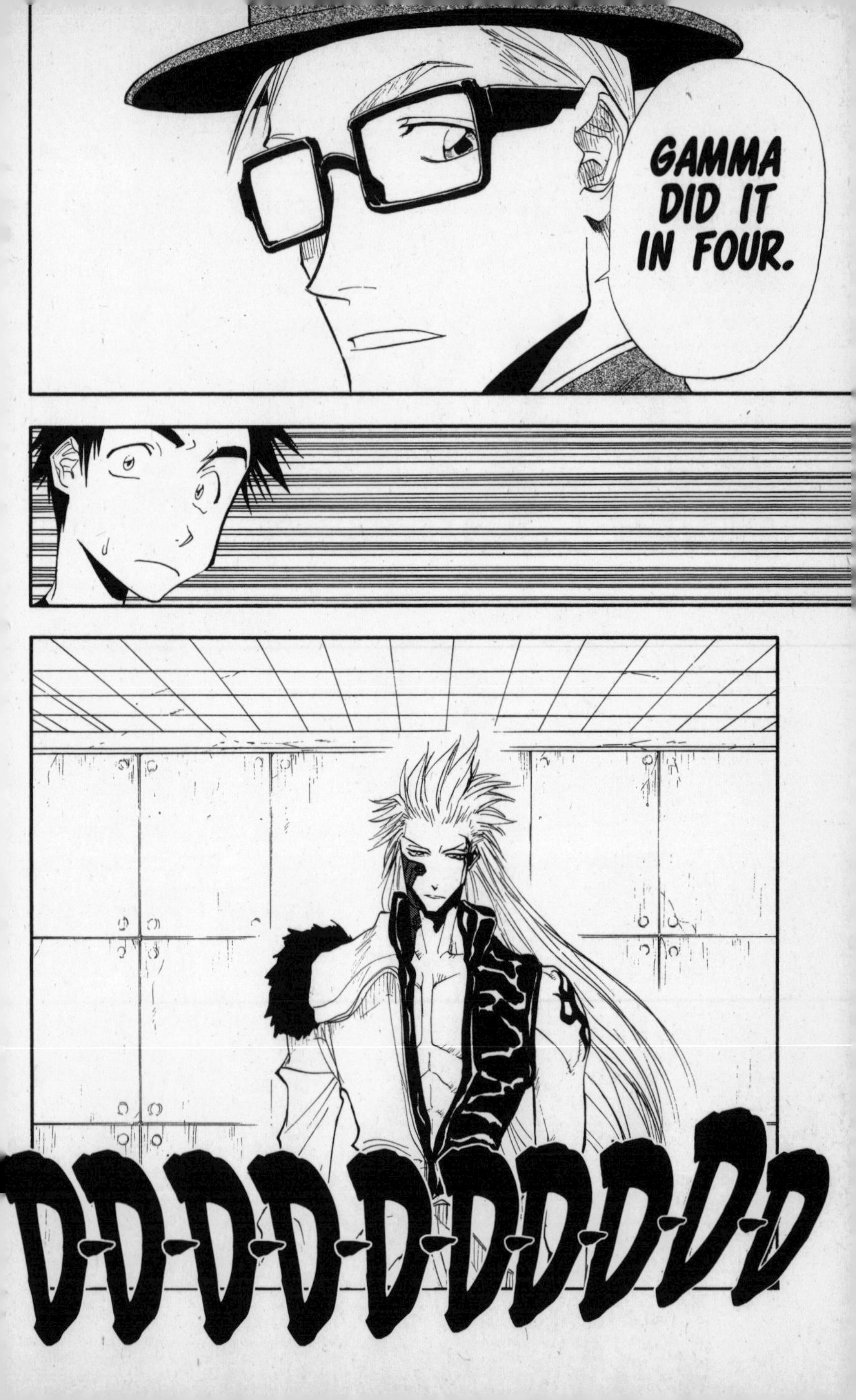
GAMMA DID IT IN FOUR.
D-D-D-D-D-D-D-D-D-D-D

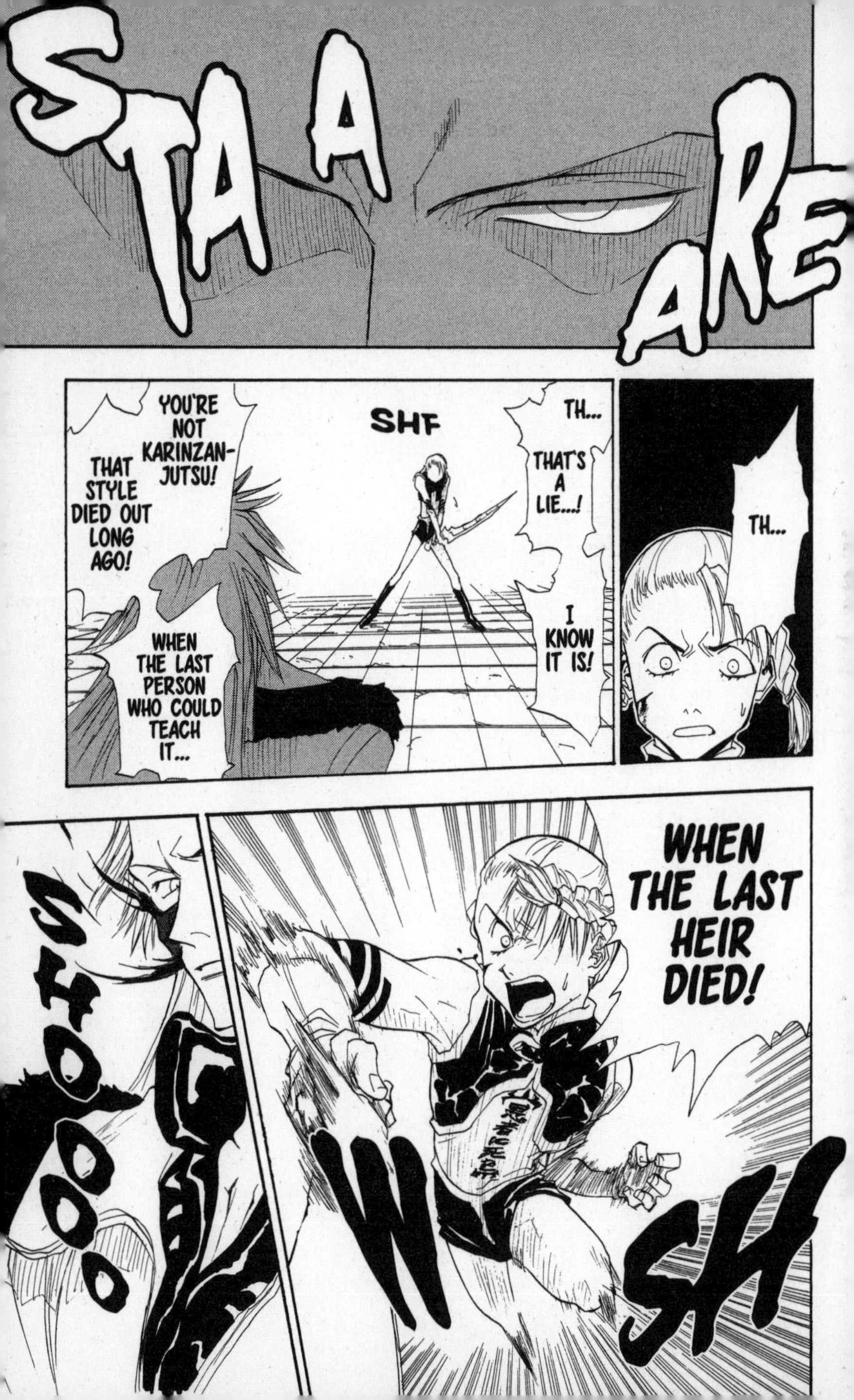
STAAARE
TH...
TH...
THAT'S A LIE...!
I KNOW IT IS!
SHF
YOU'RE NOT KARINZAN-JUTSU!
THAT STYLE DIED OUT LONG AGO!
WHEN THE LAST PERSON WHO COULD TEACH IT...
WHEN THE LAST HEIR DIED!
WHSH!
SHOOOOO

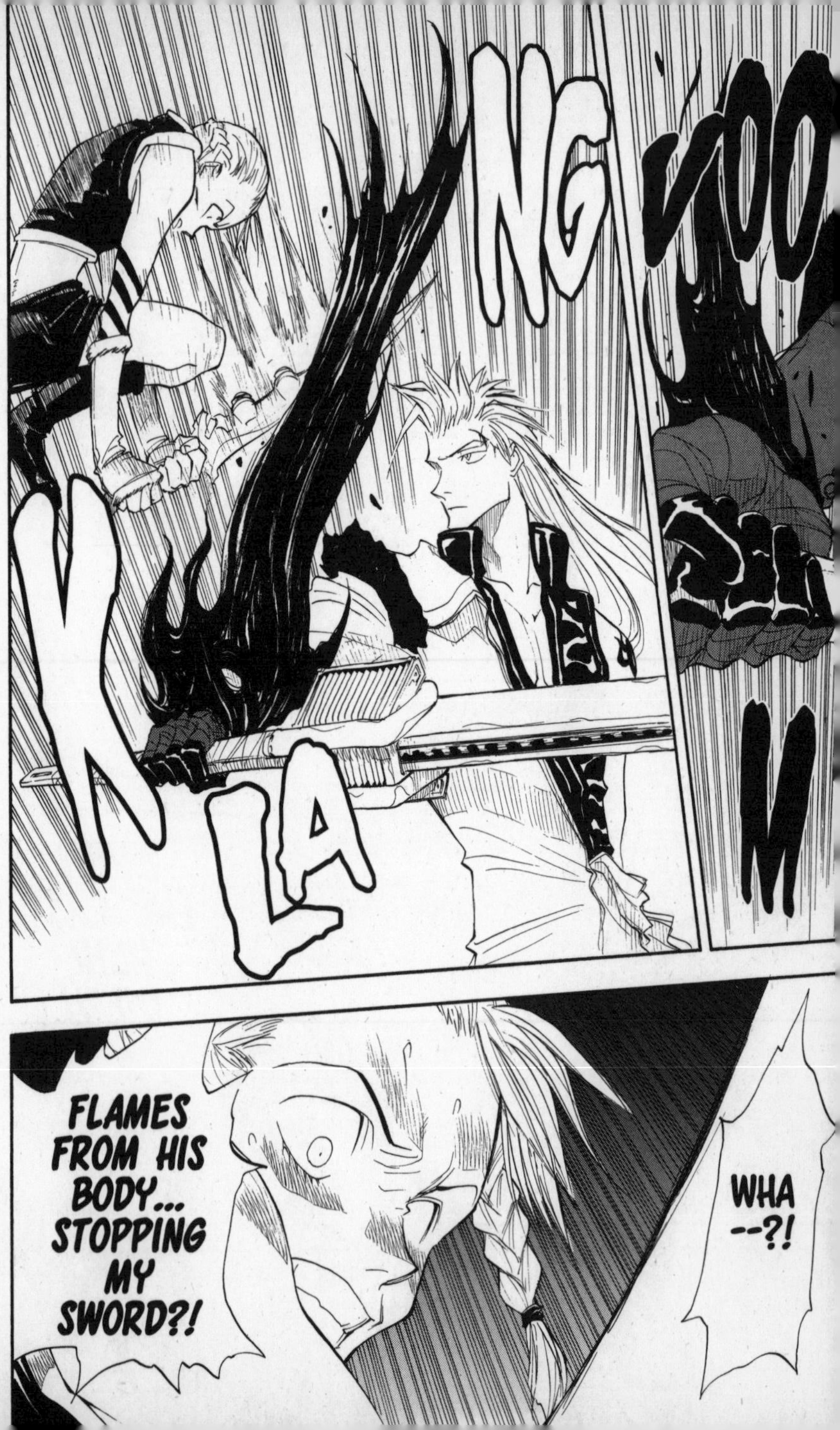
KLANG
WHA --?!
FLAMES FROM HIS BODY... STOPPING MY SWORD?!

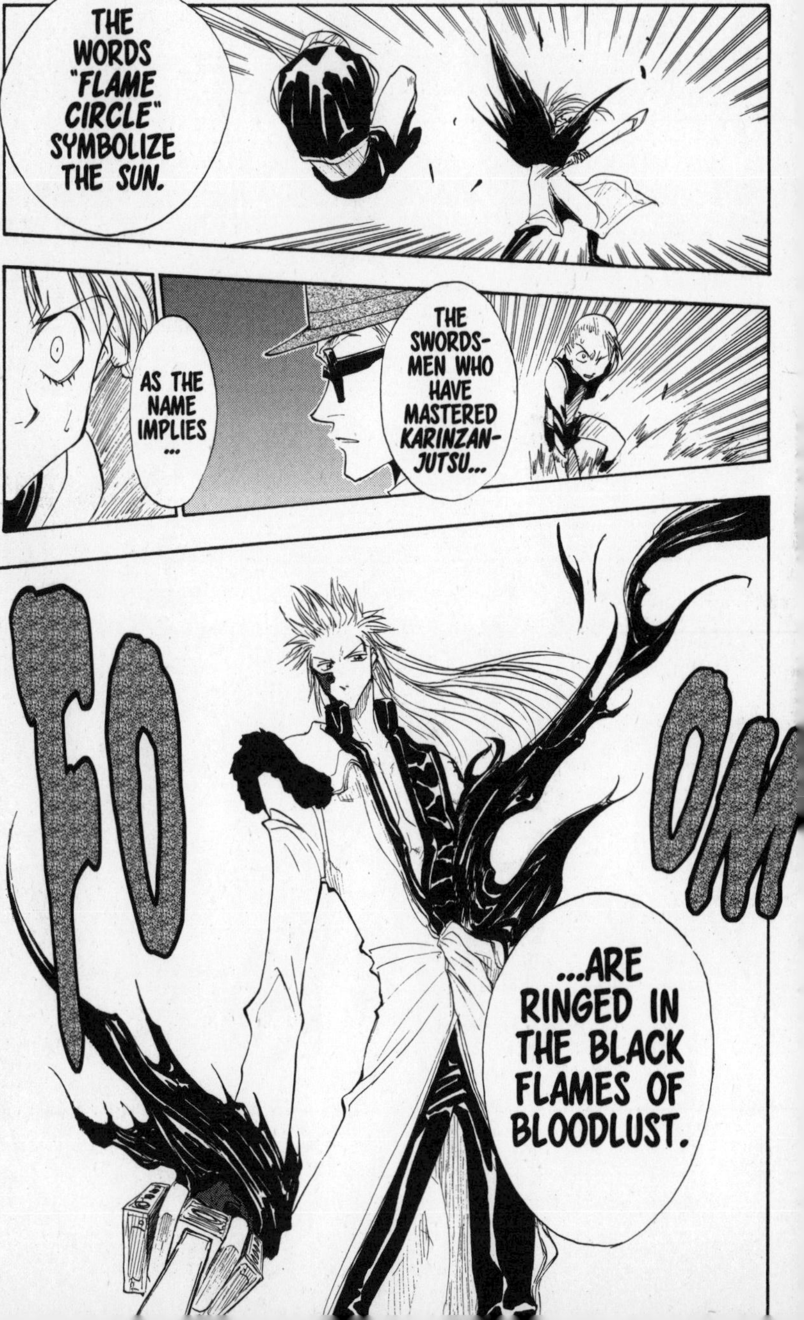
THE WORDS "FLAME CIRCLE" SYMBOLIZE THE SUN.
THE SWORDS-MEN WHO HAVE MASTERED KARINZAN-JUTSU...
AS THE NAME IMPLIES ...
FOOM
...ARE RINGED IN THE BLACK FLAMES OF BLOODLUST.

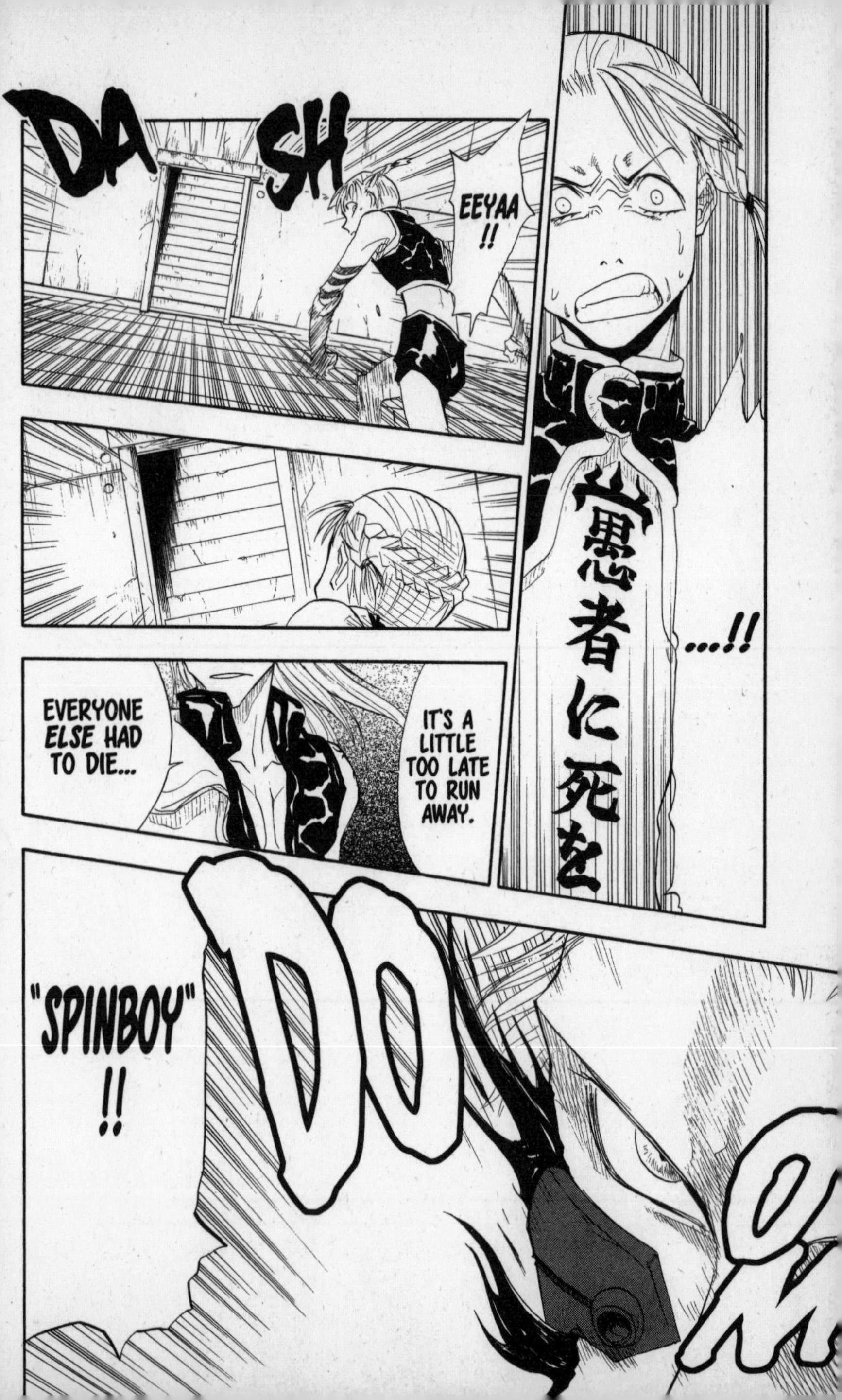
患者に死を
...!!
EEYAA !!
DASH
IT'S A LITTLE TOO LATE TO RUN AWAY.
EVERYONE ELSE HAD TO DIE...
DO
"SPINBOY" !!

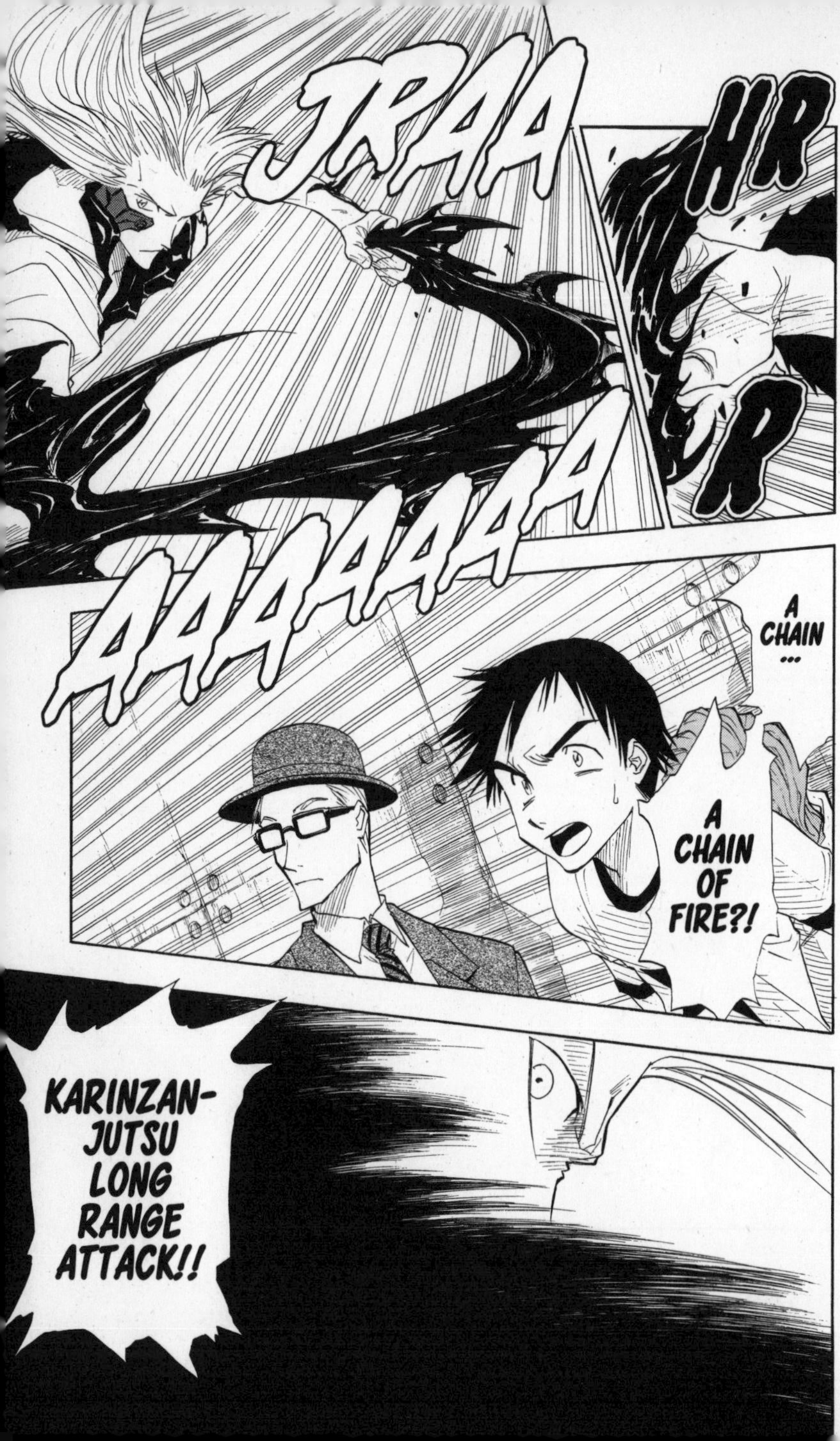
HR
R
JRAA
AAAAAAA
A CHAIN ...
A CHAIN OF FIRE?!
KARINZAN-JUTSU LONG RANGE ATTACK!!

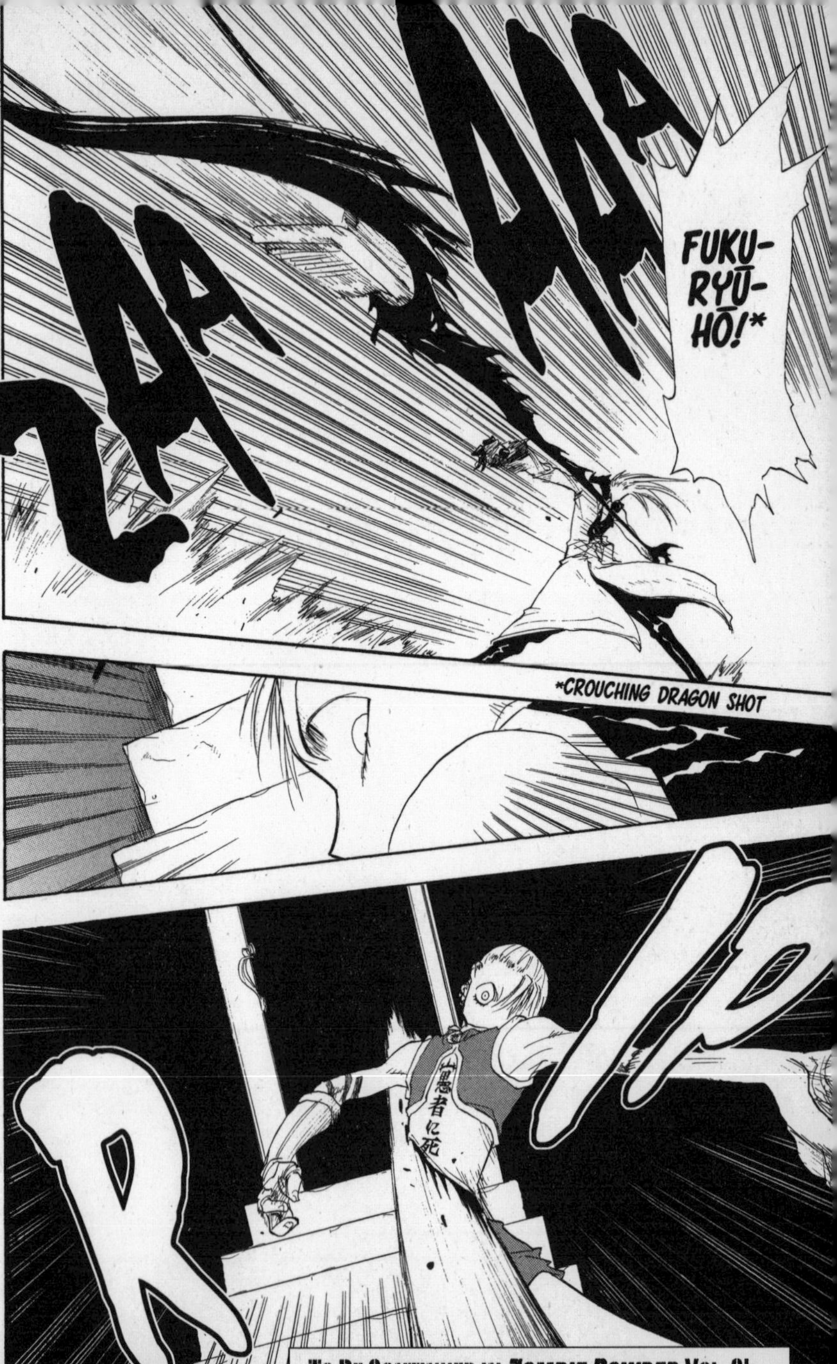
FUKU-RYŪ-HŌ!*
*CROUCHING DRAGON SHOT
TO BE CONTINUED IN ZOMBIE POWDER VOL. 2!

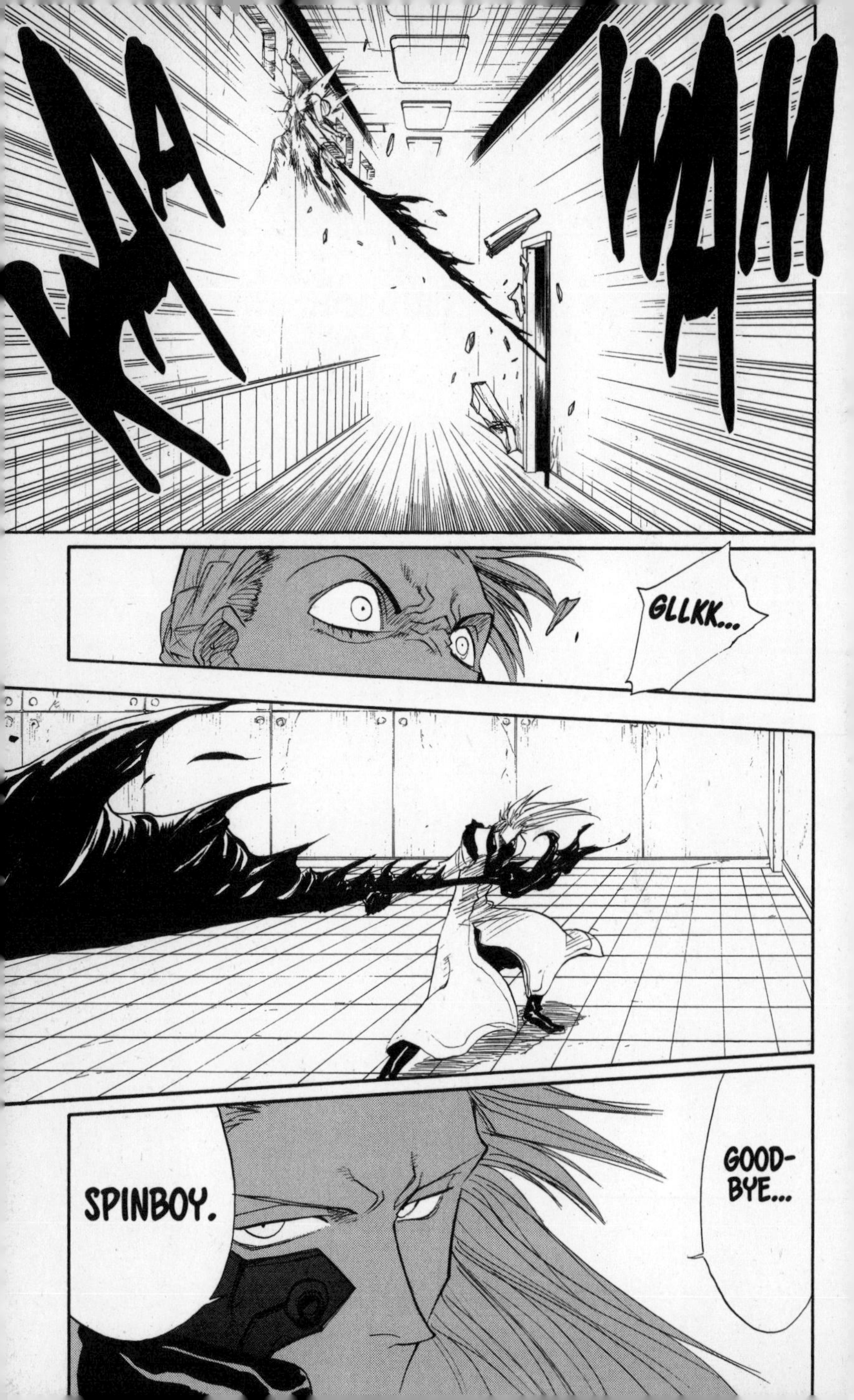
WAM
ZAA
GLLKK...
GOOD-
BYE...
SPINBOY.

CREWS

Alai Tamami

Fnats Hajime

Satow Yositaca

Tzujii Coji

Yamaula Satosi

and
some
other
technical
Naked Monkeys.

IN THE NEXT VOLUME...

Meet the newest member of Gamma Akutabi's gang, the fearless journalist Wolfina, as deadly with a camera as her friends are with a gun. But Wolfina knows the Rings' true twisted nature firsthand, having seen them turn her brother into a mindless husk. What is the true form of the Rings of the Dead? And who is the deadly Powder Hunter with powers beyond even Gamma Akutabi's? Includes a special bonus story, "Ultra Unholy Hearted Machine"!

AVAILABLE NOW!

ANIME ON hulu™

Watch Your Favorites. Anytime. For Free.

www.hulu.com

BLEACH © Tite Kubo / Shueisha, TV TOKYO, dentsu, Pierrot
SHONEN JUMP and BLEACH are trademarks of
Shueisha, Inc. in the United States and/or other countries.

NARUTO © 2002 MASASHI KISHIMOTO
SHONEN JUMP and NARUTO are trademarks of
Shueisha, Inc. in the U.S. and other countries.

DEATH NOTE © Tsugumi Ohba, Takeshi Obata/Shueisha
© DNDP, VAP, Shueisha, Madhouse
SHONEN JUMP and DEATH NOTE are trademarks of
Shueisha, Inc. in the United States and other countries.

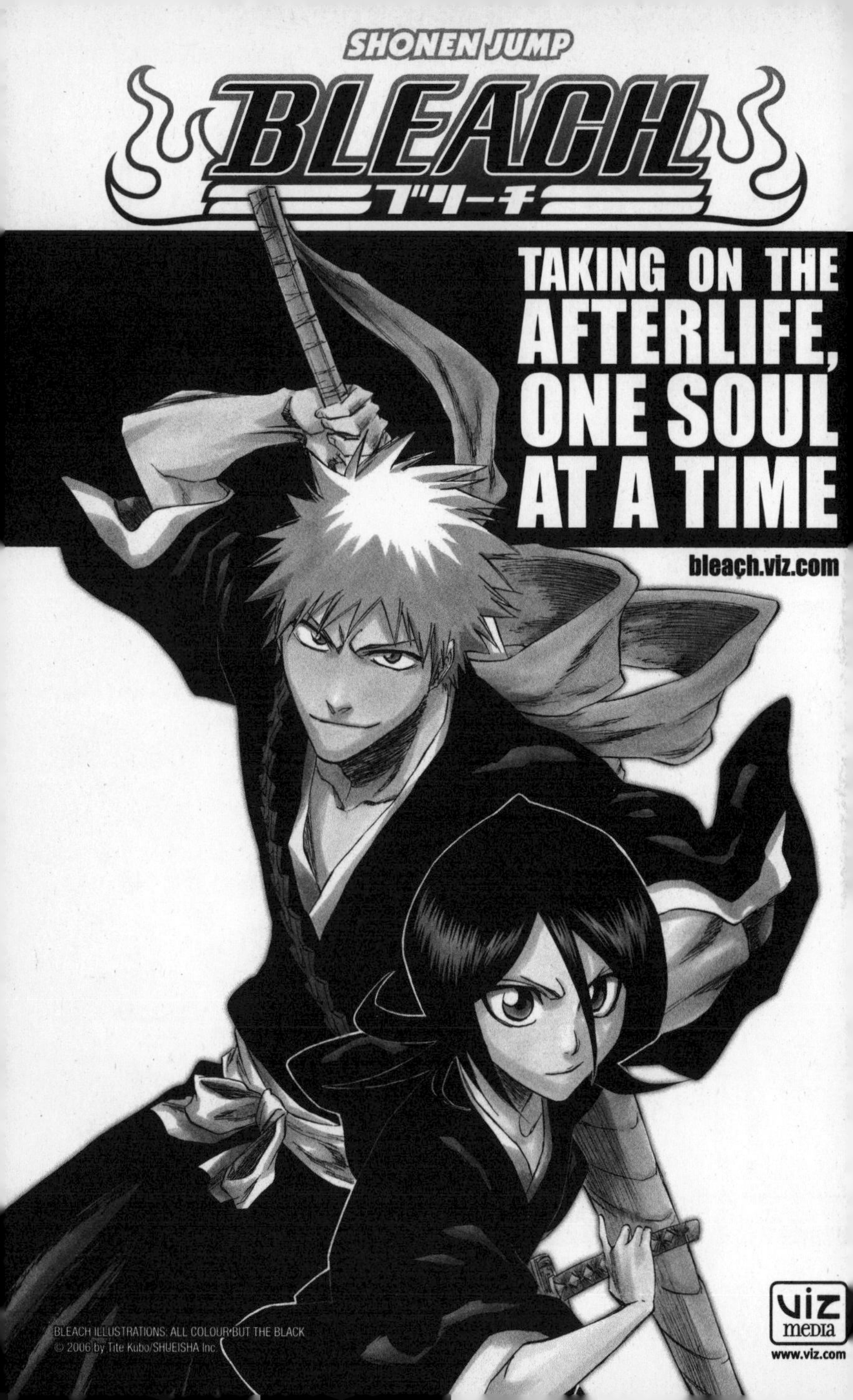
SHONEN JUMP
BLEACH
ブリーチ
TAKING ON THE AFTERLIFE, ONE SOUL AT A TIME
bleach.viz.com
BLEACH ILLUSTRATIONS: ALL COLOUR BUT THE BLACK
© 2006 by Tite Kubo/SHUEISHA Inc.
viz media
www.viz.com

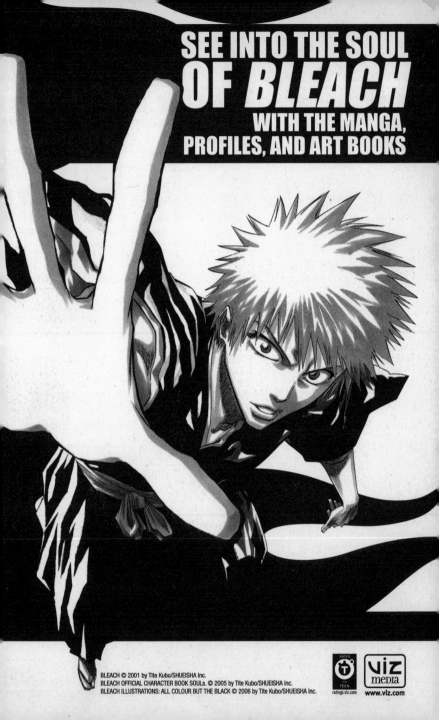

SEE INTO THE SOUL
OF *BLEACH*
WITH THE MANGA,
PROFILES, AND ART BOOKS

BLEACH © 2001 by Tite Kubo/SHUEISHA Inc.
BLEACH OFFICIAL CHARACTER BOOK SOULs. © 2005 by Tite Kubo/SHUEISHA Inc.
BLEACH ILLUSTRATIONS: ALL COLOUR BUT THE BLACK © 2006 by Tite Kubo/SHUEISHA Inc.

RATED
T
TEEN
ratings.viz.com

VIZ
MEDIA
www.viz.com

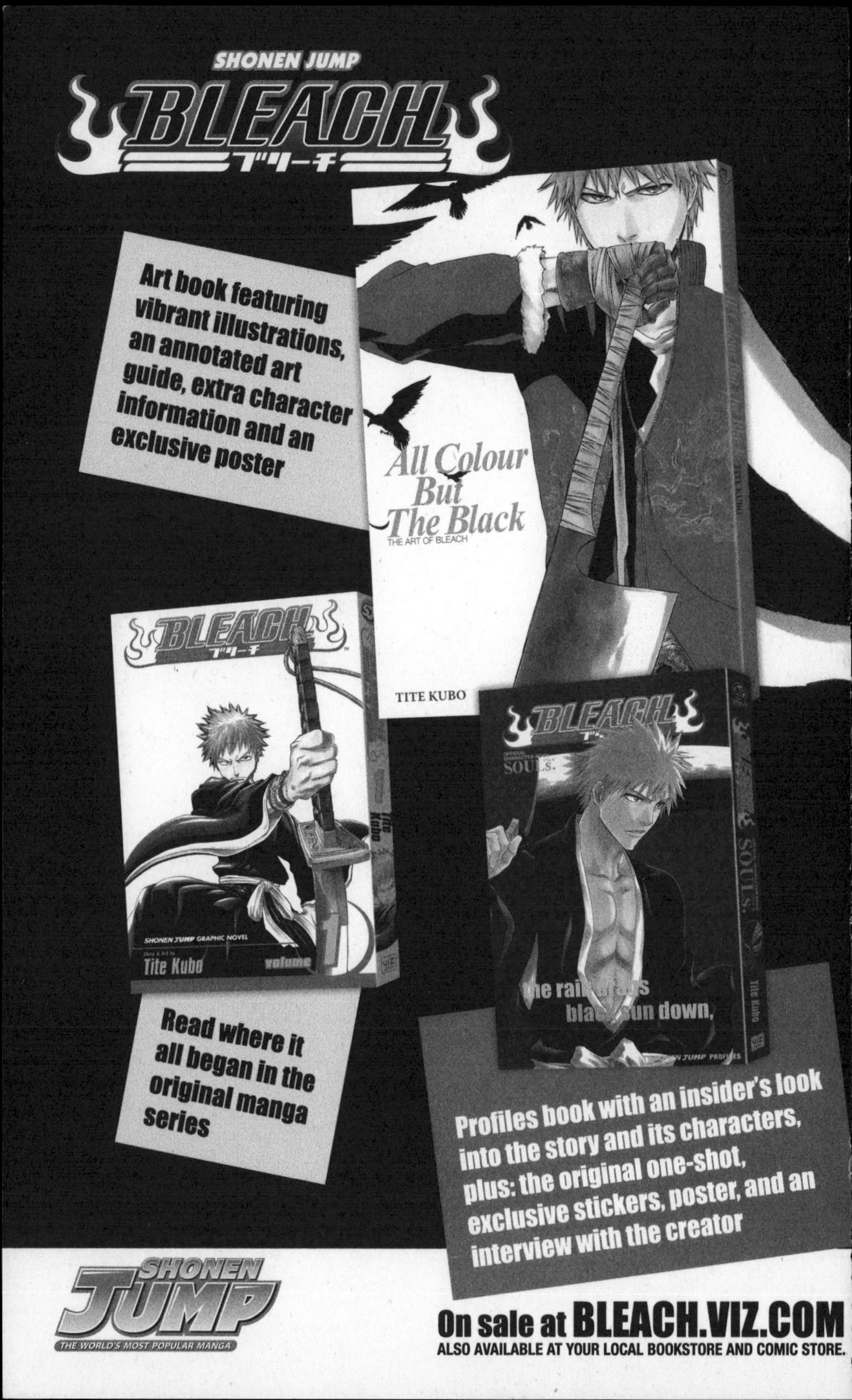
SHONEN JUMP
BLEACH
ブリーチ
Art book featuring vibrant illustrations, an annotated art guide, extra character information and an exclusive poster
All Colour But The Black
THE ART OF BLEACH
TITE KUBO
BLEACH
ブリーチ
SHONEN JUMP GRAPHIC NOVEL
Story & Art by
Tite Kubo
volume
Tite Kubo
BLEACH
SOULS.
Tite Kubo
Read where it all began in the original manga series
Profiles book with an insider's look into the story and its characters, plus: the original one-shot, exclusive stickers, poster, and an interview with the creator
SHONEN JUMP
THE WORLD'S MOST POPULAR MANGA
On sale at BLEACH.VIZ.COM
ALSO AVAILABLE AT YOUR LOCAL BOOKSTORE AND COMIC STORE.

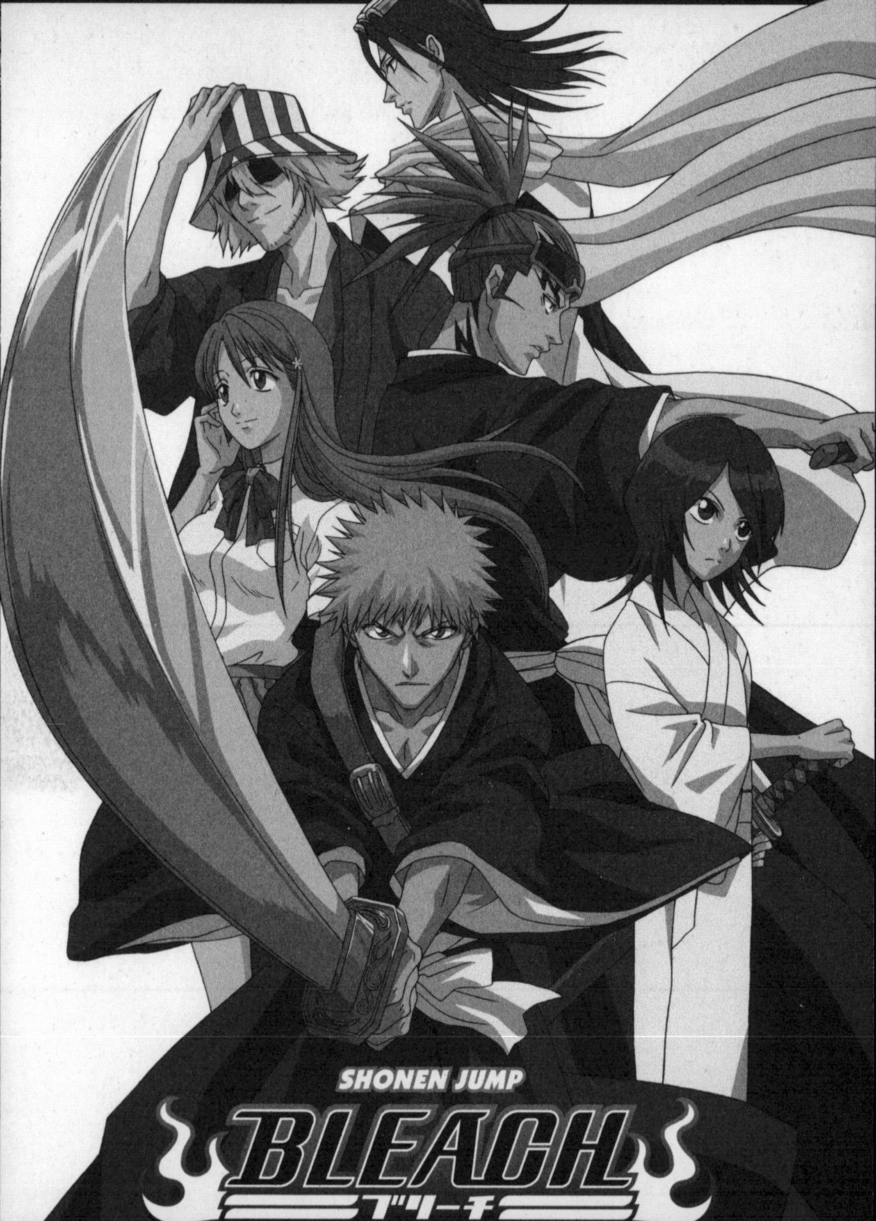

JOURNEY TO THE SOUL SOCIETY WITH THE ANIME

ORIGINAL AND UNCUT EPISODES NOW ON DVD

ANIME ALSO AVAILABLE
FOR DOWNLOAD
FIND OUT MORE AT
bleach.viz.com

GET AN ENTIRE TV SEASON IN ONE COLLECTIBLE DVD BOX SET

SHONEN JUMP

BLEACH

MEMORIES OF NOBODY

THE MOVIE

CAN THE SOUL REAPERS SAVE TWO WORLDS FROM TOTAL ANNIHILATION? FIND OUT IN THE FIRST FULL-LENGTH FEATURE FILM!

HOME VIDEO

© Tite Kubo/Shueisha, TV TOKYO, dentsu, Pierrot
© Tite Kubo/Shueisha, TV TOKYO, dentsu, Pierrot © BMP 2006

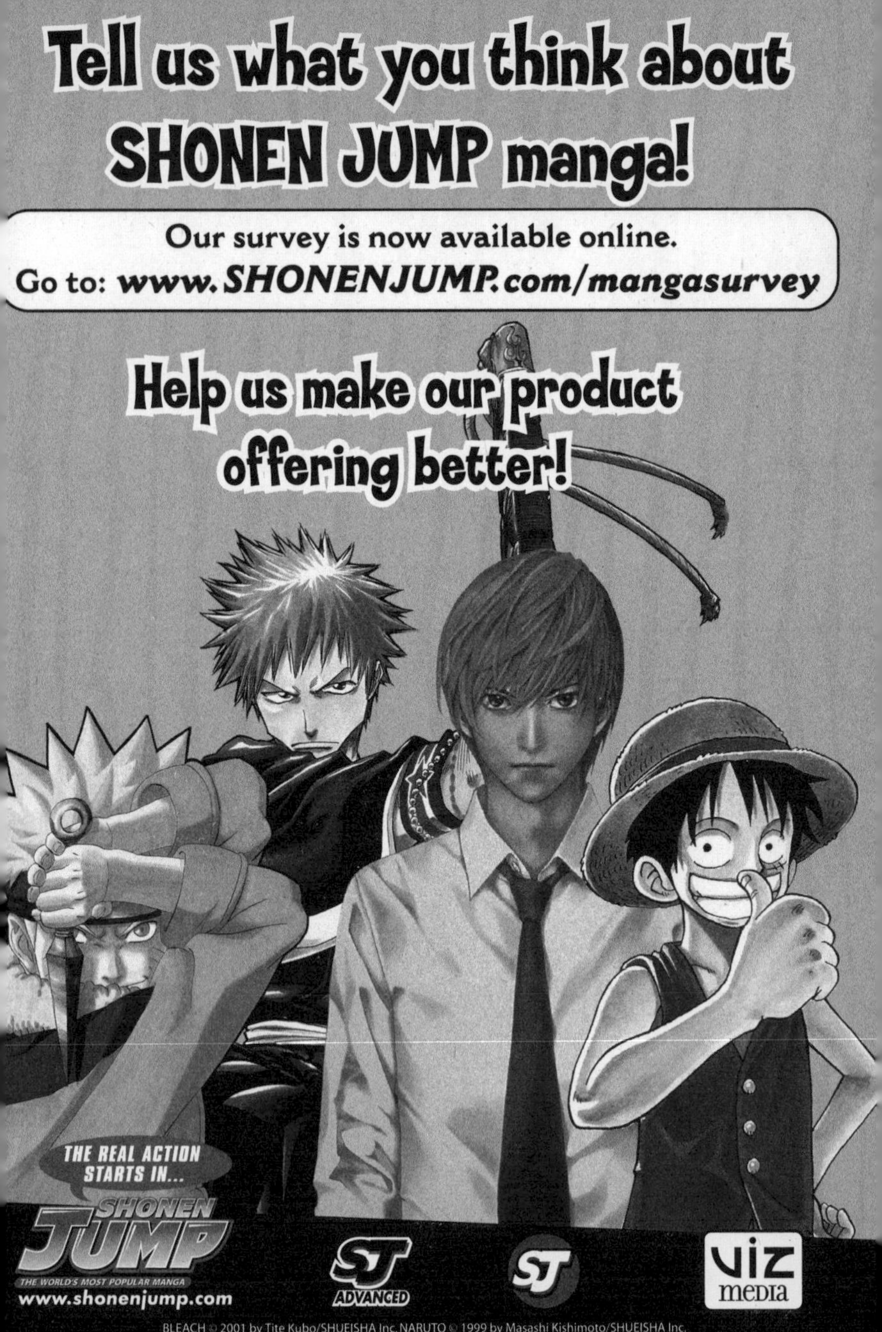
Tell us what you think about
SHONEN JUMP manga!
Our survey is now available online.
Go to: www.SHONENJUMP.com/mangasurvey
Help us make our product
offering better!
THE REAL ACTION
STARTS IN...
SHONEN JUMP
THE WORLD'S MOST POPULAR MANGA
www.shonenjump.com
SJ ADVANCED
SJ
VIZ media
BLEACH © 2001 by Tite Kubo/SHUEISHA Inc. NARUTO © 1999 by Masashi Kishimoto/SHUEISHA Inc.
DEATH NOTE © 2003 by Tsugumi Ohba, Takeshi Obata/SHUEISHA Inc. ONE PIECE © 1997 by Eiichiro Oda/SHUEISHA Inc.

SHONEN JUMP

THE WORLD'S MOST POPULAR MANGA

350+

pages of the coolest manga available in the U.S., PLUS anime news, and info on video & card games, toys AND more!

50% OFF the cover price!
That's like getting 6 issues

FREE!

12 HUGE issues for ONLY $29⁹⁵*

3 EASY WAYS TO SUBCRIBE
1 Send in a subscription order form
2 Log on to: www.shonenjump.com
3 Call 1-800-541-7919

* Canada price: $41.95 USD, including GST, HST, and QST. US/CAN orders only. Allow 6-8 weeks for delivery.

ONE PIECE © 1997 by Eiichiro Oda/SHUEISHA Inc. BLEACH © 2001 by Tite Kubo/SHUEISHA Inc.
NARUTO © 1999 by Masashi Kishimoto/SHUEISHA Inc.

SAVE 50% OFF
THE COVER PRICE!

IT'S LIKE GETTING 6 ISSUES

FREE!

OVER 350+ PAGES PER ISSUE

THE WORLD'S MOST POPULAR MANGA

This monthly magazine contains 7 of the coolest manga available in the U.S., PLUS anime news, and info about video & card games, toys AND more!

❏ **I want 12 HUGE issues of SHONEN JUMP for only $29.95*!**

NAME

ADDRESS

CITY/STATE/ZIP

EMAIL ADDRESS   **DATE OF BIRTH**

❏ **YES**, send me via email information, advertising, offers, and promotions related to VIZ Media, SHONEN JUMP, and/or their business partners.

❏ **CHECK ENCLOSED** (payable to SHONEN JUMP)   ❏ **BILL ME LATER**

CREDIT CARD: ❏ **Visa** ❏ **Mastercard**

ACCOUNT NUMBER   **EXP. DATE**

SIGNATURE

CLIP&MAIL TO:
SHONEN JUMP Subscriptions Service Dept.
P.O. Box 515
Mount Morris, IL 61054-0515

P9GNC1

* Canada price: $41.95 USD, including GST, HST, and QST. US/CAN orders only. Allow 6-8 weeks for delivery. ONE PIECE © 1997 by Eiichiro Oda/SHUEISHA Inc. BLEACH © 2001 by Tite Kubo/SHUEISHA Inc. NARUTO © 1999 by Masashi Kishimoto/SHUEISHA Inc.

www.viz.com